WHAT BIRD IS THAT?

N E V I L L E W . C A Y L E Y

The Classic Guide to the Birds of Australia

ILLUSTRATED BY THE AUTHOR

Revised and enlarged by A.H. Chisholm
K.A. Hindwood and A.R. McGill

Abridged edition prepared by Peter Roberts

This revised edition prepared by
Terence R. Lindsey

ANGUS
& ROBERTSON

A division of HarperCollins*Publishers*

AN ANGUS & ROBERTSON BOOK

First published in Australia in 1931 by
Collins/Angus & Robertson Publishers Australia
Abridged edition 1973
Reprinted 1974, 1977, 1980, 1982, 1983, 1984,
1985, 1986, 1987, 1989
This revised field edition 1991

Collins/Angus & Robertson Publishers Australia
A division of HarperCollins Publishers (Australia) Pty Limited
Unit 4, Eden Park, 31 Waterloo Road, North Ryde
NSW 2113, Australia

William Collins Publishers Ltd
31 View Road, Glenfield, Auckland 10, New Zealand

Angus & Robertson (UK)
16 Golden Square, London W1R 4BN, United Kingdom

National Library of Australia
Cataloguing-in-Publication data:

Cayley, Neville W. (Neville William), 1887–1950.
  What bird is that?

  Rev. abridged ed.
  Includes index.
  ISBN 0 207 16067 8.

  I. Birds — Australia — Indentification. I. Chisholm, Alec H.
  (Alec Hugh), 1890–1977. II. Hindwood, Keith, 1904–1971. III.
  McGill, A. R. (Arnold Robert), 1905– . IV. Roberts, Peter.
  V. Lindsey, Terence, 1941– . VI. Title.

598.2994

Cover illustration: King Parrot by Graham Pizzey
Typeset in 9/11 pt Century Old Style
Printed in Singapore

6 5 4 3 2 1
95 94 93 92 91

CONTENTS

LIST OF PLATES

EDITORIAL PREFACE

In preparing the first edition of *What Bird is That?*, Neville William Cayley executed the paintings and wrote the notes to accompany them. He was the son of Neville H. P. Cayley, himself an artist who had made a specialty of painting game-birds. The son improved upon the father in knowledge of ornithology and for several years was undoubtedly the chief artist in this field in Australia.

From the outset *What Bird is That?* was sponsored by the New South Wales Gould League of Bird Lovers, an organisation devoted to fostering an understanding of Australian native birds among school children. Neville Cayley worked for many years on the council of the league, which eventually acquired his interest in the book. The royalties for this book now go to promoting a wider interest in all aspects of conservation in schools.

In its present form, *What Bird is That?* owes much to the extensive revision performed in 1958 by three eminent ornithologists, Alec H. Chisholm, Keith Hindwood and Arnold McGill. Thanks to their work, the book is still regarded by serious students as the most reliable source of information on distribution and breeding data, and it is the undisputed all-time bestseller among Australian books on natural history.

A field edition prepared by Peter Roberts was published in 1975. In this second field edition, Terence Lindsey a respected ornithologist, has completely revised the text, including over 40 new species. His revisions ensure that this already respected field guide continues to provide informative and up-to-date details on the birds of Australia.

The format of this field edition continues to appeal to active field workers who find the hardback too heavy to carry or too large for the glove-box of a car, as well as to those with a casual interest in birdwatching who do not require all the data in the full edition. The reduction has been achieved by eliminating all the references to derivations of scientific names and removing most of the behavioural descriptions in the Notes.

INTRODUCTION

Because of the beauty of their flight and the charm of their songs, birds exercise an unfailing appeal. Australian species, numbering approximately 750, are distinctly varied, and many of them are restricted to this country. They merit appreciation and study both on aesthetic and environmental grounds.

In earlier days, canaries were used in coalmines because they responded far more quickly to dangerous gases than any instrument then devised. Birds may well be useful in a similar way today. Attention to changes in the abundance and distribution of birds may be the most convenient means of monitoring changes in our increasingly fragile environment. While birds are worth watching for this reason, even casual interest in birds can be both rewarding and worthwhile.

Birds are common, conspicuous and relatively easy to study. To indulge your interest in birds simply buy a pair of binoculars and a notebook and step outside. Birds occur almost everywhere. While the greatest number of species tends to occur in habitats undisturbed by human activities, the variety to be found even in the parks of major cities might surprise those who have not looked. For those who prefer company, most major population centres around the country have vigorous clubs and societies, with frequent well-organised meetings and field outings. All states have regional societies and there are several national groups. If you are interested, a number of universities, bird observatories and other organisations offer courses for beginners. For details about clubs or courses enquire at any zoo, museum or public library.

In this edition technical terms have been avoided where possible, but a few words used in a technical sense should be clarified. *Conspecific* means belonging to the same species. The word *morph* is used to express the situation where a species occurs in two or more forms differing only in appearance; for example, some Grey Goshawks are grey, while others are pure white. The word morph (as in grey morph, white morph) merely differentiates one from the other and carries no implication as to the significance of the phenomenon. Thus *dimorphic* simply means of two forms; the phrase 'sexually dimorphic' is often applied to the situation where the male looks different from the female. A *gregarious* bird lives in groups, not alone. *Polyandrous* indicates a situation in which a female has several mates (compare *polygynous*, in which a male has several mates, and *polygamous*, used to cover either or both possibilities without distinction). *Arboreal* means living in trees, *terrestrial* living on the ground. *Sedentary* means showing no tendency to migrate, and *irruptive* means prone to erratic and unpredictable occurrence outside the normal range; a *vagrant* is a species of rare or casual occurrence, while an *accidental* is an extreme vagrant, a specis recorded in a given area only a few times. The term *song* is not specifically distinguished from *call*, but the latter covers any vocalisation of a bird, whereas the former is normally restricted to those calls directly connected with the breeding cycle. *Subsong* is a subdued and barely audible song, of unknown function.

Foraging methods, particularly in insectivorous birds, are often so consistent and characteristic that they are useful clues to identity, and as such are sometimes referred to in the text. Birds catch insects either when perched or flying. If the bird is perched while it captures an insect that is also perched on a leaf, then the bird is said to be *gleaning*; if the insect is hidden in bark and the bird perched, it is *probing*; if the bird is perched but the insect is in flight, it is *snatching*; if both are in flight, it is *hawking*; if the bird is perched in a tree and descends to catch an insect on the ground, the bird is said to be *pouncing*.

The birds in this book are arranged in accordance with the habitats they normally occupy, rather than by their relationships with other birds (that is, in taxonomic order). This arrangement was the essence of Neville Cayley's original concept, and has been maintained through all subsequent editions and revisions of the work.

Deserts, swamps and rainforests are immediately indentifiable as different kinds of country: the first is recognisable by a total lack of trees and the last by very dense congregations, whereas swamps show an abundance of mud, reeds and water. Because conditions change from one habitat to another, the range of species of birds varies correspondingly. Chowchillas and catbirds may be found in rainforest but not in grassland, and Bustards and Gouldian Finches in grassland but not in rainforest. Each different habitat is occupied by its characteristic mix of bird species. The correspondence, of course, is not absolute, and because birds are particularly mobile many examples may be found of a particular species occupying a range of habitats rather than only one.

The concept of niche is an important consideration when discussing a bird's habitat. Generally, the word niche refers to the particular part of the habitat a bird or other animal occupies. Thus birds like Yellow-throated Scrubwrens and Logrunners are almost entirely terrestrial; Large-billed Scrubwrens and Pale-yellow Robins occupy the understorey; while Superb Fruitdoves are birds of the upper canopy — yet all share the same habitat, namely rainforest.

A brief description of some habitats mentioned in the text may be useful.
Rainforest Rainforests occur in regions of high rainfall and are characterised by a great diversity of plant species. The trees are tall, the

canopy dense and continuous, eucalypts are generally lacking, and vines, creepers, epiphytes, ferns, mosses and palms are abundant.

Forest In Australia, forests are usually dominated by eucalypts, though in interior south-eastern Queensland brigalow (a species of *Acacia*) sometimes grow as forest. The height of the visible trunk is generally much greater than that of the crown. Forests occupy much of the east coast, Tasmania and the south-west. Two types are generally distinguished: wet sclerophyll and dry sclerophyll (sclerephyllous means 'hard-leaved', indicating a characteristic shown by many Australian trees, especially eucalypts and acacias). Wet sclerophyll forests usually have continuous canopies and dense understoreys of shrubs, saplings and often tree ferns. Vines and epiphytes are scarce or absent.

Woodland This is a particularly difficult habitat to define or describe, but is significant for many bird species. A number of types may be recognised. Generally in woodland, the bole, or visible trunk, of the tree is shorter than the depth of the crown. The canopy is not necessarily continuous and woodland changes almost imperceptibly into forest on the one hand and through savannah woodland to grassland on the other. There is usually a dense ground cover of grasses, herbs and shrubs.

Scrublands Scrubs in the dry inland or semi-desert areas have growths of mallee and marlock (dwarf eucalypts), mulga, myall, gidgea, brigalow, belah, wilga, dead-finish (*Acacia*), pine (*Callitris*) and she-oak (*Casuarina*). Trees are usually less than eight metres in height, the canopy is continuous, and the ground cover may be sparse.

Heaths Heaths are characteristic of coastal areas of the south-east and south-west, but they also occur in the interior. Heaths are dense shrublands, generally less than two metres in height, and are rich in flowering plants, especially species of *Banksia, Leptospermum, Hakea, Acacia* and *Grevillea.* Grasses and herbs are scarce.

Mangroves Mangroves are trees that are tolerant of salt and flooding, and can establish themselves in soft mud; they are common in estuaries and sheltered coasts, especially in the north and east. In southern regions, mangrove swamps may consist of only one or two species, but in the north they often form very complex plant communities.

Grassland and Shrub-steppe These habitats include plains, desert and semi-desert areas. Plains are chiefly associated with Mitchell and Flinders grasses; desert areas with spinifex, porcupine and cane grasses; and semi-desert areas with saltbush, bluebush and cotton-bush.

AUSTRALIA'S LARGEST BIRDS

PLATE 1

AUSTRALIA'S LARGEST BIRDS
(Excluding seabirds)

1:1 MAGPIE GOOSE *Anseranas semipalmata*

IDENTIFICATION. The Magpie Goose is large, lanky, boldly patterned black and white, with a conspicuous knob on its crown; the sexes are similar.

DISTRIBUTION. Northern and eastern Australia (mainly coastal lowlands), south on the east coast to about Rockhampton, Queensland; casual and erratic further south (formerly to Victoria and eastern South Australia). Also found in southern New Guinea.

NOTES. A strongly gregarious bird: usually seen in flocks (sometimes huge), frequenting wetlands of all kinds, but especially shallow freshwater lagoons and swamps. It feeds by 'grubbing' or up-ending in shallows and margins. It perches freely in bushes or branches of trees. The call is a high-pitched resonant honking, and is louder and higher in the male. Food: mainly seeds, shoots, roots and tubers of aquatic plants; can sometimes cause damage to rice fields in the tropics.

BREEDING. In pairs or trios. Nest: a bulky platform of local vegetation on a trampled-down tussock of reeds, usually near the middle of a swamp. Clutch: five to eight, occasionally (when two females lay in one nest) up to fourteen or eighteen; yellowish-white. Breeding season: mainly October to March, but varying according to rainfall.

1:2 AUSTRALIAN PELICAN *Pelecanus conspicillatus*

IDENTIFICATION. The Australian Pelican is unmistakable: a very large, dignified, mainly white waterbird with a huge pink bill, with sexes of similar appearance.

DISTRIBUTION. Australia generally. Also Ambon and New Guinea; accidental to New Zealand.

NOTES. These birds are found mostly in flocks, frequenting mainly extensive shallow waters, fresh or salt. Usually they are seen fishing in groups or loafing on mud- or sand-flats. Though graceful on the water or in the air, they have a waddling gait on land, and take-off is long and clumsy. Food: mostly fish; also crustaceans.

BREEDING. Colonial. Nest: usually flimsy but sometimes substantial, the nest is a depression on the ground surrounded by plant stems, grasses and sticks gathered as incubation proceeds. Clutch: two to three, dull white or yellowish-white eggs, often irregularly coated with lime, and usually nest-stained. Breeding season: variable, but strongly influenced by local weather conditions.

1:3 SOUTHERN CASSOWARY *Casuarius casuarius*

IDENTIFICATION. This is a huge, flightless, heavily built bird with glossy blue-black plumage (dull brown in juveniles); the sexes are similar.

DISTRIBUTION. North-eastern Queensland, from the Pascoe River (Cape York Peninsula) south to near Townsville. Also found in New Guinea, the Aru Islands and Ceram (where possibly introduced).

NOTES. The bird frequents dense rainforests. It is exceptionally wary and timid, keeping to the thickest parts by day, emerging towards evening and at daybreak to visit favourite feeding trees. Although it is mostly solitary and sedentary, it can run strongly and is a good swimmer. Its call is a prolonged, harsh, guttural rumbling, or a short but deep booming grunt; also a loud hiss. Food: mainly fallen fruits.

BREEDING. Nest: a bed of sticks, leaves and other debris, about one metre in diameter, usually placed near the base of a large tree in dense jungle. Clutch: one to six, usually three to four; light pea-green, the shell being coarse and granulated. The male incubates the eggs and cares for the young. Breeding season: July to September.

1:4 CAPE BARREN GOOSE *Cereopsis novaehollandiae*

IDENTIFICATION. This bird is a large, bulky, plain smoke-grey goose with fleshy green-yellow cere.

DISTRIBUTION. Coastal southern Australia and islands offshore; Tasmania and the islands of Bass Strait.

NOTES. The Cape Barren Goose is also called Pig Goose. It occurs in pairs or small flocks, frequenting grasslands and swampy areas, where it feeds on grasses and herbage of various kinds. These birds probably mate for life, and are strongly territorial and aggressive during the breeding season. The name Pig Goose refers to its grunt-like notes; the male also utters raucous trumpeting notes. Essentially a bird of the southern coast and offshore islands, it is only rarely seen at any distance inland. Formerly much persecuted by humans but now totally protected and perhaps maintaining its numbers.

BREEDING. Nest: a large flat platform on the ground, constructed of dried grass and plants, and lined with down. Clutch: four to seven; creamy-white, glossy. Breeding season: usually May to August.

1:5 AUSTRALIAN BUSTARD *Ardeotis australis*

IDENTIFICATION. A large, stately, terrestrial bird of open plains, the Australian Bustard is mainly brown above and creamy white below with a head and neck dull white and crown dark slate grey. The sexes are similar, but the female is much smaller, and has a dull brown crown.

DISTRIBUTION. Australia generally, but now much reduced, and rare or absent over most of southern Australia. Also occurs in southern New Guinea.

NOTES. The bird is seen singly or in pairs, and occasionally in loose flocks. It has been much persecuted by humans so is wary. The male has a spectacular display, performed at a regularly used display-ground or 'lek', in which it struts about with tail thrown forward over the back, long breast feathers fanned and pendulous white breast-sac lowered to the ground, uttering a low hollow roar suggesting a distant lion. Food: insects (chiefly grasshoppers), snakes, lizards, small mammals and birds, frogs, spiders, grass and green herbage; also fruits and berries of low growing vegetation.

BREEDING. Nest: none made; instead the eggs are laid on the bare ground, sheltered by tall grass or a low bush. Clutch: one to two; buff or greenish-buff, smudged with brown. Breeding season: mainly September to December, but strongly influenced by local seasonal conditions.

1:6 BROLGA *Grus rubicunda*

IDENTIFICATION. The Brolga is a very tall, stately and elegant grey bird with red, unfeathered head and slate grey legs. The sexes are similar.

DISTRIBUTION. Throughout Australia, except Western Australia south of Onslow, and coastal south-eastern Australia; rare in Victoria.

NOTES. The bird is seen in pairs or flocks, frequenting open plains or extensive swamps; it is a permanent resident in some districts, and is nomadic in others. Its flight is easy and graceful and at times it soars to a great height. The Brolga is notable for its elaborate displays or 'corroborees', consisting of a variety of elegant dancing movements. These displays may be associated with courtship, although flocks will dance at any time of year. The call is a deep trumpeting note. The bird is sometimes kept in a tame state on country properties. Food: insects, small rodents, frogs, reptiles and herbage; occasionally damages grain crops.

BREEDING. Nest: a platform (substantial or sparse) of reeds, plants or grass in a swamp. Clutch: two to three; whitish, with a few purplish-red spots. Breeding season: mainly September to December in the south, February to June in the tropical north.

1:7 SARUS CRANE *Grus antigone*

IDENTIFICATION. The Sarus Crane is a very tall, stately plain grey bird, very similar to the Brolga but distinguished by pinkish (not slate grey) legs and the fact that the naked red skin of the head extends well down on to the neck. The sexes are similar.

DISTRIBUTION. Tropical northern Australia, mainly around the Gulf of Carpentaria from about Burketown east to the Atherton Tableland and about Ingham, Queensland. Also found in India, South-East Asia, and the Philippines.

NOTES. Very similar to the Brolga in general habits, and the two sometimes occur together in mixed flocks. It was first detected in Australia in 1966, when a flock was seen and photographed near Normanton, Queensland. It is uncertain whether the species is a recent immigrant to Australia, or whether its presence had previously been overlooked because of its close similarity to the Brolga.

BREEDING. Nest: a rough mass of reeds, grass and sticks, placed on a slight hummock on swampy ground. Clutch: usually two; pale buffy-white, blotched and freckled with dull reddish-brown and purple. Breeding season: January to March, during or just after the wet season.

1:8 BLACK-NECKED STORK *Xenorhynchus asiaticus*

IDENTIFICATION. This stork is a very tall, boldly black and white waterbird with a large, dark-grey bill and pink legs. The sexes are similar, but the female has a bright yellow, not brown, iris.

DISTRIBUTION. Northern and eastern Australia, from the Fitzroy River (north-western Australia) to (rarely) south-eastern New South Wales; accidental to Victoria. Also seen in southern Asia to New Guinea.

NOTES. The bird is seen singly, in pairs or small parties, frequenting wetlands of all kinds, but especially extensive shallow lagoons. It is generally seen stalking quietly about seeking its prey, every now and again bounding along with great strides and jabbing at fish with its huge bill. The voice, rarely heard, is reported to be a dull booming; the bird's main expression is a clapping of the mandibles. Food: fish, crustaceans and carrion.

BREEDING. Nest: a large collection of sticks and twigs, upon which a quantity of grass or rushes is laid, placed in a low tree in a swamp or in a tall forest tree; occasionally on the ground. Clutch: two to four, sometimes five; whitish unless nest-stained. Breeding season: usually February to October, but at any time after heavy rain.

1:9 BLACK SWAN *Cygnus atratus*

IDENTIFICATION. This bird is an entirely black (except white outermost flight feathers) waterfowl with long, slender neck and bright red bill. Sexes similar.

DISTRIBUTION. Australia generally, but more numerous and widespread in the south and east than in the tropical north. It was introduced into New Zealand.

NOTES. The Black Swan is found in pairs or flocks, frequenting wetlands of all kinds, including ornamental lakes and ponds in cities and towns. A trumpet-like call is uttered as it flies from one feeding ground to another. These flights are chiefly made during the evening and on moonlit nights. Black Swans gather in large flocks, often numbering thousands of birds, on extensive bodies of water to moult after the breeding season. Food: aquatic plants and animals.

BREEDING. Nest: a large, rough platform of twigs, rushes and aquatic plants, sparsely lined with down; often placed on a small island in shallow water. Clutch: four to nine, usually five to six; pale green or dull greenish-white and slightly lustrous. Breeding season: chiefly autumn and winter, sometimes as late as December.

1:10 EMU *Dromaius novaehollandiae*

IDENTIFICATION. The Emu is a very large flightless bird of open country, with shaggy dull brown plumage. The sexes are similar.

DISTRIBUTION. Australia generally, but rare or absent in closely settled coastal areas of the east and south.

NOTES. The Emu occurs in pairs or flocks, frequenting grassy plains and open woodland. Virtually omnivorous, it will feed on insects and seeds, fruit and green shoots and buds. Many pastoralists consider it a pest, charging it with breaking fences and fouling pastures. The female utters drumming noises and the male makes guttural grumbling sounds. Next to the Ostrich, the Emu is the largest of all birds (although cassowaries may be heavier).

BREEDING. Nest: a platform of trampled vegetation, frequently in the open and only slightly concealed. Clutch: usually about nine; dark green with a granulated surface; incubated by the male. Breeding season: very variable, but mainly April to November.

FOREST-FREQUENTING BIRDS

PLATE 2

BIRDS OF RAINFORESTS AND SCRUBS

2:1 LEWIN'S HONEYEATER *Meliphaga lewinii*

IDENTIFICATION. This bird is a fairly large, dark and chunky rainforest honeyeater with a yellow gape and semicircular light yellow cheek patch. The persistent staccato 'machine-gun' call is distinctive.

DISTRIBUTION. Eastern Australia, from the Rocky River (near Coen, Queensland) to eastern Victoria.

NOTES. The bird frequents rainforest and scrubs, tending to favour the middle and lower layers of foliage. Common, ubiquitous and inquisitive, it will readily approach an observer who makes squeaking noises. The Lewin's Honeyeater is mainly solitary, apparently sedentary, and very aggressive. The rapid staccato call is one of the characteristic sounds of Australian rainforests. Food: native fruits and berries and cultivated fruits, insects and nectar.

BREEDING. Nest: cup-shaped, constructed of bark strips, dry leaves and moss, bound with spiders' silk and lined with grasses and plant-down; suspended by the rim from a slender horizontal fork in the dense outer foliage of a small tree, usually 2–5 metres from the ground. Clutch: two to three; white, with reddish-brown or purplish-black markings. Breeding season: September to January.

2:2 YELLOW-THROATED SCRUBWREN *Sericornis citreogularis*

IDENTIFICATION. This dark scrubwren with yellow throat and black mask is almost always on the ground in rainforest.

DISTRIBUTION. Eastern Australia, from Cooktown to around Mount Spec near Townsville and from about Gympie, Queensland, to Mount Dromedary, New South Wales.

NOTES. The bird is usually in pairs in dense rainforest, searching for insects on the ground, on logs or among fallen leaves and other debris. Not difficult to observe, it usually ignores a quiet and patient observer. Members of the southern population (both sexes) utter a sweet and animated warbling often interspersed with the calls of many other birds; northern birds have a harsh chatter, but are seldom heard to sing.

BREEDING. Nest: bulky and pear-shaped, with a hooded side entrance; constructed mainly of rootlets and skeletons of leaves and ferns, mingled with moss; lined with feathers; attached near the end of a pendulous branch of a tree, often overhanging water, 1–10 metres from the ground. The general appearance of the nest often suggests a dangling mass of flood debris. Clutch: two to three; varying from almost pure white to chocolate brown. Breeding season: August to February.

2:3 GREY WHISTLER *Pachycephala simplex griseiceps*

IDENTIFICATION. This bird is a typical whistler in behaviour, but is rather small, and lacking any distinctive feature; its abdomen is washed yellow.

DISTRIBUTION. Coastal Queensland from Cape York to about Townsville. Also seen in the Aru Islands and New Guinea.

NOTES. The bird inhabits rainforests, where it seeks insects in the outer foliage of the largest trees or among tangled vines, mostly in the canopy. Although often seen alone, it will join mixed feeding flocks of other birds outside the breeding season. The song is a loud, clear whistle, comprising from five to ten notes; it also utters two short whistled notes. This form and the bird formerly known as the Brown Whistler (No. 23:11) are now regarded as conspecific. Food: insects.

BREEDING. Nest: loosely made, cup-shaped, constructed of fibre and dead leaves, interwoven with rootlets and tendrils, sparsely lined with dead grass and tendrils, usually placed in the upright fork of a small sapling. Clutch: two; glossy-white, well marked with spots of dark and light umber and purplish-grey. Breeding season: variable, but mainly September to February.

2:4 MAGNIFICENT RIFLEBIRD *Ptiloris magnificus*

IDENTIFICATION. This is a large, chunky bird with a long, strongly curved bill. The male is rich black with flank plumes, iridescent blue-green throat, and distinctive rustling flight; the female is warm brown above, pale below, closely barred with a bold pale eyebrow. Found on Cape York only.

DISTRIBUTION. Cape York Peninsula, Queensland, south to Weipa on the west coast and the Chester River on the east coast. Also found in New Guinea.

NOTES. Sedentary and common, the bird frequents rainforests and adjacent woodland. It is shy, and is more often heard than seen. It feeds by fossicking in epiphytes, mosses and bark of the inner limbs of trees. The usual call consists of two loud, sharp whistles; it also has harsh rasping notes. Food: native fruits and insects.

BREEDING. Nest: open, loosely built, cup-shaped, constructed of dead leaves, vine tendrils, and fibres; lined with finer material; placed in a pandanus palm, on top of a dead stub of a tree or in the crown of a sapling, usually 2–10 metres from the ground. Clutch: two; creamy-white, beautifully marked with longitudinal streaks and spots of brownish-olive, rufous-brown and slate. Breeding season: October to early February, sometimes later.

2:5 VICTORIA'S RIFLEBIRD *Ptiloris victoriae*

IDENTIFICATION. This bird is similar to the Magnificent Riflebird but is somewhat smaller. The male lacks plumes and the female is colder brown above and buff below. (Note the distribution.)

DISTRIBUTION. Eastern Queensland from near Cooktown south to the Seaview Range near Townsville.

NOTES. Victoria's Riflebird frequents rainforests of the mainland and some islands off the coast. It is active and acrobatic. Like other riflebirds, it feeds mainly by fossicking in epiphytes, bark and accumulated litter on the trunks and major limbs of trees. The characteristic call is a loud, rasping 'yaaa–sss'. Food: native fruits and insects. This and the Paradise Riflebird are sometimes regarded as conspecific.

BREEDING. Nest: open, cup-shaped, constructed of dead leaves, vine tendrils, and rootlets, and lined with finer material; cast-off snake skins are invariably worked into the walls; usually secreted in a mass of vines or foliage near the top of a tall tree in dense scrub. Clutch: two; flesh colour, beautifully marked with longitudinal streaks and spots of reddish brown and purplish-grey. Breeding season: October to December, sometimes later.

2:6 PARADISE RIFLEBIRD *Ptiloris paradiseus*

IDENTIFICATION. This bird is similar to Victoria's Riflebird but is smaller and shorter billed. The female is marked with chevrons below. (Note the distribution.)

DISTRIBUTION. Eastern Australia, from about Gympie, Queensland (perhaps locally further north to Mackay), west to the Bunya Range and south to Barrington Tops, New South Wales.

NOTES. The Paradise Riflebird frequents rainforests of the coast and contiguous ranges. Its call is a harsh 'y–a–a–ss', frequently uttered, especially during the mating season. Like other riflebirds, the male has a spectacular solitary display, performed on a favoured perch, typically the top of a stub or a bare horizontal limb of a tree several metres from the ground, often overlooking a clearing or a gorge. Food: insects, native fruits and berries; captive birds have been known to kill mice and small birds.

BREEDING. Nest: a shallow bowl of vine tendrils and dead leaves, lined with fine stems and twigs and ornamented around the rim with portions of cast-off snake skins; usually hidden in a mass of vines or in dense foliage in the crown of a tree, at heights up to 30 metres. Clutch: two; reddish-cream, beautifully marked with spots and longitudinal streaks of reddish-chestnut, purplish-red and purplish-grey. Breeding season: October to December.

2:7 SHINING STARLING *Aplonis metallica*

IDENTIFICATION. This Starling is rich glossy black with a fairly long, pointed tail and bold red eye; females and immatures have white underparts, and are heavily streaked black.

DISTRIBUTION. Eastern Queensland from Cape York south to about Townsville. Also found in Indonesia and New Guinea.

NOTES. This bird is migratory, arriving in August and departing in March, though some birds may remain throughout the year. Noisy, conspicuous, and highly social, the species associates in flocks, resembling in flight the introduced common Starling and performing many remarkable aerobatics. It breeds in colonies in tall trees, and one colony may contain as many as 300 nests. The bird utters a variety of harsh wheezy chattering notes and also a brief warbling song. Food: native fruits, principally wild nutmegs from which only the mace is eaten, and also insects.

BREEDING. Nest: large, domed, oval, with an entrance at one side, constructed chiefly of twisted tendrils of creeping plants; lined with portions of palm leaves, and a quantity of hair-like fibre; suspended from the limb of a tree, usually in or close to dense scrub. Clutch: three to four; pale bluish-white, spotted reddish-brown and purplish-grey. Breeding season: September to January.

2:8 REGENT BOWERBIRD *Sericulus chrysocephalus*

IDENTIFICATION. The male is black, with bold rich yellow wing patches and head and the female is dull brown, with slate crown and scalloped back.

DISTRIBUTION. Eastern Australia, from Clarke Range near Mackay south to the Hawkesbury River, New South Wales.

NOTES. The birds are seen in pairs or flocks according to the season; adult males often flock apart from females. The call-note is a guttural 'te–ar', long drawn out; sometimes the bird utters a squeaky 'whit–whit'. The bower is usually well hidden and rarely found. The male clears an area of ground in the centre of which it constructs a bed of sticks, well trampled down, and erects two walls, each about 25 centimetres long and 30 centimetres high, and then decorates the bower with empty land-snail shells and a few leaves and berries; macerated vegetable matter is often used to 'paint' the inner walls. Food: insects, fruits and berries.

BREEDING. Nest: a flimsy saucer-shaped structure of thin dry sticks and twigs, lined with thinner twigs; usually hidden in a mass of foliage or vines 2–20 metres or more from the ground. Clutch: two; yellowish-stone colour or dull white, with lines and hair-like markings of blackish-brown and purplish-grey. Breeding season: October to January.

2:9 GOLDEN BOWERBIRD *Prionodura newtoniana*

IDENTIFICATION. This bird is a small, stocky rainforest bowerbird. The male is golden brown, with bright yellow breast and nape and the female is plain brown above and grey below.

DISTRIBUTION. Highlands (above 900 metres) of north-eastern Queensland, from near Cooktown to Mount Spec near Townsville.

NOTES. The Golden Bowerbird frequents highland rainforest. It is usually solitary, quiet and unobtrusive away from the bower. Although the smallest of Australian bowerbirds, this species builds by far the largest bower; the walls are thick and have an average height of about one metre, although one wall may sometimes exceed two metres in height. Both walls are built around saplings growing within a few metres of each other, selected so that a vine or piece of wood extends between the two to form a 'bridge' across the bower, thus serving as a perch upon which the male can display and arrange his decorations, which consist mainly of grey-green lichen and white flowers. Most of these are attached to the higher wall and strewn on or near the bridge. Males spend much of their time perched quietly low in a tree near their bower.

Calls include a variety of harsh chattering notes. Food: native fruits, berries and insects.

BREEDING. Nest: a loosely built, deep, bowl-shaped structure of dead leaves, thin strips of bark, leaf skeletons and moss, bound with vine tendrils and rootlets; built into a hollow in the side of a tree, usually within a few metres of the ground. Clutch: two; white. Breeding season: October to January.

2:10 SATIN BOWERBIRD *Ptilonorhynchus violaceus*

IDENTIFICATION. This bird is a large stocky bowerbird. The male is rich glossy blue-black with a violet eye; the female and immature male are dull green, scalloped below; dull rufous in wings.

DISTRIBUTION. Eastern Australia (coast and associated highlands) from the Atherton Tableland south to the Seaview Range near Townsville, Queensland, and from about Rockhampton south to the Otway Ranges, Victoria.

NOTES. The birds occur in pairs in the breeding season, flocking in autumn and winter. The Satin Bowerbird is almost restricted to rainforest or wet sclerophyll forests when breeding, but winter flocks — consisting mainly of females or young males — roam widely. The species has several call-notes, chief of which is a loud 'whee–oooo'; it is also a competent mimic. Food: mainly wild fruits and berries, but also insects of various kinds.

Males build a bower on the ground, usually near a fallen log or moss-covered rock. A space of a metre or so in diameter is cleared and covered with a layer of thin sticks and twigs to a depth of about 10 centimetres, and in the centre of this platform two parallel walls of thin sticks are built to a height of about 30 centimetres. Decorations, chiefly coloured blue or yellowish green, consist of feathers, flowers, leaves, berries, snail shells, cicada shells, and such artificial items as bottle tops and plastic drinking straws. The bird customarily paints the inner walls of the bower with a paste of mixed charcoal, dark berries or wood-pulp, applied with the bill or sometimes with a wad of vegetable fibre. Males form loose clans, and often ten or twenty bowers may be found in fairly close proximity.

BREEDING. Nest: open, rather shallow, built of thin twigs and lined with dried but pliable leaves; usually in the fork of a tree (often a casuarina) or a clump of mistletoe between three and twenty-five metres from the ground. Clutch: two to three; dark cream colour, spotted brown and slaty-grey. Breeding season: October to December.

2:11 TRUMPET MANUCODE *Manucodia keraudrenii*

IDENTIFICATION. The Trumpet Manucode somewhat resembles the Shining Starling (No. 2:7), but is much larger; it has a blunt tail and conspicuous hackles at the nape.

DISTRIBUTION. Cape York Peninsula. Also occurs in New Guinea.

NOTES. The bird frequents rainforests, usually high in the canopy, singly or in pairs; it is shy and often difficult to observe. Food: mainly fruit. Its chief utterance has been described as 'a grand deep call, like the deep note of an organ', with a resonant quality imparted by a greatly extended windpipe, looped under the skin of the breast. The species may be partially migratory, moving between Cape York and New Guinea.

BREEDING. Nest: a deep saucer-shaped structure, made mainly from vine tendrils; woven into the outer fork of a leafy branch in the canopy of a tall tree, usually 10–20 metres from the ground. Clutch: two; pale purplish-pink, with longitudinal streaks and spots of chestnut and purplish-grey. Breeding season: October to January.

2:12 SPANGLED DRONGO *Dicrurus hottentottus*

IDENTIFICATION. Bold and conspicuous, this bird favours high exposed perches. It is black with a red eye and diagnostic 'fish' tail.

DISTRIBUTION. Northern and eastern Australia, west to the Kimberley and south to about Nowra, New South Wales. Vagrants are seen further south to Tasmania and South Australia. The Spangled Drongo is widespread from India and China to the Solomon Islands.

NOTES. Conspicuous, noisy and aggressive, the Spangled Drongo frequents jungle and open forest, most commonly in coastal lowlands. The bird is mainly migratory, arriving from the north during October and departing in March. Some birds wander to south-eastern New South Wales in autumn and winter. Drongos often use commanding perches on the edge of clearings or open areas, from which periodic flights are made to capture insects in mid-air; the diet also includes nectar and fruit. They also attack smaller birds at times. The calls consist of distinctive harsh chattering and metallic notes, sometimes extending into mimicry.

BREEDING. Nest: an open, shallow cup of vine tendrils and slender twigs; suspended from the rim in an outer fork (often dead) of a branch of a tall tree, often on the edge of a clearing; usually 10–20 metres from the ground. Clutch:

three to five; varying from pinkish-white to pale purplish-grey, spotted with pinkish-red. Breeding season: October to February.

2:13 COMMON KOEL *Eudynamis scolopacea*

IDENTIFICATION. The bird is slender, long-tailed, strongly arboreal, and usually unobtrusive except for loud, distinctive calls. The male is black with a red eye; the female is brown, and intricately spotted and barred.

DISTRIBUTION. Northern and eastern Australia, west to the Kimberley and south to about Wollongong, New South Wales (locally and sparingly further south). It is also widespread from India and China to New Guinea.

NOTES. The Common Koel is migratory, arriving in the south during September and returning north in March. It frequents forest country of various kinds, extending to city suburbs with extensive gardens and stands of trees. The bird feeds in the canopy of large fruiting trees (especially figs), where it keeps to dense foliage and is often difficult to see. At the height of the breeding season, however, koels are very conspicuous, calling loudly from high exposed perches or indulging in wild chases through trees and gardens. The distinctive call, 'coo–eee', may be heard at night as well as by day. Like most cuckoos, it is often pursued by other birds. Food: native fruits and berries and introduced fruits such as mulberries and figs, and also insects.

BREEDING. Nest: none built, the species being parasitic. Known foster-parents number about twelve species, mainly friarbirds, wattlebirds, mudlarks and orioles. Clutch: clutch size unknown; reddish-salmon, with dots and streaks of purplish-red. Breeding season: October to January or February.

PLATE 3

BIRDS OF RAINFORESTS AND SCRUBS

3:1 YELLOW ORIOLE *Oriolus flavocinctus*

IDENTIFICATION. The bird is mainly dull greenish-yellow, with a rather long, sturdy, pinkish bill and bold red eye. The sexes are similar, and immatures are dingier, and obscurely streaked below.

DISTRIBUTION. Tropical Australia, west to Derby, Western Australia, and south to about Ingham, Queensland. Also found in New Guinea and the Aru Islands.

NOTES. The Yellow Oriole frequents mainly trees, especially native figs, near streams, often in loose parties. It is strongly arboreal, favouring the canopy and upper levels of foliage. Its loud, bubbling notes, sometimes interspersed with mimicry of other birds, are a characteristic feature of lowland tropical rainforests, especially during the heat of the day. Food: native fruits and berries.

BREEDING. Nest: compact, cup-shaped, made of strips of soft bark and vine tendrils, lined with twigs and rootlets; usually placed in the outer branches of a tall tree, up to 20 metres from the ground. Clutch: two; pale cream, with blackish-brown and pale slate markings. Breeding season: September to December.

3:2 OLIVE-BACKED ORIOLE *Oriolus sagittatus*

IDENTIFICATION. This oriole is mainly dull green above, heavily streaked below, with a rather long, sturdy, pinkish bill and bold red eye. The sexes are similar; immatures are similar, but dingier, with a conspicuous creamy superciliary and a slate bill.

DISTRIBUTION. Northern and eastern Australia from the Kimberley east to Cape York and south to Victoria and eastern South Australia. Also found in New Guinea.

NOTES. The Olive-backed Oriole occurs singly, in pairs or sometimes small parties. It is partially migratory in the south. It frequents open forest and woodland, where it seeks native fruits, berries, and insects, usually in the canopy. The bird utters a rapid, rolling, mellow call 'olly, olly–ole', and is an assured mimic of other birds' calls.

BREEDING. Nest: deep, cup-shaped, made of strips of soft bark and leaves, lined with dried grasses; usually placed in the outer drooping branch of a tree, 1–20 metres above the ground. Clutch: two to four, usually three; pale cream, with light and dark umber and slate-grey markings. Breeding season: September to January.

3:3 FIGBIRD *Sphecotheres viridis*

IDENTIFICATION. The figbird is chunky. Males are olive green above with a black cap, and have an extensive patch of bare, bright red skin around the eye; southern males (subspecies *vieilloti*) have black throats and dull green underparts, while northern males (subspecies *flaviventris*) have bright yellow underparts. Females and immatures are dull greyish brown, heavily streaked below. There is an extensive zone of hybridisation between the two subspecies from about Cardwell to Proserpine, Queensland.

DISTRIBUTION. Northern and eastern Australia (mainly coastal lowlands), west to the Kimberley, Western Australia, and south to about Kiama, New South Wales. Also occurs in Indonesia and New Guinea.

NOTES. The bird frequents lowland forests and settled areas (including gardens and city parks), especially where figtrees occur. Strongly arboreal, it is gregarious, noisy and conspicuous, constantly uttering its peculiar chattering notes; these sometimes extend into mimicry. Food: mulberries, figs and other soft fruits.

BREEDING. Nest: open, shallow, made of vine tendrils and twigs; although only scanty, it is strongly built into the forked leafy twig of an outer branch of a tree, at heights up to 25 metres from the ground. Clutch: usually three; varying from pale apple-green to dull olive-green, with reddish or purplish-brown markings. Breeding season: October to January.

3:4 SPOTTED CATBIRD *Ailuroedus melanotis*

IDENTIFICATION. The Spotted Catbird is stocky, bright green, streaked mottled white below with contrasting black patches on its crown, chin and cheek and with a whitish bill and red eye. Both sexes are similar.

DISTRIBUTION. Northern Queensland, from Cape York to Mount Spec, near Townsville. Also found in the Aru Islands and New Guinea.

NOTES. Usually the bird occurs in pairs or small flocks in rainforest. It favours saplings and lower levels of foliage and is often secretive and difficult to observe. Its chief call is a strong, cat-like 'yowl'. Food: native fruits and berries. The Spotted Catbird is closely related to (and probably conspecific with) the Green Catbird.

BREEDING. Nest: large, bowl-shaped, of long twigs, scraps of dry wood, and broad leaves, lined with twigs and vine tendrils; usually placed near the top of a bushy sapling in dense forest, 1–10 metres from the ground. Clutch: two to three; cream coloured. Breeding season: September to December.

3:5 GREEN CATBIRD *Ailuroedus crassirostris*

IDENTIFICATION. This bird is like the Spotted Catbird but is less boldly marked, with no black patches on the head. The sexes are similar.

DISTRIBUTION. From about Gympie and Kingaroy, Queensland, south to Mount Dromedary, near Narooma, New South Wales.

NOTES. This Catbird frequents chiefly lowland rainforests. It often congregates at fruiting trees with Regent and Satin Bowerbirds. Its call, a cat–like 'me–ow', uttered most frequently at daybreak and dusk, is a common rainforest sound; a low plaintive hiss and a 'pick' note are also uttered. Food: native fruits and berries, particularly the seeds of bangalow and cabbage-tree palms; also insects, chiefly beetles.

BREEDING. Nest: bowl-shaped, of long twigs and vine stems entwined around a layer of broad leaves, occasionally moss, lined with fine twigs; usually placed in dense foliage in the crown of a small tree, or in a vine-tangle, usually 3–10 metres from the ground. Clutch: two to three; cream or pale creamy-white. Breeding season: September to January, rarely February.

3:6 TOOTH-BILLED CATBIRD *Ailuroedus dentirostris*

IDENTIFICATION. This Catbird is chunky, dull brown above and dingy white below, is heavily streaked, has a stout black bill and dark eye.

DISTRIBUTION. Highland rainforests (mainly above 600 metres altitude) of north-eastern Queensland, from Cooktown to Mount Spec near Townsville.

NOTES. The bird inhabits rainforest, favouring the understorey and lower levels of foliage. It is rather quiet and unobtrusive, except during the breeding season when the male clears a circular space, a metre or two in diameter, on the forest floor, and within it carefully arranges up to a hundred or more fresh leaves of various sizes; these are always turned upside-down. The arena is situated beneath a branch or a vine that serves as a 'singing stick', upon which the bird exercises its remarkable voice; the characteristic note is a loud 'chuck–chuck', and to this is added an extraordinary torrent of calls, partly mimetic. Food: native fruits and berries, snails and insects.

BREEDING. Nest: saucer-shaped, somewhat frail, made of thin dry sticks and lined with finer twigs; usually in dense foliage or a vine-tangle about 10–25 metres above the ground. Clutch: usually two; rich creamy-brown. Breeding season: November to January.

3:7 ROSE-CROWNED FRUITDOVE *Ptilinopus regina*

IDENTIFICATION. This bird is mainly green, and the male has an orange belly, blue-grey breast, and rose-pink cap, rimmed yellow.

DISTRIBUTION. Northern and eastern Australia (mainly coast and associated highlands) from the Kimberley and Top End east to the Sir Edward Pellew Islands, Gulf of Carpentaria (subspecies *ewingi*), and from Cape York south to the Hunter River, New South Wales (subspecies *regina*). Also occurs in Indonesia and possibly New Guinea. It is a vagrant to Victoria and Tasmania.

NOTES. The bird frequents fruiting trees of coastal rainforests, monsoon forests and mangroves. It is apparently sedentary in the Northern Territory, but strongly nomadic and possibly migratory along the east coast. The Rose-crowned Fruitdove is strictly arboreal. Although it is brightly coloured, it is a difficult bird to observe. The call, comparatively loud, is a series of 'coos' repeated about 20 times, beginning slowly then accelerating to a continuous stream of notes before dying away. There is also a distinctive soft call rendered as 'boo–uk–boo'. Food: entirely fruit.

BREEDING. Nest: a flat, flimsy platform of twigs seldom exceeding 5–6 centimetres in diameter, usually on a small outer horizontal fork in a tree, at almost any height, but usually within 10 metres of the ground. Clutch: one; lustrous white. Breeding season: October to January.

3:8 SUPERB FRUITDOVE *Ptilinopus superbus*

IDENTIFICATION. Males of the species have an orange nape, white underparts, a grey breast crossed by a bold black band, and a bright purple crown. Otherwise the bird is mainly green. The female is a bright green with a white belly. Immatures are difficult to distinguish from those of the Rose-crowned Fruitdove.

DISTRIBUTION. Northern Queensland from Cape York south to about Rockhampton; vagrant south to New South Wales (regular), Victoria and Tasmania. Also found in Indonesia and New Guinea.

NOTES. The Superb Fruitdove is similar in habits to the Rose-crowned Fruitdove. It is very common, but is strongly arboreal and difficult to observe. Its call-note is a low 'oom', exploding into 'whoops' suggesting the measured barking of a dog. Food: mainly fruit.

BREEDING. Nest: a frail platform of twigs only a few centimetres across; usually in the horizontal fork of a sapling within 3–4 metres of the ground. Clutch: one; white, with creamy tinge. Breeding season: October to February.

3:9 BROWN PIGEON *Macropygia amboinensis*

IDENTIFICATION. The Brown Pigeon is more or less plain chocolate-brown, with a very long tail. The sexes are similar.

DISTRIBUTION. Eastern Australia from Cape York south to about Bermagui, New South Wales. Also occurs in Indonesia and the Philippines.

NOTES. This pigeon is seen in pairs or small flocks, frequenting rainforests of the coast and associated highlands. It prefers the more open parts of the scrubs — second-growth, bush-tracks and clearings. The call is a deliberate 'whoop–a–whoop', uttered several times. Food: fruit and seeds, especially berries of the inkweed, wild tobacco and wild raspberry.

BREEDING. Nest: a platform of sticks, varying from scanty to substantial; in a bush or tree, usually within 10 metres of the ground. Clutch: one; creamy-white. Breeding season: very variable, but mainly October to December.

3:10 EMERALD DOVE *Chalcophaps indica*

IDENTIFICATION. Small and compact, this bird potters quietly about under shrubbery or on open forest clearings. The head and underparts are wine-pink, with the back emerald green. The sexes are similar, but juveniles are strongly barred black and chocolate.

DISTRIBUTION. Coastal Northern Territory and eastern Australia from Cape York to eastern Victoria. Also found in New Guinea and various islands of the South-west Pacific.

NOTES. Usually seen in pairs, the bird frequents wet coastal forests. Mainly terrestrial, it is quiet and unobtrusive, but usually ignores a patient observer. When flushed it rises with a whirring sound, flies rapidly through the scrub for a short distance, and then drops suddenly to the ground. Its call is a series of low, drawn-out 'coos'. Food: native fruits, berries and seeds.

BREEDING. Nest: scanty and almost flat, built of twigs; placed at the junction of leafy horizontal branches, on a mass of vines, or on top of an arboreal fern, several metres from the ground. Clutch: two; pale cream. Breeding season: variable.

3:11 TOPKNOT PIGEON *Lopholaimus antarcticus*

IDENTIFICATION. This pigeon is large and grey, with a rufous nape and a distinctive loose, backswept crest. In flight overhead it shows rather a long blackish tail crossed by a bold grey band.

DISTRIBUTION. Eastern Australia, from Cape York to north-eastern Victoria; accidental to Tasmania.

NOTES. Gregarious and highly nomadic, its movements coincide with the ripening of various native fruits and berries, especially the seeds of the bangalow and cabbage-tree palms. When not feeding it usually keeps to the topmost branches of tall trees. It is mostly silent, but one call has been described as being 'between a sniff and a snort'. Until protected, these birds were shot in large numbers.

BREEDING. Nest: a platform of fairly stout twigs, usually placed in slender branches, up to 30 metres from the ground. Clutch: one, pearly-white. Breeding season: October to December.

3:12 WHITE-HEADED PIGEON *Columba leucomela*

IDENTIFICATION. Males are dark purple-green above, with white head and underparts; females and immatures are similar but have dingy, pale brownish-grey head and underparts.

DISTRIBUTION. Eastern Australia from about Cooktown, Queensland, south to about Sydney, New South Wales; recorded south to Bermagui, but status uncertain.

NOTES. This pigeon is seen in pairs or small flocks, frequenting mainly rainforests. Its movements are regulated by the supply of food — native fruits and berries, chiefly the seeds of bangalow and cabbage-tree palms and the berries of inkweed. Generally wary, unobtrusive and strongly arboreal, birds will occasionally come to the ground to feed and drink. The call is a loud 'whooo–hoo', uttered several times.

BREEDING. Nest: a scanty platform of sticks, usually in dense foliage in the horizontal branches of a jungle tree or placed in a tangle of vines up to about 20 metres from the ground. Clutch: one, dull white or creamy-white. Breeding season: March to October.

3:13 TORRES STRAIT PIGEON *Ducula spilorrhoa*

IDENTIFICATION. Mainly pure white, the bird has black wings and tail. The sexes are similar.

DISTRIBUTION. Northern Australia, from the Kimberley, Western Australia, to the east coast and south to about Mackay, Queensland. Also found in New Guinea, the Aru Islands and the Bismarck Archipelago.

NOTES. The bird is a migrant, arriving in flocks in Australia during September or October and returning northward in March or April. It breeds in colonies, chiefly on islands off the coast and visits the mainland each day seeking food, which consists of native fruits and berries such as quandongs and wild nutmegs. Before the species was protected, many thousands were killed each year, mainly for sport.

BREEDING. Nest: a few twigs laid across each other in the fork of a small tree, chiefly mangroves or tea-trees. Clutch: one, pure white. Breeding season: August to January.

3:14 WOMPOO FRUITDOVE *Ptilinopus magnificus*

IDENTIFICATION. This is a very large fruitdove; its wine-purple breast and yellow bar on wing are diagnostic. The sexes are similar.

DISTRIBUTION. Eastern Australia from Cape York south to about the Hunter River, New South Wales. It also occurs in New Guinea.

NOTES. Mainly solitary, the bird frequents rainforests of the coast and associated ranges. It is strictly arboreal, and unobtrusive, but it has an extraordinary and very distinctive call; the deep bubbling notes resemble 'bock–bock–a–boo', or the gobble of a domestic turkey. Food: native fruits, berries, and seeds.

BREEDING. Nest: a small, flat platform of vine tendrils and twigs on an outer horizontal fork of a tree, often overhanging water; usually within 10 metres of the ground. Clutch: one; white. Breeding season: October to February, sometimes later.

3:15 BANDED FRUITDOVE *Ptilinopus cinctus*

IDENTIFICATION. This fruitdove is black above, grey below, with a white head and breast and bold black band across its lower breast. The sexes are similar.

DISTRIBUTION. Western Arnhem Land, Northern Territory. It also occurs in Indonesia.

NOTES. A little-known species, it frequents pockets of rainforest and shrubbery in gorges and stream-beds in rough sandstone areas at the western edge of the Arnhem Land plateau. The bird is found singly or in small parties. The call is a low, loud note 'best described as a hoot', and on being disturbed, the bird flushes with a loud wing-clap, and flies off with an audible wing-beat. Food: native fruits and berries.

BREEDING. Nest: a loose, flimsy platform of sticks about 20 centimetres in diameter, placed a few metres from the ground in a small tree. Clutch: one, pure white. Breeding season: uncertain, but nests with eggs have been found from May to November.

PLATE 4

BIRDS OF RAINFORESTS AND SCRUBS

4:1 WHITE-TAILED KINGFISHER *Tanysiptera sylvia*

IDENTIFICATION. This rainforest kingfisher has a bright red bill and long white tail. The sexes are similar.

DISTRIBUTION. New Guinea and north-eastern Queensland, from Cape York to Cardwell.

NOTES. This kingfisher frequents lowland rainforest, mainly in the canopy, singly or in pairs. A spring and summer migrant, this species arrives from New Guinea in November and departs in February or March, occasionally later. Numbers of birds have been reported, from time to time, in an exhausted condition at Cape York. Calls include a series of 'chop–chop' notes, a loud scream and a persistent trilling note. Food: insects and small reptiles.

BREEDING. Nest: in a cavity excavated in a termite mound, usually close to the ground. Clutch: three to four; white. Breeding season: November to January.

4:2 BRUSH CUCKOO *Cuculus variolosus*

IDENTIFICATION. This cuckoo resembles the Fan-tailed Cuckoo but is smaller, dingier; it lacks a bright yellow eye-ring, and its tail is square-tipped, and the outer webs of the tail feathers are plain grey, not notched white as in the Fan-tailed Cuckoo. The sexes are similar.

DISTRIBUTION. Coastal northern and eastern Australia. It also occurs in Indonesia and New Guinea.

NOTES. The bird is a migrant, arriving in New South Wales and Victoria in October and departing during February or March. It inhabits mainly rainforests of dense eucalypt. Usually it is unobtrusive and solitary, but is very vocal on arrival in spring; the usual call is a series of six or seven loud, shrill, measured notes, gradually descending, but increasing in volume. The bird often calls at night. Food: insects, especially hairy caterpillars.

BREEDING. Nest: none built, the species being parasitic; birds that build open, cup-shaped nests (e.g. flycatchers and monarchs) are usually chosen as foster parents. Clutch: white, with faint purplish-brown and lavender markings. Breeding season: October to January.

4:3 RUFOUS FANTAIL *Rhipidura rufifrons*

IDENTIFICATION. The bird is bright rufous above; its wings are persistently drooped and its tail is widely fanned in flamboyant manner. The sexes are similar.

DISTRIBUTION. Northern and eastern Australia, west to the Kimberley and south to Victoria, straying to Tasmania and eastern South Australia. It is also found in Indonesia, New Guinea, Micronesia and the Solomon Islands.

NOTES. The Rufous Fantail is migratory south of about Sydney, New South Wales, arriving during September and October and departing in February or March, with stragglers remaining later. It frequents mainly dense low cover in rainforest, especially tree-fern gullies, and, on migration, open forest. The song is brisk, high-pitched and penetrating. Food: insects caught on the wing, sometimes on the ground.

BREEDING. Nest: shaped like a wine glass without the base; made of dried grasses and bark-fibre, bound with spiders' silk and lined with finer materials; with a 'tail-piece' 5–6 centimetres long dangling below; constructed on a thin horizontal branch 1–10 metres from the ground. Clutch: two to three; stone or buff-coloured, with a zone of lavender around the larger end. Breeding season: November to January.

4:4 YELLOW-BREASTED BOATBILL *Machaerirhynchus flaviventer*

IDENTIFICATION. A small, active rainforest bird, the Boatbill is bright yellow below, black above, with a double white wingbar and bold yellow superciliary. Sexes are similar, but the female is noticeably duller.

DISTRIBUTION. North-eastern Queensland, from Cape York to Townsville. It is also found in New Guinea.

NOTES. The bird inhabits rainforests of coastal areas. It is a very active and lively species, often raising its tail or drooping its wings as it moves through the canopy. The birds are typically found in pairs. The Boatbill has a soft agreeable trilling song. Food: insects, caught both on the wing and among the leaves of trees.

BREEDING. Nest: saucer-shaped, constructed of plant stems matted with cobwebs, the inner portion consisting entirely of fine dried tendrils of plants; usually built in a slender horizontal fork in a sapling or bush. Clutch: two; white, with a zone of purplish-red spots around the larger end. Breeding season: September to December.

4:5 PIED MONARCH *Arses kaupi*

IDENTIFICATION. This boldly pied rainforest monarch has bright blue naked skin around eye and broad black breast band crossing white underparts. Sexes are similar, but the female is dingier, with more extensive black on the head.

DISTRIBUTION. North-eastern Queensland, from Cape York to near Townsville.

NOTES. A very active bird, it spreads its tail and erects the feathers on the nape and crest; it creeps and hops about the trunks and branches of trees in rainforests seeking insects on the bark, seldom spending more than 30 seconds or so on one tree before moving on to the next. Usually solitary or in pairs, the bird is occasionally seen in small parties. The usual call is a faint vibrant 'quarr'.

BREEDING. Nest: like a miniature basket or hammock, attached to thin parallel stems of a vine; made of thin dried fern stalks and vine tendrils, lined with fine rootlets; up to 10 metres from the ground. Clutch: two; whitish, with reddish and lavender markings. Breeding season: November to January.

4:6 FRILLED MONARCH *Arses telescophthalmus*

IDENTIFICATION. It resembles the Pied Monarch, but the underparts are entirely white. Sexes are similar.

DISTRIBUTION. Cape York Peninsula, south to the Chester River. It is also found in New Guinea.

NOTES. The Frilled Monarch inhabits lowland rainforest. It is sedentary and fairly common. The bird has similar habits to the Pied Monarch, but it extends the nape feathers (the 'frill') more often, is less restricted to rainforest, and spends comparatively more time gleaning in leaves in the canopy and less time searching the trunks of trees. It is possibly conspecific with the Pied Monarch.

BREEDING. Nest: similar to that of the Pied Monarch. Clutch: two; whitish, with purplish-red markings. Breeding season: November to January.

4:7 BLACK-FACED MONARCH *Monarcha melanopsis*

IDENTIFICATION. This bird has a smoky grey head and upperparts, with the breast and belly a brick red colour and a black chin and forehead. Sexes are similar, and the juvenile has a grey, not black, face.

DISTRIBUTION. Eastern Australia, from Cape York to the vicinity of Melbourne, Victoria. It also occurs in New Guinea.

NOTES. The Black-faced Monarch is migratory, arriving in the southern states in spring and departing during February or March. It frequents rainforest and methodically searches leaves and branches for food, or snatches insects in mid-air. The chief call is a loud cheery whistle, 'why–yew, witch–yew'. Food: insects of various kinds.

BREEDING. Nest: neat, cup-shaped, of green moss and lined with fine rootlets; usually in an upright fork of a branch 1–10 metres from the ground. Clutch: two to three; white, with reddish and lavender spots. Breeding season: November to January.

4:8 BLACK-WINGED MONARCH *Monarcha frater*

IDENTIFICATION. The bird closely resembles the Black-faced Monarch, but its wings and tail are black, not grey, contrasting with a smoke-grey back. Sexes are similar, and juvenile lacks black face. (Cape York only.)

DISTRIBUTION. Cape York Peninsula south to the Claudie River. It is also found in New Guinea.

NOTES. Singly or in pairs, the bird frequents open forest as well as jungle. It is similar in many ways to the Black-faced Monarch, but its habits are little known.

BREEDING. Nest: cup-shaped, composed of fine strips and flakes of paperbark, bound with cobweb; lined with vegetable fibres. Clutch: three; white, with small reddish-brown spots and underlying markings of pale purple. Breeding season: November to January.

4:9 SPECTACLED MONARCH *Monarcha trivirgatus*

IDENTIFICATION. This bird is much like the Black-faced Monarch, but it is darker grey above. It has a white belly, black cheeks and brick red 'moustache'. The sexes are similar.

DISTRIBUTION. Eastern Australia from Cape York to about Ourimbah, New South Wales; scattered records further south. The bird is also found in Indonesia and New Guinea.

NOTES. Sedentary populations are found in north Queensland, but the bird is migratory further south, arriving in New South Wales late in September and departing during February or March. The bird is vivacious and industrious, tumbling and fluttering in foliage or busily searching trunks, limbs and vines at all levels in rainforest. The chief calls are a fussy chattering and a whirring 'pree–pree–pree', uttered frequently. Food: mainly flying insects.

BREEDING. Nest: a deep untidy cup of fine bark and moss liberally bound with spiders' silk, lined with soft plant fibres and decorated on the outside with bits of lichen; usually only a few metres from the ground in the upright fork of a sapling. Clutch: two; dull white, with purple or reddish-brown markings. Breeding season: October to January.

4:10 WHITE-EARED MONARCH *Monarcha leucotis*

IDENTIFICATION. This monarch is mainly black above, white below, with a complex black and white pattern on its head and with a white rump. Sexes are similar.

DISTRIBUTION. Eastern Australia from Cape York south to the Clarence River, New South Wales.

NOTES. This is a very active bird, catching most of its food on the wing, and hovering about the leaves of rainforest trees, usually high in the canopy. The calls are very distinctive, and include a loud 'ta–ta–taaaa' and a drawn-out 'ee–ooo, ee–ooo'. Food: small insects.

BREEDING. Nest: cup-shaped, of moss and plant fibres, heavily bound with spiders' silk; lined with fine pieces of plant fibre and hair-like fern stems; built into a slender upright tree fork, usually 10-20 metres from the ground. Clutch: two; whitish, with small spots of reddish-brown. Breeding season: October to December.

4:11 WHITE-BREASTED ROBIN *Eopsaltria georgiana*

IDENTIFICATION. This robin is plain smoke grey above, white below, with a breast washed with grey. Sexes are similar.

DISTRIBUTION. South-western Australia, north to Geraldton, Western Australia.

NOTES. Like other robins, a common habit of this bird is to use the trunk of a tree as a vantage point and snap up insects from the ground. The chief call is 'chit–chit', somewhat harsh in tone. The bird favours dense vegetation, but at times it visits country gardens and orchards. It is often solitary. In general, it is fairly trusting.

BREEDING. Nest: cup-shaped, made of strips of bark, fine twigs and leaves; placed a metre or so up in a tree or shrub; usually in dense cover close to water. Clutch: two; olive or bronze-green, darker at the larger end. Breeding season: September to December.

4:12 GREY-HEADED ROBIN *Heteromyias albispecularis*

IDENTIFICATION. This is a fairly large robin with grey head, white throat, and light brown cheeks, dull white underparts and tawny rump. Sexes are similar.

DISTRIBUTION. North-eastern Queensland, from Cooktown to Mount Spec, near Townsville.

NOTES. The bird is found singly or in pairs, frequenting densely timbered highlands; it is seldom seen at any great height from the ground. This robin is sedentary; common but rather quiet and often unobtrusive. It is confiding, and will often come to picnic tables on the edge of forest. Its calls are three gentle notes, one high and two low, also a low, continuous whistle. Food: insects.

BREEDING. Nest: cup-shaped, made of fine twigs, rootlets and moss, lined with plant fibres; usually in the upright stem of a lawyer-vine several metres from the ground. Clutch: one to two; buffy white, with spots of umber and underlying markings of lavender. Breeding season: August to January.

4:13 WHITE-BROWED ROBIN *Poecilodryas superciliosa*

IDENTIFICATION. The bird is dark brown above, dingy white below, boldly marked with white on wings and has a conspicuous white eyebrow. Sexes are similar.

DISTRIBUTION. There are two distinct populations: subspecies *P. s. cerviniventris* occurs across northern Australia from Derby, Western Australia, east to Burketown, Queensland, and *P. s. superciliosa* occurs on Cape York Peninsula, south perhaps as far as Rockhampton.

NOTES. The bird is found singly or in pairs. Generally uncommon, local, and sedentary, it feeds largely on the ground but often searches tree trunks in heavy vegetation, mainly near streams. It is sprightly, but is quiet and unobtrusive in disposition. The call is a loud piping whistle, repeated several times; it also utters a series of soft, sweet, drawn-out whistles.

BREEDING. Nest: a neat, frail cup of grass, strips of bark and plant fibre, bound with spiders' silk and lined with leaves, placed in a sapling, often among dead foliage, a few metres from the ground. Clutch: usually two; pale green with brownish markings. Breeding season: September to February.

4:14 YELLOW ROBIN *Eopsaltria australis*

NOTES. The subspecies (*chrysorrhoa*) illustrated inhabits eastern Queensland and north-eastern New South Wales; it differs from other populations in eastern Australia by its bright yellow rump. For detailed notes on the species, see 10:4 (p. 69).

4:15 PALE-YELLOW ROBIN *Tregellasia capito*

IDENTIFICATION. This bird resembles the Yellow Robin but is smaller and much dingier; it has white lores (buff in north Queensland birds). Sexes are similar.

DISTRIBUTION. Eastern Australia from Cooktown, Queensland, south to the Williams River, New South Wales.

NOTES. This robin inhabits rainforest, especially where lawyer-vine is common. Quiet in all its movements, this bird also possesses a subdued voice. Its insect food is caught in the air or on the ground, or by foraging in foliage. Like other yellow robins, it often clings sideways to a tree trunk. It is sedentary.

BREEDING. Nest: cup-shaped, made of bark fragments and leaves, bound with cobweb and lined with small dead leaves; decorated outside with pieces of lichen; usually found in a lawyer-vine within a few metres of the ground. Clutch: two; greenish-white, with yellowish or chestnut-brown markings. Breeding season: August to December.

4:16 WHITE-FACED ROBIN *Tregellasia leucops*

IDENTIFICATION. This is a small robin, olive above, yellow below, with cheeks and crown black and face white. Sexes are similar.

DISTRIBUTION. North-eastern Queensland from Cape York to the Rocky River. The bird is also found in New Guinea.

NOTES. A quiet bird, its call, a short harsh 'chee–chee–chee', is uttered only occasionally. It is very similar in habits and habitat to the Pale-yellow Robin (4:15). Food: insects of litter and trees.

BREEDING. Nest: very similar to that of the Pale-yellow Robin. Clutch: two; greenish-white, with reddish spots. Breeding season: December to January.

4:17 GOLDEN WHISTLER *Pachycephala pectoralis*

IDENTIFICATION. Its upperparts are olive green, underparts bright yellow, head black, throat white, and it has a bold black band across the breast. The female is plain dingy brown, somewhat paler below; immatures have wing feathers edged dull rufous.

DISTRIBUTION. Eastern and southern Australia, from Cairns to Eyre Peninsula, reappearing in south-western Australia; also occurs in Tasmania.

NOTES. The Golden Whistler inhabits rainforests, scrub and open forest. It is usually solitary and deliberate in its movements. It has a sweet and ringing song, which is very freely uttered by the male in the breeding season; like other whistlers it has the distinctive habit of breaking into song after any loud, abrupt noise such as a thunder-clap or a rifle shot. Food: insects.

BREEDING. Nest: a shallow cup of rootlets and plant stems, lined with finer materials; usually in the upright fork of a sapling within about four metres of the ground. Clutch: two to three; stone-coloured or white (occasionally salmon), speckled brown. Breeding season: August to December.

4:18 OLIVE WHISTLER *Pachycephala olivacea*

IDENTIFICATION. This is a rather large, sturdy and very elusive whistler. It is olive brown above, light reddish brown below, washed grey across the breast, has a grey head and white throat, scaled grey. Sexes are similar.

DISTRIBUTION. South-eastern Queensland to eastern and southern Victoria and south-eastern South Australia, Tasmania, and islands of Bass Strait.

NOTES. The bird inhabits dense highland forests in the northern parts of its range, but often more open, coastal habitats in Victoria and Tasmania. It is sedentary, usually shy, remaining in dense thickets, but will respond to a squeaking call. All of its notes are highly melodious, with a suggestion of wistfulness; a very distinctive call of Queensland birds is a 'pee–pooo'. Food: insects and seeds.

BREEDING. Nest: cup-shaped, loosely constructed of fine twigs and dry leaves lined with finer materials; usually in the upright fork of a sapling within a metre or two of the ground. Clutch: two to three; pale yellowish-white, with markings of dull grey and umber. Breeding season: September to January.

4:19 LITTLE SHRIKE-THRUSH *Colluricincla megarhyncha*

IDENTIFICATION. The subspecies shown here (subspecies *megarhyncha*; see also No. 10:10) is dull brown above, light tan below, with pale face and light, pinkish bill. Sexes are similar.

DISTRIBUTION. Northern and eastern Australia, from the Kimberley to Cape York and south to the Bellinger River near Coffs Harbour, New South Wales. It is also found in New Guinea.

NOTES. This bird is now considered conspecific with the form once known as the Little Thrush *Colluricincla megarhyncha parvula* (No 10:10). Generally common, it is sedentary, and usually solitary. It possesses highly melodious notes, one of which is interpreted as 'tu–whee, wot–wot'; occasionally it sings a rich, sustained song; it is also an occasional mimic. Food: insects, mostly procured on the ground or in undergrowth.

BREEDING. Nest: cup-shaped, composed of dried leaves, strips of bark, and rootlets; lined with fine rootlets and grass; built in a bush or small tree or in a mass of vines. Clutch: two to three; pinkish-white, with reddish-brown and purplish-grey markings. Breeding season: September to January.

4:20 BOWER'S SHRIKE-THRUSH *Colluricincla boweri*

IDENTIFICATION. The bird is dark grey-brown above, light rufous below, and faintly streaked with a black bill. Sexes are similar.

DISTRIBUTION. Highlands (above about 400 metres) of north-eastern Queensland from Cooktown to the Seaview Range north of Townsville.

NOTES. The bird frequents dense highland rainforests. It is sedentary, generally common, but quiet, deliberate and unobtrusive in its movements. Its song is rich and melodious. Food: insects.

BREEDING. Nest: cup-shaped, composed of dead leaves, bark, and plant stems, lined with fine rootlets; placed in a dense mass of foliage or lawyer-vines up to 10 metres from the ground. Clutch: two to three; creamy-white, with dark olive or reddish-brown and dull slate markings. Breeding season: October to December.

4:21 EASTERN WHIPBIRD *Psophodes olivaceus*

IDENTIFICATION. A dark, long-tailed bird, the Eastern Whipbird is olive green with a black head and breast, white cheek and conspicuous crest. Sexes are similar.

DISTRIBUTION. Eastern Australia (mainly coast and associated highlands) from north-eastern Queensland to Victoria.

NOTES. The bird inhabits dense forest and coastal thickets. A shy bird, it seeks the seclusion of the undergrowth. It spends most of its time on the ground turning over fallen leaves and debris with its bill in search of insects. Its name is derived from its extraordinary call, an extended whistle ending on a loud 'whipcrack' note, followed instantly by two notes — 'choo–choo', or 'choo–eee'; these last are usually (but not always) uttered by the female (sometimes from the nest).

BREEDING. Nest: cup-shaped, composed of fine twigs and rootlets and lined with finer materials; built in a low bush or among undergrowth. Clutch: two; pale blue or bluish-white, with irregular markings of black and lavender. Breeding season: July to November, occasionally later.

4:22 WESTERN WHIPBIRD *Psophodes nigrogularis*

IDENTIFICATION. This whipbird resembles the Eastern Whipbird but is smaller, paler, with a smaller, grey crest. Sexes are similar.

DISTRIBUTION. South-western Australia and mallee areas of north-western Victoria and south-eastern South Australia; also found in the York Peninsula, Eyre Peninsula, and Kangaroo Island.

NOTES. An elusive species, it is extremely difficult to observe, inhabiting heath and other low, dense vegetation. It is similar in many ways to the Eastern Whipbird, but is much rarer and more specialised. Its distinctive calls have been likened to 'it's for TEAcher' and 'happy birthday to you'. Food: insects, captured mainly on the ground.

BREEDING. Nest: bowl-shaped, constructed of twigs and bark fragments, and lined with wiry grass. Clutch: two; pale blue, with spots and hieroglyphic markings of black and umber. Breeding season: September to November.

PLATE 5

NOCTURNAL BIRDS

5:1 BARN OWL *Tyto alba*

IDENTIFICATION. This owl is mottled gold above and white below, with a white, heart-shaped facial disc. Sexes are similar.

DISTRIBUTION. Throughout Australia (rare in Tasmania). Also it is found virtually worldwide.

NOTES. It is found in most types of open wooded country, but not dense forests. The bird is nomadic. During the day it usually roosts in a hollow in a tree, or in woolsheds, lofts, stables, and occasionally a canopy in a thick bush. The call is a loud screech. Food: mainly mice, also rats, bats, small birds, insects and reptiles.

BREEDING. Nest: in a cavity in a tree. Clutch: three to seven; dull white, oval. Breeding season: extremely variable, in response to plagues of mice.

5:2 SOOTY OWL *Tyto tenebricosa*

IDENTIFICATION. This is a dark, sooty, sturdy owl with stumpy tail and very large black eyes. Its upperparts are peppered white. Sexes are similar.

DISTRIBUTION. Eastern Queensland to eastern Victoria and Flinders Island (Bass Strait). It also occurs in New Guinea.

NOTES. The Sooty Owl occurs in isolated pairs in heavy forests, mainly mountainous, remaining screened by day and preying at night on possums, gliders, etc. Generally quiet, it becomes noisy when breeding; calls include a characteristic loud eerie descending whistle, suggesting a falling bomb; also a series of insect-like chirrupings. As in many birds of prey, the female is much larger than the male. It has been suggested recently that northern Queensland birds constitute a species distinct from birds of south-eastern Australia.

BREEDING. Nest: in a cavity in a tree, usually high. Clutch: two; white and oval-shaped. Breeding season: at any time according to suitable conditions.

5:3 MASKED OWL *Tyto novaehollandiae*

IDENTIFICATION. Difficult to distinguish from the Barn Owl, this bird is generally darker, browner, sturdier, usually with a brownish facial disc. Sexes are similar.

DISTRIBUTION. Coastal regions of Australia generally (has not been recorded more than about 300 kilometres from the coast). Also found in New Guinea and it has been introduced to Lord Howe Island.

NOTES. The Masked Owl frequents dense forests generally. During the day it roosts in hollows in trees or among thick foliage. Birds from Tasmania are very much larger than mainland birds. In contrast to the closely related and similar Barn Owl, Masked Owls are sedentary, mate for life, and the sexes are strikingly disparate in size. Generally they are uncommon. The call is a screech similar to, but rather louder than, that of the Barn Owl. Food: small mammals, reptiles and occasionally birds.

BREEDING. Nest: in a large hollow in a tree, usually at a considerable height; occasionally (in arid treeless regions) in a cave or blow-hole. Clutch: two to three, rarely four; pearly white, oval shaped. Breeding season: variable, according to food supply.

5:4 **EASTERN GRASS OWL** *Tyto longimembris*

IDENTIFICATION. This bird resembles the Barn Owl, but the legs are longer (extend well beyond the tip of the tail in flight), and the upperparts have large patches of dull gold and grey. Sexes are similar.

DISTRIBUTION. Coastal eastern Australia from Cape York to around Harrington, New South Wales, and from the Gulf country south through western Queensland into north-eastern South Australia.

NOTES. It frequents tussock grasslands and wallum heaths on the coast, and marshy thickets of lignum, sedge and rushes in the interior. It rests during the day in a 'squat' or 'hide', a platform of heavily trampled grass under a tussock. Food: rodents, large insects, reptiles and frogs. The population in the interior is especially affected by the periodic failure of its chief food supply (the Long-haired Rat *Rattus villolissimus*), when the birds are forced to roam widely in search of food, and may turn up almost anywhere in eastern Australia.

BREEDING. Nest: under or in a tussock of grass. Clutch: usually four; white. Breeding season: May to July.

5:5 **AUSTRALIAN OWLET-NIGHTJAR** *Aegotheles cristatus*

IDENTIFICATION. This is a dark, fluffy night bird with long tail and large dark eyes; generally grey, some individuals are washed rufous. Sexes are similar.

DISTRIBUTION. Throughout Australia, including Tasmania. It is also found in New Guinea.

NOTES. This bird frequents forest lands generally. During the day it roosts in hollows in trees, emerging in quest of insects (chiefly moths and beetles) as night approaches. The call is a double note, 'chirk–chirk', which is often uttered from the roosting hollow in daylight.

BREEDING. Nest: in a cavity in a tree or stump; lined with leaves. Clutch: three to four; white, occasionally lightly spotted. Breeding season: September to December.

5:6 MARBLED FROGMOUTH *Podargus ocellatus*

IDENTIFICATION. Delicately marbled dark grey, light grey, and rufous, this bird closely resembles the Tawny Frogmouth, but the tail is long, slender and notched; the head in profile is more rounded; it has a prominent pale eyebrow and orange eyes. Sexes are similar.

DISTRIBUTION. Extreme north-eastern New South Wales and south-eastern Queensland. They are also found in Cape York Peninsula and New Guinea.

NOTES. This Frogmouth frequents dense rainforest. During the day it shelters among masses of vines or other tangled vegetation; at night it hunts in the scrubs. The bird is generally rare, solitary, elusive and little known; although recent evidence suggests the species may be much more common than previously suspected. Its call-note is a monotonous 'kooloo, kooloo, kooloo'. Food: insects, chiefly beetles.

BREEDING. Nest: a flat platform of twigs on a branch in dense scrub. Clutch: two; white. Breeding season: August to December.

5:7 TAWNY FROGMOUTH *Podargus strigoides*

IDENTIFICATION. This bird's plumage is very variable, but delicately mottled and streaked fawn, light grey and dark grey (some individuals strongly washed rufous); it has a flat skull, bright yellow eyes, tail moderate, broad and rounded. Sexes are similar.

DISTRIBUTION. Throughout Australia, including Tasmania.

NOTES. The bird is common and widespread in most kinds of wooded country, including city parks and suburban gardens. Largely nocturnal, it reposes in an upright or semi-upright position during the day on a branch of a tree, and moves only when disturbed. When at rest it simulates the bark of the branch so closely that it is difficult to locate. The chief call is a low booming or grunting note, 'oom', repeated many times. Food: insects and mice; while seeking insects on roads the birds are often killed by motor vehicles.

BREEDING. Nest: an open platform of fine sticks and twigs loosely put together; often lined with green leaves; usually placed on a horizontal fork up to 15 metres from the ground. Clutch: two to four; white. Breeding season: August to December.

5:8 PAPUAN FROGMOUTH *Podargus papuensis*

IDENTIFICATION. This bird is very like the Tawny Frogmouth but is larger, with a proportionately bigger head, long, rather slender, graduated tail and bright red eyes. Sexes are similar.

DISTRIBUTION. North-eastern Queensland, from Cape York to Cairns. It is also found in New Guinea and the Aru Islands.

NOTES. The Papuan Frogmouth frequents open forest and scrubs. During the day it rests in an upright attitude on a branch or on the ground. At times it utters a weird laugh and a frog-like croak; it also has calls like those of the Tawny Frogmouth, a series of 'ooms', uttered for long periods at night. Like the Tawny Frogmouth, it is often flushed from roadsides at night. Food: insects, chiefly beetles, and small mammals.

BREEDING. Nest: a flimsy platform of sticks and twigs, usually on a horizontal fork up to 20 metres from the ground. Clutch: one; white. Breeding season: September to December, sometimes as late as February.

5:9 BOOBOOK OWL *Ninox novaeseelandiae*

IDENTIFICATION. This is a small, dark owl with greenish-yellow eyes and dark facial disc; its underparts are pale and densely mottled dark brown. Sexes are similar.

DISTRIBUTION. Throughout Australia, including Tasmania. The bird is also seen in Indonesia, New Guinea and New Zealand.

NOTES. The Boobook Owl is common and widespread in wooded country generally, from coastal rainforests to sparsely timbered regions of the arid interior. During the day it roosts in a tree hollow, the crevice of a rock, or the thick foliage of a tree. At dusk it emerges and searches for food, which consists of insects, small rodents and small birds. It utters a call resembling 'mo–poke' or 'boo–book', and it sometimes miews like a cat.

BREEDING. Nest: in a hollow limb or hole in a tree. Clutch: two to four; white, round. Breeding season: generally September to January.

5:10 BARKING OWL *Ninox connivens*

IDENTIFICATION. This bird is like a large Boobook Owl, but has a proportionately smaller head and very large bright yellow eyes; its underparts are densely streaked (not mottled) dark brown. Sexes are similar.

DISTRIBUTION. Most of northern and eastern Australia, also extreme south-western Western Australia; absent from Tasmania. It is also found in Indonesia and southern New Guinea.

NOTES. The bird frequents open forest lands, brushes and scrubs. During the day it rests in a hollow in a tree or in thick foliage. Its chief call, a loud 'wuk–wuk', suggests a dog's bark, but it also produces appalling nocturnal screams — calls that have given rise to the local names 'Screaming-woman Bird' and 'Murderbird'. Food: mammals and birds, also insects and sometimes fish.

BREEDING. Nest: in a cavity in a tree; occasionally in a rabbit burrow. Clutch: two to three; white. Breeding season: August to October.

5:11 RUFOUS OWL *Ninox rufa*

IDENTIFICATION. This is a large owl of the tropics. It is dark brown above, dull rufous below, closely barred dark grey. Sexes are similar.

DISTRIBUTION. North-western Australia, Northern Territory, and northern and eastern Queensland as far south as Rockhampton. It also occurs in New Guinea.

NOTES. During the day this owl inhabits, for the most part, dense foliage bordering watercourses, hunting at night in the open forest. Like other *Ninox* owls, the birds mate for life. It is highly sedentary, and its territories are maintained the year around. It has a low call-note, 'hoo–hooooo', and a modified scream in winter. Food: birds, small mammals and insects.

BREEDING. Nest: in a cavity in a tree. Clutch: two to three; white. Breeding season: July to (probably) September.

5:12 POWERFUL OWL *Ninox strenua*

IDENTIFICATION. This is a very large, impressive owl with large yellow eyes; its underparts are pale and closely marked with dark brown chevrons. Sexes are similar.

DISTRIBUTION. South-eastern Queensland to eastern and southern Victoria.

NOTES. This owl inhabits mountainous forests and scrubs. It rests during the day amid thick foliage, often grasping food remains. Like several other owls, it may have several favoured roosts, which it uses in irregular rotation. It is usually seen alone, but it lives permanently in pairs. The characteristic call of this, the largest of Australian owls, is a deep, gruff 'whoo–hoo'. Food: mammals (mainly possums and gliders) and occasionally birds.

BREEDING. Nest: a slight depression in the wood-mould on the base of a cavity in a large tree, usually one growing on a hillside in dense forest; the entrance may be up to 30 metres from the ground. Clutch: two; white. Breeding season: May to September.

PLATE 6

MOUND-BUILDING BIRDS

6:1 MALLEEFOWL *Leipoa ocellata*

IDENTIFICATION. This bird is pale fawn below, intricately barred and marbled above, in shades of grey, brown and tan, and has a bold black streak down the centre of its throat. Sexes are similar.

DISTRIBUTION. Interior southern Australia, from Shark Bay east to central New South Wales and western Victoria.

NOTES. The Malleefowl frequents dry inland scrubs, chiefly mallee country. Highly sedentary birds, males in particular rarely move more than a few hundred metres from their mounds throughout the year. It is wary, quiet and elusive. Food consists of berries, seeds and insects. The bird has been seriously reduced in numbers through the clearing of its haunts and by the inroads of foxes and shooters. The call-notes are a throaty gurgling and a deep booming.

BREEDING. Nest: a large pyramid of sand and gravel, several metres in diameter, with a core of vegetable debris, in which the eggs are buried. The male constructs the mound and continually monitors its temperature, testing it with his tongue, and regulating it by digging sand out of the mound or heaping more on as required. The sources of warmth are the fermenting vegetable material and solar heat. Clutch: fourteen to thirty-five with an average of twenty-two (several females lay in a single mound); delicate pink when fresh, but soon becoming soiled and stained a dull reddish-brown. Breeding season: variable, but mainly September to March.

6:2 ORANGE-FOOTED SCRUBFOWL *Megapodius reinwardt*

IDENTIFICATION. The bird is dark brown above, plain dark grey below, with a small crested head and large orange feet. Sexes are similar.

DISTRIBUTION. Tropical Australia, west to the Kimberley and south on the east coast to about Rockhampton, Queensland. Also, the bird is widespread from the Philippines and Indonesia to the Solomon Islands and Vanuatu.

NOTES. The bird frequents rainforests, especially in coastal lowlands; it is less common in nearby ranges. It is a more gregarious bird than either the Brush Turkey or the Malleefowl. Both sexes maintain the mound, which may be shared by several pairs. When disturbed, Scrubfowl either run or fly heavily to the lowest branch of a tree. They are noisy both by day and by night, uttering a variety of loud chortling notes and screams. Food: native fruits, berries, seeds, and the young shoots of many kinds of trees and shrubs.

BREEDING. Nest: the eggs are buried in an immense conical mound, consisting of earth and leaf-mould or sand and seaweed, usually situated in dense scrub, sheltered by large trees. Mounds tend to grow with continued use, season after season, and may reach 10–12 metres across and several metres high. The incubating factor is fermentation plus solar heat. Clutch: twelve to fifteen appear to be a normal clutch, but as many as thirty have been taken from a mound; when newly laid they are a pale pinkish-brown, soon passing into a light coffee-brown, and becoming darker after being in the mound a few days. Breeding season: mainly September to December.

6:3 BRUSH TURKEY *Alectura lathami*

IDENTIFICATION. This turkey is large, black, with a unique full, vertically folded tail; its head is naked, red. Sexes are similar.

DISTRIBUTION. Eastern Australia from Cape York south to the Hawkesbury River and (formerly) the Illawarra district, New South Wales.

NOTES. The bird inhabits rainforests near the coast and scrubs of the interior. It spends most of its time scratching among fallen leaves and debris for insects and other small creatures. It is usually shy and solitary, but in some areas it comes freely to forest picnic grounds. When disturbed, it usually runs, covering the ground with great rapidity, and only occasionally seeks refuge in trees, except for roosting at night. It is generally silent, but it utters soft grunts and crooning notes, and the male has a deep three-noted booming call. Food: insects and native fruits and seeds.

BREEDING. Nest: a large mound of earth and rotting vegetation, scraped inwards from the surrounding ground. A new mound usually measures from two to four metres in diameter and is about a metre high; an old one may reach seven metres in diameter and two metres in height. The male controls the temperature by raking over the surface of the mound or gathering in fresh material, thus advancing or retarding the rate of fermentation of the litter by varying the amount of insulation over it. The eggs are deposited on end (larger end uppermost) in holes about half a metre deep, and are then covered over. The young are completely independent on hatching; they scramble to the surface and wander off into the forest. Clutch: usually eighteen to twenty-four, but up to forty-eight have been taken from one mound; white when first deposited but soon becoming soiled and stained. Breeding season: mainly August to December.

6:4 SUPERB LYREBIRD *Menura novaehollandiae*

IDENTIFICATION. This is a very large forest bird, dark brown with a long, full tail; the males have extraordinary lyrate tail feathers and white, whispy plumes. The female is similar but has a markedly smaller tail.

DISTRIBUTION. Coastal eastern Australia, from near Stanthorpe, Queensland, south to Melbourne, Victoria; introduced to Tasmania.

NOTES. The Superb Lyrebird is usually seen singly, occasionally in pairs or small parties, inhabiting rugged forest country and brushes. It is a remarkably competent mimic, imitating most calls of the other species in its locality, as well as some sounds produced through human agency. It has several powerful calls of its own, the chief of which is a resounding 'choo–choo–choo'. The female is also a talented mimic, but less vocal than the male.

The male builds display mounds — low hillocks about a metre across — which he rakes up in soft soil. As a rule, he makes a series of these mounds and visits them in turn, stopping at each to sing and display. Nest building, incubating the egg, and rearing the nestling are performed entirely by the female. During the day lyrebirds spend most of the time on the ground sifting fallen leaves and debris, or tearing decaying logs to pieces in search of food, which consists of insects, worms, and small land molluscs. At night the birds roost in trees.

BREEDING. Nest: a bulky structure with an entrance at the side, composed outwardly of sticks, twigs, dried fern-leaves, and mosses, with an inner wall neatly made of wiry rootlets and bark-fibre; lined with downy feathers; usually built on a ledge of rock, in a cavity on top of a tall stump, or at the base of trees, occasionally high in a large tree fork. Clutch: one; varying from light stone-grey to deep purplish-brown, with streaks and spots of deep slaty-grey and blackish-brown distributed over the surface. Breeding season: May to September.

6:5 ALBERT'S LYREBIRD *Menura alberti*

IDENTIFICATION. This bird is similar to the Superb Lyrebird, but the tail is simpler and its underparts are strongly washed dull rufous. (Note distribution.)

DISTRIBUTION. Restricted to the mountain ranges of extreme south-eastern Queensland and north-eastern New South Wales.

NOTES. The bird frequents dense rainforests. It is solitary, shy and difficult to see. In addition to being smaller and more rufous in colour, this species has a much less spectacular tail than its close relative the Superb Lyrebird. The Albert's Lyrebird is an accomplished songster and mimic. It constructs display platforms of trampled vines, but also displays on the ground or on fallen logs. It is similar in general habits to its relative.

BREEDING. Nest: similar to that of the Superb Lyrebird; the sites chiefly used are rock ledges, but nests have also been found on the top of tree stumps and between the buttressed roots of jungle trees. Clutch: one; similar to that of the Superb Lyrebird. Breeding season: June to September (mainly June–July).

PLATE 7

GROUND-FREQUENTING BIRDS

7:1 NULLARBOR QUAILTHRUSH *Cinclosoma alisteri*

IDENTIFICATION. The male is boldly patterned black, white and rufous; the belly is white and chin, throat and breast are black; there is an irregular white stripe at sides of throat. The female is similar, but much paler, duller, less boldly patterned. (Note distribution.)

DISTRIBUTION. Nullarbor Plain (eastern Western Australia and south-western South Australia).

NOTES. The bird frequents sparsely vegetated gibber flats and shrub-steppe. It is territorial when breeding, but in winter it may be seen in small parties. It is very shy, usually keeping out of sight in the shelter of bushes. When flushed it rises with a whirring of wings, flies a short distance, and then alights and seeks further cover. Food: insects. It is probably conspecific with the Cinnamon Quailthrush.

BREEDING. Nest: a depression in the ground, lined with grass, usually placed under a dead bush. Clutch: three; dull creamy-white with a faint greenish tinge, with olive brown and slaty-grey markings. Breeding season: August to October.

7:2 CINNAMON QUAILTHRUSH *Cinclosoma cinnamomeum*

IDENTIFICATION. The males of the species are boldly patterned in black, white and rufous; the chin, throat and breast are black, and it is crossed at the upper breast by a broad band of white (subspecies *cinnamomeum*), warm brown (*castaneothorax*), or dull orange (*marginatum*). Females are much duller and paler, with underparts mainly dingy white.

DISTRIBUTION. Arid interior of Australia, from about Shark Bay, Western Australia, east to central New South Wales.

NOTES. The bird inhabits rather open, arid, stony country, singly, in pairs, or small parties. It is generally quiet, shy, and difficult to locate and observe. Most calls are thin and high-pitched, but include a piercing whistle. Food: insects and seeds.

BREEDING. Nest: open, cup-shaped, formed of a few twigs and dead leaves; placed under a low bush or similar shelter. Clutch: two; buffy-white to brownish grey, with streaks of umber-brown and a few underlying markings of dull bluish-grey. Breeding season: probably August to October.

7:3 CHESTNUT QUAILTHRUSH *Cinclosoma castanotum*

IDENTIFICATION. The male is mainly grey above, with mahogany rump, back and shoulders; its chin, throat and breast are black; the sides of the breast and flanks are blue-grey. The female is similar but is much paler and duller.

DISTRIBUTION. South-western New South Wales, north-western Victoria, South Australia and south-western Australia.

NOTES. The bird is seen in pairs or family parties. It is shy, unobtrusive, and wary. When flushed it rises with a whirr, flies a short distance, and alights on the ground or on a limb of a tree. It frequents open forest, mallee and mulga. The call is a soft piping whistle. Food: insects and seeds.

BREEDING. Nest: a depression in the ground, loosely lined with strips of bark and dead leaves, usually sheltered by a dead bush. Clutch: two; greyish-white, with brown and lavender markings. Breeding season: August to December.

7:4 SPOTTED QUAILTHRUSH *Cinclosoma punctatum*

IDENTIFICATION. Its upperparts are brown, streaked black, underparts are dull white, boldly spotted black, cheeks and upper breast are blue-grey, the chin and throat are black with white patch at sides, and there is a conspicuous white eyebrow stripe. The female is similar to the male, but somewhat duller, and has a dull rufous patch at the side of the throat.

DISTRIBUTION. Eastern and southern Australia, including Tasmania, from south-eastern Queensland to the vicinity of Adelaide, South Australia.

NOTES. The bird inhabits open forest country and heathy uplands, but especially rocky ridges and hillsides with abundant leaf litter and grass tussocks. The usual call is a thin soft whistle, but in springtime the male utters a series of fairly loud, plaintive short whistles. Shy and often difficult to observe, when flushed it rises like a quail, flies a short distance, and alights either on the ground or on a limb of a tree. Food: insects and seeds.

BREEDING. Nest: a depression in the ground, lined with strips of bark, leaves, and grasses; usually in the shelter of a boulder, fallen log or tree trunk. Clutch: two, sometimes three; dull white, with dark brown and lavender markings. Breeding season: August to February.

7:5 BLACK-BREASTED BUTTONQUAIL *Turnix melanogaster*

IDENTIFICATION. This bird's head and underparts are black, its breast is boldly scalloped white and it has a white eye; the male is similar but much paler, with a brown crown and a whitish throat. (It is seen in dense forests only.)

DISTRIBUTION. Extreme north-eastern New South Wales, and eastern Queensland, north to about Gladstone.

NOTES. This is a rare species, elusive and little known. It inhabits dense wet forests and rainforest (especially fond of lantana thickets). A sign of its presence is saucer-shaped depressions in the litter of the forest floor, scraped bare as the bird feeds — but the bird itself is difficult to see. Food: seeds and insects.

BREEDING. Nest: a depression in the ground under a low bush or tussock of grass; lined with grasses. Clutch: three to four; pale buffy-white, freckled light vinous-brown, chestnut-brown, and purplish-grey, with large black spots. Breeding season: mainly February to April.

7:6 PAINTED BUTTONQUAIL *Turnix varia*

IDENTIFICATION. The bird is intricately marked blue-grey and chestnut; its underparts are mottled grey, with much rufous at the shoulder, and it has a red eye. The male is similar, but duller. In flight, the bird appears spangled blue-grey above.

DISTRIBUTION. From about Cooktown, Queensland, south to Victoria, Tasmania, and south-eastern South Australia (including Kangaroo Island); also south-western Western Australia north to the Houtman Abrolhos Islands.

NOTES. The Painted Buttonquail inhabits open forest, heathlands, and lightly timbered ridges. It is partly nocturnal and has a booming note somewhat resembling that of the Common Bronzewing (No. 13:13). As in other buttonquail, the female is slightly larger and more brightly coloured than the male. She does the courting and afterwards seeks other mates, leaving the brooding and care of the chicks to the male. Food: seeds and insects.

BREEDING. Nest: a shallow depression scratched in the ground with grass forming a slight hood; lined with fine dried grasses; placed in the shelter of a low bush or rank herbage. Clutch: usually four; buffy- to greyish-white, almost obscured with chestnut-brown, dull violet, and slaty-grey markings. Breeding season: extremely variable, but usually late summer and autumn.

7:7 RAINBOW PITTA *Pitta iris*

IDENTIFICATION. The bird is stocky and stumpy-tailed; it has a bright green back and head and black underparts. Sexes are similar.

DISTRIBUTION. Tropical northern Australia from the Kimberley east to Arnhem Land.

NOTES. It inhabits coastal bamboo jungles, mangroves, and scrubs, spending almost all of its time on the ground. The call is short and sharp and may be rendered as 'walk–walk', repeated twice in quick succession. Food: insects and snails.

BREEDING. Nest: a large, loose, domed structure with a side entrance, made of dead strips of bamboo leaves and other vegetation; sometimes on the ground, otherwise up to two metres off the ground in mangroves or bamboo. Clutch: four; creamy-white, with sepia and underlying markings of dull purplish-grey. Breeding season: January to March.

7:8 NOISY PITTA *Pitta versicolor*

IDENTIFICATION. It is stocky and stumpy-tailed; the back is bright green, the head mainly black, and underparts bright buff. Sexes are similar.

DISTRIBUTION. Eastern Australia from Cape York to Barrington Tops, New South Wales; scarce and erratic further south.

NOTES. The bird inhabits dense rainforest, singly or in pairs. It can be brought within a few feet of an observer by an imitation of its resonant call, 'walk to work', or 'want to watch'. It lives mainly on the ground, feeding there on land-snails and insects, but it often calls from the branch of a tree. Its 'anvil' is a stone or small stump, where it breaks the shells of snails; sometimes a stone is worn smooth through repeated use.

BREEDING. Nest: large, dome-shaped, with a rounded side entrance, constructed of twigs and moss; built on the ground, usually between the buttresses of a hillside jungle tree, and often with a 'doormat' of moist animal dung. Clutch: three to five, usually four; creamy-white, spotted blackish-brown and with underlying markings of bluish-grey. Breeding season: mainly October to January.

7:9 BLUE-BREASTED PITTA *Pitta erythrogaster*

IDENTIFICATION. This bird is stocky and stumpy-tailed, with a breast bright blue, separated from a bright red belly by a narrow black band. Sexes are similar.

DISTRIBUTION. Cape York Peninsula. It is also widespread from the Philippines to New Guinea.

NOTES. This common bird is migratory, arriving in Australia about October, presumably from New Guinea, although there are no records of passage across Torres Strait. It inhabits dense rainforests and gallery forest, where it traverses the ground rapidly, taking food items from the leaf litter. The usual call, often uttered from high in trees, is an extended mournful whistle. Food: insects and snails.

BREEDING. Nest: dome-shaped, with a side entrance; constructed of twigs and leaves and lined with fine, hair-like fibres; usually on a stump or in a vine tangle within a few metres of the ground. Clutch: three to four; creamy-white, with purplish-brown and bluish-grey markings. Breeding season: October to December.

7:10 CHOWCHILLA *Orthonyx spaldingii*

IDENTIFICATION. The bird is very dark brown above and mainly white below. The male has a white throat; the female has an orange throat. Behaviour is distinctive; it forages in leaf litter with vigorous sideways sweeps of the large feet.

DISTRIBUTION. North-eastern Queensland from near Cooktown to Mount Spec, near Townsville.

NOTES. It inhabits dense rainforests, mainly (but not exclusively) in highlands above 450 metres. It is sedentary and almost entirely terrestrial. The bird is seen usually in small parties; it is very noisy, and is more often heard than seen. The call is a loud, ringing, rhythmic series of notes, like 'chow–chilla chow–chow, chowy chook–chook'. Occasional mimicry has been reported. Food: insects, obtained by vigorous ground-scratching.

BREEDING. Nest: domed, with a side entrance; made of sticks, twigs, dead leaves and moss; placed on the ground, in a vine tangle or on a stump within a few metres of the ground. Clutch: one; white. Breeding season: mainly May to August.

7:11 LOGRUNNER *Orthonyx temminckii*

IDENTIFICATION. Intricately patterned white, black, grey and rufous, the male has a white throat and the female has an orange throat. The behaviour is distinctive; it forages in leaf litter with vigorous sideways sweeps of the large feet.

DISTRIBUTION. Eastern Australia from about Blackall, Queensland, south to near Wollongong, New South Wales.

NOTES. Locally common, the bird is sedentary and almost entirely terrestrial. It inhabits dense rainforests, usually in pairs. It is very noisy, but possesses an agreeable song, a series of 'quicks', usually uttered in an apparently agitated manner. Its food consists of insects, chiefly beetles, and small land-snails and slugs, collected by scratching among the fallen leaves and other debris. It uses both legs and tail — the legs with a 'sideways' action, and the spine-like tips of the feathers as a prop.

BREEDING. Nest: on or near the ground; a complex, domed structure with a hooded side entrance, constructed on a platform of short, stout sticks, upon which is built a framework of more sticks and twigs, in turn covered by a thick layer of moss and leaves; usually neatly lined with rootlets, fern fibres, moss and soft bark. Clutch: two; white. Breeding season: generally May to August.

7:12 FERNWREN *Oreoscopus gutturalis*

IDENTIFICATION. A small, dark, unobtrusive bird of the rainforest floor, it has a white throat, white eyebrow, and black band across upper breast. Sexes are similar and juveniles nondescript.

DISTRIBUTION. Highland rainforests (above 650 metres) of north-eastern Queensland, from near Cooktown to Mount Spec, near Townsville.

NOTES. The bird is sedentary and almost entirely terrestrial. Usually it is seen alone or in pairs. It prefers damp places. It is quiet and unobtrusive, but tame and easily observed once located. Its food consists chiefly of insects, procured among ferns and mosses, or underneath the peeling bark of a fallen tree; the bird often tosses debris into the air, and burrows vigorously into heaped leaf litter.

BREEDING. Nest: dome-shaped, with an entrance at the side, constructed of fresh green mosses and fine black fern-stems; built on the ground among ferns or partly built into a hole in a bank. Clutch: two; white. Breeding season: July to February.

7:13 ROCK WARBLER *Origma solitaria*

IDENTIFICATION. The Rock Warbler is mainly dark grey above, brick red below, with a white throat; the sexes are similar. Behaviour is distinctive as it forages actively on exposed rock faces, cliffs and the rocky banks of streams.

DISTRIBUTION. Central-eastern New South Wales (Hawkesbury sandstone region and adjacent limestone areas).

NOTES. It frequents rocky ravines and hillsides, mainly near streams. It is very active, moving rapidly over or under rocks and fallen logs, and only occasionally perching in low trees. The calls are brisk and sharp, and sometimes extend into mimicry. Food: insects.

BREEDING. Nest: suspended from the roof of a cave or similar situation; dome-shaped, with a hooded side entrance, constructed of bark-fibre, rootlets and grasses, coated with moss and cobweb; lined with fibre and feathers; the attachment to the ceiling of the cave formed almost entirely of cobwebs. Clutch: three; white, occasionally with fine spots. Breeding season: July to December.

7:14 PILOTBIRD *Pycnoptilus floccosus*

IDENTIFICATION. The Pilotbird is dark, portly, unobtrusive, with dark brown upperparts, dull rufous face and underparts and red eye. Sexes are similar.

DISTRIBUTION. From the Blue Mountains and Port Hacking district, New South Wales, to the Dandenong Ranges, Victoria.

NOTES. The bird inhabits heavily timbered mountain ranges and dense scrubs and is more often heard than seen. Its melodious notes, especially those suggesting 'guinea–a–week', are consistently imitated by the Superb Lyrebird. Food: insects, sometimes obtained by 'piloting' (associating with) the Lyrebird.

BREEDING. Nest: a dome-shaped structure with an entrance at the side, constructed of strips of bark and fibre, with additions of leaves, rootlets, and grass; lined with bark-fibre and feathers; built on or near the ground. Clutch: two; varying from smoky-brown to dusky-grey, darker at the larger end. Breeding season: August to February.

7:15 SOUTHERN SCRUB-ROBIN *Drymodes brunneopygia*

IDENTIFICATION. A slender, long-tailed bird, it is mainly dull grey brown, with rufous rump and dark grey 'tear-mark' extending downwards from eye. Sexes are similar.

DISTRIBUTION. South-western New South Wales, north-western Victoria, southern South Australia and south-western Australia, north to Shark Bay.

NOTES. It inhabits low scrub, chiefly mallee, mulga and cypress pine. Behaviour is usually quiet and unobtrusive, but the song is loud, cheery, and vigorous. It is trustful and answers imitations of its loud call-notes, which resemble 'chip–pip–er–ee', and 'chip–pip–ee', and 'chip–peer–a–peet'. Food: insects, procured on the ground.

BREEDING. Nest: cup-shaped, constructed of strips of bark outwardly protected by a rim of criss-crossed twigs; lined with grass and a few rootlets; usually built in a slight depression scraped in the ground among scrub, but sometimes placed on top of a low thick bush. Clutch: one to two; greenish-grey, spotted and blotched brown. Breeding season: September to January.

7:16 NORTHERN SCRUB-ROBIN *Drymodes superciliaris*

IDENTIFICATION. This bird is slender, long-tailed, warm brown above and pale below; its wings are black, boldly marked with white; it has black marks on pale face, extending downward from eye. Sexes are similar. (Note distribution.)

DISTRIBUTION. Cape York Peninsula and New Guinea; also (possibly) the Roper River region, Northern Territory.

NOTES. Like its southern relative, though inhabiting much heavier vegetation, this bird runs about quietly, turning over leaves and other debris in search of insects and other invertebrates. Occurring singly or in pairs, its habits are little known. Its note is a loud shrill whistle, which it will answer if imitated.

BREEDING. Nest: a circular depression scratched in the ground, roughly lined with long wiry tendrils of plants, leaves, and fibre. Clutch: two; dull white or stone-grey, freckled and spotted with shades of brown and grey. Breeding season: November to January.

7:17 NOISY SCRUB-BIRD *Atrichornis clamosus*

IDENTIFICATION. The bird's upperparts are very dark and closely barred; the underparts are pale, the flanks washed rufous; its throat is black at the centre, white at the sides. Sexes are similar.

DISTRIBUTION. Extreme south-western Western Australia.

NOTES. Long thought extinct, this species was rediscovered in 1961 in dense coastal scrub at Two Peoples Bay, some 30 kilometres east of Albany, Western Australia, which is still the only known locality. It spends much of its time on the ground, where it moves with remarkable speed and agility; it is extremely shy, elusive and difficult to observe. The male's song is extraordinarily loud, powerful and ringing. The bird's discoverer (John Gilbert) and the bird itself are commemorated on a memorial at Drakesbrook, Western Australia.

BREEDING. Nest: a domed structure with an entrance at the side, usually placed in a grass tussock, on or close to the ground, and constructed mainly of broad grass blades, with some leaves and twigs; the lining consists of a layer of cardboard-like material. Clutch: one; pale pinkish-buff, spotted and blotched with brown. Breeding season: April to October.

7:18 RUFOUS SCRUB-BIRD *Atrichornis rufescens*

IDENTIFICATION. This bird is mainly dark brown above, closely barred blackish, washed rufous on flanks; its throat is scaly black at centre, white at sides. Sexes are similar but the female lacks black feathers on the throat.

DISTRIBUTION. Dense highland forests (generally above 400 metres) from the McPherson Range, Queensland, to the upper Williams River, New South Wales.

NOTES. It inhabits dense undergrowth of scrubs and brushes. An extremely elusive bird, rarely showing itself but running in mouse-like fashion among and beneath rotting leaves and other debris. It is a most accomplished mimic and a remarkable ventriloquist, and for its size possesses the most resonant voice of all the birds of Australia. Its 'chip–chip', repeated rapidly, is almost deafening when the bird is heard (though perhaps not seen) at close range. The female utters a single sharp 'tick' at intervals, and when anxious she may emit a loud, drawn-out squeal suggesting a small frog in distress. The bird rarely flies, and then only a few metres. Food: insects and seeds.

BREEDING. Nest: round, bulky, with an entrance at the side; the outer shell constructed of dead leaves, ferns, twigs, and broad dried blades of sedge and mat-rush; lined with wet wood-pulp that dries smoothly and suggests cardboard, perhaps the most curious lining of any Australian bird's nest; well hidden in undergrowth or sedge tussock. Clutch: two; pinkish-white or pinkish-buff, with reddish-brown and purplish-brown markings. Breeding season: September to November.

7:19 BASSIAN THRUSH *Zoothera lunulata*

IDENTIFICATION. This thrush is almost impossible to distinguish from the Russet-tailed Thrush by sight, but it is slightly larger, and its rump is olive brown, not dull rufous; sexes are similar.

DISTRIBUTION. Eastern Australia from near Cooktown, Queensland, south to Tasmania and south-eastern South Australia.

NOTES. A sedentary bird, it inhabits chiefly the floor of dense wet forests, especially highlands. Rather shy and unobtrusive, it tends to remain in dense cover, but sometimes emerges to feed on grassy clearings at forest picnic grounds and similar situations. Its food is procured on the ground among debris, and consists of insects and other small invertebrates. The song is musical but rather soft, a rambling series of whistles and trills.

BREEDING. Nest: round, cup-shaped, made of strips of bark, moss, and rootlets; usually placed in a tree fork several metres from the ground. Clutch: two to three; bluish-grey, mottled reddish-brown. Breeding season: July to December.

7:20 RUSSET-TAILED THRUSH *Zoothera heinei*

IDENTIFICATION. Almost impossible to distinguish from the Bassian Thrush by sight, it is slightly smaller, with a proportionately shorter tail; the rump is dull rufous, not olive brown; sexes are similar.

DISTRIBUTION. Eastern Australia (mainly coastal lowlands) from the vicinity of Cairns, Queensland, south to central coastal New South Wales.

NOTES. It is a sedentary bird and inhabits chiefly the floor of dense wet forests and coastal tea-tree thickets. Diet and general behaviour are similar to the Bassian Thrush. The song consists of loud, cheery series of disyllabic whistles, 'wheer-do'.

BREEDING. Nest: round, cup-shaped, made of strips of bark, moss, and rootlets; usually placed in a tree fork several metres from the ground. Clutch: two to three; pale green or greenish-blue, faintly freckled reddish-brown. Breeding season: August to January.

7:21 WHITE-THROATED NIGHTJAR *Eurostopodus mystacalis*

IDENTIFICATION. Intricately patterned in shades of buff, grey, brown, fawn and black, the bird has small white spots on primaries and a small white mark at throat. Sexes are similar.

DISTRIBUTION. Eastern Australia, mainly east of the Great Dividing Range, from Cape York south to near Melbourne, Victoria. Also found in New Guinea.

NOTES. The bird is sedentary in most of Queensland, but southern populations are migratory. It is usually met with singly during the day, resting on the ground; at night it hawks for insects. This bird has an extraordinary call, suggesting weird laughter. It prefers open forest country, keeping to the ridges separated by thickly timbered gullies. Food: insects, principally moths.

BREEDING. Nest: none, the single egg being deposited on the ground. Clutch: one; buff, stone, or cream-coloured, with black and underlying markings of bluish-grey. Breeding season: October to December.

7:22 SPOTTED NIGHTJAR *Eurostopodus argus*

IDENTIFICATION. The bird resembles a White-throated Nightjar, but it has a conspicuous white patch in the outer wing and a large white mark on the throat. Sexes are similar.

DISTRIBUTION. Cape York Peninsula and the interior of Australia, usually west of the Great Dividing Range, extending to coastal western and north-western Australia; it is also in the Aru Islands and New Ireland.

NOTES. Although some remain, the bulk of the southern population migrates to northern Australia for the winter. The bird is usually solitary and almost entirely terrestrial. When flushed, it rises and flies off to settle again on the ground. At twilight, numbers begin hawking for insects above the treetops or grasslands. The bird has a peculiar call — 'caw–caw–caw, gobble–gobble–gobble', the 'caws' being loud and the 'gobbles' gradually diminishing in volume. Food: flying insects.

BREEDING. Nest: none; the egg is deposited on the bare ground. Clutch: one; yellowish-olive to pale green, sparingly marked with reddish-purple or black spots. Breeding season: September to January.

7:23 LARGE-TAILED NIGHTJAR *Caprimulgus macrurus*

IDENTIFICATION. The bird resembles the White-throated Nightjar but is smaller, greyer, and has a conspicuous white flash in the outer wing and at the tips of the outer tail feathers. Sexes are similar.

DISTRIBUTION. Tropical northern Australia, west to about Point Keats and south along the Queensland coast to about Maryborough (although scarce and local south of Ingham). It is also widespread in South-East Asia.

NOTES. The bird inhabits the edges of rainforest, paperbark swamps, mangroves, dense vegetation along streams and similar habitats — areas which provide the bird with dense cover in which to roost during the day, and nearby open areas over which to hunt at night. A sedentary bird, it is usually seen alone, though the birds remain paired and are seldom far apart throughout the year. Its note consists of monotonous 'chopping' notes, uttered at night. Food: nocturnal flying insects.

BREEDING. Nest: none, the eggs being deposited on the bare ground. Clutch: two; pinkish-stone or reddish-cream with indistinct markings of purplish-brown and slate-grey. Breeding season: September to October.

PLATE 8

BIRDS OF THE OPEN FOREST

8:1 GREY BUTCHERBIRD *Cracticus torquatus*

IDENTIFICATION. The bird is mainly grey above, with a black head; its throat is white. Sexes are similar; immatures similar but dingier, more brownish.

DISTRIBUTION. Most of Australia south of the Tropic of Capricorn, extending north along the east coast to around Cairns, Queensland; an isolated population (subspecies *argentatus*), which occurs in the Kimberley and the Top End, is slightly smaller, has pale grey upperparts, and purer white underparts.

NOTES. Usually seen in pairs or small parties, the bird is common in open woodlands of all kinds, including suburban parks and gardens. Although not closely related, it shares the true shrike's habit of making a 'larder', hanging its prey on thorns or in small forks of trees, to be eaten at leisure. Food: insects of various kinds, also small reptiles, birds, mice, and occasionally berries.

BREEDING. Nest: cup-shaped, made of twigs, rootlets and vine tendrils, lined with rootlets and dead grass; built in the fork of a tree, 2–14 metres from the ground. Clutch: three to five; greyish-green, greyish-blue, olive, or light brown, marked with dull reddish-brown, purplish-red, or chestnut-brown. Breeding season: August to January.

8:2 PIED BUTCHERBIRD *Cracticus nigrogularis*

IDENTIFICATION. Superficially this bird resembles the Grey Butcherbird, but its throat is black. Sexes are similar; juveniles are similar, but duller.

DISTRIBUTION. Throughout most of Australia, except desert areas, the south-east (rare near Sydney), and the extreme south of Western Australia.

NOTES. Usually the bird is found in pairs. Its notes, sometimes rendered as a sub-song (and often heard at night), are among the most melodious utterances of all Australian birds; it is also an accomplished vocal mimic. Food: insects, mostly taken on the ground; also mice, reptiles and small birds.

BREEDING. Nest: open, bowl-shaped, fairly deep, made of sticks and twigs and lined with dry grass and rootlets; usually in an upright fork up to 10 or 12 metres from the ground. Clutch: three to five; greyish-green, pale olive, or pale brown, spotted with darker shades of the ground colour, or with shades of brown and some black spots. Breeding season: August to December.

8:3 BLACK-BACKED BUTCHERBIRD *Cracticus mentalis*

IDENTIFICATION. This bird resembles the Grey Butcherbird, but its back is black, not grey. Sexes are similar. (Cape York only.)

DISTRIBUTION. Cape York Peninsula, south to about Laura. It is also found in New Guinea.

NOTES. The Black-backed Butcherbird is similar in habits to the Grey Butcherbird; its notes are also similar, but are much weaker. Usually found in pairs, it comes freely to houses and camps. Food: insects and small reptiles.

BREEDING. Nest: shallow, cup-shaped, made of sticks and lined with strong grass-roots; placed in a fork of a tree in woodland, several metres from the ground. Clutch: usually three; greenish-grey or pale brown, with reddish-brown, purplish-brown, and dull slate markings. Breeding season: October to December.

8:4 MAGPIELARK *Grallina cyanoleuca*

IDENTIFICATION. This is a familiar, boldly black and white bird with pale eye and bill. Immatures have white eyebrow, black face, white throat, and adult males have white eyebrow, black face, black throat; females have black eyebrow, white face, white throat.

DISTRIBUTION. Australia generally; but few records in Tasmania.

NOTES. One of the most familiar of Australian birds, it is found commonly in open areas of all kinds, including urban parks and gardens, but usually near water. Its common name is based on the call 'pee–wee', which is usually uttered, with lifted wings, when the bird alights. It has an uncommon flight: straight with a steady, flapping motion of the wings. Food: insect life procured on the ground; also pond snails and other invertebrates.

BREEDING. Nest: bowl-shaped, constructed of mud, reinforced and lined with grass and occasionally feathers; built upon a horizontal limb of a tree. Clutch: three to six; varying from pure white to pinkish or reddish-white, with purplish-red spots and underlying markings of slate-grey. Breeding season: very variable, but especially July to January.

8:5 AUSTRALIAN MAGPIE *Gymnorhina tibicen*

IDENTIFICATION. The Australian Magpie is mainly black below, pied above, with a red eye and sturdy steel-grey bill; it has a large white patch on its nape. There are three distinct populations: eastern and northern birds (subspecies *tibicen*) have black backs; south-eastern birds (subspecies *hypoleuca*) have white backs; and western birds (subspecies *dorsalis*) have scaly backs. Sexes are similar.

DISTRIBUTION. Essentially throughout Australia, but rare, local or absent in much of the north and west. Introduced into New Zealand.

NOTES. This species is very conspicuous, and because of its fondness for foraging on green fields has probably increased with settlement; although at the same time large scale clearing has correspondingly deprived it of the woodland it needs for roosting and breeding. Very vigorous in defence of its nest, it will harass and attack even humans who inadvertently stray too close. The bird often sings in company, mainly at dawn and dusk, and sometimes at night; generally its song is one of the most characteristic features of the Australian bush. Magpies live in groups, which may routinely split up to forage, but which come together for roosting and breeding. Food: insects and their larvae; also other invertebrates and small reptiles.

BREEDING. Nest: deep, bowl-shaped, made of sticks and twigs (and sometimes scraps of wire); placed in a forked branch of a tree, usually several metres from the ground. Clutch: three to five; very variable in colour and pattern, typically greenish-blue to bluish-white, or reddish-grey to dull brown, with numerous streaks of chestnut-brown. Breeding season: July to February.

8:6 WHITE-WINGED CHOUGH *Corcorax melanorhamphos*

IDENTIFICATION. This is a large, black bird with a red eye and rather long down-curved bill; it has a white flash in the outer wing, obvious in flight. Sexes are similar.

DISTRIBUTION. Inland areas of central Queensland to New South Wales (local in a few coastal areas), Victoria and South Australia.

NOTES. A highly social bird, it is usually seen in flocks, members of which feed mainly on the ground, and when disturbed rise with grating and piping cries of alarm; then each bird hops about in trees from limb to limb, spreading and elevating its tail. The white flash in each wing, conspicuous in flight, is almost invisible when the bird is perched. The group co-operates in the construction of the nest and in rearing the brood; two females may lay in the same nest. Food: chiefly insects and their larvae; also seeds, berries and young birds in nests.

BREEDING. Nest: bulky, bowl-shaped, made of mud (sometimes cow dung) reinforced with grass and lined with strips of bark-fibre, wool, etc; built on a horizontal branch of a tree, or occasionally on an old stick nest of some other bird. Clutch: four to seven; pale creamy-white, with olive-brown, blackish-brown and slate-grey markings. Breeding season: mainly July to February.

8:7 BLACK CURRAWONG *Strepera fuliginosa*

IDENTIFICATION. This bird is large, bold, confident, with a large black bill and yellow eye; almost entirely black at rest, in flight it reveals a large white flash in outer wing. Sexes are similar.

DISTRIBUTION. Confined to Tasmania (including King Island and Flinders Island).

NOTES. It is usually seen in flocks. A bold, inquisitive and noisy bird, it is a familiar sight around campsites and picnic grounds in the highlands. It is considered a pest in some areas, since it may do considerable damage in gardens and orchards; it also sometimes attacks chickens and ducklings.

BREEDING. Nest: large, open, constructed of sticks and lined with rootlets and grass; usually built in an upright forked branch of a tall tree. Clutch: two to three; purplish-buff, spotted dull purplish-brown and reddish-brown. Breeding season: September to December.

8:8 GREY CURRAWONG *Strepera versicolor*

IDENTIFICATION. There is complex geographic variation, but essentially there are three basic plumage patterns; all have dark rumps and white undertail coverts: birds of the interior and south-eastern highlands (subspecies *versicolor*) are palest grey, with bold white flash in the outer wings; Tasmanian birds (*arguta*) are almost black, with bold white wing-flash; birds of the southern mallee woodlands (*melanoptera*) are medium grey, and lack white in the wings. Sexes are similar.

DISTRIBUTION. Southern Australia generally, including Tasmania.

NOTES. The bird is sedentary, and generally uncommon. It tends to be more wary and less gregarious than other currawongs, although some early reports mention large flocks. The most characteristic call is a loud, ringing gong-like 'clank, clank–clank', which varies in timbre according to subspecies. Food: insects, native fruits and berries.

BREEDING. Nest: untidy, loose, shallow, bowl-shaped, made of long twigs and lined with rootlets and grass; 3–14 metres from the ground in a tree in woodland. Clutch: two to three; varying from pale buff to rich pinkish-brown or grey, with blotches and freckles of darker shades. Breeding season: mainly July or August to December.

8:9 PIED CURRAWONG *Strepera graculina*

IDENTIFICATION. The bird is large, bold, black, with a large dark grey bill and yellow eye; it has a white rump, white undertail coverts, and a conspicuous flash of white in outer wing. Sexes are similar.

DISTRIBUTION. Eastern Australia, from around Cooktown south to the Grampians, Victoria. Also it is found on Lord Howe Island.

NOTES. The Pied Currawong inhabits dense coastal and highland forests, extending to urban parks and gardens. It is seen in pairs, or large flocks in winter, when it congregates at communal roosts. Once essentially mountain birds, descending in winter to coastal lowlands (and Riverina district), in recent decades the species has become increasingly abundant as a breeding resident in many eastern coastal cities. Two of the bird's names are derived from its chief calls — a loud, ringing 'curra–wa, curra–wong', and a drawn-out 'chilla–wong'; such a chorus, particularly on a mountain at dusk, is very impressive. Currawongs are omnivorous, but in season they prey heavily on phasmatids (stick-insects) and nestling birds; they also raid orchards and poultry farms.

BREEDING. Nest: large, open, constructed of twigs and sticks and lined with rootlets; built in the outer forked branches of a tall tree. Clutch: two to five; in most instances pale brown streaked with darker shades. Breeding season: September to January.

8:10 FOREST RAVEN *Corvus tasmanicus*

IDENTIFICATION. Almost impossible to distinguish from other ravens by sight, this species looks large and relatively heavily built. Its calls are very deep, harsh and guttural. Sexes are similar.

DISTRIBUTION. Tasmania; extreme south-eastern South Australia, the Otway Range and Wilsons Promontory, Victoria, and the New England Tableland and along the coast between about Tea Gardens and Urunga, New South Wales.

NOTES. This is the only raven or crow in Tasmania, where it is widespread in most habitats from high altitude moorland to dense forest and coastal woodlands. The Australian mainland populations are mainly restricted to dense forest. Adults apparently maintain territories the year around, but young birds may form roving flocks. The most distinctive call is a deep, slow 'korr–korr–korr–korr'.

BREEDING. Nest: like that of the Australian Raven. Clutch: usually four; like those of the Australian Raven but slightly larger. Breeding season: August to November.

8:11 LITTLE RAVEN *Corvus mellori*

IDENTIFICATION. Almost impossible to distinguish from other corvids by sight, this raven often looks somewhat smaller, more agile, less solidly built; it is also very gregarious, and favours open country. It has a distinctive habit of shuffling or flicking its wings when calling.

DISTRIBUTION. South-eastern Australia, mainly west of the Great Dividing Range; north to about Narrabri, New South Wales, south over most of Victoria (except coastal regions), and west to Eyre Peninsula, South Australia.

NOTES. A gregarious bird, it is usually seen in flocks, even during the breeding season. It is nomadic; it frequents a variety of open habitats including alpine woodlands, pastoral lands, and arid treeless plains of the interior. The most distinctive call is a hard, clipped 'kar–kar–kar–kar–kar'. So similar are the three ravens (Little, Forest and Australian) in appearance that until recent years they were considered all one species; although they look alike they are, however, very distinct in behaviour and ecology.

BREEDING. Nest: a shallow cup of sticks and twigs, lined with a thick pad of grass, bark and wool; usually in a small tree within 10 metres of the ground, occasionally on the ground, in bushes or on telephone poles. It often breeds in loose groups. Clutch: four; extremely variable, but usually pale green, profusely blotched and marked with shades of brown. Breeding season: mainly August to October.

8:12 AUSTRALIAN RAVEN *Corvus coronoides*

IDENTIFICATION. Almost impossible to distinguish from other corvids by sight, its behaviour when calling is a useful clue: the Australian Raven typically lowers its head when giving its territorial call, so that head, body and tail are nearly horizontal; the wings are seldom flipped (unlike the Little Raven); and the long pointed 'hackles' are conspicuous on the bulging throat.

DISTRIBUTION. Almost throughout Queensland, New South Wales, Victoria and South Australia; extending into eastern Northern Territory and southern Western Australia; absent from Tasmania.

NOTES. This is the familiar 'crow' over much of south-eastern Australia (the genus *Corvus* is widespread throughout the world, except South America; there is little real distinction between the terms 'crow' and 'raven', except that 'crow' is often applied to the smaller species, and 'raven' to the larger; the term 'corvid' is usually used to refer to either or both without distinction). It is common in most wooded habitats. Rather solitary, it is seldom seen in large flocks. It is a particularly wary bird and difficult to approach, except in suburban areas, where it is often bold. The most characteristic call is a loud and deep 'gwar–gwar–gwar–r–r', also a downward wailing 'wa–a–ah'. Food: omnivorous, including carrion.

BREEDING. Nest: a substantial, rather flat structure of sticks, lined with scraps of bark, grass and wool felted together into a thick pad; usually above 13 metres in a large tree. Clutch: three to five; very variable in colour and pattern, but usually pale green, profusely blotched and marked with shades of brown. Breeding season: July to September.

8:13 LITTLE CROW *Corvus bennetti*

IDENTIFICATION. This crow is almost impossible to distinguish from other corvids by sight, but is somewhat smaller, with a noticeably slighter, slenderer bill. Sexes are similar.

DISTRIBUTION. Interior of Australia generally, extending to the coast in Western Australia.

NOTES. The bird is gregarious; it often breeds in loose colonies, forms flocks (sometimes very large) outside the breeding season. It is a bird of the arid interior; it is less wary than any of its relatives, and is often common in the small towns and stations of the outback. Flocks may swoop and soar playfully, unlike the behaviour of the otherwise closely similar Torresian Crow. The call is a nasal 'nark', repeated several times; also a strange bubbling, warbling call. Food: chiefly insects and small reptiles.

BREEDING. Nest: a small solid basket of sticks, well lined with a variety of soft materials; characteristically with a layer of mud or clay between the lining and the outer basket. Placed in the fork of a tree, between one and ten metres from the ground. Clutch: four to six; similar to those of the Australian Raven but less profusely marked, and ground-colour tending to blue rather than green. Breeding season: typically July to October, but highly variable, apparently in response to rainfall.

8:14 TORRESIAN CROW *Corvus orru*

IDENTIFICATION. This corvid, too, is almost impossible to distinguish from other crows and ravens by sight, but is much more wary and less gregarious; it also repeatedly shuffles the wings on landing, but does not flip them when calling — both helpful clues.

DISTRIBUTION. Tropical northern Australia, extending south over most of Western Australia except the far south-west, and on the east coast to Gloucester and Port Stephens, New South Wales.

NOTES. A very versatile and common bird in most habitats; it is the typical corvid of the coastal tropics and often scavenges on beaches. It is sedentary and is usually seen singly or in pairs. Food: carrion, insects, young birds, and eggs, also cultivated fruits of all kinds. This species and the Little Crow have snowy white down at the base of the body feathers (noticeable when wind ruffles feathers); this is grey in the three species of raven. Its call is a series of nasal, high-pitched, clipped notes, 'uk–uk–uk–uk'.

BREEDING. Nest: a rough basket of sticks, usually high in a eucalypt; no mud is used in its construction (unlike the Little Crow). Clutch: four to five; like those of the Little Crow, but averaging slightly larger and paler.

PLATE 9

BIRDS OF THE OPEN FOREST

9:1 BLACK-FACED CUCKOOSHRIKE *Coracina novaehollandiae*

IDENTIFICATION. This bird appears smooth and slender, mainly smoke grey, with a black face. Sexes are similar; juveniles are similar to adult White-bellied Cuckooshrikes except that the black mask extends well behind the eye. A population in north-western Western Australia (subspecies *subpallida*) is somewhat smaller and paler than eastern birds.

DISTRIBUTION. Throughout Australia, including Tasmania. The bird is also found in Indonesia and New Guinea; it is accidental to New Zealand.

NOTES. It is seen in pairs or small parties, occasionally large flocks in winter; it is mainly a summer migrant to Tasmania, and partly nomadic elsewhere. The bird inhabits open woodlands. Its flight is undulating and the wings are always shuffled and adjusted when the bird alights. The chief call is a pleasant, trilling note with a distinctive quality, often uttered while in flight. Food: insects and their larvae, procured among the leaves of trees; also berries.

BREEDING. Nest: a small neat saucer made of dry twigs and bark bound with cobweb; built in a horizontal fork of a tree (often a eucalypt), usually high. Clutch: three; olive-green to pale olive-brown, spotted umber, chestnut-brown and dull grey. Breeding season: August to December.

9:2 WHITE-BELLIED CUCKOOSHRIKE *Coracina papuensis*

IDENTIFICATION. This bird resembles a Black-faced Cuckooshrike but is noticeably smaller, with a more compact build; the throat is white, and the black mask extends back to the eye but not beyond it. Sexes are similar; immatures are similar but duller. The southern population (subspecies *robusta*) is somewhat darker than northern birds (subspecies *hypoleuca* and *papuensis*), and has an uncommon dark morph (No. 9:2b).

DISTRIBUTION. Tropical northern Australia, and eastern Australia from Cape York to Victoria and south-eastern South Australia. The bird is also found in New Guinea.

NOTES. Usually occurring in pairs or small flocks, the bird inhabits open forest country. It is sedentary or locally nomadic. Its characteristic call is a rather reedy 'kiseek, kiseek'; other calls resemble those of the Black-faced Cuckooshrike. Food: insects, procured among branches or on the wing; also fruit.

BREEDING. Nest: small, flattish, made of grass and fine twigs, bound with cobweb; built on a horizontal fork, usually high in a eucalypt. Clutch: two; olive-green to pale olive-brown, spotted umber, chestnut-brown and dull grey. Breeding season: August to December or January.

9:3 BARRED CUCKOOSHRIKE *Coracina lineata*

IDENTIFICATION. This bird's plumage is somewhat darker grey than other cuckooshrikes; its underparts are closely barred grey and it has a yellow eye. Sexes are similar; juveniles are plain white below.

DISTRIBUTION. Eastern Australia from Cape York south to the Manning River, New South Wales. It also occurs from New Guinea east to the Solomon Islands.

NOTES. This bird frequents the canopy of rainforests and associated habitats. It is sociable, and is usually seen in flocks. It is migratory in New South Wales. The calls include an agreeable chatter and a series of soft murmuring notes. Food: wild figs, other native fruits and berries; also insects, especially stick-insects.

BREEDING. Nest: shallow, open, made of fine twigs and rootlets, bound with cobweb; built in a high tree fork. Clutch: two; white, spotted brown and purplish-grey. Breeding season: October to January.

9:4 GROUND CUCKOOSHRIKE *Pteropodocys maxima*

IDENTIFICATION. This is a slender, elongated cuckooshrike with white rump; the rump and underparts are closely barred medium grey; the wings and tail are black, the tail is forked and the eye is yellow. Sexes are similar.

DISTRIBUTION. Interior of eastern Australia and South Australia, rarely extending to the coast and mainly so in Western Australia.

NOTES. The bird occurs in pairs, trios, or larger parties, frequenting sparsely timbered grasslands and plains. It feeds on the ground, over which it moves rapidly; when disturbed it flies to the nearest trees. It has a peculiar, rippling call-note, 'kee–lick, kee–lick', usually uttered while on the wing; also, when alarmed, it utters a series of piercing cries.

BREEDING. Nest: saucer-shaped, made of grass, plant stems, rootlets or wool, bound with cobweb; placed in a horizontal tree fork. Clutch: three; dull green, with numerous fleecy markings of olive-brown. Breeding season: August to December.

9:5 APOSTLEBIRD *Struthidea cinerea*

IDENTIFICATION. The Apostlebird is dingy grey, faintly streaked white with brownish wings. Sexes are similar.

DISTRIBUTION. North-eastern Northern Territory and the interior of Queensland and New South Wales, occasionally extending into Victoria and South Australia; it is a rare visitor to coastal areas.

NOTES. Usually it is found in flocks of up to 12 or more birds, frequenting open forest lands, chiefly in the sub-interior. It feeds mainly on the ground, over which it runs and struts in a quaint manner. When disturbed the flock flies to the lower branches of a tree, ascending by a series of leaps, and meanwhile uttering harsh, grating cries. A company often establishes itself near a country homestead and soon becomes fearless. Breeding is co-operative, and all the members of the group assist in rearing the brood. Food: insects and seeds.

BREEDING. Nest: basin-shaped, made of mud reinforced with grass and lined with fine grass; placed on a horizontal limb of a tree, up to 15 metres from the ground. Clutch: four to five, sometimes up to eight; pale bluish-white, marked with blackish-brown and purplish grey. Breeding season: August to December.

9:6 CHANNEL-BILLED CUCKOO *Scythrops novaehollandiae*

IDENTIFICATION. This bird is very large, with a long tail and huge pale bill; its plumage is mainly grey. Sexes are similar.

DISTRIBUTION. Northern and eastern Australia, west to the Kimberley and south to about Moruya, New South Wales, and north-eastern South Australia. It is also seen in Indonesia and New Guinea.

NOTES. In pairs or small flocks, it frequents open forests and scrublands. It is a migrant, arriving in the south of its range during September or October and departing in March. Commonly it flies high, uttering a loud trumpeting call. Food: almost anything edible but chiefly insects, native fruits and berries.

BREEDING. Nest: none built, the species being parasitic; the chief hosts are currawongs and crows. Clutch: eggs dull white to pale yellowish-brown, marked with brown and lavender; unlike many other cuckoos, the female often deposits two or more eggs in the same nest. Breeding season: October to December.

9:7 BLUE-WINGED KOOKABURRA *Dacelo leachii*

IDENTIFICATION. This bird resembles the Laughing Kookaburra, but is much more blue in the wing; it has a pale eye, no dark face mask, males have a blue rump and tail. Females are similar but the tail is rufous and barred black.

DISTRIBUTION. From Shark Bay, Western Australia, through northern tropical Australia to south-eastern Queensland. Also it is seen in New Guinea.

NOTES. The bird inhabits open forest and mangroves beside streams. It is similar in habits to the Laughing Kookaburra, and the two species may be found together over large areas of northern Australia. The most common call suggests that of its close relative, but with a more frantic quality — it has been described as 'a raucous high-pitched trilling howl'. Food: reptiles, frogs, and small birds; insects and other invertebrates.

BREEDING. Nest: in a hole in a tree. Clutch: three to four; white. Breeding season: September to November.

9:8 LAUGHING KOOKABURRA *Dacelo novaeguineae*

IDENTIFICATION. A well known, familiar bird, it could conceivably be confused with the Blue-winged Kookaburra (note distribution), but has a bold dark mask extending on to the cheek. Sexes are similar.

DISTRIBUTION. From inland Cape York Peninsula, south throughout eastern Australia to southern South Australia (to Eyre Peninsula) and Kangaroo Island; introduced to Western Australia and Tasmania.

NOTES. It is a sedentary bird, inhabiting most kinds of wooded country. It is common, extending even into city parks and gardens; it often comes to garden bird-feeders. Usually it occurs in small groups, which jointly maintain a territory and which co-operate in raising the young. Its extraordinary laughing notes are usually heard at their strongest in the early morning and at sunset. Food: small reptiles (including snakes up to almost a metre in length), insects, crabs, and fish, including at times ornamental fish kept in garden ponds; it also robs the nests of other birds and occasionally preys on chickens.

BREEDING. Nest: in a hollow in a tree, in a chamber tunnelled into a tree termitarium or, more rarely, in an earthen bank. Clutch: two to four; white. Breeding season: September to December.

9:9 BUSH STONE-CURLEW *Burhinus grallarius*

IDENTIFICATION. The plumage is mainly fawn, delicately streaked dark grey; it has a small black bill, large glaring yellow eye, and its mannerisms are distinctively furtive and cautious.

DISTRIBUTION. Throughout most of Australia but now rare and local in most well settled areas; accidental to Tasmania.

NOTES. The bird frequents open forest with belts of trees. It is largely sedentary; it is seen in pairs when breeding, but forms small parties — which may be locally nomadic — outside the breeding season. It is very cautious and runs or flies off as an intruder approaches; occasionally it will remain stationary, either in an upright position or crouched near the ground. Its weird call, 'kee–loo', or 'koo–loo', is usually uttered after nightfall and especially on moonlit nights; when a number of birds perform in chorus the effect is distinctly eerie. Food: mainly insects.

BREEDING. Nest: a slight depression in grass or on bare ground. Clutch: usually two; varying greatly in ground colour, typical eggs are yellowish-stone or yellowish-grey, with spots of light brown, dull umber, and inky-grey. Breeding season: August to January.

PLATE 10

BIRDS OF THE OPEN FOREST

10:1 MANGROVE GOLDEN WHISTLER *Pachycephala melanura*

IDENTIFICATION. It is very difficult to distinguish this whistler from the more widespread and familiar Golden Whistler (No. 4:17), but the two species occupy distinct habitats and are not known to interbreed. The male Mangrove Golden Whistler is slightly smaller than the Golden Whistler, the yellow underparts are a richer, brighter shade, the tail is shorter and jet black, and the rump is golden; females are much more extensively yellow below than females of the Golden Whistler.

DISTRIBUTION. Coastal Western Australia from Carnarvon north to Derby; and along the coasts of the Northern Territory and Queensland south perhaps as far as Bowen. It also inhabits New Guinea.

NOTES. It is confined largely to mangroves and associated vegetation. The calls and general habits are similar to those of the Golden Whistler, except that Mangrove Golden Whistlers sometimes feed on the ground and amongst tidal debris.

BREEDING. Nest: a frail shallow cup of dry grass and rootlets, lined with finer material and placed in the upright fork of (usually) a mangrove. Clutch: two to three; eggs are almost indistinguishable from those of the Golden Whistler, but are slightly smaller. Breeding season: October to December.

10:2 HOODED ROBIN *Melanodryas cucullata*

IDENTIFICATION. The male is boldly pied, with a complete black hood; the female is pale grey-brown above, dingy white below, but with wings and tail like the male.

DISTRIBUTION. Almost throughout Australia, except Tasmania and north-eastern Queensland.

NOTES. The bird is common and widespread in most types of dry or open woodland, favouring clearings, partly cleared country, or rough paddocks. The conspicuous plumage of the male attracts attention, but the bird is unobtrusive in habits and does not often call; though at times it utters simple yet strong piping notes, by night as well as by day. Food: insects, mostly procured on the ground.

BREEDING. Nest: cup-shaped, constructed of rootlets, bark and grass, bound with cobweb; lined with soft material; usually built in an upright fork of a tree 1–7 metres from the ground. Clutch: two to three; olive to apple-green in colour, sometimes clouded with rich brown. Breeding season: August to December.

10:3 DUSKY ROBIN *Melanodryas vittata*

IDENTIFICATION. It is plain brown, somewhat paler below. Sexes are similar. (Tasmania only.)

DISTRIBUTION. Tasmania and the islands of Bass Strait.

NOTES. The Dusky Robin frequents lightly timbered country and clearings around homesteads. It is common, and largely sedentary. Unobtrusive but confiding, it closely resembles the Hooded Robin in habits and general behaviour. Its call is low and monotonous: 'choo–wee, choo–wee–er'. Food: insects.

BREEDING. Nest: cup-shaped, made of rootlets and grass; placed on the side of a stump (especially fire-blackened), at the end of a log, or in a small tree. Clutch: three to four; green, sometimes spotted reddish-brown. Breeding season: July to December.

10:4 YELLOW ROBIN *Eopsaltria australis*

IDENTIFICATION. This familiar bird is mainly plain grey above and bright yellow below; Queensland birds (subspecies *chrysorrhoa*) have bright yellow rumps, south-eastern birds (subspecies *australis*) have dull olive rumps, and south-western birds (subspecies *griseogularis*) have grey breasts. Very young juvenile birds are reddish-brown, streaked white. The sexes are similar.

DISTRIBUTION. Eastern Australia (but not Tasmania), roughly from Cooktown, Queensland, south to Adelaide, South Australia, and in south-western Australia from the Murchison River eastwards to Norseman, western South Australia and Eyre Peninsula.

NOTES. A tame and friendly bird, this robin is common in most kinds of closed-canopy woodland, both on the coast and in the interior, and including gardens and city parks. It is quiet and unobtrusive but not difficult to observe. It is one of the earliest species to awaken and one of the last to go to roost. Its calls include a loud 'choo, choo', and a conspicuous piping, usually uttered at dawn and dusk. It has a distinctive habit of perching sideways, low on a tree trunk. Food: insects, taken mainly on the ground by pouncing from a low perch.

BREEDING. Nest: cup-shaped, composed of bark and fibre and lined with small dead leaves, and often neatly decorated on the outside with strips of bark or lichen; placed in a vine or the fork of a tree, usually near the ground. Clutch: two or three; pale green with brownish markings. Breeding season: mainly July to December.

10:5 YELLOW-LEGGED FLYCATCHER *Microeca griseoceps*

IDENTIFICATION. Very similar to Lemon-bellied Flycatcher, but this bird's legs and feet are orange-yellow, not black. Sexes are similar.

DISTRIBUTION. Cape York Peninsula, south to the McIlwraith Range. Also it occurs in New Guinea.

NOTES. An uncommon, generally solitary, quiet, unobtrusive bird, it is difficult to observe; it spends much time in the canopy of rainforest trees, but also occurs in associated eucalypt and paperbark woodland. Its calls are a subdued piping note and a clear double whistle. Food: insects.

BREEDING. Nest: only one nest with eggs on record: a small neat cup made of fine black rootlets, bound with spiderweb and decorated externally with strips of paperbark and lichen; placed about 10 metres up in a Leichhardt tree. Clutch: two; pale blue, marked with dark-brown and grey specks. Breeding season: unknown; December is the only month on record.

10:6 JACKY-WINTER *Microeca leucophaea*

IDENTIFICATION. The bird is grey-brown above, dingy white below; its tail is black, with conspicuous white outer tail feathers. Sexes are similar. It spreads and flirts its tail constantly, persistently wagging it from side to side.

DISTRIBUTION. Almost throughout Australia, except Tasmania and Cape York Peninsula.

NOTES. It frequents forest clearings, orchards and parks, usually in pairs. It has a sweet, twittering song, and in addition utters calls resembling 'jacky, jacky, jacky', or 'peter, peter, peter'. The Jacky-winter commonly selects low, exposed perches, such as fence posts, stumps, or fallen timber, from which it pounces onto prey on the ground, or it captures prey in mid air in brief, fluttering sallies. Food: insects, flying or terrestrial.

BREEDING. Nest: very small, saucer-shaped, composed of fine grass mixed with horse hair, bark fragments, and lichen; built into the angle of a forked horizontal dead branch of a tree 1–20 metres from the ground. Clutch: two; greenish blue, with purplish-brown and underlying markings of greyish-lilac. Breeding season: August to December.

10:7 LEMON-BREASTED FLYCATCHER *Microeca flavigaster*

IDENTIFICATION. This flycatcher is plain greyish-olive above, dingy lemon-yellow below, with a white throat; birds of the Kimberley population (subspecies *tormenti*) are much browner above, dingy white below. Sexes are similar.

DISTRIBUTION. Tropical northern Australia from the Kimberley through the Northern Territory to northern Queensland, south to the vicinity of Mackay.

NOTES. This bird is similar in habits to the Jacky-winter. It inhabits grassy open woodland, often near water. The bird's notes are simple and cheerful, and it has an attractive song, often uttered in flight. Food: mainly insects.

BREEDING. Nest: very small, made of fibrous bark and grass, bound with cobweb; built into the fork of a dead horizontal limb. Clutch: one; faint blue, finely dotted purplish-red. Breeding season: October to January.

10:8 SHRIKETIT *Falcunculus frontatus*

IDENTIFICATION. Olive green above, yellow below, the bird has a boldly patterned black and white head and distinctive bushy crest. Sexes are similar, but the throat is dull green in females, black in males.

DISTRIBUTION. Three widely separated subspecies: *F. f. whitei* of the Kimberley and the Top End; *F. f. frontatus*, found in the eastern States from about Cairns, Queensland, south to Melbourne, Victoria, and west to about Adelaide, South Australia; and *F. f. leucogaster* of south-western Australia.

NOTES. The bird is generally common (although subspecies *whitei* apparently very rare and local), mostly sedentary. It is found in pairs or small parties, usually high in eucalypts. The Shriketit is quite acrobatic; it feeds on insects, characteristically by tearing loose bark from branches, or by rummaging in the tangles of shed bark which accumulate in forks of eucalypts. A call suggesting 'knock–at–the–door, knock–at–the–door' is frequently uttered, but the most characteristic note is a high-pitched mellow whistle.

BREEDING. Nest: a compact, neat, deep cup-shaped structure, well woven of fibre and strips of bark; built in the tallest upright branches of a tree (usually a eucalypt). Clutch: two to three; white, marked with dark olive and pale grey. Breeding season: August to December.

10:9 GREY SHRIKE-THRUSH *Colluricincla harmonica*

IDENTIFICATION. The plumage is mainly mid-grey, paler below and somewhat browner on the back, with white lores and black bill. Sexes are similar, but the female is faintly streaked on throat and breast. Birds of Western Australia (subspecies *rufiventris*) are somewhat darker grey above, buffy below, especially the undertail coverts.

DISTRIBUTION. Almost throughout Australia, including Tasmania.

NOTES. This familiar species is common and widespread in most kinds of woodland, favouring especially the lower foliage levels of eucalypts, though it often feeds also on the ground. It feeds mainly on insects. Its calls are loud, rich and melodious, and are favourite borrowings of lyrebirds. The species is mainly sedentary but wanders to some extent in the cooler months, when its melody may be heard near houses.

BREEDING. Nest: large, cup-shaped, constructed of bark, wiry roots, and grass and lined with fine rootlets and grass; the site is quite variable, but typically it is built in hollows in stumps and broken-off branches, or in an upright tree fork. Clutch: three to four; creamy-white, blotched dark olive, olive-brown and pale grey. Breeding season: August to December.

10:10 LITTLE SHRIKE-THRUSH *Colluricincla megarhyncha parvula*

NOTES. The subspecies illustrated here (*C. m. parvula*) resembles north-eastern birds, but the bill is black, not pale brown, and the upperparts are darker, greyer. It inhabits mangroves and dense coastal thickets. Once considered a distinct species, it occurs in north-western Australia, from Admiralty Gulf, Western Australia, to Arnhem Land. For further notes, see No. 4:19, p. 33.

10:11 SANDSTONE SHRIKE-THRUSH *Colluricincla woodwardi*

IDENTIFICATION. A plain bird, it is mainly dark brown above, sandy rufous below. Sexes are similar.

DISTRIBUTION. North-western Australia and Northern Territory, from Napier Broome Bay to the McArthur River.

NOTES. A characteristic bird of the sandstone cliffs and gorges and escarpments of the far north, this little known species has a variety of rich, melodious calls. It forages mainly on exposed rock surfaces, feeding primarily on insects.

BREEDING. Nest: cup-shaped, composed of roots of spinifex; placed in a rock crevice. Clutch: two to three; creamy-white, marked brownish-black, brown, and slate-grey. Breeding season: December.

10:12 RESTLESS FLYCATCHER *Myiagra inquieta*

IDENTIFICATION. This bird somewhat resembles the more familiar Willie-wagtail in size and general appearance, but the throat is white, not black. Sexes are similar. A subspecies in tropical northern Australia (*M. i. nana*) is a little smaller, and may prove to be a distinct species.

DISTRIBUTION. Throughout much of Australia (although rare in central and western areas).

NOTES. It is very confiding and will sometimes visit houses, seeking spiders in window frames. Its chief calls are a loud 'pee, pee, pee' and peculiar grinding notes (suggesting the sound of sharpening scissors at a grinding wheel), mostly uttered while the bird is hovering near the ground but sometimes when it is perched. Food: insects, usually taken on the ground.

BREEDING. Nest: cup-shaped, of fibrous materials bound with cobweb, often decorated with lichen; lined with hair or feathers; built on a horizontal tree fork 1–20 metres from the ground. Clutch: three to four; white or buff, with umber and lavender markings at the larger end. Breeding season: August to December.

10:13 GREY FANTAIL *Rhipidura fuliginosa*

IDENTIFICATION. The Grey Fantail is small, mainly grey and white, with a long tail; it has distinctive habits and mannerisms including fussing actively among outer branches of trees with tail cocked and fanned, and wings drooped. Sexes are similar. Birds inhabiting mangroves in tropical Australia (subspecies *phasiana*) are somewhat paler and plainer than those elsewhere, and are sometimes regarded as a distinct species.

DISTRIBUTION. Throughout Australia and Tasmania. It is also found in New Caledonia, Vanuatu and New Zealand.

NOTES. Generally, the species is nomadic, but southern populations are migratory. It tends to avoid dense rainforest and the harsher deserts of the interior — yet even in such environments occasional wandering birds may be seen outside the breeding season; otherwise it is one of the most common and familiar birds of the Australian bush. It is friendly, confiding, and very active — when feeding, almost hysterically so. It pursues tiny flying insects in woodland clearings or among the outer foliage of trees at almost any height, executing all manner of complicated aerial manoeuvres in its pursuit — hence the name 'Cranky Fan'. It has a sweet, high-pitched, twittering song.

BREEDING. Nest: shaped like a wine glass without the base; strongly built of fibrous material bound with cobweb and lined with fine dry grass; usually on a thin horizontal fork 1–20 metres aloft; occasionally the 'tail' of the nest is lacking. Clutch: two to three; buff-coloured, with rufous and lavender markings. Breeding season: September to December.

10:14 NORTHERN FANTAIL *Rhipidura rufiventris*

IDENTIFICATION. This fantail is similar to the Grey Fantail but is larger, much quieter and more sedate in behaviour; it is less white in face, wings and tail, it seldom fans its tail, and it perches quietly in a characteristic upright stance. Sexes are similar.

DISTRIBUTION. Tropical northern Australia. It also occurs in New Guinea and the Bismarck Archipelago.

NOTES. This tropical fantail resembles the more familar Grey Fantail, but is much less active, and seldom fans its tail in the exaggerated fashion of its relative. It inhabits rainforest edges and clearings, mangrove fringes and paperbark swamps. Usually it is quiet, inconspicuous and solitary. The most common call is a soft, musical 'chunk, chunk'.

BREEDING. Nest: cup-shaped, with a stem or tail piece several centimetres in length, made of fibre and strips of bark, bound with cobweb; usually situated within a few metres of the ground. Clutch: two; creamy-white, with a dark zone at the larger end. Breeding season: October to January.

10:15 WILLIE-WAGTAIL *Rhipidura leucophrys*

IDENTIFICATION. The bird is mainly black with a white belly and superciliary. It is very active and excitable, with a long tail frequently fanned. Sexes are similar.

DISTRIBUTION. Australia generally; accidental to Tasmania. It also occurs in New Guinea and other tropical islands.

NOTES. This bird is common, familiar, exceptionally tame, and is almost ubiquitous across Australia, inhabiting open grassland and most kinds of lightly wooded country, including city parks, often in the vicinity of water. The chief call resembles the phrase 'sweet pretty creature', uttered frequently during the day or night, especially on moonlit nights. The alarm call is a chatter that suggests the rattling of a half empty box of matches. Food: insects, chiefly flies, procured mainly in the air, but often in association with cattle, which it may follow over long distances.

BREEDING. Nest: neat, cup-shaped, strongly built of fibrous material bound with cobweb; site is variable but is usually placed on a horizontal limb of a tree, frequently one growing near water. Clutch: three to four; cream to yellowish-brown, with a darker zone on the larger end. Breeding season: August to December.

10:16 FAN-TAILED CUCKOO *Cuculus pyrrhophanus*

IDENTIFICATION. The head and upperparts are grey, underparts dull rufous; it has a bright yellow eye-ring and the underside of the tail is conspicuously 'notched' white. Sexes are similar.

DISTRIBUTION. Eastern Australia from Cape York to Tasmania and west to Eyre Peninsula, South Australia, and extreme south-western Tasmania.

NOTES. This cuckoo frequents open forest and scrub lands. The chief call is a mournful trill with a downward inflection, heard most often during spring and summer. This call is one of the most characteristic sounds of the forests of eastern Australia, but the bird itself is generally inactive and unobtrusive, and consequently not easy to locate. In autumn and winter, the bird is nomadic. Food: insects, mainly caterpillars.

BREEDING. Nest: none built, the species being parasitic; White-browed Scrubwrens and Brown Thornbills are especially favoured hosts. Clutch: eggs dull white, scattered with small spots of purplish-brown tending to concentrate in an ill-defined zone at the larger end. Breeding season: August to December.

10:17 CHESTNUT-BREASTED CUCKOO *Cuculus castaneiventris*

IDENTIFICATION. It is very similar to the Fan-tailed Cuckoo, but is smaller, darker, and more richly coloured. Sexes are similar. (Cape York only.)

DISTRIBUTION. Coastal regions of Cape York Peninsula. It also occurs in New Guinea.

NOTES. It inhabits tropical rainforest. It is placed in this group for comparison with the Fan-tailed Cuckoo; like that species, it is rather unobtrusive in behaviour. It is apparently scarce and little known in Australia. The usual call is a brief mournful trill. Food: insects, often taken on the ground.

BREEDING. Nest: none built, the species being parasitic. Clutch: apparently no formal description on record; reported to be similar to those of the Fan-tailed Cuckoo, but small and more reddish in colour.

10:18 LITTLE BRONZE-CUCKOO *Chrysococcyx malayanus*

IDENTIFICATION. The typical form is readily identified by a conspicuous red eye-ring; birds of tropical swamps and mangroves in Queensland (from about Bowen northwards, subspecies *russatus*) are somewhat browner above, with rufous outer tail feathers and rusty breasts.

DISTRIBUTION. Coastal northern and eastern Australia, west to Broome, Western Australia, and south to about Grafton, New South Wales. It is also found in Indonesia and New Guinea.

NOTES. Little has been recorded about the habits of this species; it frequents open forests, rainforests and mangroves. It is migratory in the southern parts of its range, but the northern birds are apparently sedentary. The characteristic call is a trill of silvery notes, repeated rapidly many times and strongly suggesting the stridulations of an insect; also a brisk musical 'chu–chu–chu–chu'.

BREEDING. Nest: none built, the species being parasitic; selects mainly warblers (*Gerygone* spp.) as hosts. Clutch: eggs uniform greenish-olive. Breeding season: September to January.

10:19 SHINING BRONZE-CUCKOO *Chrysococcyx lucidus*

IDENTIFICATION. This species is very like Horsfield's Bronze-cuckoo, but is paler around the eye, and coppery bars on the underparts are linked across breast and belly (bars are broken in Horsfield's Bronze-cuckoo). Sexes are similar.

DISTRIBUTION. Two distinct populations occur in Australia: *C. l. lucidus* breeds in New Zealand and migrates north to the Solomon Islands and the Bismarck Archipelago; numbers annually reach eastern Australia, and *C. l. plagosus*, which is widespread in eastern Australia from Cape York to Tasmania and in south-western Australia. The species is also found in Indonesia, New Guinea, New Caledonia and Vanuatu.

NOTES. It frequents predominantly forests; in general, its close relative the Horsfield's Bronze-cuckoo prefers drier, more open habitats, whereas Shining Bronze-cuckoos tend to be more common in denser, more humid forest-lands. It is migratory in southern Australia, though birds are occasionally seen in winter. The call is a high-pitched monotone, suggesting the syllable 'pee', long drawn-out and uttered many times. It feeds mainly on caterpillars.

BREEDING. Nest: none built, the species being parasitic; usually selecting as host those that build domed nests, especially the Yellow-rumped Thornbill (19:10). Clutch: eggs pale greenish-olive or a distinct bronze-brown; if rubbed with a damp cloth the colouring may be removed, disclosing a pale blue shell. Breeding season: August to December.

10:20 HORSFIELD'S BRONZE-CUCKOO *Chrysococcyx basalis*

IDENTIFICATION. Easily confused with the Shining Bronze-cuckoo, this species has a dark brownish mask extending through the eye, and the bars on underparts do not meet across breast and belly. Sexes are similar.

DISTRIBUTION. Throughout Australia, including Tasmania. It also occurs in Indonesia and New Guinea.

NOTES. The species frequents open forest and heathlands. It is in general a migrant to the southern parts of Australia and Tasmania, arriving in early spring and departing at the end of summer, though some birds remain in the south during the winter. Its call is a piercing and mournful whistle with a downward inflection. In the breeding season the call is often uttered at night. Food: insects, mainly caterpillars.

BREEDING. Nest: none built, the species being parasitic, selecting as hosts from those species that build domed nests near the ground. Clutch: pinkish, with small red spots. Breeding season: July to December.

PLATE 11

BIRDS OF THE OPEN FOREST

11:1 RUFOUS WHISTLER *Pachycephala rufiventris*

IDENTIFICATION. The male is mainly grey above, pale rufous below, with a conspicuous black band across the upper breast; the throat is white; the female is nondescript brownish grey above, dull white or pale buff below and faintly streaked grey.

DISTRIBUTION. Throughout Australia, except Tasmania.

NOTES. A common bird, it is seen in southern Australia mainly in spring and summer, when its ringing 'ee–chong', followed by rippling notes, is one of the most characteristic sounds of forests and orchards. Most common in open woodlands (especially eucalypt, mallee and mulga), it tends to avoid dense humid forests. Both members of a pair sing, and co-operate in defending their joint territory. Highly vocal and animated during the breeding season, it is generally quiet and solitary at other times. Like other whistlers, it often sings in response to any loud and sudden noise, such as a gun-shot or a peal of thunder. Food: insects.

BREEDING. Nest: open, cup-shaped, made of dry twigs and grasses, lined with fine grass and rootlets; built in a tree or bush, usually 1–12 metres from the ground. Clutch: two to three; dull olive to olive-brown, with shades of brown. Breeding season: September to January.

11:2 WHITE-WINGED TRILLER *Lalage sueurii*

IDENTIFICATION. During breeding the male is mainly black above, white below, with grey rump and boldly marked black and white wings; at other seasons, head and back are light grey-brown. Females and immatures resemble non-breeding males, but are duller and browner.

DISTRIBUTION. Throughout continental Australia. It also occurs in New Guinea and Timor and is a straggler to Tasmania.

NOTES. This species is migratory, usually arriving in southern Australia in September and departing in February. It is unusual among Australian birds in that the male has two distinct plumages a year — the non-breeding plumage (worn generally in winter quarters in northern Australia) resembles that of the female. It is noisy, active and conspicuous. Aptly named triller, the male has a persistent, intense and spirited song; the high-pitched trills and 'joey–joey' notes are often uttered in flight. In some years the species is plentiful and in others curiously scarce. Food: insects procured in foliage and on the ground.

BREEDING. Nest: small, open, shallow; made of fine rootlets and dry grass, bound with cobweb; placed in a tree fork 1–10 metres from the ground. Clutch: three; bluish-green, heavily marked chestnut-brown. Breeding season: variable, but mainly September to January.

11:3 VARIED TRILLER *Lalage leucomela*

IDENTIFICATION. It somewhat resembles the breeding male White-winged Triller, but with conspicuous white superciliary, underparts faintly barred, and belly and undertail washed warm buff. Sexes are similar, but females are rather duller than males, and more distinctly barred below.

DISTRIBUTION. Coastal northern and eastern Australia, west to the Kimberley and south to the Myall Lakes, New South Wales. It is also found in New Guinea.

NOTES. The Varied Triller frequents scrubby open forest on the edge of jungle and is more or less nomadic. It is quieter than its smaller relative the White-winged Triller. The characteristic call is a reflective 'kar–r–r', but at times the bird utters a trilling song. Food: insects, native fruits and berries.

BREEDING. Nest: small, shallow, saucer-shaped, made of rootlets and grasses, bound with cobweb; usually on a slender horizontal tree fork a metre or so from the ground. Clutch: one; green, spotted chestnut-brown. Breeding season: October to January.

11:4 LEADEN FLYCATCHER *Myiagra rubecula*

IDENTIFICATION. The male has head, breast and upperparts glossy blue-grey and belly white; the female is mainly brownish-grey above, white below, with suffused rusty wash on throat and upper breast. It is active, and often perches bolt upright, tail held vertical, and shivers rapidly from side to side (a distinctive mannerism of most *Myiagra* flycatchers).

DISTRIBUTION. North-western Australia, Northern Territory and eastern Australia (from Cape York to Victoria). It also occurs in New Guinea and is a straggler to Tasmania and south-eastern South Australia.

NOTES. An interstate migrant, this flycatcher arrives in New South Wales in September and departs during March. It is chiefly a coastal bird; it is very active, with a peculiar and distinctive trembling of the tail. Its calls include a clear whistle 'too–whee', and a grating noise resembling that of certain species of frogs, hence the name 'Frogbird' used in some districts. Food: insects, chiefly flies, caught on the wing or among the leaves of tall trees.

BREEDING. Nest: cup-shaped, made of fine bark bound with cobweb, lined with fine rootlets and decorated outside with fragments of bark and lichen; typically built on a dead branch immediately below a living, leafy limb, usually 10–25 metres from the ground. Clutch: three; white or faint bluish-white, spotted brown and lavender. Breeding season: October to January.

11:5 SATIN FLYCATCHER *Myiagra cyanoleuca*

IDENTIFICATION. This bird closely resembles the Leaden Flycatcher in size, general appearance and mannerisms, but the head and upperparts are richly blue-black and highly glossed. The female is more difficult to distinguish from the female Leaden Flycatcher, but it is noticeably more richly coloured, the throat and breast is a deeper chestnut, and is more sharply separated from white underparts.

DISTRIBUTION. Eastern Australia (rarely to south-eastern South Australia) and Tasmania.

NOTES. It arrives in south-eastern Australia and Tasmania during September and departs in February. Similar in habits to the Leaden Flycatcher, but it has a deeper note, 'chee–ee, chee–ee'. The two species often occur together, but in general the Satin Flycatcher tends to favour denser, taller, more mature forest, while the Leaden Flycatcher often occurs in dry open woodland. Food: insects, procured chiefly on the wing.

BREEDING. Nest: cup-shaped, constructed of bark fragments bound with cobweb, usually lined with slender rootlets; built on a horizontal dead branch, sometimes one situated beneath a living limb, at a considerable height. Clutch: two to three; dull white to greenish-white, spotted brown and lavender. Breeding season: November to January.

11:6 BLACK-EARED CUCKOO *Chrysococcyx osculans*

IDENTIFICATION. This cuckoo is pale grey-brown above, dull white below, with a black mask, pale eyebrow, and grey rump. Sexes are similar.

DISTRIBUTION. Sparingly spread through the interior of Australia generally, rarely extending to coastal areas.

NOTES. This bird is mostly solitary, quiet and unobtrusive. It is generally uncommon. Apparently migratory in the south, it is nomadic elsewhere. It procures most of its food, insects, on or near the ground. The flight is similar to that of the other bronze-cuckoos. The most characteristic call is a long drawn-out whistle, gradually fading away, often uttered from a conspicuous perch on a high dead twig.

BREEDING. Nest: none built, the species being parasitic; the Redthroat and the Speckled Warbler seem to be the chief hosts. Clutch: eggs uniform dark chocolate in colour. Breeding season: August to January (New South Wales and Victoria); March (central Australia).

11:7 PALLID CUCKOO *Cuculus pallidus*

IDENTIFICATION. This is a rather large, slender cuckoo, grey above, paler below, with a yellow eye-ring and a distinctive white mark at the nape. Sexes are similar, but immatures are browner, and intricately marked and spotted buff and reddish-brown.

DISTRIBUTION. Throughout continental Australia, where suitable conditions exist, and Tasmania.

NOTES. It arrives in south-eastern Australia in July or August and departs during February or March, though a few birds remain throughout the year. The species tends to favour dryer, more open country than the other larger cuckoos. It has an undulating flight with the true cuckoo habit of elevating its tail when alighting. The call is a series of loud crescendo notes, ascending the scale, varied occasionally by a few harsh notes. Food: insects, especially hairy caterpillars, which few other species of birds eat.

BREEDING. Nest: none built, the species being parasitic; most species selected as hosts build open nests. Clutch: eggs uniform flesh-colour; some have a few dots of a darker hue. Breeding season: September to January.

11:8 ORIENTAL CUCKOO *Cuculus saturatus*

IDENTIFICATION. Adults are large, grey, closely barred below; immatures are darker and browner above, flecked and scaled buff.

DISTRIBUTION. Widespread in eastern Asia and the Oriental region, wintering south to Indonesia, New Guinea, and northern and eastern Australia, south (occasionally) as far as Sydney, New South Wales.

NOTES. Recorded in Australia in almost all months, but it is mainly seen in January to May. It is a close relative of the European Cuckoo. A strong, hawk-like flier, it is usually shy but may become trustful when feeding on caterpillars, etc. In Japan the call is said to be a two-syllabled 'po–po' or 'pon–pon'; in Australia the species has been heard to utter a low, harsh churring and a laugh-like 'kuk–kuk–kuk'.

BREEDING. It does not breed in Australia.

11:9 CICADABIRD *Coracina tenuirostris*

IDENTIFICATION. This is a typical cuckooshrike, but the male is almost entirely dark blue-grey; the female is brownish above, underparts buff, closely barred grey.

DISTRIBUTION. Northern and eastern Australia, west to the Kimberley and south to Melbourne, Victoria — although becoming progressively rarer and more local south of about Sydney. It also occurs in Indonesia and New Guinea.

NOTES. An interstate migrant, it arrives in the south early in October and departs in March. Strictly arboreal, it spends most of its time high in the woodland canopy, and is more often heard than seen. The chief call of the male is a distinctive, loud and continuous trilling or buzzing which suggests the stridulation produced by a large cicada; the species also calls 'chuck–chuck'. Food: insects, including cicadas, obtained among leaves and branches of trees.

BREEDING. Nest: small, open, made of short dry twigs bound with cobweb and draped with lichen; usually on a horizontal tree fork 10–25 metres above the ground. Clutch: one; varies from pale bluish to greenish-grey, with umber, slaty-brown, and underlying markings of lavender. Breeding season: October to January.

11:10 RUFOUS SONGLARK *Cinclorhamphus mathewsi*

IDENTIFICATION. This is a slender, rather long-tailed, nondescript bird of woodland clearings. It is brown above, streaked blackish, has a rufous rump and plain dingy white underparts. Sexes are similar.

DISTRIBUTION. Throughout Australia, except northern Queensland and the heavily forested regions of south-western and eastern Australia.

NOTES. It arrives in eastern New South Wales and Victoria from August to October and departs in February. It frequents grassy woodland, rough pasture with scattered timber, and similar lightly wooded habitats. The song — 'wicha–poo, a whicha–poo' — is very animated but somewhat monotonous; it is rendered by the male bird as he flies from tree to tree or post to post. The species is believed to be polygamous. Food: insects and seeds, procured on the ground.

BREEDING. Nest: cup-shaped, composed of dried grasses; lined with finer grasses and horse hair when available; built in a depression in the ground, well concealed in grass. Clutch: three to four; pure white to reddish and faint purplish-white, almost obscured with freckles of reddish- or purplish-brown. Breeding season: September to December.

11:11 SACRED KINGFISHER *Halcyon sancta*

IDENTIFICATION. It is common and conspicuous, with greenish blue above, pale buff below and no white in the wing. Sexes are similar.

DISTRIBUTION. Australia generally, including Tasmania. Also occurs from Sumatra and Borneo to New Guinea, Vanuatu, New Caledonia and New Zealand.

NOTES. This kingfisher arrives in southern Australia in August or early September and departs in March; odd birds may remain throughout the year. It has a loud note 'kee–kee–kee' uttered several times, occasionally during the night; it emits harsh cries if its nest is approached, and will attack an intruder. Food: mainly insects and small reptiles, also fish and crabs.

BREEDING. Nest: in a cavity in a tree, a bank, or in a termite nest. Clutch: four to five; white. Breeding season: October to January.

11:12 FOREST KINGFISHER *Halcyon macleayii*

IDENTIFICATION. Often confused with the Sacred Kingfisher, this species is bright blue (not greenish) above, and white (not buff) below; it has a white patch in the outer wing, is obscure at rest but conspicuous in flight. Sexes are similar.

DISTRIBUTION. Northern and eastern Australia, west to the Kimberley and south to about Taree, New South Wales. It also occurs in New Guinea.

NOTES. It is a sedentary species in northern Australia, but at least partly migratory in New South Wales, arriving in September and departing in March. It is a common and conspicuous bird in the north, often perching on roadside fence posts or telephone wires. The loud call is uttered intermittently throughout the day. Food: large insects, small lizards, fish and crabs.

BREEDING. Nest: a hollowed-out cavity in a termite nest on a tree, usually 2–25 metres from the ground. Clutch: four to five; white and rounded. Breeding season: October to December.

11:13 RED-BACKED KINGFISHER *Halcyon pyrrhopygia*

IDENTIFICATION. This species has a shaggy dull white crown, copiously streaked greenish blue and a dull rufous rump. Sexes are similar.

DISTRIBUTION. Interior of Australia, extending to coastal districts, as far south-east as Melbourne, on rare occasions.

NOTES. It arrives in the south during September and departs in March. It is characteristic of the arid interior, inhabiting more open country than other kingfishers, but is not uncommon in many coastal areas, especially in winter. It perches conspicuously on telephone posts, wires and other exposed places.

The call is a single mournful note, uttered at short intervals. Food: large insects and small reptiles.

BREEDING. Nest: a tunnel in a bank of a dry creek, or in a termite nest. Clutch: four to five; white, rounded. Breeding season: September to December.

11:14 DOLLARBIRD *Eurystomus orientalis*

IDENTIFICATION. This bird appears dark and colourless at a distance, but with a distinctive silhouette — big-headed and short-tailed, with large, blunt, reddish bill. Sexes are similar.

DISTRIBUTION. Northern and eastern Australia (breeding). It occurs on migration and during the winter in the Moluccas, Celebes, New Guinea and the Bismarck Archipelago. It is a straggler to South Australia, Tasmania, New Zealand and Lord Howe Island.

NOTES. The Dollarbird arrives in southern Australia in late September or early October, departing at the end of February or March. It spends much of its time perched on the highest dead branch of a tall tree, from which it will fly out in pursuit of some insect. At dusk it hawks continuously above tree tops, often remaining on the wing for a lengthy period. It is named Dollarbird (also Star-wing) from the round, pale blue spot on each wing, seen when in flight, and also named Roller from its habit of somersaulting in mid-air. The characteristic note 'kak–kak–kak–kak' is peculiarly harsh and discordant; it is uttered chiefly when the bird is in flight, and particularly towards sunset. Food: large flying insects.

BREEDING. Nest: in a hole in a dead tree, always at a considerable height. Clutch: three to five; white, rounded. Breeding season: October to December.

11:15 TREE MARTIN *Cecropis nigricans*

IDENTIFICATION. This is a square-tailed swallow, with rump dull white and crown bluish black. Sexes are similar.

DISTRIBUTION. Throughout Australia where suitable habitats exist, though rare in far northern areas. It is also seen in Timor, the Moluccas, Aru Islands and New Guinea.

NOTES. The Tree Martin arrives in southern Australia in flocks during August and departs about the end of March, though some birds are likely to remain throughout the year. Usually it is seen in flocks. The species is common in the interior as well as in coastal districts, particularly those areas studded with tall and spreading trees.

BREEDING. Nest: usually in a cavity in a tree or in a crevice in a cliff, but sometimes in suitable cavities in buildings; lined with dead leaves and dry grass; mud may be used to narrow the entrance. Clutch: four to five; creamy-white, occasionally with flecks of reddish-brown. Breeding season: August to January.

11:16 RAINBOW BEE-EATER *Merops ornatus*

IDENTIFICATION. It is mainly blue and green, with yellow-orange throat and black crescent across breast. Wings show a distinctive burnt orange colour in flight. Sexes are similar.

DISTRIBUTION. Almost throughout Australia, excluding Tasmania. Also from Indonesia to New Guinea and the Solomon Islands.

NOTES. It arrives in southern Australia in September or October and departs in February or March; most birds appear to winter in islands north of Australia but many remain in the northern parts of the continent. It is a gregarious, conspicuous bird, with a graceful erratic flight, and a shrill whirring call-note. It prefers open areas and procures its food on the wing, but often perches on the limbs of trees, on wires and on stumps, from which positions it will dart out in pursuit of insects.

BREEDING. Nest: a tunnel in sandy soil, up to a metre in length, with a cavity at the end. Clutch: five to seven; white and glossy. Breeding season: October to January and February.

11:17 MASKED WOODSWALLOW *Artamus personatus*

IDENTIFICATION. The bird is smooth grey above and white below with black face, cheeks and throat. Sexes are similar.

DISTRIBUTION. Interior of Australia, extending in fewer numbers to coastal areas (except Cape York and the extreme south of Western Australia); it is a straggler to Tasmania.

NOTES. The Masked Woodswallow arrives in southern Australia in flocks, often in the company of the White-browed Woodswallow (in such mixed flocks, White-browed numbers tend to dominate in the east, Masked in the west), during September or October and departs at the end of January. The two species are very similar in habits, and both may visit a locality regularly year after year, then, without any known reason, be absent for several seasons. Food: mainly insects.

BREEDING. Nest: cup-shaped, made of thin twigs and grasses; built in a bush, stump, or post, 1–7 metres from the ground. Clutch: two to three; greyish-white to light greenish-grey, with shades of brown and a few underlying spots of pale grey. Breeding season: August to December or January.

11:18 WHITE-BREASTED WOODSWALLOW *Artamus leucorhynchus*

IDENTIFICATION. The head and upperparts are dark grey, underparts are white; it is the only woodswallow with a white rump. Sexes are similar.

DISTRIBUTION. From Shark Bay, Western Australia, through northern and eastern Australia to central Victoria and to eastern South Australia; it is a straggler to Tasmania. Also it is found in islands of the Western Pacific.

NOTES. A graceful and attractive species, this bird is usually seen near water, either on the coast or along rivers of the sub-interior. It has a loose association with the Magpielark, the old nests of which it uses freely for breeding purposes. Like other woodswallows it catches most of its insect-food in the air and, again like others of its group, it is given to animated chirruping and chattering.

BREEDING. Nest: cup-shaped, composed of dried grasses; the site is highly variable but is usually in the fork of a small tree or in a hollow spout. Clutch: Three to four; creamy-white, spotted pale brown and faint bluish-grey. Breeding season: August to January.

11:19 BLACK-FACED WOODSWALLOW *Artamus cinereus*

IDENTIFICATION. It is plain sooty-brown, slightly paler below, with a small black mask. Sexes are similar. The population in north-eastern Queensland (subspecies *albiventris*) differs slightly in having white, not black, undertail coverts.

DISTRIBUTION. Interior of Australia generally, extending to coastal regions in the west and north. It also occurs in Timor.

NOTES. It is seen usually in pairs or small flocks. It is common, almost ubiquitous, in most kinds of open country in the arid interior, and a familiar sight on telephone and fence wires along the roadsides. It is mainly sedentary, or only locally nomadic. The calls include a scratchy 'chiff, chiff' and a soft but animated song.

BREEDING. Nest: open, cup-shaped, composed of rootlets and small twigs; lined with finer materials, occasionally horse hair; placed in a shrub or stump. Clutch: usually four; fleshy-white, spotted with umber-brown and underlying bluish-grey. Breeding season: September to December.

11:20 WHITE-BROWED WOODSWALLOW *Artamus superciliosus*

IDENTIFICATION. The head and upperparts are deep grey, underparts rich chestnut; it has a conspicuous white superciliary. Sexes are similar.

DISTRIBUTION. Australia generally, except Cape York Peninsula and the extreme south-west; it is rare in Tasmania.

NOTES. The bird is strongly gregarious — feeding, travelling, roosting and even nesting in loose companies. Flocks often consist of hundreds of birds, and are often accompanied by the Masked Woodswallow. Migratory over much of southern Australia, it arrives during September or October and departs in January; it is highly nomadic elsewhere. Its notes when uttered high in the air are contented chirps, they become a harsh scolding when the nest is disturbed. Food: flying insects and occasionally nectar.

BREEDING. Nest: a frail, open, shallow structure, composed of dried grasses and thin twigs; built in a variety of situations, but generally in a bush, tree, or cleft in a stump. Clutch: two to three; whitish-brown to greyish-green, spotted and blotched with pale umber. Breeding season: October to January.

PLATE 12

SOME HONEYEATERS OF THE OPEN FOREST

12:1 TAWNY-BREASTED HONEYEATER *Xanthotis flaviventer*

IDENTIFICATION. The underparts are warm buff, obscurely streaked dull white; the crown and face are grey, with a small patch of naked dull orange skin around eye. Sexes are similar.

DISTRIBUTION. North-eastern Queensland, from Cape York to the Claudie River. It also occurs in New Guinea.

NOTES. The species frequents rainforest, open forest and mangroves. It is common, seen singly or in small parties. The bird is often active, noisy and conspicuous. Food: insects and nectar.

BREEDING. Nest: cup-shaped, made of bark and fibre; lined with fibre and fine rootlets; usually suspended from a horizontal fork up to 16 metres from the ground. Clutch: two; pinkish-white, with small spots of bright brownish-red. Breeding season: probably November to January or February.

12:2 WHITE-GAPED HONEYEATER *Lichenostomus unicolor*

IDENTIFICATION. It is plain grey-brown, with a prominent white mark at the gape. Sexes are similar.

DISTRIBUTION. Tropical northern Australia west to Broome, Western Australia, and south to Townsville, Queensland.

NOTES. The bird frequents scrubs bordering streams and swamps. It is common, active, noisy, pugnacious and conspicuous, often visiting urban parks and gardens. It utters a wide variety of rich melodious whistles and loud rollicking calls — one of them suggesting the chirrup of the House Sparrow. It also has the habit, unusual for a honeyeater, of erecting its tail. Food: insects, nectar, native fruits and berries.

BREEDING. Nest: cup-shaped, constructed of bark and grass; usually placed in a bushy tree. Clutch: two; pale pinkish-white, profusely marked with reddish-brown, chestnut and purple. Breeding season: August to January.

12:3 SPINY-CHEEKED HONEYEATER *Acanthagenys rufogularis*

IDENTIFICATION. The species is large, has a white rump, buff throat, white cheeks, and pink bill, tipped black. Sexes are similar.

DISTRIBUTION. Interior of Australia generally, extending to coastal areas in various parts.

NOTES. The bird is common in most arid and semi-arid environments, including mallee, but also in some areas coastal tea-tree scrubs and similar habitats. It is an attractive, noisy, pugnacious and conspicuous bird. It is nomadic. It has a pleasant song, a series of gurgling notes, which frequently ends abruptly — often given in flight. Food: insects and nectar.

BREEDING. Nest: cup-shaped, made of grass and rootlets bound with cobweb; lined with fur, wool or other soft materials; usually suspended by the rim from

a horizontal fork or a clump of mistletoe, up to 20 metres from the ground.
Clutch: two to three; pale olive-green, with dark to light umber and purplish
grey markings. Breeding season: August to January.

12:4 STRIPED HONEYEATER *Plectorhyncha lanceolata*

IDENTIFICATION. This is a pale, brownish honeyeater with distinctive shaggy
head, boldly streaked black and white. The sexes are similar.

DISTRIBUTION. Eastern Australia, broadly east of a line from Cairns,
Queensland, to Yorke Peninsula, South Australia, but excluding south-eastern
New South Wales, eastern Victoria and Tasmania.

NOTES. The bird is seen in pairs or small parties, inhabiting mainly open
woodlands of the hot, dry inland, especially mallee, mulga and saltbush, but
also coastal thickets of melaleuca, banksia and casuarina. It is active, noisy and
conspicuous. The song, bold, rolling and melodious, is one of the most
agreeable of all utterances by honeyeaters. Food: insects and nectar, procured
among the blossoms and foliage.

BREEDING. Nest: cup-shaped, deep, composed of grasses and rootlets, neatly
woven with plant-down, sheep's wool, and occasionally emu feathers; lined
with fine grasses, hair, and feathers; suspended near the extremity of a
drooping and swaying branch of a tree (often a casuarina). Clutch: three to
four; pale pinkish-white, spotted with reddish-brown and purplish-grey.
Breeding season: August to December.

12:5 BLUE-FACED HONEYEATER *Entomyzon cyanotis*

IDENTIFICATION. It is a large honeyeater, green above, white below, with
bright blue cheeks (greyish-green in immatures). The sexes are similar.

DISTRIBUTION. Northern and eastern Australia, west to the Kimberley and
south to the Riverina.

NOTES. The species is seen in pairs or small flocks, inhabiting open forest
country. It is abundant in north-eastern Queensland, where, because of its
attachment to the pandanus tree, it is often termed Pandanus-bird; it is also
common in various other areas and since about the 1930s it has become
established in parts of south-eastern Australia that it previously did not
inhabit. It has a loud and monotonous call 'queet', and an alarm note like that of
the Noisy Miner. Food: insects, nectar, native fruits and berries.

BREEDING. Nest: usually refurbishes the abandoned nest of some other bird; otherwise builds a flattish structure of bark strips lined with fine bark and grass; usually placed high on an outer branch of a tree. Clutch: two to three; rich salmon to fleshy-buff, sparingly spotted chestnut-brown. Breeding season: June to January.

12:6 NOISY MINER *Manorina melanocephala*

IDENTIFICATION. The bird is mainly pale grey, with a white face and forehead, black crown and cheeks, grey rump, and yellow bill. Sexes are similar.

DISTRIBUTION. Eastern Australia, from about Cairns, Queensland, south to Tasmania and west to about Adelaide, South Australia.

NOTES. It frequents open forest and partly cleared lands. It is a restless, bold, and noisy bird, keeping up a constant chatter of loud and sharp notes, especially at sight of intruders, hence the name Soldierbird. The birds live in colonies, co-operating in defending the colony's territory and in raising the young. Food: insects, procured among the leaves and blossoms and on the ground; also pollen, native fruits and berries.

BREEDING. Nest: cup-shaped, made of twigs, strips of bark and grass, frequently decorated outside with wool; lined with fine grass and hair; placed in a bush or tree, up to 7–8 metres from the ground. Clutch: three to four; pinkish-white, profusely spotted reddish-chestnut and purplish-grey. Breeding season: July to December or January.

12:7 BLACK-EARED MINER *Manorina melanotis*

IDENTIFICATION. It is very difficult to distinguish either of the other two miners, but it is somewhat duskier grey, the crown is grey, it has a dusky black mask extending to lores and the rump is grey. Identify with extreme caution. Sexes are similar.

DISTRIBUTION. Restricted to a small area at the junction of New South Wales, Victoria and South Australia.

NOTES. Once locally common, but now it is generally rare, shy and little known, and is now possibly Australia's rarest bird, hovering on the brink of extinction. Usually it is found in small parties, inhabiting mainly mallee country. It is similar in habits to the Noisy Miner. Food: insects, native fruits and berries. The so-called Dusky Miner of south-western Australia, once regarded as belonging to this species, has been shown to be a subspecies of the White-rumped Miner.

BREEDING. Nest: a loose untidy bowl of grass and fine twigs, lined with fine grass and other soft materials; placed in a mallee eucalypt up to 7–8 metres from the ground. Clutch: three to four; salmon-buff, spotted reddish-brown and purplish-brown. Breeding season: August to February.

12:8 YELLOW-THROATED MINER *Manorina flavigula*

IDENTIFICATION. The bird is similar to the Noisy Miner, but the crown and forehead are yellow and the face and throat are faintly tinged yellow; birds in eastern Australia have white rumps, but western populations have grey rumps like the Noisy Miner. Sexes are similar.

DISTRIBUTION. Australia generally, except eastern coastal regions.

NOTES. The species frequents open forest and scrub lands. It replaces the Noisy Miner in the west and over most of the arid interior; the ranges of the two species abut in some areas, and hybrids have been reported. It is generally similar in habits to the Noisy Miner, but tends to form larger colonies, and is rather less assertive than the Noisy Miner. It is fairly tame and sometimes visits gardens of inland homesteads. Food: insects, nectar, native fruits and berries.

BREEDING. Nest: a loose, substantial cup of grass and twigs; lined with fine grass, hair, wool, and other soft materials; placed in a bush or tree, usually 2–7 metres from the ground. Clutch: three to four; rich salmon-pink, spotted reddish-brown and purplish-grey. Breeding season: July to December.

12:9 LITTLE FRIARBIRD *Philemon citreogularis*

IDENTIFICATION. This is a small friarbird, lacking a knob on the bill; it also has a patch of naked, bluish grey skin around the eye. Sexes are similar; immatures have yellowish throat, upperparts scaled pale grey.

DISTRIBUTION. Northern and eastern Australia, west to about Port Hedland, Western Australia and south to the Riverina. It is also found in New Guinea.

NOTES. The bird frequents open forest country of inland districts, especially along watercourses, and occasionally coastal areas. It utters a wide variety of loud calls, including a loud, monotonous 'ar–coo' and a mellow, liquid 'gee–whit'. Food: insects, nectar, native fruits and berries.

BREEDING. Nest: cup-shaped, made of grass, rootlets and strips of bark, bound with cobweb and lined with fine grass; usually placed near the end of a drooping branch of a tree, sometimes overhanging water. Clutch: two to three;

pinkish-buff, with chestnut and purplish-brown markings. Breeding season: August to February.

12:10 SILVER-CROWNED FRIARBIRD *Philemon argenticeps*

IDENTIFICATION. This species is very difficult to distinguish from the Helmeted Friarbird, but the crown, throat and breast are a cleaner white, and less dingy grey-buff; there is a faint white tip to tail. Sexes are similar.

DISTRIBUTION. Tropical northern Australia, from about Derby, Western Australia, east to about Cooktown, Queensland; extending inland to Mount Isa.

NOTES. The bird frequents flowering trees of forests, and also mangroves. Gregarious but aggressive, it has similar habits to the Noisy Friarbird. Its calls are loud, varied, and raucous; one especially distinctive call sounds a little like 'more tobacco', repeated. Food: insects, nectar, native fruits and berries.

BREEDING. Nest: similar to that of the Noisy Friarbird. Clutch: two; pale pinkish-buff, marked reddish-brown, purplish-brown, and purplish-grey. Breeding season: August to January or even March.

12:11 HELMETED FRIARBIRD *Philemon buceroides*

IDENTIFICATION. Easily confused with Silver-crowned Friarbird, but this bird's crown, nape and throat are dingy grey-brown, not pale silvery-grey; a naked black face patch extends backwards on to side of neck. Sexes are similar.

DISTRIBUTION. There are three very similar subspecies in Australia: *P. b. gordoni* and *P. b. ammitophila* of western Arnhem Land, Melville Island and nearby coast of the Northern Territory; and *P. b. yorki* (Helmeted Friarbird) of north-eastern Queensland, from Cape York south to about Mackay. The species also occurs in Indonesia and New Guinea.

NOTES. It frequents rainforests, mangroves, and dense vegetation along watercourses; it is usually seen singly or in pairs, but congregates at blossoming trees to form large, active flocks. It is quarrelsome and aggressive, as well as being exceptionally noisy; its call, resembling 'poor devil, poor devil', is constantly repeated. Food: insects, nectar, native fruits and berries.

BREEDING. Nest: a large untidy cup of grass, rootlets and strips of bark, closely woven, and lined with fine grass and rootlets; usually slung from the rim in a high horizontal fork amid foliage. Clutch: three to four; pinkish-white, with reddish-brown and dull purple markings. Breeding season: August to January.

12:12 NOISY FRIARBIRD *Philemon corniculatus*

IDENTIFICATION. This is a large, active, raucous bird which is dull grey-brown above, dingy white below; its head is naked, entirely black (except chin whitish). Sexes are similar.

DISTRIBUTION. Eastern Australia, from Cape York to eastern and southern Victoria.

NOTES. A noisy and pugnacious bird, of nomadic habits, it sometimes does damage to orchards. Often uttered in company are an extraordinary jumble of notes, one of which has been interpreted as 'four–o'clock'. Food: insects, nectar, native fruit, berries and cultivated fruits.

BREEDING. Nest: cup-shaped, made of bark and grasses woven together with cobweb and neatly lined with dry grass; it is usually suspended from a drooping branch, often overhanging water. Clutch: two to four; pinkish-buff, with clouded markings of chestnut and dull purplish-grey. Breeding season: August to December or January.

12:13 RED WATTLEBIRD *Anthochaera carunculata*

IDENTIFICATION. This bird is easily confused with the Little Wattlebird (No. 24:17), but its belly is clear lemon yellow and it has grey outer wings (round red wattle often inconspicuous). Sexes are similar.

DISTRIBUTION. From southern Queensland to Victoria, South Australia, and south-western Australia; it is accidental to New Zealand.

NOTES. The species is nomadic, following the blossoming of eucalypts and banksias. In the spring and summer it frequents chiefly open forest country, where it breeds, and often in autumn and winter it visits heathlands. At one time great numbers were killed each year for the table, but the species is now protected by law. It utters a wide variety of loud, harsh and raucous calls; perhaps most characteristic is a loud emphatic 'tchock!'. Food: insects and nectar, also cultivated fruits.

BREEDING. Nest: an untidy bowl of twigs, grass and bark, lined with softer materials; placed in a bush or tree. Clutch: two to three; pinkish-buff, spotted reddish-brown and purplish-grey. Breeding season: July to December.

12:14 YELLOW WATTLEBIRD *Anthochaera paradoxa*

IDENTIFICATION. This is a very large honeyeater, mainly streaked, with yellow wash on belly and long dangling yellow wattles behind the eye. Sexes are similar.

DISTRIBUTION. Restricted to Tasmania (rare on King Island, absent from Flinders Island).

NOTES. It is seen in pairs or flocks, according to season; the bird is active, acrobatic and conspicuous. It frequents open forests and scrub-lands alike where it feeds among the flowering eucalypts and banksias; it is also seen in gardens and parks. The characteristic call of this largest of Australia's honeyeaters is an extraordinary gurgling, discordant noise, sometimes described as suggesting the sound of a person vomiting. Food: insects and nectar.

BREEDING. Nest: bulky, loose, open, saucer-shaped, of twigs and strips of bark, lined with fine grass and wool; placed in a fork of a bush or tree. Clutch: two to three; pinkish-buff, spotted reddish-brown and purplish-grey. Breeding season: July to December.

PLATE 13

GROUND-FEEDING PIGEONS AND DOVES

13:1 PEACEFUL DOVE *Geopelia placida*

IDENTIFICATION. This bird is small; its neck is closely barred black and white and its eye-ring is powder blue. Sexes are similar.

DISTRIBUTION. Northern and eastern Australia generally, except Tasmania, but including almost all of Queensland, New South Wales and Victoria; absent from the south-west and most of the arid western interior, but on the west coast occurs south to about Carnarvon. The species also occurs in New Guinea, with closely related (and possibly conspecific) forms occurring widely in Malaysia and Indonesia.

NOTES. This is a common and familiar bird, found usually in pairs or small flocks, frequenting open forest country. It is mainly sedentary. The bird is fond of sun-bathing, and is often seen along roadsides and near homesteads, also in

towns in some areas. The call is a melodious coo sounding like 'doodle–doo'.
Food: seeds of grasses and shrubs.

BREEDING. Nest: a frail platform of thin twigs; usually placed on a horizontal fork within a few metres of the ground. Clutch: two; white. Breeding season: virtually year-round, but only sporadically during the dry season (May to July) in the north, and during the colder months (May to August) in the south.

13:2 DIAMOND DOVE *Geopelia cuneata*

IDENTIFICATION. This species is very small; its back is brown and finely dotted white and the eye-ring is red. Sexes are similar.

DISTRIBUTION. Australia generally except the coastal districts of south-eastern Australia and South Australia; sparsely distributed in the south-west of Western Australia.

NOTES. It occurs in pairs or small flocks, frequenting mainly the vicinity of rivers and permanent water in lightly wooded savannah country. Although its distribution broadly overlaps that of the Peaceful Dove in eastern Australia, in general it replaces its larger relative over most of the arid interior of the continent. It is generally common, but highly nomadic. The call is a plaintive and somewhat prolonged yodelling coo. Food: seeds of grasses and herbaceous plants, taken on the ground.

BREEDING. Nest: a frail structure of thin twigs and grasses; placed in a fork of a low bush or tree, sometimes on top of a stump. Clutch: two; white. Breeding season: generally August to December, but highly variable in response (apparently) to rainfall.

13:3 BAR-SHOULDERED DOVE *Geopelia humeralis*

IDENTIFICATION. The back is brown, the nape rufous, both are closely barred black. Sexes are similar.

DISTRIBUTION. Northern and eastern Australia, mainly in coastal regions, west to about Onslow, Western Australia, and south to about Newcastle, New South Wales. Apparently the species is expanding its range southwards and westwards. It also is found in New Guinea.

NOTES. The bird is similar in general habits to the Peaceful Dove, but in general it prefers more humid environments and denser vegetation; it inhabits palm thickets, dense scrubs and mangroves. Its characteristic call is a loud 'hop–off, hop–off'. Food: seeds of various plants and native fruits and berries.

BREEDING. Nest: a platform of thin twigs and grass; placed in a low bush or tree in mangroves or scrub. Clutch: two; white. Breeding season: variable, but mainly August to March.

13:4 SPINIFEX PIGEON *Geophaps plumifera*

IDENTIFICATION. The breast and upperparts are sandy-rufous and it has a long, pointed vertical crest. Sexes are similar. Western populations (including subspecies *ferruginea* , No. 13:4b) tend, among other differences, to be more extensively reddish below than eastern birds.

DISTRIBUTION. The species occurs in several often widely separated populations across northern Australia, west to the Kimberley, east to Cape York Peninsula (interior) and south to north-eastern South Australia and the MacDonnell Ranges, Northern Territory.

NOTES. It inhabits open stony country — especially arid mountain ranges — studded with scrubby bushes and spinifex; it avoids sandy deserts. It is unusual among birds of Australia's arid interior in being essentially sedentary rather than nomadic. The species is seen in pairs or small flocks and is generally very tame. It prefers to walk rather than fly; when flushed, it rises with a loud whirr and flies a short distance. The call is a loud 'coo'. Food: seeds of grasses and herbaceous plants.

BREEDING. Nest: a slight, grass-lined depression in the ground sheltered by a low bush or clump of spinifex. Clutch: two: creamy white. Breeding season: variable, but after rains.

13:5 WHITE-QUILLED ROCK-PIGEON *Petrophassa albipennis*

IDENTIFICATION. The bird is rather large, terrestrial, dark brown, scaled paler brown, with a white flash in the wings (obvious in flight). Sexes are similar.

DISTRIBUTION. From the Kimberley to extreme north-western Northern Territory.

NOTES. The bird is sedentary. It occurs in pairs or small flocks, frequenting sandstone country. A common but shy bird, it is difficult to flush, relying on its protective colouration to render it inconspicuous. Almost entirely terrestrial, it seldom perches in trees. If flushed it rises with a whirr of wings, but only flies a short distance and usually alights on a bare rock.

BREEDING. Nest: a slight hollow scooped in ground near a tuft of spinifex or a stone; lined with dead grass. Clutch: two; creamy-white. Breeding season: uncertain, but eggs have been found in July and October.

13:6 CHESTNUT-QUILLED ROCK-PIGEON *Petrophassa rufipennis*

IDENTIFICATION. It looks like the White-quilled Rock Pigeon, but the wing-flash is chestnut, not white. Sexes are similar. (Note distribution.)

DISTRIBUTION. Arnhem Land, Northern Territory.

NOTES. The species is found in pairs or small flocks, frequenting rocky sandstone gorges and plateaus. It is a shy bird, usually crouching and hiding among rocks, the colours of which harmonise perfectly with its plumage. It has habits like those of the White-quilled Rock-pigeon. Food: seeds of grasses and herbaceous plants.

BREEDING. Nest: a substantial platform of sticks supporting a pad of leaves and spinifex stems; built on a shaded rock ledge or in a crevice. Clutch: two; creamy-white. Breeding season: uncertain, but nests have been found in June, July and October.

13:7 CRESTED PIGEON *Ocyphaps lophotes*

IDENTIFICATION. A common, widespread and familiar bird whose plumage is mainly fawn and pale grey, with a long, pointy, vertical black crest. Sexes are similar.

DISTRIBUTION. Australia generally, except areas with high rainfall in the far south-east, north-eastern Queensland, and the Top End; it is also absent from Tasmania. The species has expanded its range considerably since European settlement, and is apparently still doing so in some eastern coastal areas.

NOTES. It is seen in pairs, small parties of five or six and sometimes large flocks, frequenting mainly inland districts. Its favourite haunts are lightly wooded savannah country, usually near waterways or dams. The bird is sedentary and common. Its flight is rapid and is marked by a metallic whistling of the wings; on alighting, it tips its tail in a highly characteristic manner. Food: seeds of grasses and herbaceous plants.

BREEDING. Nest: a frail platform of twigs, usually placed in a bushy horizontal branch several metres from the ground. Clutch: two; white. Breeding season: practically throughout the year, but chiefly during spring and summer.

13:8 WONGA PIGEON *Leucosarcia melanoleuca*

IDENTIFICATION. This is a large and plump bird with upperparts smooth blue-grey, underparts white, boldly spotted black, with a broken band of grey across breast. Sexes are similar.

DISTRIBUTION. Generally coastal eastern Australia from about Rockhampton, Queensland, south to Melbourne, Victoria; possibly also an isolated population in the Carnarvon Range, southern Queensland.

NOTES. Usually found in pairs, it inhabits rainforest and heavily timbered gullies. The bird forages mainly on the ground. Often it comes to forest picnic grounds, where it may become tame. When flushed, it rises with a loud clapping noise of the wings and flies a short distance before alighting. As a rule, it alights on a horizontal limb, where it remains motionless with its back towards the observer, relying on its colouration to escape detection. Its call is a monotonous 'woop–woop–woop', which may be heard up to a kilometre away and which may be uttered more than one hundred times in succession. Food: seeds of grasses and herbaceous plants, native fruits and berries, and insects.

BREEDING. Nest: open, almost flat, made of twigs; usually placed on a horizontal tree fork several metres from the ground; often in relatively open situations. Clutch: two; white. Breeding season: very variable, but normally October to January.

13:9 SQUATTER PIGEON *Geophaps scripta*

IDENTIFICATION. The bird is mainly brown above (paler feather edges produce scallopped effect), white below, the breast is grey-brown and the face, cheeks and throat are boldly patterned black and white. Sexes are similar.

DISTRIBUTION. Eastern Queensland except the high-rainfall areas of the far north and south-east, extending south into New South Wales (to about Inverell).

NOTES. Seen in pairs or small flocks, the bird frequents lightly wooded country near water, in arid inland districts. When flushed, a flock rises with a loud whirring noise of the wings, the individuals scattering to seek cover in the grass. The population has declined markedly since European settlement, and is now rare or absent over much of its former range. The name 'Squatter' alludes to the bird's habit of crouching to hide itself when approached. It only rarely perches in trees. The call is a deep 'coo'. Food: seeds of grasses.

BREEDING. Nest: a shallow depression scraped in the ground, lined with dry grass and a few dry leaves. Clutch: two; creamy-white. Breeding season: normally August to October.

13:10 PARTRIDGE PIGEON *Geophaps smithii*

IDENTIFICATION. The species somewhat resembles the Squatter Pigeon but is paler, with *smooth* brown upperparts; the extensive bare skin around the eye is red (eastern subspecies *blaauwi*) or yellow (Kimberley subspecies *smithii*). Sexes are similar.

DISTRIBUTION. Tropical northern Australia from the MacArthur River, Northern Territory, west to the Kimberley.

NOTES. Birds are seen in pairs or family parties during the breeding season, but at other times in small flocks. Favourite haunts are open woodlands adjacent to water. It is similar in habits to the Squatter Pigeon. Food: seeds of grasses and herbaceous plants.

BREEDING. Nest: a shallow depression in the ground, lined with soft grasses, and usually sheltered by a tuft of grass or low bush. Clutch: two; creamy-white. Breeding season: normally August to October.

13:11 FLOCK BRONZEWING *Phaps histrionica*

IDENTIFICATION. The bird is plain sandy-brown above and grey below; the head is mainly black, with a white face and patch on the lower throat. Sexes are similar, but the female is somewhat duller than the male.

DISTRIBUTION. Essentially western Queensland and the Barkly Tableland, Northern Territory, but highly irruptive, and flocks or scattered individuals may occur almost anywhere across the arid north and west of the continent.

NOTES. A bird of vast treeless grass plains, it is highly gregarious and nomadic, its movements being regulated by seasonal conditions and food supply. At one time this pigeon was seen in countless numbers on the inland plains, but now is seldom recorded in substantial numbers. When flushed, flocks rise with a loud whirring noise and, after circling in the air, alight again. Food: seeds of grasses and herbaceous plants.

BREEDING. Nest: on bare ground in the shelter of a tussock or low bush. Clutch: usually two; creamy-white. Breeding season: highly variable.

13:12 BRUSH BRONZEWING *Phaps elegans*

IDENTIFICATION. The bird is mainly smooth warm brown above and grey below; the throat and nape are rich chestnut, the forehead golden and the crown grey. Sexes are similar.

DISTRIBUTION. Coastal southern Australia, from Fraser Island, Queensland, to the Houtman Abrolhos Islands, Western Australia, including Tasmania; this range is interrupted by a stretch of generally unsuitable habitat along the Great Australian Bight between (approximately) Eyre and Ceduna.

NOTES. The species is seen usually in pairs, inhabiting chiefly scrub and heathlands of coastal districts. It is essentially a bird of the ground, over which it runs rapidly. The call is a low mournful 'coo', mainly uttered at evening. The species has declined markedly since European settlement. Food: seeds of grasses and herbaceous plants, also native fruits and berries.

BREEDING. Nest: saucer-shaped, composed of twigs; placed in a thick bush or in the branches of a fallen tree, or on the ground in the shelter of a bush. Clutch: two; white. Breeding season: usually October to January.

13:13 COMMON BRONZEWING *Phaps chalcoptera*

IDENTIFICATION. This bird is very like the Brush Bronzewing, but is somewhat paler, with upperparts scalloped, throat plain pinkish grey, forehead golden and crown dark brown. Sexes are similar, but the female is markedly duller than the male.

DISTRIBUTION. Throughout Australia, including Tasmania.

NOTES. Usually seen in pairs, the bird is common in almost any kind of wooded country. It is usually seen on the ground. It prefers to freeze rather than fly when disturbed, but when flushed it rises with a loud whirring noise, flies rapidly for a short distance, and then alights on a tree branch. Its call is a low 'oom', repeated many times. Food: seeds of grasses and herbaceous plants, also native fruits and berries.

BREEDING. Nest: a frail saucer of twigs, placed in a tree fork several metres from the ground. Clutch: two; white. Breeding season: usually October to January.

PLATE 14

BIRDS OF BLOSSOMS
AND OUTER FOLIAGE

14:1 YELLOW-SPOTTED HONEYEATER *Meliphaga notata*

IDENTIFICATION. Very like Lewin's Honeyeater, but this bird is smaller, with a relatively short bill and rounded pale yellowish patch near the ear. Sexes are similar.

DISTRIBUTION. North-eastern Queensland, south to about Townsville. It is also found in New Guinea.

NOTES. The bird frequents coastal rainforests and mangroves. Some of its calls resemble those of its close relative, the Lewin's Honeyeater, but are less robust and rather sharper; it also utters a melodious 'chip' and a sharp 'queak–queak–queak'. Food: native fruits, berries, insects and nectar.

BREEDING. Nest: fragile, cup-shaped, made of soft bark and dead leaves, bound with spider web and wild cotton, lined with plant down and decorated outside with lichen; suspended by the rim from a low horizontal fork in a bush or sapling. Clutch: two; white, spotted chestnut and purplish-brown. Breeding season: October to March.

14:2 GRACEFUL HONEYEATER *Meliphaga gracilis*

IDENTIFICATION. This species is very difficult to distinguish from the Yellow-spotted Honeyeater, but is rather smaller and slimmer, with a proportionately longer, more slender bill, and diamond-shaped earpatch. Sexes are similar.

DISTRIBUTION. North-eastern Queensland south to about Ingham. It also occurs in New Guinea.

NOTES. The bird frequents rainforest and adjacent woodlands. Generally it is solitary, quiet and inconspicuous. The most characteristic call is an abrupt 'pick'. Food: insects, nectar, native fruits, berries.

BREEDING. Nest: cup-shaped, constructed of bark shreds, usually covered with green moss, and lined with silky plant material; suspended from a low leafy branch. Clutch: two; salmon-pink, with chestnut and purplish-grey spots. Breeding season: October to January.

14:3 MACLEAY'S HONEYEATER *Xanthotis macleayana*

IDENTIFICATION. The bird is mainly brown above, greyish below, obscurely streaked and mottled dull white; the crown is dark grey and it has a large patch of naked pinkish-orange skin around the eye. Sexes are similar.

DISTRIBUTION. North-eastern Queensland, south to about Townsville.

NOTES. It frequents rainforest and associated woodlands, and comes freely to bird-tables in forest areas. The bird is deliberate in its movements, rather quiet and unobtrusive. The call is similar to that of the Yellow-faced Honeyeater. Food: insects, native fruits, berries.

BREEDING. Nest: cup-shaped, constructed of fibre, leaves, and other materials, and lined with fine rootlets; placed in a bush. Clutch: two; fleshy-buff colour, with reddish-chestnut spots intermingled with lilac and slate markings. Breeding season: October to December.

14:4 WHITE-STREAKED HONEYEATER *Trichodere cockerelli*

IDENTIFICATION. The bird is dark brown above, with wing and tail feathers conspicuously edged yellow; it has a shaggy yellow plume on the side of its neck, its underparts are dingy white, and it is streaked grey on throat and breast. Sexes are similar.

DISTRIBUTION. Cape York Peninsula, south to about Cooktown.

NOTES. The bird inhabits tea-tree thickets, coastal heaths, and small shrubs growing beneath forest trees. It is active, gregarious and noisy. Food: insects and nectar.

BREEDING. Nest: rather frail, cup-shaped, composed of dried twigs and vine-tendrils, bound with cobweb; placed in a small tree. Clutch: two; salmon-pink, with markings of dull reddish-brown. Breeding season: January to May.

14:5 YELLOW HONEYEATER *Lichenostomus flavus*

IDENTIFICATION. This is a plain dull yellow honeyeater of tropical Queensland, lacking obvious markings. Sexes are similar.

DISTRIBUTION. Northern Queensland, south to about Mount Isa and Mackay.

NOTES. The species inhabits open forest and scrub lands, frequently visiting orchards and gardens. It is sedentary, fairly common, but somewhat patchy in distribution, and is usually encountered alone or in pairs. The most frequent call is a brisk 't–wheet', but the bird also has an agreeable song. Food: insects, procured among flowers and leaves; also nectar.

BREEDING. Nest: shallow, cup-shaped, made of bark and grasses; usually in a bush or small tree within a metre or two of the ground. Clutch: two; white with a pale pinkish tinge, spotted reddish-brown and purplish-grey. Breeding season: August to November.

14:6 YELLOW-FACED HONEYEATER *Lichenostomus chrysops*

IDENTIFICATION. This is a plain olive-grey honeyeater; a narrow, bright yellow band extends backward from gape below the eye to the ear-coverts, bordered above and below by parallel black bands. Sexes are similar.

DISTRIBUTION. Eastern Australia, from about Cooktown, Queensland, to near Adelaide, South Australia.

NOTES. This common and sprightly bird is usually seen in the canopy of woodlands generally. Sedentary in the north, but migratory in the south, it gathers in flocks and travels by day; spectacular movements can be seen, for example, in the Blue Mountains west of Sydney, New South Wales. Food: mainly insects; also nectar.

BREEDING. Nest: cup-shaped, very neat, made of fibre and moss and lined with fine dry grass; suspended amid the foliage of a low bush or tree. Clutch: two to three; pinkish-buff, spotted reddish-chestnut and purplish-grey. Breeding season: July to January.

14:7 FUSCOUS HONEYEATER *Lichenostomus fuscus*

IDENTIFICATION. This is one of the plainest of honeyeaters, mainly dull grey, tinged olive yellow on wings and tail, with an inconspicuous yellow plume behind ear-coverts; breeding adults are blackish around the eye. Sexes are similar.

DISTRIBUTION. From Cairns, Queensland, through New South Wales and Victoria to the east of South Australia.

NOTES. This common species is found in pairs or small flocks frequenting open forest country. The chief call is a cheery 'kitty–lin–toff–toff–toff', but it has a wide variety of other notes. Food: insects, procured among the blossoms and leaves or in the air; also nectar.

BREEDING. Nest: cup-shaped, neat, made of fibre bound with cobweb and plant-down; lined with wool or plant-down; suspended from a slender branch a few metres from the ground. Clutch: two to three; rich salmon, sometimes spotted reddish-brown and purplish-brown. Breeding season: July to December.

14:8 WHITE-LINED HONEYEATER *Meliphaga albilineata*

IDENTIFICATION. This dull grey-brown bird has a faintly mottled breast, blue eye, a narrow white line extending from the gape backwards below the eye, almost linking with a small, inconspicuous white plume behind the ear-coverts. Sexes are similar. (Note habitat and range.)

DISTRIBUTION. Restricted to the Kimberley and Arnhem Land, tropical northern Australia.

NOTES. Rare and little known, this species frequents pockets of rainforest and associated scrub in rocky gorges of sandstone hills. Often solitary and unobtrusive, but it gathers in flocks at flowering trees. Its call is a loud clear whistle, 'tu–u–u–heer, tu-u-u-in'. Food: insects, nectar, native fruits and berries.

BREEDING. Nest: a deep cup of vine-tendrils and plant stems, the rim bound with spiderweb, lined with fine plant stems and fibre, slung from a slender fork within a few metres of the ground. Clutch: two; pale salmon with a wreath of brown dots at the larger end, overlaying scattered grey-brown dots. Breeding season: uncertain; the only recorded nest was found in September.

14:9 BRIDLED HONEYEATER *Lichenostomus frenatus*

IDENTIFICATION. This rather large, active, grey-brown honeyeater has a black throat, intricate face pattern, and bicoloured bill. Sexes are similar.

DISTRIBUTION. North-eastern Queensland (mostly above 300 metres), from about Cooktown south to the Seaview Range near Townsville.

NOTES. A common honeyeater of highland rainforests, it is generally found in pairs or small groups. It is often sedate in behaviour, quietly gleaning for insects in foliage at any height — but large noisy flocks may gather at flowering trees and mistletoe. At times the bird will come to forest picnic tables for bread and scraps. Calls are varied and distinctive; the most characteristic is an imperious, intense rattle of whistled notes. Food: insects, nectar, native fruits, berries.

BREEDING. Nest: cup-shaped, constructed of twigs and fern stems; suspended in a scrub tree. Clutch: two; white, spotted reddish-brown, brownish-grey, and purplish-grey. Breeding season: October to January.

14:10 EUNGELLA HONEYEATER *Lichenostomus hindwoodi*

IDENTIFICATION. This species somewhat resembles the Bridled Honeyeater, but it is smaller; it has a grey throat and the underparts are faintly and narrowly streaked white. Sexes are similar. (Note distribution.)

DISTRIBUTION. Highlands of the Clarke Range, near Mackay, Queensland.

NOTES. It is usually seen alone or in pairs, although numbers congregate at flowering trees, or (especially) mistletoe. Common within its restricted range, the species frequents rainforest and rainforest edges. The calls resemble those of the closely related Bridled Honeyeater, but are more variable. Often quiet and unobtrusive, at other times it is noisy and conspicuous. Recently described from specimens taken in 1978, the species had previously been confused with the Bridled Honeyeater.

BREEDING. Nest: the only nest reported was described as deeply cup-shaped, made of grey-green moss and lined with fine fibres, placed in a rainforest tree about 3 metres from the ground. Clutch: two; buffy-cream, blotched brown. Breeding season: October is the only month on record.

14:11 YELLOW-TUFTED HONEYEATER *Lichenostomus melanops*

IDENTIFICATION. Dark olive brown above and yellow below, this bird has a bright yellow throat, large black mask with conspicuous yellow plume at the rear and a yellowish crown. Sexes are similar.

DISTRIBUTION. East-central Queensland to Victoria and south-east of South Australia.

NOTES. The Yellow-tufted Honeyeater occurs in loose colonies, frequenting various kinds of wooded country from scrub lands near the coast to flowering eucalypts of the sub-interior. Populations west of the Dividing Range are generally nomadic; coastal birds are mainly sedentary. The species has a considerable variety of notes, including a harsh screeching as it flutters over the ground, feigning injury, when disturbed at a nest containing young. Food: almost exclusively insects, but also, on occasion, nectar and fruit; the species is sometimes troublesome in orchards. A small, more or less sedentary population inhabits a restricted area east of Melbourne, Victoria. Once regarded as a distinct species, *L. cassidix* (the Helmeted Honeyeater) is seriously threatened, mainly as a result of subdivision and clearing of its habitat. This form is slightly larger and darker than the Yellow-tufted Honeyeater, and, in particular, is distinguished by a golden head-tuft, or 'helmet', which is usually elevated into a slight crest.

BREEDING. Nest: cup-shaped, composed of strips of bark and grasses and lined with hair or plant-down; usually suspended from the branch of a bush or low shrub. Clutch: two to three; pinkish-buff, spotted reddish-brown and purplish-grey. Breeding season: June to December, sometimes later.

14:12 YELLOW-TINTED HONEYEATER *Lichenostomus flavescens*

IDENTIFICATION. A plain bird, very similar to the Fuscous Honeyeater, but paler, and strongly washed yellow; ear coverts are narrowly rimmed black at rear, and it has a narrow, inconspicuous yellow plume. Sexes are similar.

DISTRIBUTION. Northern tropical Australia.

NOTES. Common in open forests and scrub lands, it is found especially along rivers and streams, feeding among blossoms and leaves of eucalyptus trees. The bird is similar in habits to the White-plumed Honeyeater, but somewhat more gregarious. Food: insects and nectar. It is almost certainly conspecific with the Fuscous Honeyeater.

BREEDING. Nest: cup-shaped, constructed of fine bark and grasses bound with cobweb, occasionally wool or hair; lined with rootlets or wool; suspended from thin twigs of a drooping branch of a small tree or bush. Clutch: two; pale salmon-pink, spotted dark reddish-brown and pale purplish-grey. Breeding season: July to November.

14:13 WHITE-PLUMED HONEYEATER *Lichenostomus penicillatus*

IDENTIFICATION. Mainly greenish grey above and pale below, the bird is strongly washed yellow on head, wings and tail (inland birds are more strongly washed yellow, eastern birds tinged green); its cheeks are yellow, narrowly rimmed black at rear, with a small white plume. Sexes are similar.

DISTRIBUTION. Australia generally, except the far north, the south-west, and Tasmania.

NOTES. This widely distributed and engaging bird ranges from various coastal areas (including parks of Sydney, Melbourne and Adelaide) to the trees fringing streams of the interior (where it is often the most numerous bird). It is apparently expanding its range in some areas. It is lively and assertive, constantly active in seeking nectar and insects among flowers and foliage, and meanwhile chattering and uttering its resonant 'chick–o–wee'.

BREEDING. Nest: cup-shaped, neat, made of grass bound with cobweb, lined with wool or hair; suspended from thin twigs of a drooping branch of a tree (usually a eucalypt) several metres from the ground. Clutch: two to three; pinkish-white, spotted reddish-brown and purplish-grey. Breeding season: June to December, sometimes later.

14:14 PAINTED HONEYEATER *Grantiella picta*

IDENTIFICATION. The species is mainly black above, white below, with bright yellow patches in wings and tail and with a bright pink bill. Sexes are similar.

DISTRIBUTION. From the Northern Territory to southern Victoria, mainly in the sub-interior but near the coast in forest areas carrying its food plants.

NOTES. This curious honeyeater lives almost entirely on the berries of mistletoe, and its movements are therefore regulated by the fruiting of the plants; it usually appears in south-eastern Australia in September and departs in February or March. The calls are loud and clear, the chief one being a resonant 'georgie–georgie–georgie'; others include a burring note and chattering calls like those of the Jacky-winter.

BREEDING. Nest: small, cup-shaped, lace-like, made of fine rootlets and fibre and bound with cobweb; placed in the outermost drooping branches of a eucalypt, melaleuca or casuarina, usually 3–20 metres from the ground. Clutch: two to three; salmon-pink, spotted reddish-brown and lilac. Breeding season: October to February.

14:15 REGENT HONEYEATER *Xanthomyza phrygia*

IDENTIFICATION. A striking, black and yellow honeyeater, its head is black, with a bare, warty, pinkish face; the underparts are pale yellow, heavily scaled black and it has bright yellow flashes in wings and tail. Sexes are similar.

DISTRIBUTION. South-eastern Australia, approximately from Adelaide, South Australia, to Rockhampton, Queensland.

NOTES. It often occurs in flocks. The bird is a nomad, following the flowering of eucalypts, among the blossoms of which it feeds on insects and nectar. It is a somewhat pugnacious bird, fighting its own kind as well as other species. Its chief call is a rich, bell-like note, interspersed with a clicking sound. There is some evidence to suggest that the species is declining in numbers.

BREEDING. Nest: rounded, cup-shaped, made of fibre and strips of bark; lined with thistledown and other soft material; usually placed in the upright or horizontal fork of a tree several metres from the ground. Clutch: two to three; rich reddish-buff, becoming darker at the larger end, spotted reddish- and purplish-brown. Breeding season: August to January.

14:16 BELL MINER *Manorina melanophrys*

IDENTIFICATION. This bird is mainly olive green, with bright yellow bill and legs. Sexes are similar.

DISTRIBUTION. Coastal and mountain areas of eastern Australia from south-eastern (Mary Valley) Queensland to south-western Victoria.

NOTES. In flocks, it frequents leaves of tall eucalypts as well as undergrowth beneath the trees. Large colonies of these birds establish themselves on timbered ridges or beside creeks, and remain in the same locality for years. Their notes, uttered by a number of birds, sound like the chiming of small bells; when alarmed they utter a harsh screech, rather like that of their relative the Noisy Miner. Food: mainly leaf-insects, with some nectar.

BREEDING. Nest: cup-shaped, made of grass, thin strips of bark, and twigs, bound with cobweb; suspended from a forked twig of a small tree or bush several metres from the ground. Clutch: two to three; rich flesh-colour, spotted reddish-brown, purplish-brown and purplish-grey. Breeding season: mainly June to November.

14:17 SINGING HONEYEATER *Lichenostomus virescens*

IDENTIFICATION. An alert, active, conspicuous honeyeater, it is mainly grey-brown, with a very faintly and obscurely streaked breast; it has a narrow black mask through the eye, bordered below by a yellow streak ending in bushy white plume. Sexes are similar.

DISTRIBUTION. Australia generally, except Tasmania, the east coast and the far north.

NOTES. Occurring in pairs or small flocks, the bird frequents for the most part arid scrubby areas. Common, aggressive and conspicuous, it spends much of its time in bushes and small trees within a few metres of the ground, but often calls from conspicuous perches in the tops of bushes and trees. The name 'Singing Honeyeater' is misleading, since the bird's calls, though resonant, vigorous and loud, are much less melodious than those of various other honeyeaters. Food: mostly insects; also nectar.

BREEDING. Nest: cup-shaped, constructed of bark strips and grasses and lined with wool or other soft materials; suspended from a fork of a bush. Clutch: two to three; pinkish-buff, with brownish specks. Breeding season: variable, but mainly August to December.

14:18 YELLOW-PLUMED HONEYEATER *Lichenostomus ornatus*

IDENTIFICATION. The species is plain grey-brown, with a conspicuous yellow plume behind the ear, and a distinctly streaked breast. It can be easily confused with the Grey-fronted Honeyeater. Sexes are similar.

DISTRIBUTION. North-western Victoria, south-western New South Wales, South Australia and south-western Australia.

NOTES. A common, conspicuous and characteristic bird of mallee scrubs, it also occurs in other kinds of low scrubby woodland. It is sedentary and is usually seen singly or in pairs. It is a very active species, with many loud and animated notes. Food: insects and nectar.

BREEDING. Nest: cup-shaped, constructed of grasses and strips of bark; placed in a bush or small tree. Clutch: two; salmon-pink, spotted reddish-brown and purplish-grey. Breeding season: August to November, sometimes later.

14:19 GREY-FRONTED HONEYEATER *Lichenostomus plumulus*

IDENTIFICATION. This honeyeater is very similar to the Yellow-plumed Honeyeater, but the breast is faintly and obscurely streaked, the yellow ear plume is broader, and the lores are dusky grey, not olive green. Sexes are similar.

DISTRIBUTION. The arid interior of Australia generally.

NOTES. It inhabits tall eucalypts, also mallee in some areas, and feeds among the blossoms and leaves. Generally it is solitary and wary, but flocks gather at flowering trees. Food: insects and nectar.

BREEDING. Nest: small, cup-shaped, composed chiefly of dry grasses and wool and lined with wool or horse hair; suspended from the branch of a bush or small tree. Clutch: two; pale salmon, with minute spots of reddish-brown. Breeding season: August to December or January.

14:20 GREY-HEADED HONEYEATER *Lichenostomus keartlandi*

IDENTIFICATION. Plain, mainly grey-brown, with faintly yellowish underparts, it has a grey crown, dark mask through eye, and is bordered below with a narrow yellow plume ending in a small tuft. Sexes are similar.

DISTRIBUTION. Central Australia, ranging to the coast in mid-western and north-western Australia, northward to the Gulf of Carpentaria and south to northern South Australia.

NOTES. The bird is found in pairs or small flocks, frequenting mulga, stunted eucalypts and scrub. It is similar in behaviour to the White-plumed Honeyeater. One characteristic call has been described as 'chee–toyt, chee–toyt'. Food: largely insects; also nectar.

BREEDING. Nest: small, cup-shaped, made of dry grass matted with plant-down; suspended from the extremity of a small leafy branch of a tree a few metres from the ground. Clutch: two; fleshy-buff, with spots of dull reddish-brown. Breeding season: July to November or after rain.

14:21 PURPLE-GAPED HONEYEATER *Lichenostomus cratitius*

IDENTIFICATION. The head is grey, with a dusky black mask, narrow yellow malar streak and inconspicuous yellow plume below the ear; the gape is narrow, naked, lavender-purple and the breast plain and unstreaked. Sexes are similar.

DISTRIBUTION. Two populations: western Victoria and south-eastern South Australia, and a limited area in south-western Australia.

NOTES. The species is almost confined to mallee, but extends into open woodland in Western Australia. It is generally shy, uncommon and not especially gregarious. Food: insects and nectar.

BREEDING. Nest: cup-shaped, constructed chiefly of thin strips of bark and lined with grass; suspended from a branch of a bush or small tree, often within a metre or so of the ground. Clutch: two; pinkish-white, with reddish-brown markings. Breeding season: August to December.

PLATE 15

BIRDS OF BLOSSOMS
AND OUTER FOLIAGE

15:1 SILVEREYE *Zosterops lateralis*

IDENTIFICATION. This species is common and widespread; its plumage varies with locality, but essentially it is olive green above, whitish below, with a pale grey back and narrow (but conspicuous) white ring around the eye. Sexes are similar.

DISTRIBUTION. Eastern and southern Australia, from Cape York south to Tasmania, west to Perth and north to about Carnarvon, Western Australia. Several populations, including *Z. l. gouldi* of Western Australia, *Z. l. halmaturina* of South Australia and western Victoria, and *Z. l. lateralis* of Tasmania. The species also inhabits New Zealand and islands of the south-western Pacific to Fiji.

NOTES. The Silvereye disperses in pairs to breed, but is highly mobile and gregarious at other times. Southern populations are migratory, often travelling in flocks of hundreds. The species is common in almost all kinds of wooded country, including gardens, orchards and urban parks. The chief call is a rather peevish 'cheee'; its song is fragile, but melodious and sustained; the bird is also a competent vocal mimic. Food: insects, native fruits and berries and cultivated soft fruits.

BREEDING. Nest: small, neat and cup-shaped, made of fine grass, horse hair and other soft materials, bound with cobweb; suspended in the low horizontal fork of a bush or sapling. Clutch: three to four; pale bluish-green. Breeding season: August to December.

15:2 PALE WHITE-EYE *Zosterops citrinella*

IDENTIFICATION. This bird is similar to the Silvereye, but the back is yellowish-olive, the throat yellow and the breast white. Sexes are similar. (Note habitat and distribution.)

DISTRIBUTION. Islands off the coast of Cape York Peninsula and in Torres Strait. It also occurs in Indonesia and New Guinea.

NOTES. In pairs or flocks, according to the season, the Pale White-eye frequents the branches of flowering trees or shrubs, mainly on small islands. It is sedentary; otherwise it is similar to the Silvereye in general habits. Food: insects, native fruits and berries.

BREEDING. Nest and clutch similar to that of the Silvereye. Breeding season: unknown.

15:3 GREEN-BACKED HONEYEATER *Glycichaera fallax*

IDENTIFICATION. Looking much like a female Fairy Warbler, the species can be identified by a slender pointed bill and white, not red, eye. Sexes are similar. (Note distribution.)

DISTRIBUTION. Northern Cape York Peninsula. The species also inhabits Indonesia and New Guinea.

NOTES. This little known species frequents mainly the canopy of rainforest and associated vegetation. It is an active, but nondescript and inconspicuous bird. Usually it is seen singly or in pairs, but often joins mixed feeding flocks of other species. Calls include a variety of thin twittering notes. Food: insects.

BREEDING. Unknown.

15:4 SCARLET HONEYEATER *Myzomela sanguinolenta*

IDENTIFICATION. A very small honeyeater, the male is mainly brilliant red, with black wings and tail and white belly. The female is nondescript brown, with pinkish chin.

DISTRIBUTION. Eastern Australia from about Cooktown, Queensland, south to eastern Victoria.

NOTES. The bird is seen in pairs or flocks, arriving in southern areas during early spring; in the winter months it is nomadic. It frequents flowering eucalypts, melaleucas, banksias, etc., seeking insects and nectar — usually in the canopy. The male utters a succession of melodious tinkling notes, often heard during the midday heat of summer when most other birds are silent. Occasionally, members of this species are seen in the south during winter.

BREEDING. Nest: small, cup-shaped, made of hair, thin strips of bark and rootlets, lined with fine grass; usually suspended from a slender, drooping tree fork several metres from the ground. Clutch: two to three; white with a faint pinkish tinge, spotted dull chestnut, reddish-brown, and purplish-grey. Breeding season: October to January.

15:5 RED-HEADED HONEYEATER *Myzomela erythrocephala*

IDENTIFICATION. The male is mainly black, with a brilliant red head and rump; the female is a nondescript, dull brown, with a pinkish chin and forehead.

DISTRIBUTION. Tropical northern Australia, from about Derby, Western Australia, to Cape York. It is also found in Indonesia and New Guinea.

NOTES. The species is seen in pairs or flocks, frequenting mangroves and open forests, seeking insects and nectar from the flowers. It is very active, flitting from one cluster of flowers to another, uttering at the same time a brisk and hard 'chiew–chiew–chiew'.

BREEDING. Nest: like that of the Scarlet Honeyeater, usually placed in the tops of tall mangroves. Clutch: two; white, finely spotted reddish-brown and purplish-grey. Breeding season: October to January.

15:6 BANDED HONEYEATER *Certhionyx pectoralis*

IDENTIFICATION. This honeyeater is black above, white below, with a white rump and narrow black band across the breast. Sexes are similar; immatures have creamy, pale brown backs.

DISTRIBUTION. Tropical northern Australia, from the Kimberley to Townsville.

NOTES. The species is highly nomadic; it frequents swamp woodlands, open eucalypt woodland, mangroves and vegetation along watercourses. It is often seen in pairs or small parties, but large flocks gather at abundant blossom. The bird utters a variety of brisk sharp notes, also a crisp and cheerful song. Food: insects and nectar.

BREEDING. Nest: small, cup-shaped, constructed of strips of bark and fine grasses, bound with cobweb; suspended from a fork at the extremity of a small leafy branch of a tree or bush. Clutch: two; buffy-white, becoming darker towards the larger end. Breeding season: mainly October to January.

15:7 BLACK HONEYEATER *Certhionyx niger*

IDENTIFICATION. The male has a black head and upperparts, plain black wings and white belly. The female is a nondescript, grey-brown, paler below and with a pale streak behind the eye.

DISTRIBUTION. Inland Australia generally, where suitable habitats occur.

NOTES. The species is highly nomadic and is active, darting and conspicuous. Found in pairs or flocks, it frequents scrubby vegetation on dry hillsides or flats, including areas through which bushfires have passed. The bird often shows a conspicuous preference for flowering emu-bush (genus *Eremophila*). Its chief call is an insect-like 'seeeee', varied by a sparrow-like chirp. The male has a distinctive song-flight — a steep upward flight to about 15 metres, followed by a stepped descent on stiff, quivering, down-arched wings. Food: insects and nectar.

BREEDING. Nest: small, open, shallow, made of twigs, grass, and rootlets, bound with spiderweb; usually placed in a dead fork or in fallen branches within a few metres of the ground. Clutch: two; yellowish-buff, with a band of minute spots of pale slate and umber. Breeding season: mainly September to December.

15:8 BAR-BREASTED HONEYEATER *Ramsayornis fasciatus*

IDENTIFICATION. This is a small grey-brown honeyeater, mainly white below, and conspicuously barred black. Sexes are similar.

DISTRIBUTION. Tropical northern Australia, from western Cape York Peninsula west to about Derby, Western Australia.

NOTES. The species is usually found in pairs, but large flocks gather where blossom is abundant. It frequents vegetation along watercourses, fringes of mangrove swamps, and especially melaleuca (tea-tree) swamps. Its chief call is a shrill, piping note, repeated rapidly. Food: insects and nectar.

BREEDING. Nest: bulky, dome-shaped, constructed of strips of soft paper-bark and fine rootlets bound with cobweb and lined with soft bark; usually suspended from a pendent branch overhanging water. Clutch: three to four; white, with reddish-brown markings. Breeding season: mainly October to January.

15:9 GREY HONEYEATER *Conopophila whitei*

IDENTIFICATION. This very nondescript bird is plain grey, slightly paler below and the tail has a white tip. Sexes are similar.

DISTRIBUTION. Mid-western Australia, east to Alice Springs, Northern Territory, and the Musgrave and Everard Ranges, South Australia.

NOTES. The species is rare, elusive, nondescript and little known. It is probably nomadic and usually occurs in pairs, frequenting semi-arid country where mulga bush grows. It is reported to associate with thornbills. Its call-notes have been described as a succession of five or six monotonous notes, high-pitched but musical, and uttered in a rapid, sibilant manner. Food: insects, procured in foliage.

BREEDING. Nest: a frail structure of fibre, loosely woven and bound with cobweb; placed near the extremity of a slender branch within a few metres of the ground. Clutch: two; white, with small reddish-brown spots and underlying markings of dull purplish-grey. Breeding season: August to (probably) November.

15:10 RUFOUS-THROATED HONEYEATER *Conopophila rufogularis*

IDENTIFICATION. This small, dull grey-brown honeyeater has a small rufous throat patch and wings and tail strongly washed yellow. Sexes are similar.

DISTRIBUTION. Tropical northern Australia, from about Broome, Western Australia, east to about Coen and the Atherton Tableland, Queensland, extending (though rare and highly local) to the east coast between Ingham and Noosa.

NOTES. The species is active, noisy and conspicuous. Seen in pairs or flocks, it frequents flowering trees, shrubs and tall grass, seeking insects and nectar; it often catches insects on the wing. Calls include a sharp 'zit–zit' and chattering notes.

BREEDING. Nest: small, purse-shaped, with the rim on one side lower than on the opposite side, made of soft pieces of bark and grass, kept in shape with stiff grass; suspended from a pendent branch of a tree several metres from the ground. Clutch: two to three; white, with reddish-brown and slate-grey markings. Breeding season: October to February or March.

15:11 BLACK-HEADED HONEYEATER *Melithreptus affinis*

IDENTIFICATION. The upperparts are olive green, underparts white and head black. Sexes are similar. (Tasmania only.)

DISTRIBUTION. Tasmania and islands of Bass Strait.

NOTES. The species is common and sedentary. Usually found in flocks, it is active and quarrelsome. Frequenting chiefly the outer foliage and blossoms of eucalypts, it also visits gardens and orchards, where it may do considerable damage to small fruits. Flocks occasionally associate with Strong-billed Honeyeaters. The call is a sharp whistle. Food: insects, nectar and cultivated fruits.

BREEDING. Nest: cup-shaped, constructed of fine strips of bark, wool and cobweb and lined with fur or feathers; suspended from small twigs at the end of a drooping branch of a eucalypt, frequently at a considerable height. Clutch: two to three; flesh-pink, with reddish-brown and dull purplish-grey markings. Breeding season: October to December.

15:12 WHITE-NAPED HONEYEATER *Melithreptus lunatus*

IDENTIFICATION. The head is black, throat and underparts white, upperparts olive green and it has a narrow white band across the nape. The bird is very like the White-throated Honeyeater, but the naked skin around the eye is red, not dull blue; the white nape band does not reach the eye and the black cheek extends somewhat further down, just barely reaching the chin. Sexes are similar.

DISTRIBUTION. From Cairns through eastern Australia to south-eastern South Australia and Kangaroo Island; south-western Australia (Moora to Esperance); also in the Kent Group (Bass Strait).

NOTES. The species is nomadic and southern populations are migratory. The bird usually occurs in small flocks. It is a common bird throughout the coastal districts, timbered mountain ranges, and open forest country inland, and is seen chiefly in eucalyptus trees seeking insects and nectar. The calls are a single piping whistle and many cheery chattering notes. This bird often alights on horses and cows to obtain hair for nest-lining.

BREEDING. Nest: cup-shaped, composed of fine strips of bark matted with cobweb and lined with grass, fur or hair; suspended from a drooping branch of a tree, usually at a considerable height. Clutch: two to three; pale buff, finely spotted reddish-brown and pale purplish-grey. Breeding season: July to November.

15:13 WHITE-THROATED HONEYEATER *Melithreptus albogularis*

IDENTIFICATION. This bird is very similar to the White-naped Honeyeater, but naked skin around the eye is bluish, not red; the white nape band extends further forward, just reaching the eye and the throat is entirely white, including the chin. Sexes are similar.

DISTRIBUTION. From near Broome, Western Australia, through northern and eastern Australia, south to about Nambucca Heads, New South Wales. Also, the species is found in New Guinea.

NOTES. The bird frequents most kinds of wooded country. It is similar in habits to the White-naped Honeyeater, but is sedentary or nomadic rather than migratory. Its calls include a peevish 'psee', a flat hard trill, and a loud, ringing series of 'chick' notes. Food: insects and nectar.

BREEDING. Nest: resembles that of the White-naped Honeyeater. Clutch: two; pale salmon-pink, with reddish-brown markings. Breeding season: July to January.

15:14 BLACK-CHINNED HONEYEATER *Melithreptus gularis*

IDENTIFICATION. The bird resembles the White-naped Honeyeater, but is larger and duller, with upperparts grey-green, underparts dingy grey, and with a black chin; the naked skin around the eye is dull blue, not red. Populations in northern and north-western Australia (subspecies *laetior*) are golden green above, pale buff below, with golden green naked eye-ring. Sexes are similar.

DISTRIBUTION. Much of northern and eastern Australia, in Western Australia from about Shark Bay northwards, most of the Northern Territory and Queensland; eastern New South Wales, and most of Victoria.

NOTES. It frequents open forests, where it seeks nectar and insects among the outer foliage and also forages under bark on trunks and branches. Gregarious, active and highly vocal, the species utters many vigorous, animated and pleasing notes.

BREEDING. Nest: cup-shaped, constructed of fine bark and similar materials, bound with cobweb and lined with hair or fur; suspended from the foliage of a drooping branch of a tree, usually a eucalypt, at a considerable height. Clutch: two to three; pale salmon-pink, spotted reddish-brown and purplish-grey. Breeding season: July to December.

15:15 STRONG-BILLED HONEYEATER *Melithreptus validirostris*

IDENTIFICATION. The bird is very similar to the Black-chinned Honeyeater but is somewhat darker and the back is more brownish. Sexes are similar. (Tasmania only.)

DISTRIBUTION. Tasmania, King Island and the Flinders Group.

NOTES. Found in pairs or flocks, it frequents leaves and blossoms of trees, chiefly eucalypts, in search of insects and nectar; it forages often over the trunks and branches of trees, searching in crevices of the bark for insect life.

Its chief call is a short sharp 'cheep'. Possibly it is conspecific with the Black-chinned Honeyeater.

BREEDING. Nest: cup-shaped, constructed of bark, grasses, and wool; suspended from drooping branches of a tree or shrub, sometimes at a considerable height. Clutch: three; pinkish-white, spotted dark reddish-brown and purplish-grey. Breeding season: July to December.

15:16 BROWN-HEADED HONEYEATER *Melithreptus brevirostris*

IDENTIFICATION. This bird is much like the White-naped Honeyeater but is smaller, browner and dingier; the bill is entirely black, the head dull brown, the nape band dull white and the naked eye ring dull ochre. Sexes are similar.

DISTRIBUTION. Widespread across southern Australia, except the arid interior; north to a point inland of about Bowen, Queensland, on the east coast, and around Shark Bay on the west coast.

NOTES. The species is common and is usually seen in small flocks frequenting, for the most part, the outer foliage and blossoms of gum trees, searching for insects and nectar. The chief calls are made up of brisk, staccato 'chips' uttered singly or, with variations, strung together in a cheerful, rapid animated series. The bird often perches on horses and cows to obtain hair for nest-lining.

BREEDING. Nest: deep, cup-shaped, firmly woven of bark, grass and animal hair and bound with spiderweb; usually suspended from a drooping branch high in a eucalypt. Clutch: two to three; pale reddish-buff, spotted reddish-brown and purplish-grey. Breeding season: August to December.

15:17 EASTERN SPINEBILL *Acanthorhynchus tenuirostris*

IDENTIFICATION. The bird's long, curved, very slender bill is distinctive; the bird is mainly dark blue-grey above, warm buff below, rusty at nape and with a small throat patch, head black, throat white and with white outer tail feathers which are conspicuous in flight. Sexes are similar.

DISTRIBUTION. Eastern Australia, from Cairns, Queensland, south to Tasmania and west to about Adelaide, South Australia.

NOTES. The bird is vivacious and very active. Usually seen in pairs, it frequents heathlands and open forest country; it is also a familiar bird in gardens, there flitting from flower to flower and probing them with its long, spine-like bill. Its call is a succession of shrill, musical notes, uttered very quickly. Often, when in flight, its wings make a distinct flicking sound. Food: insects and nectar.

BREEDING. Nest: cup-shaped, made of bark, grass and moss, lined with fine grass and feathers; suspended from a thin horizontal branch in a thick bush, usually within a few metres of the ground. Clutch: two to three; pale buff, marked chestnut and dull purplish-grey. Breeding season: mainly August to December.

15:18 WESTERN SPINEBILL *Acanthorhynchus superciliosus*

IDENTIFICATION. The long, curved, very slender bill is distinctive; the bird is mainly grey above, pale buff below, with rufous throat and nape. The female is similar, but much duller with a buff not rufous throat.

DISTRIBUTION. South-western Australia, extending north and east to Moora, the Stirling Range and Israelite Bay.

NOTES. The bird is usually seen in pairs, frequenting banksia and tea-tree country; it is sometimes seen in gardens in Perth and other centres. In habits it is similar to the Eastern Spinebill. Food: insects and nectar.

BREEDING. Nest: like that of the Eastern Spinebill, but slightly smaller. Clutch: one to two; pinkish-white, with spots of chestnut and dull purplish-grey. Breeding season: August to December.

15:19 YELLOW-BELLIED SUNBIRD *Nectarinia jugularis*

IDENTIFICATION. The bird is olive green above, bright yellow below and males have brilliant blue throats.

DISTRIBUTION. Northern Queensland from Cape York to about Gladstone. The species also inhabits Indonesia, New Guinea and the Solomon Islands.

NOTES. This is a common, vivacious and familiar bird of the tropics. It is often found in gardens and is usually seen in pairs, flitting among flowering trees and shrubs seeking insects and nectar, occasionally darting out to capture an insect on the wing; it has the hummingbird-like habit of hovering near flowers. The male bird utters a goldfinch-like 'tsee–tsee', and its song is a rapid and melodious warble.

BREEDING. Nest: long, oval-shaped, with a tail-piece and an entrance in the side protected by a hood; constructed of bark-fibre, dried grasses, and dead leaves, bound with cobweb and lined with fine grasses and plant-down;

suspended from a twig of a small bush, often close to the ground and also frequently fastened to pieces of rope or wire about houses, especially verandahs. Clutch: two to three; pale greenish-grey, speckled and mottled with umber. Breeding season: mainly September to January.

P L A T E   1 6

B I R D S   O F   B L O S S O M S
A N D   O U T E R   F O L I A G E

16:1 WEEBILL *Smicrornis brevirostris*

IDENTIFICATION. The Weebil is plain yellowish below, olive above, with a straw-yellow eye and tiny blunt bill. Sexes are similar. Populations in the interior north and west (subspecies *flavescens*) are generally paler than those in the south and east (subspecies *brevirostris*).

DISTRIBUTION. Throughout mainland Australia, although avoiding high rainfall areas in far north-eastern Queensland, southern Victoria, and extreme south-western Australia.

NOTES. This common bird is usually found in pairs or small parties, but often joins roving feeding flocks of other birds. Very active, it usually keeps to the outer foliage on saplings and taller trees, often hovering. The call-note is spirited and loud in proportion to the bird's size. The chief calls are a clear insistent 'weebill, weebill' and a hard and brisk chatter, uttered very freely and sometimes suggesting a child's rattle. Food: small insects.

BREEDING. Nest: small, dome-shaped, with a narrow side entrance protected by a hood; constructed of fibre mingled with plant-down, and lined with plant-down or feathers; usually built among the outer foliage of a tree. Clutch: two to three; creamy-buff with purplish-brown markings. Breeding season: variable, but usually August to November.

16:2 WHITE-THROATED WARBLER *Gerygone olivacea*

IDENTIFICATION. The bird's plumage is neutral grey above, bright yellow below with a white throat; it has a small white spot behind the bill, much white in the tail and a red eye. Sexes are similar.

DISTRIBUTION. Northern and eastern Australia, west to the Kimberley and south to about Melbourne, Victoria, rarely to the Mount Lofty Ranges, South Australia. It is also found in New Guinea.

NOTES. This species is a migrant, arriving in south-eastern Australia in early spring and departing during autumn. It frequents sapling scrubs and open woodland, seeking insects among the twigs and leaves. Its spring song, a falling cadence uttered at frequent intervals, is one of the most attractive Australian bird-songs.

BREEDING. Nest: pear-shaped, with a hooded side entrance and a tail-piece; made of fine bark strips bound with cobweb, lined with plant-down and feathers; usually attached to a thin, leafy branch at almost any height in a eucalypt sapling. Clutch: three to four; white, with fine spots of purplish-red. Breeding season: August (in the north) or September to January.

16:3 WESTERN WARBLER *Gerygone fusca*

IDENTIFICATION. This species is nondescript grey above, dingy white below, with a small white spot behind the bill, much white in the tail and a red eye. Sexes are similar.

DISTRIBUTION. Australia generally, but distribution apparently fragmented, and absent over large areas: in particular absent from the Top End, Cape York Peninsula, most of the east coast and South Australia, eastern Western Australia and Tasmania.

NOTES. Although this bird of the open forests is found near the coast in south-western Australia (it is common about Perth), in the east of the continent it is mainly restricted to the sub-interior. It inhabits mallee scrubs and open eucalypt and acacia scrubs. It is common, active but unobtrusive, and frequents the outer foliage. The song is melodious and persistent, with a frail, elusive quality somewhat suggestive of that of the White-throated Warbler. The species appears to be a partial migrant, or to move seasonally at least short distances.

BREEDING. Nest: pear-shaped, with a tail-piece dangling beneath and a hooded side entrance near the top; compact and well made of fine bark strips and dry grass, bound with cobweb and lined with feathers; suspended from the leafy end of a slender branch of a bush or sapling. Clutch: three; pinkish-white with reddish-brown markings. Breeding season: October to December.

16:4 BROWN WARBLER *Gerygone mouki*

IDENTIFICATION. This bird is dull brown above, dingy white below, with a small, distinct white spot between bill and eye and with outer tail feathers tipped white. Sexes are similar. Southern populations (subspecies *richmondi*) are somewhat browner than north-eastern birds (subspecies *mouki*).

DISTRIBUTION. Eastern Australia (mainly coast and adjacent highlands) from around Cooktown, Queensland, to eastern Victoria.

NOTES. The bird is seen in pairs or small parties, and is very common in rainforest and extending to open forest in the cooler months. It is very active when searching for food among the twigs and leaves, and often hovers and flutters at sprays of foliage. The call-note is a brisk pleasing twitter, resembling 'which–is–it, which–is–it', repeated incessantly. Food: small insects.

BREEDING. Nest: dome-shaped, with a spout-like entrance near the top, and a tail-piece; constructed of grasses and lichen, bound with spiders' webbing, and decorated with lichen; attached to a thorny vine or a thin leafy twig of a tree in rainforest. Clutch: two to three; white or reddish-white, spotted and blotched purplish-red. Breeding season: September to January.

16:5 FAIRY WARBLER *Gerygone palpebrosa*

IDENTIFICATION. The bird resembles the White-throated Warbler but is a little duller and the upperparts are tinged green rather than grey. Males of the southern population (subspecies *flavida*) have a dull yellow throat and black chin; males of the Cape York population (subspecies *palpebrosa*) have black throats with a prominent white malar streak.

DISTRIBUTION. Cape York Peninsula and eastern Queensland south to about Maryborough. Two subspecies in Australia: *G. p. flavida* occurs from the Atherton Tableland southward, and *G. p. personata* on Cape York Peninsula. The species also occurs in New Guinea and the Aru Islands.

NOTES. The bird is seen in pairs or small parties, inhabiting margins of rainforest and mangroves and vegetation bordering creeks. It is fairly common. Its song is very agreeable, suggesting that of the White-throated Warbler but less wistful. Food: insects.

BREEDING. Nest: roughly spherical, with a wispy tail-piece and a hooded side entrance near the top; made of thin strips of bark bound with cobweb, lined with plant-down and often decorated with scraps of moss or lichen; usually slung from the leafy end of a horizontal tree branch several metres above the ground. Clutch: two to three; fleshy-white, speckled purplish-brown or red. Breeding season: September to March.

16:6 MANGROVE WARBLER *Gerygone levigaster*

IDENTIFICATION. This bird is rather like the Western Warbler except for the conspicuous white superciliary and less white in the tail. It is seldom away from mangroves. Sexes are similar.

DISTRIBUTION. Coastal northern and eastern Australia, from about Derby, Western Australia, east to about Normanton, Queensland, and from about Cairns, Queensland, south to Newcastle, New South Wales, erratically further south.

NOTES. The species inhabits tidal mangroves and associated vegetation, especially smaller mangroves close to the sea. Generally common, it is seen singly or in pairs, actively searching among the leaves of the canopy and outer branches for small insects. The calls consist of fragile twittering, and a frail, sweet song. The form illustrated here is the northern form (subspecies *levigaster*), which is somewhat paler and browner in tone than the east coast form (subspecies *cantator*, No. 23:4, p. 175), with faintly buff-tinted breast.

BREEDING. Nest: dome-shaped, with a hooded entrance and a pendent tail; constructed of fine roots, grass stalks and similar materials; suspended from a slender branch of a mangrove several metres from the ground. Clutch: two to three; white or pale pink, with small reddish-brown markings. Breeding season: usually October to March in the tropical north, August to December in the east.

16:7 YELLOW THORNBILL *Acanthiza nana*

IDENTIFICATION. This small, plain, active thornbill is yellowish below and greenish above, with grey eyes, finely streaked ear-coverts, and plain, unstreaked breast. Sexes are similar.

DISTRIBUTION. Eastern and south-eastern Australia from the Atherton Tableland to south-eastern South Australia, north to the Flinders Range.

NOTES. The bird is seen in pairs or small parties, frequenting the upper and outer branches of trees, especially wattles and casuarinas. It is very active, searching among the leaves for insects. The chief call is a simple 'tiz–tiz'.

BREEDING. Nest: very small, domed, with an entrance near the top; constructed of bark and grasses, often ornamented with moss and lined with feathers or fur; placed among the outer or top branches of a leafy tree. Clutch: two to four; whitish, freckled reddish-brown and lavender. Breeding season: August to December.

16:8 STRIATED THORNBILL *Acanthiza lineata*

IDENTIFICATION. The bird is dull brown above, dingy white below, with a hint of tawny on the crown and a hint of green on the back; the breast is finely streaked dull grey and the forehead narrowly streaked white. Sexes are similar. The species is easily confused with the Brown Thornbill (the two species often occur together), but the Brown Thornbill has bright red (not brown) eyes, the forehead is scalloped (not streaked), and the rump is distinctly reddish.

DISTRIBUTION. South-eastern Australia (except Tasmania), from about Charleville, Queensland, south and west to about Adelaide and Kangaroo Island, South Australia.

NOTES. This is perhaps the commonest and most widespread thornbill in forests of the south-east; it avoids rainforest, but otherwise is found in most kinds of wooded country. Usually it is seen in small parties, sometimes in company with other thornbills, frequenting the topmost foliage of tall trees and also small shrubs. It is very active, searching diligently for small insects and maintaining an animated twittering.

BREEDING. Nest: pear-shaped, with a hooded side entrance; made of bark fragments and grass matted with cobweb and lined with feathers or other soft material and usually decorated on the outside with moss and lichen; usually placed in thick foliage of a eucalypt sapling within a few metres of the ground. Clutch: three; pinkish-white or creamy-white, freckled reddish-brown. Breeding season: July to December.

16:9 WESTERN THORNBILL *Acanthiza inornata*

IDENTIFICATION. This species is very similar to the Buff-rumped Thornbill in general appearance, behaviour and habitat, but is much plainer, with a dull olive rump. Sexes are similar. (Far south-west only.)

DISTRIBUTION. South-western Australia, extending north to Moora and east to the Stirling Range.

NOTES. The bird is seen in pairs or small parties frequenting leaves and branches of trees or shrubs, but occasionally feeding on the ground. It has a rapid staccato twitter, suggesting that of the Buff-rumped Thornbill, but it is also a competent vocal mimic.

BREEDING. Nest: domed, oval; constructed of grass and lined with feathers; usually placed in a crevice or cavity in a bushy tree. Clutch: three; flesh-coloured, freckled reddish-brown. Breeding season: September to December.

16:10 TASMANIAN THORNBILL *Acanthiza ewingii*

IDENTIFICATION. This bird is very similar to the Brown Thornbill, but the forehead is plain tawny (not scalloped), the breast greyish and faintly mottled (not streaked) and the flanks are white (not yellowish). Sexes are similar.

DISTRIBUTION. Tasmania, Flinders Island and King Island (Bass Strait).

NOTES. The species is common and sedentary; it frequents forests and woodlands. It is similar in habits to the Brown Thornbill, but where they occur together, this species shows a preference for denser, wetter forests. The usual call is a soft 'tsirp', repeated several times.

BREEDING. Nest: dome-shaped, with a rounded side-entrance; made of thin bark strips, grass and moss and lined with feathers and fur; suspended in dense foliage low in a bush or sapling. Clutch: three; white, freckled purplish-red. Breeding season: August to December.

16:11 MOUNTAIN THORNBILL *Acanthiza katherina*

IDENTIFICATION. The bird is very like the Brown Thornbill, but the eye is white and the breast is plain dingy white and unstreaked. Sexes are similar. This is the only thornbill in its range and habitat.

DISTRIBUTION. Highlands (above 350 metres) of north-eastern Queensland from about Cooktown to Mount Spec near Townsville.

NOTES. This thornbill frequents mainly the canopy of highland rainforest; it is common but difficult to observe. The species occurs in pairs or small parties. It is a sedentary bird, similar in general habits to the Brown Thornbill, to which it is closely related.

BREEDING. Nest: bulky, domed, with slightly hooded side entrance near the top; made of dry grass and vine tendrils and covered with green moss and lined with finer material; usually placed in outer foliage high in a rainforest tree.

Clutch: two; white, freckled reddish-brown or purplish-red. Breeding season: September to December or January.

16:12 BROWN THORNBILL *Acanthiza pusilla*

IDENTIFICATION. This species is dull brown above, faintly greyish and yellowish below, the breast is obscurely streaked grey, the forehead is rusty and finely scalloped white, the rump is reddish and the eye bright red. Sexes are similar.

DISTRIBUTION. Central Queensland to Victoria, South Australia (to Eyre Peninsula) and Tasmania.

NOTES. This bird is sedentary and is usually found in pairs or family parties frequenting thickets and low scrub; it also visits gardens and orchards. It is not a gregarious bird, though it sometimes joins mixed feeding parties of other thornbills in winter. It is active, restless and acrobatic. The bird has a wide variety of calls, including a harsh churring alarm call and it sometimes mimics the notes of other birds. Food: small insects.

BREEDING. Nest: dome-shaped, with an entrance near the top; constructed of bark, grasses, and webbing and lined with feathers and other soft materials; it is usually attached to bracken fern or a low bush. Clutch: three; white, freckled reddish-brown or purplish-red. Breeding season: August to December.

16:13 SLATE-BACKED THORNBILL *Acanthiza robustirostris*

IDENTIFICATION. This bird's upperparts are slate grey, underparts dingy white, rump chestnut, forehead finely streaked black and the eye red. Sexes are similar.

DISTRIBUTION. From extreme south-western Queensland west across southern Northern Territory and northern South Australia into Western Australia.

NOTES. Found in pairs or small parties, the species frequents mulga scrubs, especially in the vicinity of low mountain ranges. The bird usually feeds in foliage and seldom on the ground. It has a low-pitched, twittering call and a number of clear and animated notes. Food: small insects and spiders.

BREEDING. Nest: oval, with an entrance near the top; constructed of fine dried grasses bound with spiders' web and cocoons; placed among slender branches of a bush. Clutch: three; white with a tinge of pink, speckled reddish-brown. Breeding season: July to October.

16:14 INLAND THORNBILL *Acanthiza apicalis*

IDENTIFICATION. This thornbill is greyish above and dingy white below, the breast is obscurely streaked grey, the rump is bright rufous and the eye is red. Sexes are similar.

DISTRIBUTION. Southern and interior Australia generally, west of the Great Dividing Range, north to the Tanami Desert, Western Australia, and near Winton, Queensland, but excluding Tasmania and most of Victoria. This is a widespread and variable species, with several populations differing slightly in appearance, including: *A. a. apicalis* of Western Australia, *A. a. whitlocki* of the Nullarbor Plain region, *A. a. hamiltoni* of north-western Victoria, and *A. a. albiventris* of western New South Wales and Queensland.

NOTES. The species is common and is usually seen in pairs. It inhabits arid scrubs and woodlands in the interior, extending to coastal heaths, dense forests and even mangroves in the far south-west. The bird feeds mostly in foliage and seldom on the ground. Several of its calls are like those of the Brown Thornbill; it also utters a high-pitched 'tsee–tsee' and mimics other birds. It often carries the tail cocked like a wren. The species is closely related to the Brown Thornbill, with which it is often considered conspecific.

BREEDING. Nest: domed, with a side entrance near the top; made of bark fragments and dry grass, bound with cobweb and lined with soft grass and feathers; usually placed in a shrub near the ground. Clutch: three; white with reddish blotches and freckles. Breeding season: July to December.

16:15 MISTLETOEBIRD *Dicaeum hirundinaceum*

IDENTIFICATION. The male is glossy blue-black above, white below, with a brilliant red throat and breast and undertail coverts, and black band down centre of belly. The female is dull and identifiable by dull pink undertail coverts.

DISTRIBUTION. Throughout Australia, except Tasmania. The species is also found in the Aru Islands and Indonesia.

NOTES. This species is common in a wide range of habitats, from dense rainforest to mallee and mulga scrubs of the interior. It feeds to some extent on insects, but its staple food is the smaller type of mistletoe berries, and the bird is found wherever these occur. It is seen singly or in pairs, usually feeding unobtrusively in the crowns of trees. Its calls are a piercing, high-pitched 'wit–a, wit–a' and other brisk notes; in addition it may use a pretty warbling song which sometimes extends into mimicry of other birds' voices.

BREEDING. Nest: neat, pear-shaped, with a side entrance; made of plant fibre thickly bound with cobweb, and usually decorated with the brown castings of wood-boring insects or the dried brown heads of flowers; it is suspended from a slender branch of a leafy tree several metres from the ground. Clutch: usually three; pure white. Breeding season: mainly October to March.

16:16 SPOTTED PARDALOTE *Pardalotus punctatus*

IDENTIFICATION. The crown is black and closely spotted white; the throat is bright yellow and rump bright red. Sexes are similar, but females are somewhat duller than males.

DISTRIBUTION. Eastern Australia from about Cairns, Queensland, south to Tasmania and west to about Adelaide, South Australia; also far south-western Australia.

NOTES. It is usually found in pairs, frequenting the outer foliage of eucalypts and other trees, moving among the leaves in search of insects. The species occurs in most kinds of wooded country, and may be common even in shade trees along suburban streets in many towns and cities. It has a monotonous call-note, like 'slee–p ba–bee'. The call is ventriloquial, and a characteristic feature of the bush.

BREEDING. Nest: domed; made of bark and placed in a hollowed-out chamber at the end of a tunnel in the ground. Clutch: four to five; white. Breeding season: August to December.

16:17 YELLOW-RUMPED PARDALOTE *Pardalotus xanthopygus*

IDENTIFICATION. This bird is very similar to the Spotted Pardalote, but the upperparts are somewhat greyer and the rump is bright yellow. Sexes are similar.

DISTRIBUTION. Southern Australia from about Dubbo, New South Wales, west to the Stirling Ranges, Western Australia.

NOTES. The species is similar in habits to the Spotted Pardalote, but it is largely a bird of mallee areas of the inland; occasionally it will be seen in mulga or tall eucalypt woodlands. The usual call suggests that of the Spotted Pardalote, but is slower, more plaintive, and has a ringing, metallic quality. It is now usually considered a subspecies of the Spotted Pardalote.

BREEDING. Nest: similar to that of the Spotted Pardalote. Clutch: four to five; white. Breeding season: August to November.

16:18 STRIATED PARDALOTE *Pardalotus striatus*

IDENTIFICATION. This is the most widespread pardalote. It is greyish above, mainly white below and variably washed buff. The crown is black, either plain (northern populations) or narrowly streaked (*not* spotted) white (southern populations); it has a yellow spot between eye and bill and a narrow white streak along the folded wing. Sexes are similar.

DISTRIBUTION. Australia generally, including Tasmania. A complex number of populations, including: *P. s. striatus* breeds in Tasmania and the islands of Bass Strait, and winters in south-eastern mainland Australia, north to about Rockhampton, Queensland; *P. s. substriatus* occurs virtually throughout southern Australia; *P. s. melanocephalus* occurs across northern and eastern Australia, west to the Kimberley and south to about Newcastle, New South Wales.

NOTES. The species is usually seen in pairs, but the Tasmanian subspecies forms large flocks in its winter quarters on the mainland. Calls vary geographically; the northern subspecies ('Black-headed Pardalote') has an insistent 'chip–chip, chip–chip'; other calls elsewhere may be rendered 'pick-it–up' or 'wit–e–chu'. It is common and widespread in most types of woodland, but especially in open eucalypt forest. The bird mainly frequents the crowns and outer sprays of foliage gleaning insects and occasionally it feeds on the ground.

BREEDING. Nest: cup-shaped or partly domed; made of bark fibre and grass and sometimes lined with feathers; placed in a small hollow in a tree, or in a tunnel in the ground. Clutch: four; white. Breeding season: August to December.

16:19 FORTY-SPOTTED PARDALOTE *Pardalotus quadragintus*

IDENTIFICATION. The bird is a dull greenish colour, with freckled crown and spotted wings (juvenile Spotted Pardalote is similar but brownish, not greenish, and has a red rump). Sexes are similar.

DISTRIBUTION. Tasmania, including King Island (where probably now extinct) and Flinders Island.

NOTES. It is usually found in pairs, although roving flocks form during the colder months. It frequents the crowns and outer foliage of trees (especially the White Gum *Eucalyptus viminalis*) in search of food, rarely descending near the ground. The call is a soft, nasal 'whi–whi', with the accent on the first syllable. Food: insects procured among foliage and from under the bark.

Formerly widespread, the species is now restricted to a few scattered localities and is possibly nearing extinction — the total population has been estimated at less than a thousand individuals.

BREEDING. Nest: domed or cup-shaped; made of bark fibre and lined with fine grass; placed in a cavity in a tree. Clutch: three to four; white. Breeding season: September to January.

16:20 RED-BROWED PARDALOTE *Pardalotus rubricatus*

IDENTIFICATION. The bird's crown is black, it is boldly spotted white, has a reddish superciliary and pale eye. Sexes are similar.

DISTRIBUTION. Queensland, Northern Territory, north-western Australia (south to the Gascoyne River), interior of New South Wales, extreme northern South Australia, and central Australia.

NOTES. The species inhabits arid open woodland and mulga scrub. Usually seen in pairs, it frequents the outer foliage of trees. The call is a series of five mellow, ventriloquial whistled notes. Food: insects.

BREEDING. Nest: cup-shaped; constructed of fine strips of bark and placed at the end of a tunnel in a bank. Clutch: three to four; white. Breeding season: July to October.

PLATE 17

BIRDS OF TREE TRUNKS AND BRANCHES

17:1 VARIED SITTELLA *Neositta chrysoptera*

IDENTIFICATION. This bird is small, greyish, streaked, with orange or white wing flashes (depending on subspecies) conspicuous in flight. Its behaviour is very distinctive; it is seen in flocks or small parties, scuttling nimbly over twigs and branches at the tops of trees.

DISTRIBUTION. Throughout mainland Australia. Six distinct populations, substantially differing in appearance: *N. c. leucoptera* occurs across much of northern Australia from the Kimberley to central Queensland; *N. c. striata* on

Cape York Peninsula and in northern Queensland; *N. c. pileata* over most of Western Australia, South Australia, south-western Queensland, and western New South Wales and Victoria; *N. c. leucocephala* in south-eastern Queensland and north-eastern New South Wales; and *N. c. chrysoptera* in eastern New South Wales and Victoria. A sixth form, *N. c. albata*, is enigmatic, known from several specimens taken many years ago near Bowen, Queensland, and apparently not recorded since.

NOTES. In behaviour and habits the various forms are very similar and, despite their distinctive appearance, interbreed freely wherever their ranges abut or overlap. In general, the northern forms have white wing flashes, the southern forms orange. It inhabits most kinds of open woodlands, but avoids rainforests. Usually seen in small flocks, the bird is constantly on the move. It is very active; flocks typically land in the outer twigs of a tree and work inward towards the trunk, running along the branches with the greatest ease, seeking insect life in the crevices of bark. Occasionally it feeds briefly on the ground. While feeding, and when in flight from tree to tree, birds constantly utter twittering notes.

BREEDING. Nest: cup-shaped, beautifully made of bark fibre matted with cobweb, and decorated on the outside with small pieces of bark fastened on like shingles, often forming a perfect imitation of the bark of the tree in which the nest is built; placed high in an upright forked limb of a dead branch. Clutch: three; very variable, a typical clutch being greyish-white with dark olive and slate markings. Breeding season: August to January.

17:2 RUFOUS TREECREEPER *Climacteris rufa*

IDENTIFICATION. The face and underparts are rusty red and it has a buff wing flash. A closely streaked patch in centre of breast is black and white in males and chestnut and white in females.

DISTRIBUTION. South-western Australia (north to Geraldton and Kalgoorlie), and Eyre Peninsula, South Australia.

NOTES. The bird is usually seen in pairs, frequenting open forest. It is similar in habits to the Brown Treecreeper, often seeking its food, insects of various kinds, on the ground. Its note is a single piercing call, 'peet!', uttered rapidly and loudly when disturbed.

BREEDING. Nest: similar in site and construction to that of the Brown Treecreeper. Clutch: two to three; pinkish-buff, spotted reddish-brown and dull purple. Breeding season: September to December.

17:3 BROWN TREECREEPER *Climacteris picumnus*

IDENTIFICATION. The bird is grey-brown with lightly streaked underparts and conspicuous buff superciliary. Sexes are similar, but a small patch on the lower throat is black and white in males and dull rufous and white in females. Birds in northern Queensland (subspecies *melanota*) are very much darker than southern birds (subspecies *picumnus*).

DISTRIBUTION. Eastern Australia generally, excluding Tasmania, from the vicinity of Adelaide, South Australia, to Cape York Peninsula.

NOTES. The species is common and widespread. It is usually seen in pairs or small parties, showing a preference for lightly timbered forests and partly cleared lands where it feeds upon the ground or hops up the trunks of trees, stumps or fence posts. When disturbed it flies with a skimming motion to the nearest tree, usually settling near the base and ascending the trunk spirally. It has a loud abrupt call 'spink!', uttered as a single note or in series, especially when alarmed. Food: mostly ants.

BREEDING. Nest: made of fur, hair and fine feathers; placed in a cavity several metres up in a dead tree, or sometimes in a fence post or stump (rarely in a creek bank). Clutch: two to three; pinkish-white, covered with small spots of pinkish-red and purple. Breeding season: mainly July to December.

17:4 WHITE-THROATED TREECREEPER *Cormobates leucophaea*

IDENTIFICATION. This is the common treecreeper of eastern forests; it is rather dark with a conspicuous white throat. The female has a small patch of dull rufous under the eye; immature females have rufous rumps. Birds of north-eastern rainforests (subspecies *minor*) are even darker and somewhat smaller.

DISTRIBUTION. Eastern and southern Australia, excluding Tasmania, from the vicinity of Cairns, Queensland, south to Victoria and west nearly to Adelaide, South Australia.

NOTES. The bird is usually solitary, strongly territorial and sedentary. It frequents forest country generally. It is strictly arboreal, ascending tree trunks rapidly in search of insects. The species has a wide variety of calls, including a characteristic loud shrill piping note, repeated in a rapid burst which gradually slows and falls in pitch; also a series of liquid warbling notes may be uttered in the breeding season. Food: mostly ants.

BREEDING. Nest: placed in a tree cavity, lined with bark, grass and fur and usually at a considerable height. Clutch: two to three; white, sparingly marked reddish-brown and purplish-brown. Breeding season: August to December.

17:5 RED-BROWED TREECREEPER *Climacteris erythrops*

IDENTIFICATION. This bird is often difficult to distinguish from the more common and widespread White-throated Treecreeper in the field, but streaks on the underparts extend noticeably further up the breast, and both sexes have a rich chestnut superciliary, the female with breast streaked chestnut and white.

DISTRIBUTION. Coastal and mountain areas of eastern Australia, from south-eastern Queensland to Victoria.

NOTES. This is a social bird usually seen in small groups; it inhabits dense eucalypt forests. It is similar in habits to the White-throated Treecreeper, but is usually quieter and less conspicuous; the two species often occur together. The usual call suggests that of the White-throated Treecreeper but is softer and less sustained; it also has a high-pitched hissing chatter. Food: mostly ants.

BREEDING. Nest: a compact mass of bark fragments lined with fur, placed in a cavity in a tree. Clutch: two; pinkish-white, densely marked with brown and dull purple. Breeding season: August to January.

17:6 WHITE-BROWED TREECREEPER *Climacteris affinis*

IDENTIFICATION. This bird is rather like the White-throated Treecreeper, but has conspicuous white superciliary and black and white streaked ear-coverts. Sexes are similar. (Inhabits arid interior.)

DISTRIBUTION. Central-western Australia through central Australia to south-western Queensland, western New South Wales, north-western Victoria, and inland South Australia.

NOTES. Usually seen in pairs or small parties, the bird frequents scrub-lands of the interior. It secures insects by spirally ascending tree trunks or searching fallen timber; often it feeds on the ground. The calls resemble those of the White-throated Treecreeper; one call suggests the 'peter–peter' of a Jacky-winter.

BREEDING. Nest: made of fur, hair, fragments of bark, dry grass and plant-down; placed in a cavity in a tree; usually close to the ground. Clutch: three; pinkish-white, spotted pinkish-red and purplish-red. Breeding season: September to December.

17:7 BLACK-TAILED TREECREEPER *Climacteris melanura*

IDENTIFICATION. This large, dark treecreeper of the tropical north and north-west, lacks a pale superciliary; its tail is black and the belly and flanks are unstreaked. The male has a black and white streaked throat; the female has a white throat and white and rufous streaked upper breast.

DISTRIBUTION. Tropical northern Australia, in two separate populations: *C. m. melanura* occurs from the Kimberley east to about Mount Isa, Queensland; *C. m. wellsi* occurs roughly between the de Grey and Gascoyne Rivers, central coastal Western Australia.

NOTES. The species usually occurs in pairs or small parties and inhabits timbered river flats, open woodlands and savannah. It is similar in habits to the other treecreepers; it often feeds on the ground. Calls include a clear strident 'pee, peepeepeepeepeepee, pee, pee'. Food: insects, mainly ants.

BREEDING. Nest: constructed of soft bark, fur, and dead grasses, and placed in a cavity in a tree. Clutch: two; pinkish-white, with numerous markings of pinkish-red and purple. Breeding season: September to January.

PLATE 18

SOME BIRDS OF SCRUBLANDS

18:1 RED-LORED WHISTLER *Pachycephala rufogularis*

IDENTIFICATION. The species is mainly grey-brown, with buff belly and dull rufous lores, face and throat. Sexes are similar.

DISTRIBUTION. Mallee areas of north-western Victoria, south-eastern South Australia, and south-western New South Wales.

NOTES. Usually shy and solitary, the bird is difficult to observe. It is sedentary and inhabits mainly mallee scrubs, especially those with broombrush or spinifex. It usually keeps to the densest foliage of trees and shrubs, but feeds much on the ground. The calls are wistful, highly melodious, and somewhat ventriloquial; the bird is far more often heard than seen. Food: insects.

BREEDING. Nest: cup-shaped; constructed of strips of fine bark and grass bound with cobweb and lined with fine grasses and usually having green tendrils around the rim; placed in a low bush or cluster of porcupine grass. Clutch: two to three; creamy or buff, spotted dark brown or umber and lavender. Breeding season: September to December.

18:2 GILBERT'S WHISTLER *Pachycephala inornata*

IDENTIFICATION. The species is similar to the Red-lored Whistler, but the male has black lores and face (throat dull rufous) and the female has a grey face and dull white throat.

DISTRIBUTION. Southern Australia, from western New South Wales and central Victoria (very rarely near the coast in the east and south) to inland south-western Australia.

NOTES. This bird is usually found in pairs, inhabiting mallee, mulga and lignum scrubs, and open forests. It is inconspicuous and deliberate in its movements, but is much less shy than the Red-lored Whistler, and is common in a wider variety of habitats. It has a wide vocabulary of loud, rich and haunting notes, some of which are ventriloquial; one call suggests the whistle of a man calling a dog. Food: insects, taken on the ground or in trees and shrubs.

BREEDING. Nest: cup-shaped; constructed mainly of dry bark; placed in a low bush or on top of an old nest of a babbler. Clutch: two to three; creamy or buff, spotted dark brown or umber and lavender. Breeding season: September to November.

18:3 CRESTED BELLBIRD *Oreoica gutturalis*

IDENTIFICATION. The bird is mainly greyish brown, with white face, black breastband and shaggy black crest. Sexes are similar.

DISTRIBUTION. Inland parts of continental Australia generally wherever suitable habitats occur; closer to the coast in certain areas.

NOTES. The species occurs singly or in pairs, inhabiting dry open forests and scrub lands, where it feeds mainly on grass-frequenting caterpillars. Perching aloft (usually on a dead branch), it produces a rolling, highly melodious and ventriloquial song of bell-like notes, perhaps best transliterated as 'pan–pan–panella'. Once heard, this call is difficult to confuse with that of any other bird.

BREEDING. Nest: cup-shaped; made of strips of bark, twigs, leaves and often scraps of cloth, lined with dry grass and rootlets; usually placed in a tree fork or hollow stump. Nests with eggs usually have, on the rim or in the chamber, numbers of semi-paralysed caterpillars which the bird injures and 'stores' for unknown reasons. Clutch: three to four; white, spotted and blotched sepia and black. Breeding season: mainly August to December.

18:4 CHIRRUPING WEDGEBILL *Psophodes cristatus*

IDENTIFICATION. This bird has mainly pale dull brown plumage, with a prominent shaggy pointed crest and a breast very faintly and obscurely streaked grey. Sexes are similar.

DISTRIBUTION. South-western Queensland, western New South Wales, and eastern South Australia (west to about Oodnadatta and Bookaloo).

NOTES. The species is seen in pairs or small parties frequenting low shrublands and steppe in arid areas. Recent research has indicated that there are two distinct forms of the wedgebill, almost identical in appearance, but with marked differences in calls, behaviour and ecology. This species is gregarious, relatively tame, and inhabits more open environments; pairs regularly sing duets, the song is sometimes transcribed as 'chip–chir–cherooo'. Food: insects and seeds.

BREEDING. Nest: a loose flattened cup of twigs; placed in a low shrub. Clutch: two to three; blue or pale greenish-blue, sparingly marked or spotted with black or purplish-grey. Breeding season: variable, but usually August to December.

18:5 CHIMING WEDGEBILL *Psophodes occidentalis*

IDENTIFICATION. This species is virtually identical in appearance to the Chirruping Wedgebill, but differs in calls and habitat. Sexes are similar.

DISTRIBUTION. Central Australia, from about the Queensland/Northern Territory border and Oodnadatta, South Australia, west to coastal Western Australia.

NOTES. This species was recognised as distinct in 1973. It is very similar to the Chirruping Wedgebill in appearance, but inhabits denser environments, is much more solitary and shyer, and does not sing duets. The call is a series of four to six notes in a descending chime-like series.

BREEDING. Nest and eggs: like those of the Chirruping Wedgebill.

18:6 HALL'S BABBLER *Pomatostomus halli*

IDENTIFICATION. This bird is very similar to the White-browed Babbler, but its underparts are nearly as dark as the back, more or less sharply marked off from white throat and upper breast; the white superciliary is broad and very conspicuous. Sexes are similar.

DISTRIBUTION. Western Queensland and north-central New South Wales; approximately north to Winton, west to Windorah, east to Charleville in Queensland, and south to Mootwingie, New South Wales.

NOTES. This species is closely related and similar in general habits to the White-browed Babbler. Usually seen in small parties and occasionally in pairs, it frequents arid mulga scrub, open eucalypt woodland and treeless spinifex country. It forages actively in shrubs and the lower branches of trees. Calls include a variety of chuckling and chattering notes. This species was first described in 1963 from specimens taken near Charleville, Queensland.

BREEDING. Nest: bulky, domed, with a side entrance near the top; made of sticks and twigs, thickly lined with grass, fur and plant-down; usually well concealed in a bush. Clutch: usually two; pale brownish- or greyish-white; densely marked with small blotches and streaks of blackish-brown. Breeding season: variable and influenced by rainfall; mainly July to September.

18:7 GREY-CROWNED BABBLER *Pomatostomus temporalis*

IDENTIFICATION. This is a large babbler with yellow eyes and pale grey crown. Sexes are similar. Eastern birds are grey below; populations in the north and north-west have dull reddish underparts.

DISTRIBUTION. Northern and eastern mainland Australia generally. Two groups of populations, once regarded as distinct species: '*rubeculus*' forms (Red-breasted Babbler) occur across northern Australia from about Shark Bay, Western Australia, east to about Winton, Queensland, and south to about Boulia and Oodnadatta (South Australia); '*temporalis*' forms (Grey-crowned Babbler) occur from Cape York south to about Melbourne and west to about Adelaide, although generally avoiding coastal regions. The species also occurs in New Guinea.

NOTES. The bird is usually seen in flocks of from eight to twelve birds frequenting scrub and open forest. It is highly sociable, noisy and very active, and spends much time on the ground in search of insects. Owing to its incessant fussy chattering or cackling notes and its playful habits, it is a general favourite. Many calls are nondescript, but the loud 'arco' or 'ya–ho' cannot be mistaken.

BREEDING. Nest: bulky, dome-shaped, with a spout-like entrance; made of sticks and twigs loosely interwoven, lined with bark fibre, feathers, grass or wool; usually placed in a tree fork several metres from the ground. Communal roost nests are also built. Clutch: three to six; varying from pale brown to purplish-brown and buff, covered with hair-like markings of dark brown. Breeding season: mainly August to December.

18:8 WHITE-BROWED BABBLER *Pomatostomus superciliosus*

IDENTIFICATION. This bird has a dark brown crown, dark eye, and underparts markedly paler than the back. Sexes are similar.

DISTRIBUTION. Inland areas of southern Western Australia, through central Australia to South Australia, southern Queensland, western New South Wales, and central Victoria.

NOTES. The species occurs in small flocks, frequenting scrub and open forest. In habits it resembles the Grey-crowned Babbler — very noisy, active and sociable. The calls are a harsh and animated chatter.

BREEDING. Nest: bulky, dome-shaped with a side entrance; made of twigs and lined with grass, wool or other soft materials; placed in a tree, several metres from the ground. Clutch: three to five; various shades of brown, covered with hair-like markings of dark brown. Breeding season: July to December.

18:9 CHESTNUT-CROWNED BABBLER *Pomatostomus ruficeps*

IDENTIFICATION. This is the only babbler with white in the wing; it has a rich chestnut crown. Sexes are similar.

DISTRIBUTION. Interior of southern Queensland, western New South Wales, north-western Victoria, and eastern South Australia.

NOTES. The species inhabits arid scrub lands, and it is highly social, living in groups of about twelve to twenty birds. It feeds mainly on the ground. Like other babblers, it is noisy and very active, but in general is shyer. Food: insects.

BREEDING. Nest: similar to the nests of other babblers. Clutch: four to five; light stone-colour or various shades of brown, with hair-like markings of sepia or blackish-brown. Breeding season: July to December.

18:10 SPOTTED BOWERBIRD *Chlamydera maculata*

IDENTIFICATION. This bird is very similar to the Western Bowerbird but is paler. The throat and breast are faintly streaked and mottled grey and fawn, a pale streak extends backwards from gape, and it has a greyish patch at hind neck. Sexes are similar. (Note distribution.)

DISTRIBUTION. From interior of Queensland (near coast in suitable areas) through inland New South Wales to north-western Victoria and the upper Murray River in South Australia.

NOTES. The species is seen in pairs or small flocks frequenting scrub and open forests of inland districts. The species is familar about many pastoral homesteads, where it sometimes becomes a nuisance by raiding cultivated fruits. The natural calls are harsh (and include a cat-like cry), but the bird is a remarkable mimic, rendering perfectly all manner of bush sounds. It builds bowers averaging about 60 centimetres in length and 25 centimetres in height, and decorates them with an assortment of bones (in sheep country) or bleached shells (in cattle country), pieces of glass and bright objects of many kinds. It also 'paints' the interior wall with macerated vegetable matter. The lilac mantle worn by males is assumed also by old females. Food: insects, seeds, fruits and berries.

BREEDING. Nest: saucer-shaped and shallow; made of thin dead twigs, lined with fine twigs and sometimes dry grass; placed in a leafy tree. Clutch: two; greenish-yellow, with numerous lines of umber and blackish-brown and underlying lines of pale purplish-grey. Breeding season: usually October to December.

18:11 WESTERN BOWERBIRD *Chlamydera guttata*

IDENTIFICATION. The species is very similar to the Spotted Bowerbird, but is somewhat darker, browner, and more boldly spotted buff on the head, breast and back. Sexes are similar.

DISTRIBUTION. From mid-Western Australia through central Australia to the Musgrave and Everard Ranges.

NOTES. The bird is seen in pairs or small flocks, inhabiting scrub and open forests. It is similar to the Spotted Bowerbird in habits and mimetic ability. Decoration of the bower includes pieces of white or grey limestone, bleached bones and green fruits. Food: insects, seeds, fruits and berries.

BREEDING. Nest: similar to that of the Spotted Bowerbird. Clutch: two; pale greenish-grey, marked with a tangled network of lines. Breeding season: mainly September to December.

18:12 FAWN-BREASTED BOWERBIRD *Chlamydera cerviniventris*

IDENTIFICATION. The head and breast are pale grey, and obscurely streaked dull white; belly and undertail coverts are a warm reddish buff. Sexes are similar. (Note distribution.)

DISTRIBUTION. North-eastern Queensland, from Cape York to about Cape Flattery. The species also occurs in New Guinea.

NOTES. The bird is found in pairs or small flocks, frequenting scrub, open forest and mangroves. It is shy, wary and generally difficult to observe; it is less inclined to come around dwellings than other bowerbirds. The bower is a compact structure comprising two walls of interwoven sticks and twigs; decorations are mostly green berries. Like all other Australian bowerbirds, this species is a competent vocal mimic. Food: seeds, native fruits and berries.

BREEDING. Nest: saucer-shaped; made of twigs and bark and lined with grass and other fine materials; placed in a tree. Clutch: one; creamy-white, with a network of lines and hair-like markings of olive-brown, umber, purplish-grey and blackish-brown. Breeding season: September to December.

18:13 GREAT BOWERBIRD *Chlamydera nuchalis*

IDENTIFICATION. This large bird has a pale grey head and breast and is unmarked. Sexes are similar.

DISTRIBUTION. From the Kimberley through tropical northern Australia to a point below Mackay, Queensland.

NOTES. The species is found in pairs or small flocks, frequenting scrub and open forest. The bower is usually built in isolated patches of scrub; bowers average about 60 centimetres in length by 45 centimetres in width and 37 centimetres in height. Decorations are usually bleached shells of land-snails, pieces of bleached coral, or bleached bones, but many other oddments are used. Like the Spotted Bowerbird, this species is often seen near homesteads and, again like its smaller relatives, it is renowned as a vocal mimic. Food: seeds, native fruits and berries, and insects.

BREEDING. Nest: like that of the Spotted Bowerbird; placed in a thick bunch of twigs several metres from the ground. Clutch: one to two; greyish-green, with a tangled tracery of lines and hair-like markings of olive-brown, umber, blackish-brown and purplish-grey. Breeding season: September to February.

PLATE 19

BIRDS OF FOREST BORDERS
AND GRASSLANDS

19:1 SCARLET ROBIN *Petroica multicolor*

IDENTIFICATION. This is a small, rotund robin. Males have a black head and throat, bright red breast, conspicuous white patch on forehead and boldly black and white wings; females are dull and brownish, but usually show at least a hint of the male colour pattern.

DISTRIBUTION. South-eastern Queensland (rarely), eastern New South Wales, Victoria, south-eastern South Australia to southern Eyre Peninsula, Kangaroo Island, south-western Australia, and Tasmania. The species is also found on Norfolk Island and some other Pacific Islands.

NOTES. The bird is usually seen in pairs frequenting open forests and orchards during spring and summer and more open country during the cooler months. Its call-note is a slight trill; it also has a modest but agreeable song. Food: insects, mainly taken on the ground.

BREEDING. Nest: cup-shaped; made of bark strips, mosses, and dry grass, bound with cobweb and thickly lined with fur, feathers or plant-down; usually decorated on the outside with small pieces of bark or lichen; built in a charred stump, or in an open fork or hollow spout at almost any height above the ground. Clutch: three; greenish-white, with brown and underlying markings of purplish-grey. Breeding season: July to December.

19:2 RED-CAPPED ROBIN *Petroica goodenovii*

IDENTIFICATION. This species is very similar to the Scarlet Robin but the forecrown is bright red, not white; the female is dull brownish, but usually with a hint of red on forehead and upper breast.

DISTRIBUTION. The interior of Australia generally, extending to coastal areas in suitable parts.

NOTES. The bird is found in pairs, frequenting chiefly scrub-lands and open forests of inland districts. The species is common, generally tame and confiding, and is usually seen sitting watchfully on stumps or low branches. It has a call somewhat like the ticking of a clock or the gentle tapping of wood. Food: terrestrial and flying insects.

BREEDING. Nest: small, cup-shaped; made of fine shreds of bark and dry grass, liberally bound with cobweb and lined with hair or fur; built in a tree fork (either horizontal or vertical); usually within a metre or two of the ground. Clutch: two to three; bluish-white, minutely dotted with shades of brown and underlying spots of violet-grey. Breeding season: September to December.

19:3 PINK ROBIN *Petroica rodinogaster*

IDENTIFICATION. The male of this species has black head and upperparts, rose-pink breast and plain black tail (no white); the female is mainly brown, paler below, with two rich buff wingbars.

DISTRIBUTION. Tasmania, southern Victoria, and south-eastern New South Wales.

NOTES. The bird is seen in pairs, frequenting heavily timbered mountain ranges and gullies during spring and summer and moving to more open country in autumn. It is usually tame, but unobtrusive, usually feeding low in dense cover. The call is a slight 'tick', but at times the bird utters a simple yet pleasant warble. Food: terrestrial and flying insects.

BREEDING. Nest: cup-shaped; constructed of green moss bound with cobweb, lined with fur and down from fronds of tree ferns, and decorated on the outside with lichen; usually built into a low forked horizontal branch. Clutch: three to four; greenish-white, with pale brown spots and underlying markings of lavender. Breeding season: October to January.

19:4 ROSE ROBIN *Petroica rosea*

IDENTIFICATION. This bird is very similar to the Pink Robin, but the male is grey above (not black) and has white flashes in the tail; the female is somewhat duller and greyer than the female Pink Robin, with fawn wingbars and white flashes in the tail.

DISTRIBUTION. Eastern mainland Australia from about Rockhampton (possibly Mackay), Queensland, south to Melbourne, Victoria and west to about Adelaide, South Australia.

NOTES. The species is found in pairs, frequenting coastal rainforests and contiguous mountain ranges where it breeds; during autumn and winter it frequents more open country. It feeds mainly high in the canopy of trees. Its chief call is a faint 'churring', but it also has a slight but agreeable song. Food: insects, mainly taken in the trees and the air.

BREEDING. Nest: small, cup-shaped; constructed of soft fibre and moss, bound with cobweb, lined with fur or plant-down, and decorated on the outside with lichen; usually built at a considerable height in a tree fork. Clutch: two to three; bluish-grey, spotted purplish-brown. Breeding season: October to December.

19:5 FLAME ROBIN *Petroica phoenicea*

IDENTIFICATION. The male is brilliant orange below, including the throat; the female is very like the female Scarlet Robin but underparts are dingy grey-white, clouded brown on the breast.

DISTRIBUTION. From south-eastern Queensland through south-eastern Australia to south-eastern South Australia, Kangaroo Island, the islands of Bass Strait and Tasmania.

NOTES. The bird groups in pairs during spring and summer, breeding in cleared areas in coastal ranges, and flocking during the colder months throughout the lowlands, where it frequents farmlands, golf courses, parks and open woodlands. It is usually seen perched on a fence post, stump or low branch, watching the ground for insects. The species is common in Tasmania and there may be some migration between that island and Victoria. Calls include a pleasing lilting song and a soft short 'peep'.

BREEDING. Nest: cup-shaped; constructed of strips of soft bark, grasses, and rootlets, coated with mosses and cobweb and lined with fur or plant-down; built in a tree fork or a cavity in a tree. Clutch: three; bluish-white, finely dotted with shades of brown and dull lavender. Breeding season: September to January.

19:6 SOUTHERN WHITEFACE *Aphelocephala leucopsis*

IDENTIFICATION. The species is mainly dingy grey, with white face and pale grey breast; western birds (subspecies *castaneiventris*) have dull reddish flanks. Sexes are similar.

DISTRIBUTION. Mainland southern Australia generally, north to about the Tropic of Capricorn in the west and about Chinchilla, Queensland, in the east.

NOTES. Frequently in flocks, the bird is often in the company of the Yellow-rumped Thornbill. The Southern Whiteface is locally common, but is patchy in distribution. It is sedentary, and frequents chiefly open forest country and cleared lands, obtaining most of its food on the ground. It is a sociable species and possesses a cheerful though simple song. Food: insects and seeds.

BREEDING. Nest: domed; loosely constructed of strips of bark and grasses and lined with soft materials; usually placed in the cavity of a stump or post or in a thick shrub, often in a shed or dwelling. Clutch: three to five; white to pale buff, profusely spotted brown and purplish-grey. Breeding season: June to November.

19:7 CHESTNUT-BREASTED WHITEFACE *Aphelocephala pectoralis*

IDENTIFICATION. The bird is similar to the Southern Whiteface in size, behaviour and general appearance, but the back is reddish, and it has a warm rufous band across the breast. Sexes are similar.

DISTRIBUTION. Interior of South Australia, from Port Augusta to Oodnadatta.

NOTES. The bird is found in pairs or flocks, frequenting open country and open scrublands. It is similar in habits to the other whitefaces, but this species is rare, remote and little known. The call is low and plaintive. Food: insects and seeds.

BREEDING. Nest: domed but lacking spout; first example found was built of small twigs in bluebush (Kochia). Clutch: three; pale pink, marked purplish-grey; not glossy and smaller than eggs of the Eastern Whiteface. Breeding season: uncertain (very few nests recorded).

19:8 BANDED WHITEFACE *Aphelocephala nigricincta*

IDENTIFICATION. This bird is similar to the Southern Whiteface, but has a narrow black band across lower breast and the back is reddish. Sexes are similar.

DISTRIBUTION. From inland Western Australia through central Australia to northern South Australia and south-western Queensland.

NOTES. The species is found in pairs or flocks, frequenting open country. It feeds mainly on the ground, taking cover in bushes when alarmed. It is similar in habits to other whitefaces, but its call is sweeter; the song is often uttered in flight. Food: insects and seeds.

BREEDING. Nest: bulky, dome-shaped, with a spout-like entrance; constructed of rather thick twigs and lined with flower pods and other soft materials; usually placed in a prickly shrub. Clutch: two to three; pinkish-white, spotted pale reddish-brown and purplish-grey. Breeding season: April and May.

19:9 SAMPHIRE THORNBILL *Acanthiza iredalei*

IDENTIFICATION. This bird is a nondescript grey-brown, with white eye and pale buff rump; it is easily confused with the Buff-rumped Thornbill, but the plumage is somewhat greyer in tone, and the rump patch smaller. Its habitat is distinctive. Sexes are similar.

DISTRIBUTION. Southern Western Australia, most of South Australia, and extreme western Victoria. There are three similar subspecies: *A. i. iredalei* (Samphire Thornbill) occurs west of about Port Augusta, South Australia; *A. i. rosinae* is confined to the eastern shore of St Vincents Gulf, South Australia; and *A. i. hedleyi* inhabits the Little Desert, western Victoria.

NOTES. The species is found in pairs or flocks, frequenting samphire flats, open country studded with low bushes, and similar semi-desolate spots with very low vegetation. It feeds on the ground or in low shrubs. It is inconspicuous in habits, and generally shy; it has a feeble song and a call-note resembling 'tip–tip–tip', uttered rapidly. Food: insects.

BREEDING. Nest: oblong, domed, with an opening near the top; loosely constructed of thin strips of bark and soft plant stems, bound with cobweb and lined with plant-down; placed in a low bush. Clutch: three; pinkish-white, with small spots of dull reddish-brown. Breeding season: July to October.

19:10 YELLOW-RUMPED THORNBILL *Acanthiza chrysorrhoa*

IDENTIFICATION. The crown is black and spotted white; the rump is clear yellow. Sexes are similar.

DISTRIBUTION. Australia generally, south of the Tropic of Capricorn, and extending north in Queensland to the Gulf of Carpentaria.

NOTES. Found in pairs or flocks, the bird frequents open forest and partly cleared lands; it is also common in orchards, parks and gardens. It is mostly seen on open ground, and when flushed rarely flies any distance. The song is a succession of sweet and animated notes; the usual flight call is 'check'. Food: insects, mainly obtained on the ground.

BREEDING. Nest: an unusual double structure, consisting of a domed nest with a narrow hooded side entrance and a cup-shaped addition on top; made of dry grass, plant stems, wool or other soft materials, liberally bound with cobweb and lined with fine dry grass, hair, wool, fur or feathers. The function of the upper nest is unknown. The structure is usually built in the leafy end of a drooping branch, several metres from the ground. Clutch: three to four; white or flesh-colour, often speckled pale red or reddish-brown at the larger end. Breeding season: mainly July to December.

19:11 BUFF-RUMPED THORNBILL *Acanthiza reguloides*

IDENTIFICATION. The bird's upperparts are neutral grey-brown with a hint of green, underparts pale, eye white and rump and base of tail are yellowish buff. North Queensland birds (subspecies *squamata*) are strongly washed yellow. Sexes are similar.

DISTRIBUTION. Eastern and southern mainland Australia from the Atherton Tableland south to Melbourne, Victoria, and west to about Adelaide, South Australia.

NOTES. The bird is usually in small flocks, frequenting scrublands, lightly timbered ranges, and open forests where there is much rough litter and fallen branches. It feeds mainly on or close to the ground. When in flight it spreads its tail and flits along with a jerky motion. Food: insects.

BREEDING. Nest: dome-shaped, with a side entrance; constructed of bark and grass bound with cobweb and lined with feathers, hair or fur; the site is particularly variable, but is usually in a low bush or tree cavity or crevice. Clutch: three to four; white or fleshy-white, with freckles of light red to rich brownish red. Breeding season: August to December.

19:12 CHESTNUT-RUMPED THORNBILL *Acanthiza uropygialis*

IDENTIFICATION. The bird is grey above, dull white below with a white eye and chestnut rump. (The Inland Thornbill is very similar, but has a red eye and faintly streaked breast). It is the only red-rumped thornbill to feed habitually and persistently on the ground. Sexes are similar.

DISTRIBUTION. Central Western Australia to the southern part of the Northern Territory and south to about Esperance, Western Australia; South Australia, Victoria, western New South Wales and south-western Queensland.

NOTES. Usually seen in small flocks, the species is common and widespread in the interior in a variety of arid environments, but with a preference for scrubby woodland with much fallen timber. A restless species, it utters a subdued twittering as it searchs for insects on the ground or in bushes; it also has a cheerful song.

BREEDING. Nest: domed, with a side entrance; constructed of bark and grass, bound with cobweb and lined with feathers; usually placed in a tree cavity or crevice. Clutch: three; fleshy-white, with reddish-brown markings. Breeding season: July to December.

19:13 WHITE-FRONTED CHAT *Ephthianura albifrons*

IDENTIFICATION. The head and underparts are mainly white, with a broad black band across the breast; the female is much duller, greyer, with an obscure smudgy slate crescent on upper breast.

DISTRIBUTION. Southern Queensland to Victoria and South Australia (except north-west), southern Western Australia (north to Point Cloates), Kangaroo Island and Tasmania.

NOTES. The species is found in pairs or small flocks, frequenting open country studded with low bushes, samphire flats or swampy localities. In certain districts it is resident, but generally it is nomadic. It is a sprightly bird, usually seen hurrying over the ground in search of insects. The chief call is a metallic 'tang'. Both male and female are much given to feigning injury when they suppose their eggs or nestlings to be in danger.

BREEDING. Nest: cup-shaped; neatly constructed of twigs, grass, and fine rootlets and lined with hair; placed in a low shrub or tall grass. Clutch: three to four; white, with reddish-brown spots on the larger end. Breeding season: mainly July to December.

19:14 CRIMSON CHAT *Ephthianura tricolor*

IDENTIFICATION. The male has a white throat and a brilliant red crown, breast and rump; the female is nondescript, brownish with underparts mottled red.

DISTRIBUTION. Eastern Australia (generally west of the Great Dividing Range) from the Gulf of Carpentaria to north-western Victoria, northern South Australia and central Australia; in Western Australia from the Kimberley south to the Moore River.

NOTES. In pairs or flocks, the bird frequents open country studded with low bushes. It is nomadic and irruptive, with numbers suddenly appearing in regions where the species has not been recorded for years. Like the White-faced Chat, it is usually seen seeking insects on the ground. The call-note is a metallic 'ting-ting'.

BREEDING. Nest: cup-shaped; constructed of grass and rootlets and lined with finer materials; placed in a low bush or in a tuft of grass. Clutch: three to four; white, sparingly spotted reddish-purple. Breeding season: mainly October to December (east); July to March (west).

19:15 ORANGE CHAT *Ephthianura aurifrons*

IDENTIFICATION. The male is mainly brilliant orange, with black mask and throat. The female is dull, pale, yellowish, with orange eye.

DISTRIBUTION. Western Queensland, western New South Wales, north-western Victoria, northern South Australia and central Australia; Western Australia south of the Kimberley to Morawa and Eucla.

NOTES. The bird occurs in pairs or flocks, frequenting open country studded with low bushes or samphire flats. It is highly nomadic and, although chiefly found inland, sometimes visits samphire swamps nearer the coast. In habits it is similar to the Crimson Chat.

BREEDING. Nest: cup-shaped; constructed of grass and rootlets, and lined with finer materials; placed in a low bush or a tuft of long grass. Clutch: three; white, with purplish-red markings. Breeding season: September to February.

19:16 YELLOW CHAT *Ephthianura crocea*

IDENTIFICATION. The male has bright yellow head and underparts, with a small black crescent on breast, variable in extent. The female is very similar to the female Orange Chat, but has straw-yellow, not orange eye.

DISTRIBUTION. Poorly known; occurs in isolated populations across northern Australia, from about the Fitzroy River, Western Australia, east to western Queensland.

NOTES. Found in pairs, the species frequents marshy swamps and reedy growth around bore drains; when disturbed it seeks safety among grasses. It procures its insect food in grass or small bushes or along muddy margins of lagoons and ponds. The call is slight and simple. Its habits are little known.

BREEDING. Nest: cup-shaped; constructed of grasses and rootlets; placed in a low bush. Clutch: three; white, dotted purplish-red. Breeding season: November to January.

19:17 GIBBERBIRD *Ashbyia lovensis*

IDENTIFICATION. The species is yellow below, sandy brown above with the rump same colour as back. Sexes are similar.

DISTRIBUTION. From south-western Queensland and north-western New South Wales through northern South Australia to Oodnadatta.

NOTES. It is seen in pairs or family parties, frequenting arid country, chiefly gibber plains. It is strictly a ground bird, in many ways suggesting a pipit, but occasionally it mounts in the air, and during the descent utters a sharp 'whit–whit–whit'. The bird is not easily seen unless accidentally flushed. It is remarkably adept at feigning injury. Food: insects and seeds.

BREEDING. Nest: cup-shaped; constructed of small twigs and dry grasses, neatly lined with rootlets; built in a depression in the ground. Clutch: three; white, with reddish-brown spots on the larger end. Breeding season: May to October or after rain.

19:18 SPECKLED WARBLER *Chthonicola sagittata*

IDENTIFICATION. The face is whitish, the crown dull reddish, narrowly streaked white and the underparts are heavily streaked black. Sexes are similar.

DISTRIBUTION. Victoria, eastern New South Wales, and Queensland north to about Mackay.

NOTES. In pairs or small parties, the bird frequents shrubs and fallen timber in open forest country and feeds on insects of the ground, though often perching in trees. The chief note is a 'charring' chatter, but the species also utters a sweet song that sometimes extends into mimicry. It is the chief host of the Black-eared Cuckoo, which lays an egg of the same distinctive colour.

BREEDING. Nest: domed, with a side entrance; constructed of dried grasses and bark, and lined with fur and feathers; built in a slight depression in the ground. Clutch: three to four; glossy reddish-brown, with a darker zone at the larger end. Breeding season: August to January, sometimes in autumn.

PLATE 20

PARROTS AND COCKATOOS
OF FOREST LANDS

20:1 RED-CHEEKED PARROT *Geoffroyus geoffroyi*

IDENTIFICATION. The bird is mainly green. The male has a red face, blue nape and crown and the female has a dingy brown head. (Cape York only.)

DISTRIBUTION. Cape York Peninsula, from the Pascoe River to the Rocky River. The species also occurs in Indonesia and New Guinea.

NOTES. The species is relatively common in rainforest and associated vegetation and is found in pairs or small flocks. Its flight is swift and usually high with characteristically brisk, shallow wingbeats. The bird is noisy and conspicuous, but wary.

BREEDING. Nest: in a hollow in a rainforest tree. Clutch: three; white. Breeding season: August to December.

20:2 PRINCESS PARROT *Polytelis alexandrae*

IDENTIFICATION. This is a graceful pastel-hued parrot with a long slender tail. The wing coverts are golden green, the throat pink and the crown and rump are lilac. Sexes are similar, but females are somewhat duller than males.

DISTRIBUTION. Arid interior, from central and northern Western Australia to the southern Northern Territory and northern South Australia.

NOTES. This tame bird is found in pairs or small flocks, usually frequenting belts of timber near watercourses. The species is strongly nomadic, moving over long distances searching for seeds of various plants, chiefly porcupine grass. The bird feeds mostly on the ground. Both flocks and pairs maintain a continuous chatter when perched in trees.

BREEDING. Nest: in a hole in a tree or stump, usually beside a creek. Clutch: four to six; white. Breeding season: mainly September to December.

20:3 SUPERB PARROT *Polytelis swainsonii*

IDENTIFICATION. This parrot is mainly green, with a long slender tail. The male has bright yellow face and cheeks and a red band across the lower throat; the female has a dull bluish face and throat.

DISTRIBUTION. From the Murray River (between about Albury and Barham) north and east to the upper Lachlan and Castlereagh Rivers, New South Wales; it is partially migratory, breeding in the Riverina and wintering in the Lachlan-Castlereagh region.

NOTES. The species usually occurs in small flocks, frequenting chiefly belts of timber bordering watercourses and adjoining grasslands. It feeds on the seeds of grasses and other plants, and also seeks nectar and other food in the eucalypts. It often feeds on spilled grain along roadsides. Most active in the early morning and evening, the bird spends the heat of the day resting quietly in dense foliage in the crowns of trees. Calls have a characteristic gruff quality.

BREEDING. Nest: in a hole in a tree, at a considerable height from the ground. Clutch: four to six; white. Breeding season: September to December.

20:4 REGENT PARROT *Polytelis anthopeplus*

IDENTIFICATION. The bird is mainly smoky yellow, with black wings and tail, black bill and red patches on inner wings. Sexes are similar, but females are much duller than males.

DISTRIBUTION. Northern Victoria and adjacent parts of New South Wales to the mallee areas of south-eastern South Australia; also in south-western Australia, extending east as far as Esperance.

NOTES. This species is rather rare and local in the east, but common in Western Australia where it sometimes becomes a pest to wheat farmers. It occurs in flocks up to perhaps twenty birds, which in flight make a very beautiful sight. Females and immature males are much duller in colour than the adult males.

BREEDING. Nest: in a hole in a tree. Clutch: four to six; white. Breeding season: September to December.

20:5 RED-WINGED PARROT *Aprosmictus erythropterus*

IDENTIFICATION. This parrot is mainly green. Males have black backs and a large bright red patch on upper wing. Females are similar but very much duller. The bill is pink.

DISTRIBUTION. Northern and eastern Australia, west to the Kimberley and south to northern New South Wales (chiefly west of the Great Dividing Range) and north-eastern South Australia. The species is also found in New Guinea.

NOTES. Seen in pairs or small flocks, the bird frequents scrub and open forest, especially along watercourses. The call is musical, the flight is buoyant, and when on the wing the bird's colouring makes it a very pretty sight. Food: seeds, berries, nectar and insect larvae.

BREEDING. Nest: in a tree hollow, usually far below the entrance. Clutch: three to six; white. Breeding season: September to December.

20:6 KING PARROT *Alisterus scapularis*

IDENTIFICATION. The bird's upperparts are mainly green and underparts red. The male has a bright red head and deep blue rump; the female has a dingy green head and breast.

DISTRIBUTION. Eastern Australia, from Cooktown to southern Victoria.

NOTES. The species occurs in pairs or flocks, inhabiting chiefly heavily timbered ranges and brushes. The bird is common and conspicuous, but rather wary. Although its usual call is a shrill grating 'eek–eek–eek', at times it utters a soft and musical whistle. The species feeds on native seeds, fruits and berries; in certain districts it does damage to ripening maize crops.

BREEDING. Nest: in a tree hollow, sometimes several metres below the entrance. Clutch: three to five; white. Breeding season: October to December.

20:7 ECLECTUS PARROT *Eclectus roratus*

IDENTIFICATION. This large stocky parrot is big headed and short tailed. The male is mainly green, with pink bill and orange eyes; the female is mainly red, with bright blue breast and shoulders and black bill. (Cape York only.)

DISTRIBUTION. Cape York Peninsula, from the Pascoe River south to Massey Creek. The species also occurs in Indonesia and New Guinea.

NOTES. This parrot frequents rainforests, feeding on nuts and seeds of tall trees. It is common, noisy and conspicuous, and is found in pairs or small parties. Its general behaviour and mannerisms often suggest a cockatoo rather than a parrot. The call-note of the male is a casual 'quork', but the bird also utters a resonant clanging; the call of the female is a screeching whistle.

BREEDING. Nest: in a large hole in a tall tree, often 20 metres or more above the ground. Clutch: two; white. Breeding season: October to December.

20:8 GALAH *Cacatua roseicapilla*

IDENTIFICATION. This bird is powder grey above and pink below. Sexes are similar.

DISTRIBUTION. Continental Australia generally, chiefly inland areas; accidental to Tasmania.

NOTES. This common and familiar bird is found in pairs or flocks, frequenting open country, chiefly inland plains interspersed with belts of timber, or trees bordering watercourses. Numbers of the birds feed together on seeds of grasses and other plants; when disturbed they rise with loud cries. A flock in flight presents a most striking spectacle of colour as the wheeling birds alternately reveal their rosy breasts and grey backs. Galahs cause considerable damage to cultivated crops, but also devour large quantities of seeds of noxious plants.

BREEDING. Nest: on the base of a hollow in a tall tree; it is lined with green leaves. Clutch: three to five; white. Breeding season: usually September to November.

20:9 LITTLE CORELLA *Cacatua pastinator*

IDENTIFICATION. This is a plain white cockatoo with a short, shaggy white crest and patch of naked blue skin around the eye; some populations have pink feathers between bill and eye. The species is easily confused with the Long-billed Corella. Sexes are similar.

DISTRIBUTION. Arid interior of Australia generally. The species also occurs in New Guinea.

NOTES. This bird is common and widespread. It is found in pairs or flocks (often numbering thousands of birds), frequenting open country interspersed with belts of scrub or timber bordering watercourses. Some coastal cities (such as Sydney) have substantial feral populations, originating from escaped aviary birds. The Little Corella roosts in flocks, close to water. It feeds on seeds of grasses and other plants, and also on bulbs and roots.

BREEDING. Nest: in a hole in a tree and occasionally in a hollow in a large termite mound. Clutch: usually three; white. Breeding season: August to October.

20:10 LONG-BILLED CORELLA *Cacatua tenuirostris*

IDENTIFICATION. This bird is very similar to the Little Corella, but it has a longer bill, and usually conspicuous amounts of pink, splashed irregularly on forehead, chin, face and throat. Sexes are similar.

DISTRIBUTION. Far south-western New South Wales, western Victoria, and extreme south-eastern South Australia. (The populations of 'long-billed' corellas in Western Australia have recently been shown to belong not to this species but to the Little Corella.)

NOTES. Occurring in pairs or flocks, the bird frequents plains or timber bordering watercourses. It is noisy and conspicuous and often associates with flocks of Little Corellas. The bird is locally common, but is in general rare and perhaps threatened with extinction; although there is some evidence within the last two decades that its decline has been arrested and numbers are apparently on the increase. It feeds on seeds of grasses and other plants and on bulbous roots; sometimes it damages crops.

BREEDING. Nest: in a hole in a tree. Clutch: two to four; white. Breeding season: August to November.

20:11 SULPHUR-CRESTED COCKATOO *Cacatua galerita*

IDENTIFICATION. This cockatoo is large, more or less plain white, with a conspicuous, recurved yellow crest. Sexes are similar.

DISTRIBUTION. Northern and eastern Australia, west to the Kimberley and south to Tasmania and south-eastern South Australia. The species also occurs in New Guinea.

NOTES. The species is common and familiar, even in many towns and cities. It is the best known member of its group, and is a familiar cage-bird. It is seen in pairs or large flocks, frequenting heavily timbered mountain ranges, open forests, paddocks and timber bordering watercourses. The normal food of this cockatoo is seeds and bulbous roots, but the species sometimes does damage to crops. The bird is noisy, with a variety of calls, the most common being a raucous ear-splitting screech.

BREEDING. Nest: in a hole in a tree. Clutch: two to three; white. Breeding season: August to November.

20:12 PINK COCKATOO *Cacatua leadbeateri*

IDENTIFICATION. This bird resembles the Sulphur-crested Cockatoo in general appearance, but is noticeably smaller, with pronounced (but delicate) pink wash on face, neck, breast and underwing; it has a striking white, deep pink and yellow crest.

DISTRIBUTION. From north-western Australia through central Australia to south-western Queensland, western New South Wales, western Victoria, and the inland parts of South Australia.

NOTES. This cockatoo is seen in pairs or small flocks, frequenting thickly timbered scrub (mallee chiefly) and semi-arid lands. It feeds on bulbous roots and seeds of shrubs and grasses. When disturbed, it rises with a loud screech, sometimes alighting on a dead tree but usually on the ground again. The bright colouring of the under-wings and the crest render the bird very beautiful when agitated or in flight.

BREEDING. Nest: in a hole in a tree. Clutch: three to four; white. Breeding season: September to December.

20:13 PALM COCKATOO *Probosciger aterrimus*

IDENTIFICATION. This very large cockatoo is black with a naked red face and huge shaggy crest. Sexes are similar. (Cape York only.)

DISTRIBUTION. Cape York Peninsula, south to the Rocky River. The species also inhabits New Guinea and the Aru Islands.

NOTES. It is seen in pairs or small flocks, frequenting jungle and open forests. It breeds in forest country and feeds in jungle on the kernels of large fruits and on grubs torn out of rotten wood by its large bill. Calls include a short, harsh screech and a low, short whistle, 'hweet–hweet', but many other notes are uttered.

BREEDING. Nest: in a high tree cavity, lined with masses of splintered twigs. Clutch: one; white. Breeding season: August to January.

20:14 GLOSSY BLACK COCKATOO *Calyptorhynchus lathami*

IDENTIFICATION. The male is dusky black (not especially glossy), with large bright red panels in the tail; the female has a brown head with variable patches of yellow, and tail panels yellow or yellow-orange, speckled black.

DISTRIBUTION. South-eastern Australia from central-eastern Queensland to Victoria; also on Kangaroo Island.

NOTES. This cockatoo is generally uncommon and mainly sedentary. Seen in pairs or small flocks, it frequents heavily timbered mountain ranges and open forests. It feeds almost exclusively on the seeds of casuarinas. When feeding it is easy to approach, and when alarmed it moves with a distinctive, buoyant flight to an adjacent tree. The chief call-notes are prolonged squeaky grating 'caws'.

BREEDING. Nest: on chips of wood in a high tree cavity. Clutch: one; dull white. Breeding season: March to August.

20:15 YELLOW-TAILED BLACK COCKATOO *Calyptorhynchus funereus*

IDENTIFICATION. This is a very large, stately, black cockatoo with a yellow ear patch and large yellow panels in the tail. A population in south-western Australia (subspecies *latirostris*) has yellow replaced with white, and is extremely difficult to distinguish from the Long- billed Black Cockatoo.

DISTRIBUTION. From central Queensland to Victoria and southern South Australia; extending west to southern Eyre Peninsula; also found on King Island and Kangaroo Island, and in Tasmania.

NOTES. The species occurs in pairs or flocks, frequenting heavily timbered mountain ranges and adjacent open forest, and banksia scrubs during the winter months. It has a slow and laboured flight, and on the wing it usually utters loud wailing cries, 'kee–ah, kee–ah'. The food consists mostly of banksia, casuarina and hakea seeds, also large white grubs found in eucalypts and pines; to reach these insects it tears the bark and wood with its powerful bill, often making holes of considerable depth in a branch or tree trunk. It also visits plantations of introduced pines.

BREEDING. Nest: in a high tree cavity. Clutch: usually two; white. Breeding season: March to July in the north, usually later in the south.

20:16 LONG-BILLED BLACK COCKATOO *Calyptorhynchus baudinii*

IDENTIFICATION. This is a very large, stately cockatoo with a white ear patch and large white panels in the tail. Confusingly, it has recently been shown that there are two distinct populations of 'white-tailed' cockatoos in south-western Australia which do not interbreed. One of these populations (*latirostris*) is regarded as a subspecies of the eastern Yellow-tailed Black Cockatoo; the other (*baudinii*) appears to be a distinct species. Both forms share the white patches in the tail, and they are extremely difficult to tell apart. The Long-billed Black Cockatoo is slightly smaller and longer-billed than the other form, is somewhat browner in plumage, and is largely restricted to marri and karri forests.

DISTRIBUTION. South-western Australia, north to the Murchison River and east to Esperance.

NOTES. Large, noisy and conspicuous, this cockatoo is found in pairs or flocks frequenting heavily timbered lands and feeding largely on marri and karri nuts, wood-boring grubs and fruit. The chief call is 'wee–loo', which subsides to a murmuring chatter when a flock settles in a tree.

BREEDING. Nest: in a high tree cavity. Clutch: two; white. Breeding season: August to October.

20:17 GANG-GANG COCKATOO *Callocephalon fimbriatum*

IDENTIFICATION. This rather small, scaly grey cockatoo has a unique 'feather-duster' crest. The head and crest are bright red in males and grey in females and immatures.

DISTRIBUTION. Eastern Australia, from near Muswellbrook, New South Wales, south to Victoria and King Island, Bass Strait; it was introduced to Kangaroo Island, South Australia.

NOTES. The bird occurs in pairs or small flocks, frequenting chiefly heavily timbered mountain ranges; although it is also common in dense coastal forests in Victoria. It procures most of its food in trees, feeding on the seeds of eucalypts as well as various species of acacia. It is confiding and oblivious when feeding, and will often permit an observer to approach almost within touching distance. It has a peculiar wheezy call-note, and utters a curious growling sound when feeding.

BREEDING. Nest: in a hole in a tree; usually at a considerable height. Clutch: usually two; white. Breeding season: October to January.

20:18 RED-TAILED BLACK COCKATOO *Calyptorhynchus magnificus*

IDENTIFICATION. The male superficially resembles the Glossy Black Cockatoo (often confused by unwary observers), but is much larger, its plumage is a richer blue-black with a striking 'Roman helmet' crest, and it has a very different habitat and behaviour (it feeds often on open ground, for example, which the Glossy Black Cockatoo almost never does). The female has orange-yellow tail panels, freckled black; the head is black, minutely speckled (not blotched) yellow.

DISTRIBUTION. Australia generally, but absent from the south-east, most of South Australia, and eastern Western Australia.

NOTES. The species is seen in pairs or flocks (sometimes very large), frequenting alike heavily timbered and open forest (especially along rivers and creeks), and also banksia scrubs. Its food consists of eucalypt, casuarina, and banksia seeds, and also large white grubs. The bird is noisy, wary and conspicuous. It is arboreal in heavily forested areas, but feeds much on the ground in more arid environments.

BREEDING. Nest: in a hole in a tree; usually high. Clutch: one to two; white. Breeding season: April to August.

PLATE 21

PARROTS OF OPEN FOREST AND SCRUBLANDS

21:1 HOODED PARROT *Psephotus dissimilis*

IDENTIFICATION. This is a graceful parrot with a long slender tail. The male is mainly turquoise blue below and dark brown above, with a black cap and forehead, and a bright yellow wing patch; the female is mainly dull olive, with a pale bluish face and belly and dull salmon undertail coverts.

DISTRIBUTION. Top End of the Northern Territory.

NOTES. This species is usually seen in pairs or small flocks, inhabiting open forests and spinifex country. It feeds mainly on grass seeds. Their flight is swift and slightly undulating. It is similar in habits to the Golden-shouldered Parrot with which it is often considered conspecific.

BREEDING. Nest: in a termite mound on the ground, usually the large magnetic and spire-shaped termitaria. Clutch: four to six; white. Breeding season: probably May to January.

21:2 GOLDEN-SHOULDERED PARROT *Psephotus chrysopterygius*

IDENTIFICATION. The male is mainly blue below, pale brown above, with black crown and yellow forehead. The female is similar to the female Hooded Parrot, but has mainly pale blue undertail coverts (dull salmon in female Hooded Parrot).

DISTRIBUTION. Cape York Peninsula, from about the Flinders River (south) north to the Watson and Rocky River areas.

NOTES. This parrot is usually seen in pairs or small flocks, inhabiting the open forest country dotted with large mounds of termites. It has a soft and pleasing whistle. Now rare and much restricted in range, it is vulnerable and perhaps endangered. Food: seeds of grasses and herbaceous plants.

BREEDING. Nest: in a termite mound. Clutch: four to six; white. Breeding season: mainly April to June.

21:3 PARADISE PARROT *Psephotus pulcherrimus*

IDENTIFICATION. Almost certainly extinct, this parrot somewhat resembles Golden-shouldered Parrot, but has a bright red forehead, wing patch and belly. The sexes are similar, but females are very much duller than males.

DISTRIBUTION. Queensland and extreme north-central and (occasionally) north-eastern New South Wales.

NOTES. Although moderately common when first found (1844) and for some decades afterwards, this very beautiful bird declined abruptly in numbers — probably during the first two decades of the twentieth century. Its decline has been attributed to a combination of severe drought and overgrazing. Despite persistent rumours, there have been no verifiable reports since 1927, and the species must now be considered extinct or very close to extinction. It is recorded as frequenting sparsely timbered grasslands, usually in pairs. It feeds (or fed) mainly on the ground, but occasionally in trees. Its chief call, 'queek', and other notes are more musical than those of most parrots. Food: seeds of grasses and herbaceous plants.

BREEDING. Nest: a chamber in a termite mound on the ground. Clutch: three to five; white. Breeding season: usually August to December.

21:4 RED-RUMPED PARROT *Psephotus haematonotus*

IDENTIFICATION. The male is mainly bright green, with a bright yellow belly and a patch of red on its lower back; females and immatures are very plain, mainly khaki.

DISTRIBUTION. Southern Queensland to Victoria (occasionally near the coast) and southern and north-eastern South Australia.

NOTES. A common bird, it is seen in pairs or flocks, frequenting sparsely timbered grasslands, including roadsides and suburban golf courses and playing fields. It is more often seen on the ground than in trees. The call-note is a pleasing whistle, almost a song, which is uttered while the bird is perched in a tree or when in flight. Food: seeds of grasses and other plants.

BREEDING. Nest: in a hole in a tree. Clutch: four to seven; white. Breeding season: September to December.

21:5 MULGA PARROT *Psephotus varius*

IDENTIFICATION. The male is mainly bright green, with a golden forehead and a small patch of red on its hind crown and on its rump. Its lower belly and undertail coverts are red and yellow, and it has a bright yellow patch at the bend of the wing. The female is somewhat similar but very much duller and browner.

DISTRIBUTION. Central Australia, south-western Queensland to north-western Victoria and the inland areas of South Australia and Western Australia.

NOTES. This parrot is usually seen in pairs or small parties, frequenting scrublands and open forests. Common and confiding, but generally quiet and unobtrusive, it spends much time on the ground in search of seeds of grasses and herbaceous plants. The call is a slight chattering, or whistle, often repeated.

BREEDING. Nest: in a hole in a tree. Clutch: four to six; white. Breeding season: July to December.

21:6 BLUEBONNET *Psephotus haematogaster*

IDENTIFICATION. This bird is mainly brownish-grey, with a blue face and a yellow or tawny patch at the bend of the wing. Its belly is red and yellow, and it has much deeper blue in its outer wings. Sexes are similar.

DISTRIBUTION. Western New South Wales, north-western Victoria, and eastern South Australia. A distinctive population (sometimes considered a separate species), *P. h. narethae* (Naretha Parrot or Little Bluebonnet), inhabits the western fringes of the Nullarbor Plain.

NOTES. Found in pairs or small flocks, this bird inhabits timber bordering watercourses. It also frequents mallee, mulga and callitris scrubs. The harsh, abrupt 'cluck–cluck' notes, given especially in flight when disturbed, are difficult to confuse with those of any other parrot. Food: seeds of grasses and herbaceous plants.

BREEDING. Nest: in a hole in a tree. Clutch: three to seven; white. Breeding season: August to December.

21:7 COCKATIEL *Nymphicus hollandicus*

IDENTIFICATION. Unmistakable, this small grey parrot with a long slender tail, long pointed crest, and conspicuous white wing patch has a dull orange patch on its cheek. The face and crest are pale yellow in males, greyish in females.

DISTRIBUTION. Inland parts of Australia generally where suitable habitats exist, rarely extending to coastal areas.

NOTES. Usually in pairs or flocks, this bird inhabits timber bordering watercourses and open country dotted with scrub. It is migratory in the southern parts of its range and nomadic elsewhere. The species utters a pleasant, chattering note. Though superficially resembling a parrot, it has been shown that this species is actually an aberrant cockatoo. Food: seeds of grasses and herbaceous plants.

BREEDING. Nest: in a hole in a tree or stump. Clutch: four to seven; white. Breeding season: August to December.

21:8 EASTERN ROSELLA *Platycercus eximius*

IDENTIFICATION. This bird has a red head and breast, white cheeks, and yellow belly. Sexes are similar. (This bird, the Northern Rosella and the Pale-headed Rosella, together are now usually regarded as forms of a single species, the White-cheeked Rosella, *Platycercus eximius*; the three forms are, however, so different in appearance that they are allowed to stand here as species, purely for convenience of presentation.)

DISTRIBUTION. From south-eastern Queensland to Victoria and south-eastern South Australia (west to Adelaide); and Tasmania.

NOTES. Usually found in pairs or flocks, inhabiting open forest country and partly cleared lands, it feeds in trees but spends much time on the ground in search of seeds of grasses, which, with wild fruits and berries, constitute its normal food. In some areas it is destructive in orchards and cultivated paddocks. The call is a pleasant whistling note. This is the commonest and best known of all the broad-tailed group of parrots; it has been freely kept in captivity since its first discovery near Rosehill (Parramatta) in the early days of settlement; the name Rosella (originally Rosehiller) is derived from Rosehill.

BREEDING. Nest: in a hole in a tree, stump, or fence post; rarely in a rabbit burrow. Clutch: four to nine; white. Breeding season: September to January.

21:9 NORTHERN ROSELLA *Platycercus venustus*

IDENTIFICATION. This bird has a black head, white cheeks and pale dingy yellow underparts. Sexes are similar.

DISTRIBUTION. Tropical northern Australia from the Kimberley east to the Queensland border.

NOTES. Found in pairs or small flocks, inhabiting open forest, sometimes mangroves. Generally uncommon, it is local in distribution, and seldom seen in large flocks. It frequently utters a rapid succession of double notes resembling 'trin–se, trin–se'. Food: seeds of grasses and herbaceous plants, also native fruits.

BREEDING. Nest: in a hole in a tree. Clutch: two to three; white. Breeding season: August to October.

21:10 PALE-HEADED ROSELLA *Platycercus adscitus*

IDENTIFICATION. This parrot has a pale yellow head, white cheeks (pure white in southern birds, strongly tinged blue in birds inhabiting Cape York Peninsula), light blue breast and belly. Sexes are similar.

DISTRIBUTION. North-eastern and eastern Queensland and north-eastern New South Wales.

NOTES. Usually found in pairs or small flocks, inhabiting open forests, savannah woodland, and coastal heathland, the birds show considerable variation in plumage. It interbreeds with the Eastern Rosella in northern New South Wales. Also closely related to the Northern Rosella, all three may prove to be conspecific.

BREEDING. Nest: in a hole in a tree or stump; sometimes well below the opening. Clutch: three to six; white. Breeding season: mainly September to December.

21:11 CRIMSON ROSELLA *Platycercus elegans*

IDENTIFICATION. This rosella is mainly bright red, with blue cheeks, wings and tail. Sexes are similar, but immatures are mainly dull green (but with blue cheeks, wings and tail), irregularly daubed with red. (This form, the Yellow Rosella, Green Rosella and Adelaide Rosella are all very closely related, and are now usually regarded as comprising a single species, the Blue-cheeked Rosella, *Platycercus elegans*. However, as in the case of the Eastern Rosella (above), they differ so strongly in appearance that it seems useful to allow them to stand here as species, purely for convenience of presentation.)

DISTRIBUTION. Eastern Australia from the Atherton Tableland, Queensland south to Victoria and extreme south-eastern South Australia. This species was introduced to Norfolk Island and New Zealand.

NOTES. A common and familiar species, it often comes around picnic tables in parks. In pairs or flocks, it frequents mainly heavily timbered ranges and rainforests, but also occurs in more open forests and partly cleared lands. It feeds on the ground upon the seeds of grasses and other plants, and on blossom, fruit, and berry-bearing trees. It is occasionally destructive in orchards, but it also often eats scale insects. Its chief call is somewhat shrill but it has many musical notes which are favourite borrowings of Lyrebirds.

BREEDING. Nest: in a hole in a tree. Clutch: five to eight; white. Breeding season: October to January.

21:12 YELLOW ROSELLA *Platycercus flaveolus*

IDENTIFICATION. This rosella is similar to Crimson Rosella, but its body plumage is bright straw yellow, not red, and it has a narrow red band across its forehead. Sexes are similar.

DISTRIBUTION. The valleys of the Lachlan, Murrumbidgee, and lower Darling Rivers in southern New South Wales, Victoria, and eastern South Australia.

NOTES. In pairs or small flocks, it inhabits chiefly timber bordering watercourses and the adjoining open country. It is usually seen on the ground in search of seeds of grasses and other plants. When disturbed, it flies to the nearest timber, uttering its whistling call while on the wing.

BREEDING. Nest: in a hole in a tree. Clutch: four to five; white. Breeding season: September to December or January.

21:13 GREEN ROSELLA *Platycercus caledonicus*

IDENTIFICATION. This bird is dull yellow-green, with blue cheeks, wings and tail, and a narrow red band across its forehead. Sexes are similar.

DISTRIBUTION. Tasmania and islands of Bass Strait.

NOTES. Generally common, it is found in pairs or flocks, inhabiting partly cleared areas as well as heavily timbered country, and sometimes orchards. It is usually seen either feeding among blossoms of eucalypts or searching on the ground for seeds of grasses and other plants. In certain districts it approaches homesteads and raids cultivated fruits. The chief call has been rendered as 'kussick, kussick'.

BREEDING. Nest: in a hole in a tree. Clutch: four to five; white. Breeding season: November to February.

21:14 ADELAIDE ROSELLA *Platycercus adelaidae*

IDENTIFICATION. Though like the Crimson Rosella, the Adelaide Rosella has body plumage which is mainly rich orange, irregularly daubed yellow. Sexes are similar.

DISTRIBUTION. South Australia (Mount Lofty and Flinders Ranges).

NOTES. In pairs or flocks, it inhabits timbered country. It is similar in habits to the Crimson Rosella.

BREEDING. Nest: in a hole in a tree. Clutch: five to seven; white. Breeding season: September to December.

21:15 WESTERN ROSELLA *Platycercus icterotis*

IDENTIFICATION. A small rosella, the male has red head and underparts, with a yellow cheek patch. The female is very much duller, with a mainly dull green crown, nape and breast.

DISTRIBUTION. South of Western Australia, north to Moora and east to Dundas.

NOTES. Fairly common, it occurs in pairs or small flocks, inhabiting open forests and cleared country. It is also seen about homesteads and gardens. Calls include a rather soft 'tink, tink'. Food: seeds of grasses and other plants, also wild fruits and berries and sometimes cultivated fruits.

BREEDING. Nest: in a hole in a tree. Clutch: three to seven; white. Breeding season: August to November.

21:16 RINGNECK PARROT *Barnardius zonarius*

IDENTIFICATION. Common and widespread, this parrot is mainly green, with a prominent bright yellow band across the nape. Sexes are similar. It occurs in four rather different populations, now widely regarded as subspecies of a single variable species: interior and western forms are somewhat darker than eastern birds, with black heads; the far south-western form (subspecies *semitorquatus*, the 'Twenty-eight Parrot') has a black head with a narrow red band on the forehead and a green belly; birds of the western interior (subspecies *zonarius*, the 'Port Lincoln Ringneck') have plain black heads and yellow bellies; eastern birds (subspecies *barnardi*, the 'Mallee Ringneck') have green heads, with a narrow red band across the forehead; and birds of the north-eastern interior (subspecies *macgillivrayi*, the 'Cloncurry Parrot') are much paler than the others, with plain bluish-green heads.

DISTRIBUTION. Australia generally, mainly interior and west, avoiding tropical far north and humid east coast.

NOTES. This bird is usually found in pairs or small flocks, inhabiting scrub, open forest, and timber bordering watercourses. It is especially common in mallee. It is usually seen on the ground searching for the seeds of grasses and other plants. It also feeds on flower buds of eucalypts and when thus engaged it maintains a continuous chatter.

BREEDING. Nest: in a hole in a tree. Clutch: four to six; white. Breeding season: July to December.

21:17 RED-CAPPED PARROT *Purpureicephalus spurius*

IDENTIFICATION. This bird has a deep purple breast, red crown and undertail coverts, yellow rump and cheeks. Sexes are similar.

DISTRIBUTION. South-western Australia, north to the Moore River and east to Esperance.

NOTES. Common, but rather secretive, this bird is mainly sedentary. Found in pairs or small flocks, it inhabits forest and scrublands. It feeds on the seeds of eucalypts (especially the marri *Eucalytus calophylla*) and of grasses and other small plants. At times it is destructive to cultivated crops of various kinds and therefore is frequently shot. The chief call is a peculiar grating note, 'krurr–rak', repeated several times.

BREEDING. Nest: in a hole in a tree. Clutch: five to six; white. Breeding season: August to November.

PLATE 22

PARROTS OF TREETOPS AND OPEN SPACES

22:1 BLUE-WINGED PARROT *Neophema chrysostoma*

IDENTIFICATION. This parrot is mainly olive green, with deep blue wings, yellow belly and face. It has a narrow blue band across its forehead which extends backwards to the eye, but not over it. Sexes are similar, but females are much duller than males.

DISTRIBUTION. Tasmania, King Island, Victoria, southern South Australia, western New South Wales, south-western Queensland.

NOTES. Found in pairs or small flocks, it frequents grasslands and sparsely timbered country, both on coastal sandhills and inland areas. Mainly migratory in Tasmania and other more southern parts of the range, although small numbers remain through the winter months. When disturbed, the birds usually rise simultaneously, uttering feeble call-notes, but soon settle again, either on the ground or in a tree. Food: seeds of grasses and herbaceous plants.

BREEDING. Nest: in a hole in a tree or stump. Clutch: five to seven; white. Breeding season: October to January.

22:2 ORANGE-BELLIED PARROT *Neophema chrysogaster*

IDENTIFICATION. This bird is difficult to distinguish from the Elegant Parrot but its upperparts are grass-green rather than olive-green; the adult has an orange patch on its belly. Sexes are similar.

DISTRIBUTION. Tasmania, southern Victoria, and coastal south-eastern South Australia.

NOTES. Usually found in pairs or small flocks, it frequents mainly coastal habitats, including sand dunes, samphire flats, scrubland, paddocks and farmland. Apparently confined as a breeding species to south-western Tasmania, it migrates to southern Victoria (especially around Port Phillip Bay) and the Coorong, South Australia, to spend the winter months. Now very rare and probably seriously endangered, it is similar in general habits to the Blue-winged Parrot.

BREEDING. Nest: in a hole in a tree or stump. Clutch: four to five; white. Breeding season: November to January.

22:3 ELEGANT PARROT *Neophema elegans*

IDENTIFICATION. This bird is difficult to distinguish from Blue-winged Parrot, but its upperparts are yellow-green rather than olive green; its blue wing patch is much less extensive; and its narrow blue frontal band extends backwards over the eye. Sexes are similar.

DISTRIBUTION. Extreme south-western New South Wales, western Victoria, South Australia (north through the Flinders Ranges); widespread in south-western Australia, north to about the Fortescue River and east to Esperance.

NOTES. Usually found in scattered flocks upon grasslands, often on plains away from trees, on barren sandy belts bordering the coast, and on sparsely timbered areas. It is apparently spreading and increasing in numbers in Western Australia. When flocks are flushed they often rise, sharply, to a considerable height. Similar in habits to the Blue-winged Parrot, and the two species occasionally occur in mixed flocks. Food: seeds of grasses and plants.

BREEDING. Nest: in a hole in a tree. Clutch: four to six; white. Breeding season: August to October.

22:4 ROCK PARROT *Neophema petrophila*

IDENTIFICATION. This parrot resembles Elegant Parrot, but is very much duller being olive brown above, dingy yellow below, with a bluish face. Note habitat and range. Sexes are similar.

DISTRIBUTION. Coast and islands of south-western and southern Australia, from Shark Bay to south-eastern South Australia.

NOTES. Occurring in pairs or small flocks, it frequents islands off the coast and swampy parts of coastal areas, seldom occurring more than a few hundred metres from the sea. Its flight is swift and erratic; at times it mounts to a considerable height. It appears to select the most exposed and bleak situations in which to breed. The calls usually uttered in flight are a series suggesting 'zit–zeet'. Food: seeds of grasses and herbaceous plants, especially seeds of a species of pigface.

BREEDING. Nest: in a hole in a cliff or in a cavity under a rock. Clutch: four to five; white. Breeding season: September to December.

22:5 TURQUOISE PARROT *Neophema pulchella*

IDENTIFICATION. This bird is bright green above, yellow below, with an extensively blue face; males have a bright chestnut patch on the shoulder.

DISTRIBUTION. From about Maryborough, Queensland, south through eastern New South Wales to the Victorian border.

NOTES. Found in pairs or small flocks, it frequents rough grasslands bordering open forest, especially along ridges, mountain slopes or creeks. It feeds on the ground and when flushed flies swiftly to the nearest timber, uttering a feeble call-note. This pretty bird was once common, but suffered a marked decline around the turn of the century and was widely regarded as in danger of extinction. The past few decades have however seen a marked increase in numbers. The female resembles the female Scarlet-chested Parrot. Food: seeds.

BREEDING. Nest: in a hole in a tree; occasionally a stump. Clutch: four to five; white. Breeding season: usually August to December.

22:6 SCARLET-CHESTED PARROT *Neophema splendida*

IDENTIFICATION. This parrot resembles Turquoise Parrot. The males have a bright scarlet breast; deep blue forehead, face and throat, but no red on wing. The female is very difficult to distinguish from the female Turquoise Parrot, but has blue (not dull whitish) lores and light blue (not deep blue) wing patch.

DISTRIBUTION. Western New South Wales, through northern South Australia to the coastal areas of the Great Australian Bight, and inland in scattered colonies in Western Australia.

NOTES. A rare species, it frequents dry inland areas interspersed with patches of low scrub, often far from water. It is nomadic and apparently subject to marked fluctuations in numbers. During the present century it has frequently been bred in aviaries. Food: seeds of grasses and herbaceous plants.

BREEDING. Nest: in a hole in a tree. Clutch: three to five; white. Breeding season: August to December.

22:7 BOURKE'S PARROT *Neophema bourkii*

IDENTIFICATION. Unmistakable, this parrot is pastel brown, blue and pink. Sexes are similar.

DISTRIBUTION. From south-western Queensland and far western New South Wales through central Australia and extreme northern South Australia to some inland parts of Western Australia.

NOTES. Found in pairs or small flocks, it frequents acacia and mulga scrubs in the arid interior. It spends much time on the ground searching for the seeds of grasses, herbaceous plants, and acacia trees. It is generally quiet and inconspicuous in behaviour. Being crepuscular, and to some extent nocturnal, it makes a practice of visiting watering places after dark or before dawn.

BREEDING. Nest: in a hole in a tree. Clutch: four to five; white. Breeding season: August to October.

22:8 DOUBLE-EYED FIGPARROT *Psittaculirostris diophthalma*

IDENTIFICATION. This bird is small and tubby with a large head and very short tail. Its plumage is mainly green, with patches of red and blue on the head.

DISTRIBUTION. Eastern Australia, in three separate populations: *P. d. marshalli* of Cape York Peninsula, south to about Massey Creek, Queensland; *P. d. macleayana* of north-eastern Queensland from near Cooktown to about Cardwell; and *P. d. coxeni* of south-eastern Queensland and north-eastern New South Wales, from about Gympie south perhaps as far as Kempsey. This species is also found in New Guinea.

NOTES. Usually found in small flocks, it inhabits rainforests. It frequents tall fruit-bearing trees, chiefly the various species of native figs. It is exceptionally quiet and difficult to observe except when travelling between feeding trees. Common in the north, but the southern population (*P. d. coxeni*) is very seldom reported and may be close to extinction.

BREEDING. Nest: in a hole in a tree. Clutch: two; white. Breeding season: mainly September to December.

22:9 LITTLE LORIKEET *Glossopsitta pusilla*

IDENTIFICATION. Mainly green, this bird is rather similar to Musk Lorikeet, but smaller. It has a black bill, red chin and green cheek. Sexes are similar.

DISTRIBUTION. Eastern Australia, from near Cairns, Queensland, south to Victoria and (possibly) Tasmania, and west to extreme south-eastern South Australia.

NOTES. Found in flocks, it mostly frequents flowering eucalypts and other blossom or fruit-bearing trees. It is remarkably fearless when feeding and generally noisy both while feeding and in flight. Its flight is swift, and flocks of the birds travel long distances in search of flowering trees. The chief call is 'gizz, gizz'. Food: nectar, pollen, native and cultivated fruits and grain.

BREEDING. Nest: in a hole in a tree; usually at a considerable height. Clutch: four; white. Breeding season: June to December.

22:10 PURPLE-CROWNED LORIKEET *Glossopsitta porphyrocephala*

IDENTIFICATION. This bird is mainly green, but distinctly bluish on throat and breast. It has an orange band across the forehead, dark blue crown, and orange ear coverts. Sexes are similar.

DISTRIBUTION. Victoria and occasionally the adjacent parts of New South Wales, southern South Australia and Kangaroo Island; also southern and south-western areas in Western Australia.

NOTES. Generally common, especially in dry mallee scrubs, it is found in flocks, frequenting flowering eucalypts and other blossom or fruit-bearing trees. It is similar in habits to the Little Lorikeet, and, like that species, is nomadic, its movements being regulated by the flowering of eucalypts. Its flight is swift and it utters its screeching notes when on the wing, also frequently while feeding. Food: nectar, pollen, native and cultivated fruits and berries.

BREEDING. Nest: in a hole in a tree. Clutch: four; white. Breeding season: September to November.

22:11 MUSK LORIKEET *Glossopsitta concinna*

IDENTIFICATION. Mainly green, this bird somewhat resembles Little Lorikeet, but it has red ear coverts (not green), a green chin (not red) and a black bill, tipped red. Sexes are similar.

DISTRIBUTION. Eastern Australia, from about Rockhampton, Queensland, south to Tasmania and west to about Adelaide, South Australia.

NOTES. Usually found in flocks, it frequents flowering eucalypts and other blossom or fruit-bearing trees. It is nomadic in habits, and is often found in the company of other lorikeets. It at times does considerable damage in orchards. The screeching call is stronger than those of its smaller relatives. Food: nectar, native and cultivated fruits and berries.

BREEDING. Nest: in a hole in a tree; usually high. Clutch: two; white. Breeding season: August to December.

22:12 VARIED LORIKEET *Psitteuteles versicolor*

IDENTIFICATION. A small tropical lorikeet, this parrot is mainly greenish, obscurely streaked, with conspicuous white eye-ring and red cap. Sexes are similar.

DISTRIBUTION. Tropical northern Australia from the Kimberley east to about Townsville, Queensland (although decidedly rare and erratic in the north-east).

NOTES. This bird frequents flowering eucalypts and tea-trees in tropical lowlands. It is usually found in small parties, although large numbers congregate where blossom is abundant. Highly nomadic in habits, it utters a shrill screech in flight, and a constant high-pitched chatter while feeding. Food: nectar and pollen.

BREEDING. Nest: in a hollow in a tree. Clutch: two to four; white. Breeding season: recorded throughout the year, but mainly April to August.

22:13 SCALY-BREASTED LORIKEET *Trichoglossus chlorolepidotus*

IDENTIFICATION. This bird is plain green, variably scaled yellow below, with a pink bill. Sexes are similar.

DISTRIBUTION. Eastern Australia, from near Cooktown, Queensland south to about Wollongong, New South Wales.

NOTES. Usually found in flocks, it inhabits open forests and cultivated fields. It is nomadic, and often occurs in mixed flocks with the 'Bluey' — Rainbow Lorikeet. Food: nectar, pollen, flowers and fruits. Like the Rainbow Lorikeet, it will come to feeding stations for sweet mash.

BREEDING. Nest: in a hole in a tree. Clutch: two; white. Breeding season: May or June to January.

22:14 RAINBOW LORIKEET *Trichoglossus haematodus*

IDENTIFICATION. Gaudy, this parrot is unmistakable. It has a green back, blue head and orange breast. Populations west of the Gulf of Carpentaria (subspecies *rubritorquis*) have a band of bright orange across the nape.

DISTRIBUTION. Northern and eastern Australia from the Kimberley through the Top End to Cape York, and along the east coast, south to Tasmania and west to Kangaroo Island and Eyre Peninsula, South Australia; introduced around Perth, Western Australia. This species is also found in Indonesia, New Guinea, the Solomon Islands, Vanuatu and New Caledonia.

NOTES. Found in flocks, it frequents flowering eucalypts, often in the company of the Scaly-breasted Lorikeet. It gathers in flocks to roost, from which point flocks may travel considerable distances seeking blossom-laden trees. Calls include high-pitched chattering notes and a sharp shrill screech when on the wing. This beautiful bird sometimes causes damage in orchards. In some areas flocks visit houses and can be hand-fed. Food: nectar, pollen, flowers, and native and cultivated fruits and grain.

BREEDING. Nest: in a hole in a tree. Clutch: two; white. Breeding season: usually September to January.

22:15 BUDGERIGAR *Melopsittacus undulatus*

IDENTIFICATION. Unmistakable.

DISTRIBUTION. Inland areas of Australia generally, extending irregularly to many coastal localities.

NOTES. Usually found in flocks, this bird inhabits open country, chiefly areas interspersed with belts of timber, or isolated patches of scrub. It is highly nomadic, but in southern areas is more regularly migratory, appearing in late winter or early spring and departing during February or March. When disturbed from the ground the flocks settle in trees, thereby often causing dead branches to appear to be blossoming. While feeding, or when perched in a tree, the birds are constantly warbling and chattering in a most amiable manner. The species suffers heavily in times of drought, dying in thousands near drying waterholes. Budgerigars have been bred into many colour varieties in aviaries. Food: seeds.

BREEDING. Nest: in a hole in a tree. Clutch: four to eight; white. Breeding season: usually October to December.

22:16 GROUND PARROT *Pezoporus wallicus*

IDENTIFICATION. Mainly green, this parrot is intricately marked yellow and black, with a narrow red band across the forehead. Sexes are similar.

DISTRIBUTION. Coastal areas of southern Queensland, New South Wales, Victoria, south-eastern South Australia, south-western Australia; also Tasmania.

NOTES. This shy and uncommon parrot inhabits swampy heathlands. Largely nocturnal or crepuscular, it is very difficult to observe, and rarely seen until flushed. When disturbed it flies rapidly, in swallow-like fashion, above the swampy grass or (in Tasmania) button grass plains, and then suddenly hurls itself down into cover again. The call is a thin clear high-pitched 'tee, tee, stit', uttered especially at dawn and dusk. Food: seeds of grasses and herbaceous plants.

BREEDING. Nest: a substantial platform of grass and rootlets on the ground in the shelter of a tussock. Clutch: four to five; white. Breeding season: August to December.

22:17 NIGHT PARROT *Geopsittacus occidentalis*

IDENTIFICATION. Stocky and rather short-tailed, this parrot is mainly green, intricately marked yellow and black, with no red on the forehead. Sexes are similar.

DISTRIBUTION. Restricted and scattered localities in central Australia, northern South Australia, and inland Western Australia; probably also western Queensland and western New South Wales.

NOTES. This extremely rare and little-known species inhabits sandstone ranges, spinifex country, and shrubby samphire flats. It is nocturnal, seeking cover in tussocks of spinifex during the day and emerging at dusk to drink and to feed on the seeds of grasses. Only rarely has the bird been kept in captivity; one was studied in the London Zoo for two months in 1867-68; this specimen was obtained in the Gawler Range, South Australia, and was sent to England by Dr F. von Mueller. Calls have been described as a 'low, disyllabic whistle' and 'a double note, loud and harsh'. The last specimen taken was in 1912, and the few subsequent reports were so vague and unsatisfactory that it was suspected that the species might be extinct until several were seen in extreme north-eastern South Australia in 1979 on an expedition specifically mounted in search of them.

BREEDING. Nest: a depression in the ground, usually under spinifex-grass. Clutch: four to five; white. Breeding season: not recorded.

22:18 SWIFT PARROT *Lathamus discolor*

IDENTIFICATION. Mainly green, with small patches of red and bright blue on face and shoulders, and a dark maroon-red tail, it much resembles a lorikeet in general appearance and behaviour.

DISTRIBUTION. This species breeds in Tasmania and winters mainly in Victoria, but has been recorded north to about Bowen, Queensland, and west to about Adelaide, South Australia.

NOTES. Usually gathering in small parties, occasionally large flocks, it frequents flowering eucalypts and other nectar-bearing trees, and is therefore nomadic in habits. Its flight is remarkably rapid and is accompanied by a torrent of high-pitched notes — 'clink–clink, clink–clink'. Food: nectar, scale insects, and caterpillars.

BREEDING. Nest: in a hole in a tree. Clutch: two; white. Breeding season: November to January.

PLATE 23

SOME BIRDS OF MANGROVES

23:1 LARGE-BILLED WARBLER *Gerygone magnirostris*

IDENTIFICATION. This is a rather dark, nondescript warbler with narrow white eye-ring but no white in front of the eye. Sexes are similar.

DISTRIBUTION. Coastal Northern Territory and northern Queensland south to about Mackay. This species is also found in New Guinea.

NOTES. Usually seen singly or in pairs, it inhabits lowland rainforests, mangroves, swampy woodlands, and vegetation bordering streams, where it searches leaves and blossoms for small insects. It has an agreeable twittering song.

BREEDING. Nest: dome-shaped, with a hooded entrance at the side; constructed of fine bark and fibre, and in general (especially because it usually overhangs water) suggesting debris left by a flood. Clutch: two to three; white, with reddish-brown markings. Breeding season: September to April.

23:2 GREEN-BACKED WARBLER *Gerygone chloronota*

IDENTIFICATION. The throat and underparts are dingy white, the rest of the head is grey, without white markings; and the upperparts are greenish. Sexes are similar.

DISTRIBUTION. Coastal tropical Australia from the Kimberley east to Groote Eylandt. This species is also found in New Guinea.

NOTES. It inhabits mangroves, bamboo thickets, paperbark swamps, and dense vegetation near water. It is rather shy and difficult to locate among the leaves of the trees as it moves about in search of the small insects upon which it subsists. Its voice is slight but cheerful.

BREEDING. Nest: domed, with a side entrance. It is constructed of grass and fine rootlets and suspended from a twig of a mangrove tree. Clutch: two to three; white, with reddish-brown dots. Breeding season: October (probably) to December.

23:3 DUSKY WARBLER *Gerygone tenebrosa*

IDENTIFICATION. This species is rather like Western Warbler, but paler and greyer, with a white (not red) eye, and no white in the tail. Sexes are similar.

DISTRIBUTION. Coastal mid- and north-western Australia, from Carnarvon, Western Australia, to Port Keats, Northern Territory.

NOTES. It inhabits mangroves. Mostly seen singly or in pairs, it is apparently sedentary. It is little known and difficult to observe. It has a plaintive little song, also a deliberate 'chew chew chew wee'.

BREEDING. Nest: domed, rather compact, with a side entrance and a short 'tail', made of shreds of bark and bound with cobweb; suspended in a mangrove several metres from the ground. Clutch: two; white, with reddish-brown dots. Breeding season: October (Port Hedland).

23:4 MANGROVE WARBLER *Gerygone levigaster cantator*

NOTES. The form illustrated here is the east coast population (subspecies *cantator*), which is a slightly darker, cooler brown than the northern subspecies *levigaster*, with dingy white underparts. For further notes see No. 16:6, p. 123.

23:5 DUSKY HONEYEATER *Myzomela obscura*

IDENTIFICATION. The plumage of this bird is plain dusky brown. Sexes are similar.

DISTRIBUTION. Northern and eastern Australia, west to Port Keats, Northern Territory, and south to about Brisbane, Queensland. This species is also found in Indonesia and New Guinea.

NOTES. This bird inhabits rainforests, mangroves, adjacent scrubs, and open forests, searching the leaves and blossoms for insects and nectar. It is common, gregarious, aggressive, very active, and often inquisitive. The voice is simple but animated.

BREEDING. Nest: small, frail, cup-shaped; constructed of rootlets, thin grasses, and sometimes hair; suspended near the extremity of a leafy branch of a tree or bush. Clutch: two; white with a pinkish tinge, minutely spotted reddish-brown, chestnut, and purplish-grey. Breeding season: September to December.

23:6 BROWN-BACKED HONEYEATER *Ramsayornis modestus*

IDENTIFICATION. A small, nondescript honeyeater, it is mainly brown above, dingy white below, with pinkish bill and a narrow white streak below the eye. Sexes are similar.

DISTRIBUTION. North-eastern Queensland, south to about Mackay. This species is also found in the Aru Islands and New Guinea.

NOTES. This bird inhabits mangroves, tea-tree swamps, and scrubs adjacent to water, where it searches leaves and blossoms for insects and honey. It has an abrupt sharp call and a brisk, chattering song. Migratory, it arrives in early August and departs in April. Its wintering grounds are unknown, possibly Cape York Peninsula. It is very closely related to the Bar-breasted Honeyeater (No. 15:8).

BREEDING. Nest: domed, with a hooded side entrance, made of fine strips of paperbark, lightly bound with cobweb; suspended from a slender branch in a tree or bush, usually over water. Clutch: two to three; white, finely spotted dark brown. Breeding season: August to April.

23:7 RUFOUS-BANDED HONEYEATER *Conopophila albogularis*

IDENTIFICATION. This honeyeater has brown upperparts, wings strongly washed yellow; a grey head, white underparts, crossed at breast with broad band of dull rufous. Sexes are similar.

DISTRIBUTION. Coastal Northern Territory and the west coast of Cape York Peninsula. This species is also found in the Aru Islands and New Guinea.

NOTES. It inhabits mangroves and tea-tree swamps and nearby open forest. It is an active bird, constantly flitting from branch to branch and making irregular flights, during which it utters a pretty song. Males also have a repeated rising note, 'zzheep'. Food: insects and nectar.

BREEDING. Nest: small, cup-shaped; constructed of fine strips of bark matted with webbing and lined with fine grass; suspended from the extremity of a thin branch; often overhanging water. Clutch: three; white, finely spotted bright chestnut-red. Breeding season: October to January.

23:8 MANGROVE HONEYEATER *Lichenostomus versicolor*

IDENTIFICATION. This is a bold, active, noisy, olive green honeyeater with black mask extending back to the shoulder and a yellow malar streak ending in a conspicuous, shaggy white plume. The northern subspecies *versicolor* is yellow below, faintly spotted grey; the southern subspecies *fasciogularis* is grey below, obscurely streaked white on the belly, and narrowly barred yellow on the throat. Sexes are similar.

DISTRIBUTION. Coastal eastern Australia; the northern subspecies *versicolor* occurs in New Guinea and from Cape York south to about Townsville, Queensland. The southern subspecies *fasciogularis* occurs from about Townsville south to the vicinity of Macksville, New South Wales.

NOTES. It frequents coastal mangroves and nearby woodlands, foraging in the canopy, but at low tide often descends to fossick among mangrove roots. It often associates in small flocks and its resonant and melodious notes, mostly uttered in company, ranks it as one of the best singers among the honeyeaters. Food: insects and nectar.

BREEDING. Nest: open, cup-shaped; constructed of dry sea grasses, weeds, and dead leaves; lined with fine rootlets; usually placed in the foliage of a mangrove, within a metre or two of the mud or water. Clutch: two to three; pinkish-buff, with reddish-buff on the larger end, there finely spotted purplish-red. Breeding season: August to December, sometimes later.

23:9 BROAD-BILLED FLYCATCHER *Myiagra ruficollis*

IDENTIFICATION. This flycatcher is very difficult to distinguish from female Satin Flycatcher (No. 11:5, p. 79), but is very slightly smaller, darker, and glossier above. Its throat is slightly paler rufous than its breast. Sexes are similar.

DISTRIBUTION. Coastal northern Australia from the Kimberley to Cape York. This species is also found in Indonesia and New Guinea.

NOTES. Inhabiting mangroves and associated vegetation, it is seen singly or in pairs. It is generally quiet and deliberate while searching for insect-life among the foliage. The song is a clear 'hrinney, hrinney, hrinney'; also soft chattering notes.

BREEDING. Nest: cup-shaped; constructed of strips of bark, bound with webbing, and decorated on the outside with lichen; usually built on a dead twig just beyond high-water mark. Clutch: two; whitish, with a zone of brownish and lavender spots on the larger end. Breeding season: November to February.

23:10 MANGROVE ROBIN *Eopsaltria pulverulenta*

IDENTIFICATION. This robin is dusky grey-blue above, white below, with white panels in the tail.

DISTRIBUTION. Coastal northern Australia, from Exmouth Gulf, Western Australia, to about Ingham, Queensland. This species is also found in the Aru Islands and New Guinea.

NOTES. Inhabiting mangroves, it obtains insects among the leaves or on the ground. Not shy, but quiet, unobtrusive and difficult to observe, it is usually seen in dense mangroves sitting on exposed roots close to the mud. The call is a short, low whistle, most frequently uttered in the breeding season.

BREEDING. Nest: compact, cup-shaped, made of strips of bark bound with cobweb, lined with grass, and decorated on the outside with bark fragments; usually in a mangrove fork. Clutch: two; light green to dark olive green, with small spots of reddish-brown and underlying markings of lilac. Breeding season: August and September to January.

23:11 GREY WHISTLER *Pachycephala simplex simplex*

NOTES. The form illustrated here (subspecies *simplex*) is very similar to the north-eastern subspecies (*P. s. peninsulae*, No. 2:3), but is dingy white (not pale yellow) below, and the upperparts are browner in tone. It occurs in coastal Northern Territory, from Port Keats to the Roper River, inhabiting mangroves and adjoining rainforest and swamps. For further notes, refer No. 2:3, p. 11.

23:12 YELLOW WHITE-EYE *Zosterops lutea*

IDENTIFICATION. This bird is is like Silvereye (No. 15:1, p. 111) but its plumage is strongly washed yellow, with an olive green back. Sexes are similar.

DISTRIBUTION. Coastal northern Australia, from Shark Bay, Western Australia, to Cape York, Queensland.

NOTES. Common and sedentary, it is usually seen in small flocks, frequenting mangroves and associated vegetation. It is very active while searching among the leaves for insects, meanwhile uttering low, tinkling notes. Food: insects, berries, and seeds.

BREEDING. Nest: small, fibrous, cup-shaped; usually suspended in a mangrove. Clutch: three; pale bluish-green. Breeding season: probably September to January.

23:13 WHITE-BREASTED WHISTLER *Pachycephala lanioides*

IDENTIFICATION. This is a typical whistler restricted to mangroves. It is rather large; the male black-headed, with grey upperparts, plain white underparts, with broad black band across breast; the female looks rather like a female Rufous Whistler, but is much larger and heavier in build.

DISTRIBUTION. Coastal northern Australia from about Carnarvon, Western Australia, to near Normanton, Queensland.

NOTES. Fairly common though sedentary, it is usually found in pairs, frequenting mangroves. It feeds in the foliage, or on mud between exposed roots at low tide. The song is loud, rich and animated; calls include a clear slow whistle. Food: insects and small crustaceans (mainly small crabs).

BREEDING. Nest: open, rather frail; made of twigs and rootlets lined with finer rootlets and anchored with cobweb; usually in a mangrove fork. Clutch: two; stone-coloured or buff, with a zone of umber and lavender spots at the larger end. Breeding season: November to January.

23:14 BLACK BUTCHERBIRD *Cracticus quoyi*

IDENTIFICATION. This is like other butcherbirds, but entirely black. Sexes are similar. Between about Cooktown and Mackay, Queensland, juvenile birds are dull reddish-brown (elsewhere they are black like adults).

DISTRIBUTION. Northern and eastern Australia, west to Port Keats, Northern

Territory, and south to about Rockhampton, Queensland. This species is also found in New Guinea.

NOTES. This bird inhabits rainforests (including highlands), mangroves and adjacent scrub. Generally secretive and rather solitary, it has a deep, rich bubbling melody. Food: crustaceans, insects, reptiles, and small birds and their eggs.

BREEDING. Nest: substantial, open, cup-shaped, made of sticks and twigs; placed in an upright fork, usually seven or eight metres from the ground. Clutch: four; greyish-green or cream, with spots of umber and dull slate. Breeding season: October to January.

23:15 MANGROVE KINGFISHER *Halcyon chloris*

IDENTIFICATION. This kingfisher is difficult to distinguish from Sacred Kingfisher, but it is somewhat larger, with green (not blue) rump; back and crown darker, sootier green; white (not buff) underparts; proportionately longer, heavier bill. Sexes are similar.

DISTRIBUTION. Coastal northern and eastern Australia, west to Carnarvon, Western Australia, and south to Tweed Heads, New South Wales.

NOTES. In Australia it inhabits mangroves almost exclusively, but in other parts of its range it is common in coconut plantations and other coastal habitats. Some of its notes suggest the Sacred Kingfisher, but others, much louder, resemble the 'laughter' of the Laughing Kookaburra. Food: small fish and crustaceans.

BREEDING. Nest: in a hole in a termite nest; or in a tree cavity. Clutch: three to four; white. Breeding season: October to December.

23:16 YELLOW-BILLED KINGFISHER *Halcyon totoro*

IDENTIFICATION. This is rather like a Sacred Kingfisher in general appearance, except for its unique dull orange head and yellow bill. The female has a black crown (Cape York only).

DISTRIBUTION. Cape York Peninsula, between the Claudie and Chester Rivers. This species is also found in New Guinea.

NOTES. It inhabits lowland rainforests, monsoon forest and margins of open woodland (not usually in mangroves). It has a mournful, trilling call, ascending the scale. Perching quietly for long periods low in dense cover, it is often hard to see. Food: insects, small reptiles, crustaceans.

BREEDING. Nest: in a chamber at the end of a short tunnel in a termite nest, usually a few metres high in a tree. Clutch: three to four; white. Breeding season: November to January.

23:17 WHITE-BROWED CRAKE *Poliolimnas cinereus*

IDENTIFICATION. This bird is dull brown above, streaked black, mainly dingy white below, with a distinctive black and white head pattern. Sexes are similar.

DISTRIBUTION. Northern and eastern Australia, west to the Kimberley and south to about Townsville, Queensland. This species is also widespread from south-east Asia, the Philippines, Indonesia and New Guinea to islands of the south-western Pacific.

NOTES. It inhabits freshwater marshes, dense vegetation bordering creeks and lagoons, and mangroves. It wanders on mud, over floating vegetation, or among branches of trees, where it climbs with ease. The call is a distinctive loud chattering and it is especially noisy and active at dawn and dusk. Food: insects, worms, and leaves of aquatic plants.

BREEDING. Nest: placed on the ground or in tussocks in swamps; formed of coarse grasses and lined with finer materials. Clutch: three to six; greenish-white, with fleecy markings of chestnut-brown or yellowish-brown. Breeding season: mainly January to April.

23:18 SHINING FLYCATCHER *Myiagra alecto*

IDENTIFICATION. The male is entirely blue-black, strongly glossed. The female has a black head, white underparts, and rich chestnut upperparts.

DISTRIBUTION. Coastal northern and eastern Australia, west to Broome, Western Australia, and south to about Noosa, Queensland. This species is also found in Indonesia and New Guinea.

NOTES. This bird inhabits mangroves, tea-tree swamps and margins of coastal streams. Common, it is usually seen singly or in pairs, sometimes in small parties. It is very active but sometimes rather shy. Calls are extremely varied; the chief utterance of the species is a melodious trilling, also an extended 'cheeee'. Food: insects, caught in the air and on logs in streams.

BREEDING. Nest: open; constructed of strips of bark bound with cobweb and decorated on the outside with bark and lichen; usually built in trees or vines overhanging water. Clutch: three; greenish-white, spotted brown and lavender. Breeding season: October to February.

BIRDS OF THE HEATHLANDS AND OPEN COUNTRY

PLATE 24

SOME BIRDS OF HEATH AND UNDERGROWTH

24:1 SCRUBTIT *Acanthornis magnus*

IDENTIFICATION. This small warm brown bird has a dark, white-tipped tail and whitish face. Sexes are similar.

DISTRIBUTION. Tasmania.

NOTES. Similar in habits to the scrubwrens, it inhabits dense undergrowth in temperate rainforests and fern gullies. A shy bird, it moves rapidly in a rather mouse-like manner among tree ferns and fallen logs while searching for insects. It also forages on tree trunks and lower branches. The call is a simple 'to–wee–to', reinforced by a pleasant whistling.

BREEDING. Nest: dome-shaped, made of grass, moss, bark fragments, and fern down, lined with fur and feathers; placed near the ground among dense herbage, or in a low tree fork. Clutch: three; white, with purple markings. Breeding season: August to January.

24:2 WHITE-BROWED SCRUBWREN *Sericornis frontalis*

IDENTIFICATION. This bird is brownish above, dingy white below, with a straw-yellow eye. White superciliary and white malar streak contrasts with slate grey ear coverts. Several populations, differing slightly in appearance: Queensland birds (subspecies *laevigaster*) have dingy yellowish-buff underparts; south-eastern birds (subspecies *frontalis*) have whitish underparts; western and south-western birds (subspecies *maculatus*, South Australia and Western Australia) have spotted underparts; and Tasmanian birds (subspecies *humilis*) are generally much darker and browner than mainland birds, with a less distinct face pattern. All of these forms are usually regarded as conspecific, but some evidence has recently emerged to suggest that Tasmanian birds (*humilis*) should be regarded as a distinct species.

DISTRIBUTION. Eastern and southern Australia, from about Cairns, Queensland, south to Tasmania, and north on the west coast to about Carnarvon, Western Australia.

NOTES. Widespread in dense undergrowth in most types of forest, it is also often quite common in gardens and city parks. It is seen in pairs or small parties and is active, excitable, and inquisitive. Calls include a variety of insistent, fussy scolding notes, and also a sharp whistling song. Food: insects procured on the ground or in shrubs.

BREEDING. Nest: dome-shaped, with a side entrance, made mainly of dry ferns and lined with feathers; situated in thick undergrowth. Clutch: two to four; brownish, with purplish-brown markings forming a zone at the larger end. Breeding season: mainly August to December.

24:3 TROPICAL SCRUBWREN *Sericornis beccarii*

IDENTIFICATION. This is rather like White-browed Scrubwren, but with a reddish eye (not yellow) and a plainer face, with markings less distinct. It has a narrow broken white eye-ring, and double narrow white wingbar. Sexes are similar, but the female is much duller than the male (Cape York only).

DISTRIBUTION. North-eastern Queensland, from Cape York to about Cooktown. It also inhabits New Guinea.

NOTES. In pairs or small parties, it is fairly common in tropical rainforests where it searches for insects among fallen leaves and debris or among masses of vines and fallen trees.

BREEDING. Nest: dome-shaped, with a side entrance; constructed of leaves and rootlets, and lined with tendrils and a few feathers; placed near the ground in a scrubby tree. Clutch: three; faint reddish-brown, with a zone of light brown on the larger end. Breeding season: October to December.

24:4 LARGE-BILLED SCRUBWREN *Sericornis magnirostris*

IDENTIFICATION. This scrubwren is brownish and very plain, its face light buff, producing a sharp contrast with its dark reddish eye and rather long black bill. Sexes are similar.

DISTRIBUTION. Eastern Australia, from Cooktown, Queensland, to near Melbourne, Victoria, occasionally extending short distances inland.

NOTES. It frequents rainforests, from sea level to an altitude of about 1500 metres and is seen singly or in small groups. The most arboreal of the scrubwrens, it procures its food, insects, among branches and leaves of tall trees, in the undergrowth and, occasionally, on the ground. The calls include simple chattering notes and a penetrating chanting 's'chee–s'chee–s'chee'.

BREEDING. Nest: large, oval-shaped, with a side entrance; constructed of leaves, moss and grass; lined with feathers; placed in a drooping branch of a leafy tree, in a tree fern, or in vines; whenever possible a deserted nest of the Yellow-throated Scrubwren is used. Clutch: three; whitish or grey, finely spotted brown. Breeding season: August to January.

24:5 ATHERTON SCRUBWREN *Sericornis keri*

IDENTIFICATION. This bird is very difficult to distinguish from Large-billed Scrubwren, but its face is relatively much darker, producing less contrast with the dark red eye. It is also slightly larger, longer-legged, and with darker brown plumage. It persistently forages on the ground rather than in bushes or trees (Atherton Tableland only). Sexes are similar.

DISTRIBUTION. Highlands of the Bellenden Ker Range (above about 650 metres) in north-eastern Queensland, possibly south to Mount Spec.

NOTES. Generally solitary or in pairs, it frequents the ground and understorey of highland rainforests. The calls have not been described. It is so similar to the Large-billed Scrubwren in appearance that its existence as a distinct species was not demonstrated until 1964.

BREEDING. Nest: the only nest so far reported was domed, with a side entrance near the top; made of plant fibres and leaf skeletons, lined with feathers; hidden in vegetation near the ground. Clutch: two; purplish-white, freckled dark brown at the larger end. Breeding season: uncertain; eggs reported in November.

24:6 BEAUTIFUL FIRETAIL *Emblema bellum*

IDENTIFICATION. This bird has plumage which is largely olive brown, closely barred black, with a bright red rump, black face, white eye-ring, and pink bill. Sexes are similar.

DISTRIBUTION. South-eastern Australia, from near Newcastle, New South Wales, south to Tasmania and west to Kangaroo Island and the Mount Lofty Ranges, South Australia.

NOTES. It is seen in pairs or small parties, frequenting heath and low scrub, rarely far from water. It is a shy and quiet bird, keeping to the undergrowth and tall grasses. The call is a low, plaintive whistle. Food: insects and seeds.

BREEDING. Nest: shaped like a bottle on its side; constructed of thin dried grass, green grass, and a few leaves; placed in thick foliage of a bush or tree. Clutch: five to eight; white. Breeding season: September to January.

24:7 RED-EARED FIRETAIL *Emblema oculatum*

IDENTIFICATION. The plumage of this bird is mainly olive brown, closely barred with black. The belly is boldly spotted white; the rump and ear coverts bright red; mask black, with a conspicuous white eye-ring. Sexes are similar.

DISTRIBUTION. Coastal south-western Australia, from the Darling Range to Esperance.

NOTES. Usually alone or in pairs, it seldom forms flocks. It frequents swampy heathlands, dense wet gullies, or undergrowth in dense forest; and is sedentary. It is secretive in habits, always keeping to the undergrowth. The calls include a soft, mournful 'oo–wee', sometimes uttered in a series. Food: seeds and insects.

BREEDING. Nest: well-made, bottle-shaped, made of green grass; usually placed at the extremity of a horizontal branch of a swamp banksia or other bush. Clutch: four to six; white. Breeding season: mainly August to December.

24:8 NEW HOLLAND HONEYEATER *Phylidonyris novaehollandiae*

IDENTIFICATION. This bird is mainly black and white, with underparts heavily streaked, and bright yellow flashes in wings and tail. It resembles White-cheeked Honeyeater but has white eyes, and black cheeks. Sexes are similar.

DISTRIBUTION. Eastern and southern Australia, from about Gympie, Queensland, south to Tasmania and west to Eyre Peninsula, South Australia; also Western Australia from about Moora to Israelite Bay.

NOTES. A common bird, it is seen in pairs or small flocks, chiefly in heathlands of coastal districts, especially where banksias are abundant. It also visits open timbered country and is common in gardens. It is active, restless and aggressive. The call-note is sharp and shrill; when alarmed the bird utters harsh chattering notes. Food: insects and nectar.

BREEDING. Nest: open, cup-shaped, made of strips of bark, grasses, and twigs, lined with plant-down (often brown velvety down from the dead cones of banksias); placed low in a banksia or other dense shrub. Clutch: two to three; pinkish-buff, spotted reddish-chestnut and slate-grey. Breeding season: mainly June to January.

24:9 WHITE-CHEEKED HONEYEATER *Phylidonyris nigra*

IDENTIFICATION. This bird resembles New Holland Honeyeater except for a dark eye and large white cheek patch. Sexes are similar.

DISTRIBUTION. Eastern Australia from about Cairns, Queensland, south to about Ulladulla, New South Wales; also Western Australia from Israelite Bay to the Murchison River.

NOTES. Found in pairs or flocks, it inhabits heathlands and open timber. It is more restricted in habitat and is rather more wary and less conspicuous, pugnacious and active than the New Holland Honeyeater. The calls are an animated chatter; the male has a conspicuous song-flight.

BREEDING. Nest: cup-shaped; constructed chiefly of strips of bark and dried grasses, and lined with soft plant-down, often the brown velvety tufts from the cones of banksias; placed close to the ground in thick foliage. Clutch: two; pale buff, with a zone of reddish-brown and purplish-grey. Breeding season: July to February.

24:10 CRESCENT HONEYEATER *Phylidonyris pyrrhoptera*

IDENTIFICATION. This honeyeater is mainly grey, with conspicuous bright yellow flashes in wings and tail, and a bold black crescent on the side of the breast. Sexes are similar.

DISTRIBUTION. South-eastern Australia, from Barrington Tops, New South Wales, south to Tasmania and west to Kangaroo Island and about Adelaide, South Australia.

NOTES. It inhabits tall forest country carrying dense undergrowth, creekside vegetation, and occasionally thick heathy country. Common, it is usually seen singly or in pairs, but numbers gather where nectar is abundant. It retreats from higher altitudes in winter. The most characteristic call is a brisk 'egypt, egypt'. Food: insects and nectar.

BREEDING. Nest: cup-shaped; constructed of strips of bark and twigs; lined with grass and a little soft material; placed low in a dense bush. Clutch: two to three; pale flesh-coloured, spotted reddish-chestnut and purplish-grey. Breeding season: July to December.

24:11 TAWNY-CROWNED HONEYEATER *Phylidonyris melanops*

IDENTIFICATION. This honeyeater is mainly dull grey-brown, streaked above.

Its crown is pale rufous, with a conspicuous black crescent extending from eye to sides of breast. Sexes are similar.

DISTRIBUTION. South-eastern Australia from about Grafton, New South Wales, south to Tasmania and west to Eyre Peninsula and Kangaroo Island, South Australia; also Western Australia from Israelite Bay to the Murchison River.

NOTES. Usually found in pairs, it inhabits low, dry, open heath and dwarf scrub, often seen on the ground. The song, although simple, is melodious, wistful, and ventriloquial; it may be uttered while the bird is perched on top of a shrub or while it is indulging in acrobatics above a heathland. Food: insects and nectar.

BREEDING. Nest: cup-shaped; constructed of bark and grass, matted with cobweb, and lined with plant-down; placed near the ground in a tussock of grass or a small bush. Clutch: two to three; white, sparsely spotted dull chestnut-brown. Breeding season: mainly June to February.

24:12 WHITE-FRONTED HONEYEATER *Phylidonyris albifrons*

IDENTIFICATION. This bird rather resembles New Holland Honeyeater in general appearance and behaviour, but has a plain black breast and conspicuous white forehead, a dark eye, with small pink wattle. Sexes are similar.

DISTRIBUTION. Western Australia (north to the Fortesque River), through central and South Australia to western New South Wales and north-western Victoria; very rare near the coast in the east and south.

NOTES. Usually seen in pairs or small parties, it inhabits heath and dwarf scrub of the sub-interior. Though very active and aggressive, darting among foliage and blossoms in search of insects and nectar, at all times it is wary. It is highly nomadic. It has a variety of strange, metallic calls; the song is spirited and melodious, suggesting that of the Reed Warbler.

BREEDING. Nest: cup-shaped, made of bark and grass, lined with plant-down; placed in a low bush. Clutch: usually two; pinkish-white, spotted reddish-brown and dull purple. Breeding season: August to January.

24:13 BROWN HONEYEATER *Lichmera indistincta*

IDENTIFICATION. A small, plain brownish honeyeater, it has a yellow wash on its wings and a small yellow plume behind its eye. Sexes are similar.

DISTRIBUTION. Most of Western Australia, and northern Australia south to northern South Australia and New South Wales (south to about Sydney). It also inhabits the Aru Islands and New Guinea.

NOTES. Its habitat is extremely varied, from dense forest and rainforest margins to mangroves, heaths, and arid stunted scrubs. A resident in northern Australia, it is migratory in the south. It occurs alone, in pairs or in flocks. The calls are loud and spirited — perhaps the strongest of any Australian bird of its size — and resemble those of the Reed Warbler. Food: insects and nectar.

BREEDING. Nest: small, cup-shaped; constructed of soft bark and fibre, lined with plant-down, suspended in a small forked branch of a shrub, often overhanging water. Clutch: usually two; white, with a few specks of pale chestnut on the larger end. Breeding season: June to January.

24:14 PIED HONEYEATER *Certhionyx variegatus*

IDENTIFICATION. This is a small, boldly black and white honeyeater with black head, white shoulder patch and panels in the tail, and small blue wattle under the eye. The female is dingy brown, with wing feathers edged white, and breast obscurely streaked.

DISTRIBUTION. From mid-Western Australia through central Australia to western Queensland, western New South Wales, northern South Australia, and north-western Victoria.

NOTES. Found in pairs or small parties, it is unobtrusive and fairly quiet, frequenting arid heaths and savannahs, and flowering semi-desert shrubs, feeding among flowers and foliage on insects and nectar. Migratory in the southern parts of its range, it is nomadic elsewhere. The male has a distinctive song-flight display, flying some distance aloft with tail fanned, meanwhile uttering a piercing whistling song 'tee–titee–tee–tee'.

BREEDING. Nest: shallow, cup-shaped, made of small twigs and grass, bound with cobweb and lined with fine grass; usually placed low in a small bush or tree. Clutch: usually two; white, with a few specks of pale chestnut on the larger end. Breeding season: June to January.

24:15 WHITE-EARED HONEYEATER *Lichenostomus leucotis*

IDENTIFICATION. This bird is mainly rich yellow-green, with a black head, grey crown and white ear patch. Sexes are similar.

DISTRIBUTION. Central Queensland to Victoria, southern South Australia, Kangaroo Island, and south-western Australia.

NOTES. Usually seen in pairs or small parties, it frequents alike heathlands, mallee and open forest country. It is noisy, conspicuous, pugnacious and inquisitive. The bird utters various loud ringing notes, among them an abrupt 'chop, chop'. During the breeding season it becomes very tame; there are many instances on record of the female alighting on the heads and clothes of observers, seeking hair and wool for nesting material. The bird usually feeds in scrub, but it sometimes frequents tall trees and occasionally seeks insects on trunks and branches in the fashion of treecreepers. Food: insects and nectar.

BREEDING. Nest: cup-shaped, made of bark and grasses bound with cobweb; lined with fur, hair or other soft materials; placed in a low bush or sapling. Clutch: two to three; flesh-coloured or white, spotted pinkish-red and reddish-brown. Breeding season: July to December.

24:16 YELLOW-THROATED HONEYEATER *Lichenostomus flavicollis*

IDENTIFICATION. This honeyeater is mainly rich olive green above, and grey below. Its head is grey, and throat bright yellow. Sexes are similar.

DISTRIBUTION. Tasmania and islands of Bass Strait (King Island and the Flinders Group).

NOTES. Seen in pairs or small flocks, it frequents open forests, orchards and gardens. It calls 'tonk, tonk', and utters various other notes, while perched on the topmost twig of a low tree. It is similar in general habits to the closely related White-eared Honeyeater. Food: insects and nectar.

BREEDING. Nest: cup-shaped; constructed of bark and grasses and lined with hair, fur, or other soft materials; placed in a thick bush close to the ground. Clutch: two to three; pinkish-white, spotted reddish-brown and purplish-grey. Breeding season: mainly July to November.

24:17 LITTLE WATTLEBIRD *Anthochaera chrysoptera*

IDENTIFICATION. This bird is is similar to Red Wattlebird (No. 12:13, p. 93), but has more contrast between dark crown and silvery cheek. Its belly is grey-streaked (not yellow), and there is a dull rufous wash on outer wing feathers, evident in flight. Sexes are similar.

DISTRIBUTION. South-eastern Australia, from about Noosa Heads, Queensland, south to Tasmania and west to about Adelaide, South Australia; also south-western Australia from about Israelite Bay to Geraldton.

NOTES. Seen in pairs or small parties, it frequents scrubs and heathlands, also parks and gardens, especially where banksias are abundant. Mainly coastal, it also occurs locally in some highland districts. It is active, noisy, and extremely pugnacious, especially during the breeding season, constantly uttering a variety of harsh notes. There is persuasive evidence to indicate that the south-western population might be best regarded as a distinct species. Food: insects and nectar.

BREEDING. Nest: cup-shaped; constructed of small twigs, lined with grasses and soft bark, sometimes also plant-down; placed in a fork of a low tree or bush. Clutch: one to three; pinkish-buff, spotted reddish-brown and purplish-grey. Breeding season: August to December.

PLATE 25

BIRDS OF THE HEATHLANDS

25:1 REDTHROAT *Pyrrholaemus brunneus*

IDENTIFICATION. This bird is a rather plain, greyish brown, with dull rufous throat and white-tipped tail. Sexes are similar, but the female has a white throat.

DISTRIBUTION. Central Australia, including inland areas of all States (possibly excluding Queensland), extending to near the coast in mid-Western Australia.

NOTES. Usually seen in pairs, it inhabits stunted scrub in arid regions. It spends much time on the ground, over which it moves rapidly. The bird possesses a very sweet song, usually uttered from the topmost twig of a low bush; it is also a competent mimic. Food: insects, procured on the ground or in undergrowth.

BREEDING. Nest: round, with a side entrance; constructed of bark fibre and grass; sometimes lined with feathers; usually built in a low bush close to the ground, but sometimes placed in a hollow log. Clutch: three to four; purplish-brown with a darker shade at the larger end. Breeding season: mainly August to November.

25:2 SPINIFEXBIRD *Eremiornis carteri*

IDENTIFICATION. This bird somewhat resembles Clamorous Reedwarbler in appearance, but its crown and nape are rufous, and its tail long, graduated, and frequently held cocked. Sexes are similar.

DISTRIBUTION. Northern Australia, from Cloncurry, Queensland, to the Fitzroy River, Western Australia, and south to the Minilya River and Alice Springs, Northern Territory.

NOTES. Locally common, it is sedentary, and usually seen in pairs, inhabiting spinifex and other low scrub, especially in hilly or rocky country. It is customarily shy and is essentially a bird of the ground. The song of the male has been likened to the French words 'je suis a vous', and the notes of the female to 'thrip–thrip'. Another call is rendered as 'chutch'. Food: insects.

BREEDING. Nest: cup-shaped; built of shredded grass and lined with fine roots; placed in a bunch of spinifex. Clutch: two; pinkish-white, covered with minute markings of pale lilac and reddish-brown. Breeding season: August to November.

25:3 SOUTHERN EMUWREN *Stipiturus malachurus*

IDENTIFICATION. Very small, this bird is streaked brown above, buff below, with an extraordinary long, filamentous tail. The male has a dull reddish crown, streaked dark slate-brown, and a bright blue face and throat.

DISTRIBUTION. Eastern Australia (mostly coastal) from central Queensland to southern Victoria, south-eastern South Australia, and south-western Australia from Shark Bay to Israelite Bay; also Tasmania and Kangaroo Island.

NOTES. Seen in pairs or small parties, it inhabits swampy heathlands, mostly coastal but locally in highlands. It is very shy, keeping to dense undergrowth, through which it moves easily in a mouse-like manner. Its chief call is a slight twitter, also a thin 'seee', so high-pitched as to be almost inaudible. Food: insects.

BREEDING. Nest: oval, with a side entrance near the top; constructed of grass, lined with finer grasses; built in a tuft of grass or a low bush. Clutch: three to four; white, spotted red. Breeding season: August to December.

25:4 MALLEE EMUWREN *Stipiturus mallee*

IDENTIFICATION. This is very like Southern Emuwren but is slightly smaller and relatively short-tailed; its crown is unstreaked, rich rufous.

DISTRIBUTION. The mallee districts of north-western Victoria and south-eastern South Australia.

NOTES. Usually found in pairs or small parties, it inhabits undergrowth of mallee scrubs, especially mature 'bull' spinifex under a canopy of low eucalypts. May be common locally, but in general it is rare and patchy in distribution — apparently very exacting in its habitat requirements. Similar in habits to the other two species of emuwren, this population should probably be regarded as conspecific with one or the other, but there is some difficulty in deciding which one.

BREEDING. Nest: roughly spherical, with slightly hooded side entrance; made of spinifex, grass-stems and fibres, bound with cobweb and lined with fur, feathers and plant-down. Usually well-hidden in a tussock of spinifex. Clutch: two to three; white, freckled and blotched with rust-red and mid-brown. Breeding season: September to October.

25:5 RUFOUS-CROWNED EMUWREN *Stipiturus ruficeps*

IDENTIFICATION. This species is like Mallee Emuwren, but its crown and nape are rich rufous (Mallee Emuwren has a brownish, streaked nape).

DISTRIBUTION. From mid-coastal Western Australia east across the interior of northern Australia into western Queensland (to about Opalton and Winton) and south to the Great Victoria Desert and the Simpson Desert.

NOTES. Seen in pairs or small parties, it inhabits arid spinifex country or stunted scrub. Like other emuwrens, it is rather secretive. Its flight is feeble and reluctant. Calls include a thin, high-pitched, rapid trill. Food: small insects.

BREEDING. Nest: domed, with a side entrance; made of fine bark and grass bound with cobweb; lined with feathers or plant-down; well-hidden in a spinifex tussock. Clutch: two to three; white, tinged pinkish-buff, with spots of reddish-brown and light umber. Breeding season: variable, usually August to November.

25:6 CHESTNUT-RUMPED HEATHWREN *Hylacola pyrrhopygia*

IDENTIFICATION. This is a skulking, scrubwren-like bird with white superciliary, streaked breast, a bright rufous rump, and white-tipped tail habitually cocked, an unstreaked back, and no white in the wing. Sexes are similar.

DISTRIBUTION. South-eastern Australia, from extreme south-eastern Queensland south to Victoria and west to Kangaroo Island and the Flinders Ranges, South Australia.

NOTES. Found in pairs or small parties, it frequents heathlands and dense undergrowth. A shy bird, it keeps mainly to the ground, but often sings from the branch of a shrub up to about three metres high. The song is very sweet and spirited and it is also a highly skilled mimic; the alarm-call is a single sharp 'chip'. Food: insects.

BREEDING. Nest: dome-shaped, with a side entrance; constructed of grasses and fine bark and lined with feathers; placed on the ground or in a low bush or tussock. Clutch: two to three; pinkish-white to buff, spotted purplish-brown. Breeding season: July to November.

25:7 SHY HEATHWREN *Hylacola cauta*

IDENTIFICATION. This bird is very similar to Chestnut-rumped Heathwren, but is darker, with a bolder colour pattern, and a small white patch in the wing. Sexes are similar.

DISTRIBUTION. Southern Australia, from about West Wyalong, New South Wales, to the Murchison River, Western Australia.

NOTES. It frequents mallee, low scrubs on rocky hillsides, and shrub woodland. It is similar in habits and voice to the Chestnut-rumped Heathwren but not such an assured mimic.

BREEDING. Nest: dome-shaped, with a side entrance; constructed of bark and grasses and lined with finer grasses or other soft material; placed on or near the ground. Clutch: two to three; buff, freckled purplish-brown. Breeding season: September to November.

25:8 EASTERN FIELDWREN *Calamanthus fuliginosus*

IDENTIFICATION. A skulking, scrubwren-like bird of south-eastern moors and wet heaths, this wren is dull olive brown, boldly streaked above and below, with a tail habitually cocked. Sexes are similar.

DISTRIBUTION. South-eastern South Australia, Tasmania, southern Victoria, and south-eastern New South Wales, north to about Ulladulla.

NOTES. Seen in pairs or small parties, it frequents heathlands, alpine tussocks, rough grasslands bordering swamps and marshes, stunted scrub, and other open habitats. Sedentary, the pairs are said to maintain territories throughout the year. The song is spirited and ventriloquial, and is usually uttered from a perch on the topmost twig of a bush, a fence post, or similar exposed situation. It is shy, however, and dives to cover on the least disturbance. It moves actively in undergrowth, tail often cocked. This and the next species, the Western Fieldwren, have often been regarded as conspecific. Food: insects.

BREEDING. Nest: domed, with a side entrance, an untidy structure made of moss, dry grass, and leaves, lined with feathers; placed in dense vegetation near the ground. Clutch: three to four; reddish-buff, thickly freckled and marked with darker shades at the larger end. Breeding season: July to December.

25:9 WESTERN FIELDWREN *Calamanthus campestris*

IDENTIFICATION. This fieldwren has variable plumage according to subspecies. Though very similar to Eastern Fieldwren, it is paler; grey rather than brown in colour, variably washed rufous on the head; and eye pale yellow (not red). Sexes are similar.

DISTRIBUTION. Southern Australia generally, except the south-east. Several populations differing slightly in plumage, including: *C. c. campestris* of western New South Wales (east to about Menindee Lakes) and much of South Australia; *C. c. isabellinus*, which occurs locally over southern Western Australia (except the south-west); and *C. c. montanellus* of extreme southern South Australia and south-western Western Australia.

NOTES. It inhabits saltbush and bluebush plains, stunted scrub in claypans or gibber country in the interior, heathlands and rocky hillsides in the south-west. It is difficult to observe, being inconspicuous and shy, running mouse-like between grass-clumps and other cover. Tail generally cocked. It has a subdued but clear, sweet song. Food: insects.

BREEDING. Nest: globular, with side entrance, made of dry grass lined with feathers; placed beneath a low bush, occasionally on open ground. Clutch: three to four; uniform pale chocolate, shading to a darker cap at the larger end. Breeding season: variable, but mainly July to December.

25:10 THICK-BILLED GRASSWREN *Amytornis textilis*

IDENTIFICATION. This bird has plumage more or less entirely reddish brown, narrowly and copiously streaked white. Its bill is stout. The female has rufous flanks. Western birds (subspecies *textilis*) are somewhat more richly coloured and more heavily streaked with white.

DISTRIBUTION. Southern Western Australia, south-western Northern Territory, and much of South Australia. Two subspecies: *A. t. modestus* occurs in the central and eastern interior, and *A. t. textilis* inhabits the far west.

NOTES. Seen in pairs or small parties, it frequents saltbush, spinifex, and other low scrub. The bird is almost always on the ground, carrying its tail erect, and scampering over the ground and through undergrowth with great speed. It utters a low and somewhat plaintive song while at rest, and also possesses a faint, high-pitched call. Locally common, but it is extremely difficult to observe. Food: insects and seeds.

BREEDING. Nest: domed, occasionally cup-shaped, made of bark, grass, and plant stems; lined with finer materials; placed in the centre of a low bush. Clutch: two to four; white or pinkish, freckled with rich red and a few underlying markings of lilac-grey. Breeding season: August to October.

25:11 DUSKY GRASSWREN *Amytornis purnelli*

IDENTIFICATION. This wren is very like Thick-billed Grasswren but somewhat darker and browner, with a proportionately more slender bill. The female has reddish flanks. It favours open herb fields and plains.

DISTRIBUTION. Central Australia, east to about Mount Isa, Queensland, and west to about Rawlinson, Western Australia.

NOTES. Gregarious, it occurs in pairs or small groups during the breeding season, and in parties of up to a dozen or more at other times. It inhabits open plains, with spinifex, canegrass, saltbush or similar vegetation. It also likes flood debris in dry sandy riverbeds. Sedentary, it is very common in a suitable habitat, and relatively less shy and secretive than other grasswrens. The song is a sweet twittering. Food: insects and seeds.

BREEDING. Nest: like that of the Thick-billed Grasswren. Clutch: two to four; creamy-white, spotted and freckled with reddish-brown. Breeding season: variable; after rain.

25:12 STRIATED GRASSWREN *Amytornis striatus*

IDENTIFICATION. Somewhat resembling Thick-billed Grasswren but smaller, its plumage is strongly reddish in tone, with underparts paler than upperparts, substantially unstreaked. It has a slender bill, and a conspicuous black malar streak. The female has reddish flanks.

DISTRIBUTION. Central and western Australia, from about Cobar, New South Wales, and north-western Victoria north and west to the Pilbara and North West Cape, Western Australia. Two populations, once regarded as distinct species: *A. s. striatus* (Striated Grasswren) of the east and south, and *A. s. whitei* (Rufous Grasswren) of the interior and west.

NOTES. Seen in pairs or small parties, it frequents spinifex on sandy areas, often associated with mallee, acacia and other shrubs. It is similar in habits to other grasswrens. The male utters a pleasing song, long-sustained, also a clear musical call-note, 'tu–tu–tu'.

BREEDING. Nest: partly domed; constructed of bark fibre and grass blades, built on a foundation of bark; placed close to the ground, in or under a spinifex tussock. Clutch: two; white, with spots of reddish-brown and lilac. Breeding season: after rain.

25:13 EYREAN GRASSWREN *Amytornis goyderi*

IDENTIFICATION. This grasswren is reddish above, narrowly and copiously streaked white. Its underparts are white. There is no black malar streak, and it has a stout bill. The female has reddish flanks.

DISTRIBUTION. South Australia (Lake Eyre district).

NOTES. This small grasswren, discovered by an exploratory party in 1874, remained virtually unknown (with very few specimens in museums) until September 1961; it is restricted to the most arid and inhospitable regions of the Simpson Desert favouring spinifex and canegrass in sandhill country. The calls include a faint two-syllable whistle 'swi–it, swi–it'. It also has a beautiful silvery song.

BREEDING. Nest: deep, cup-shaped or partly domed; made of grass, lined with fine grass and plant-down, placed in a canegrass tussock. Clutch: three; off-white, freckled with minute spots of lavender-grey, and blotched dull reddish-brown, light purplish-grey and light olive. Breeding season: September (the only set of eggs on record).

25:14 WHITE-THROATED GRASSWREN *Amytornis woodwardi*

IDENTIFICATION. This grasswren has rich red-brown upperparts, a black head, narrowly and copiously streaked white; underparts dull brown (male) or rusty (female), the throat and upper breast white; and a prominent black malar streak.

DISTRIBUTION. Western Arnhem Land, Northern Territory.

NOTES. It occurs singly or in small parties and frequents sandstone escarpments. Difficult to observe, it runs in bursts over rock faces and hides in crevices. Calls include a strong sharp 'tzzzt'; also a rich song of trills and rising and falling notes.

BREEDING. Nest: bulky, domed, made of grass, leaves and bark strips, hidden in the top of a spinifex tussock. Clutch: two; pale pink, sparingly blotched and marked with red-brown, purple-grey and olive. Breeding season: December to March.

25:15 CARPENTARIAN GRASSWREN *Amytornis dorotheae*

IDENTIFICATION. This bird resembles Striated Grasswren but is more richly coloured, and has a darker head.

DISTRIBUTION. Eastern Northern Territory, in the Macarthur River region.

NOTES. Little known, it is sedentary, and very restricted in distribution. It occurs in pairs or small parties and frequents spinifex on rock ledges and plateaux in sandstone country. It is very shy and elusive, hiding among the rocks.

BREEDING. Nest: bulky, domed; made of spinifex stems, grass and leaves, loosely woven; lined with finer grass, placed in the top of a spinifex clump. Clutch: two to three; pale pink, marked with red-brown and purplish-grey. Breeding season: December to March.

25:16 BLACK GRASSWREN *Amytornis housei*

IDENTIFICATION. A large, dark grasswren, it has black head, wings and tail, the head boldly streaked white. Upperparts are rich red. The belly is black (male) or chestnut (female).

DISTRIBUTION. Restricted to a small area of the Kimberley (Mount Elizabeth, Manning Creek and the Charnley River), Western Australia.

NOTES. Little known, but it is apparently common within its restricted habitat — exceedingly rough country, strewn with piled-up masses of sandstone. Generally seen in small parties, it is not especially shy, but extremely difficult to observe. The birds scuttle over rocks and boulders with head and tail lowered. Perhaps more vocal than other grasswrens, the calls include a trilled staccato 'tschrrrk', a sharp 'tick', and a song described as a 'brief full-throated swirling whistle' with a 'quick-fire, metallic quality'. Food: insects and seeds.

BREEDING. Nest: only a few have ever been found. A bulky, domed structure with side entrance; made of grass and spinifex stems, lined with fine grass. Clutch: unknown. Breeding season: unknown.

25:17 GREY GRASSWREN *Amytornis barbatus*

IDENTIFICATION. This wren is long-tailed with plumage greyish sand-coloured, with an intricate black and white face pattern.

DISTRIBUTION. Goyders Lagoon, north-eastern South Australia and the Bulloorine area of extreme southern Queensland and north-western New South Wales.

NOTES. Usually seen in small parties, it frequents dense lignum and canegrass thickets in swamps and overflow channels. Generally uncommon and patchily distributed, it may be locally abundant. Said to be more vocal than other grasswrens, and the calls have been rendered 'tsi–tsi–tsit'. First described from specimens taken in 1967 (although birds seen as early as 1921 may have been of this species). Food: seeds and insects.

BREEDING. Nest: a loose and bulky structure of grass, usually with an incomplete hood; lined with soft grass and sometimes a few feathers; usually not well-hidden in a lignum bush, or in canegrass clumps. Clutch: two; pinkish-white, irregularly spotted with nutmeg-brown, often at the larger end. Breeding season: July to September.

25:18 EASTERN BRISTLEBIRD *Dasyornis brachypterus*

IDENTIFICATION. This bird is mainly plain brown, and somewhat paler on the face, throat and breast, with a pronounced rufous wash in the wing. Sexes are similar.

DISTRIBUTION. Restricted areas from extreme south-eastern Queensland to eastern Victoria; mainly coast and associated highlands.

NOTES. It inhabits swampy heathlands and grassy undergrowth amid forest country in mountainous areas; also occurring in coastal areas. Although still locally common, it is now generally rare and very restricted in range. Skulking and elusive, it is extremely difficult to observe, but it has several loud, distinctive calls, including an alarm note, 'szwit', and a clear, resonant, 'ip–

per–tee–chee'. It scampers rapidly through the thickest vegetation, sometimes with its tail partly erect. It rarely flies, and then only for short distances. The voice is sweet and resonant. Food: insects and seeds.

BREEDING. Nest: dome-shaped, with a side entrance; loosely constructed of dry leaves and grass blades, and lined with fine dried grass; placed near the ground in a tussock or a low bush. Clutch: two; white or whitish-brown, with dots of purplish-brown. Breeding season: August to December, occasionally January.

25:19 RUFOUS BRISTLEBIRD *Dasyornis broadbenti*

IDENTIFICATION. This bird is mainly plain warm brown, with a greyish, scaled breast and rich rufous head, with a small pale spot between bill and eye. Sexes are similar.

DISTRIBUTION. Coastal southern Victoria (west of Port Phillip) and south-eastern South Australia; also in a narrow strip of coastal plain in the south-west of Western Australia.

NOTES. Apparently this bird once extended right across the coastal area of southern Australia, but the intermediate links of the chain have been lost. Secretive and extremely difficult to observe, the species inhabits dense low scrub and is practically confined to the ground. It is most common in south-western Victoria, where its clear calls may often be heard; the chief notes are 'chip, chip, chewee', and 'chip–chowee', followed by a softer 'chew–a'; the alarm-note is a brisk 'queeek'. The bird also exercises its rich voice at times in a charming whisper-song. Food: insects and seeds.

BREEDING. Nest: oval, with a side entrance; constructed of dry leaves and grasses and lined with finer materials; placed in a low thick bush or tussock. Clutch: two; pinkish-white, dotted purplish-brown. Breeding season: September to December.

25:20 WESTERN BRISTLEBIRD *Dasyornis longirostris*

IDENTIFICATION. This bird is very similar to Eastern Bristlebird, but somewhat smaller, and slightly more distinctly scaled on breast and upperparts. Sexes are similar.

DISTRIBUTION. Coastal corner of south-western Australia.

NOTES. Rare, sedentary, and apparently now confined to Two Peoples Bay, Waynchinicup River and Fitzgerald River National Park, in the neighbourhood of Albany, Western Australia, where it frequents wet heathland and dense coastal scrub. Usually seen in pairs, it is secretive and extremely difficult to observe. Territories are maintained throughout the year. The song has been rendered 'chip–pee–tee–peetle–pet', answered by the mate's 'quick three beers'. Food: insects and seeds.

BREEDING. Nest: oval, with a side entrance; constructed of dried grass stalks, with finer grasses for lining; placed in thick herbage near the ground. Clutch: two; dull white, spotted purplish-brown. Breeding season: October to January.

PLATE 26

FAIRYWRENS OF HEATH AND SHRUBS

26:1 SUPERB FAIRYWREN *Malurus cyaneus*

IDENTIFICATION. The male is brilliant blue and black, with a white belly, and no chestnut in the shoulder. The female and young are dull brown, with a sooty brown tail, pale reddish bill, and dull rufous patch around the eye.

DISTRIBUTION. From about Springsure and Brisbane, Queensland, south to Tasmania and west to Kangaroo Island and Eyre Peninsula, South Australia; also much of the Riverina.

NOTES. Usually seen in family parties, its favourite haunts are thickets in the fringes of scrubs and the banks of watercourses. It is also plentiful in orchards and gardens and is therefore one of Australia's best-known birds. It feeds often on open ground close to cover. It has a pretty, reeling song, which may be said to suggest a tiny and musical alarm clock; this is sometimes rendered at night. The young male resembles the female for several months. The first change of plumage is the appearance of a dark blue tail and black bill; other changes follow quickly, black feathers appearing on the nape and chest, and blue feathers on the crown, cheeks and back. Young birds of an early brood often assist in feeding later ones. Food: insects.

BREEDING. Nest: dome-shaped, with a side entrance; constructed of grasses, bark fibre and cobweb; lined with feathers, wool, or other soft materials; placed near the ground in shrubs or grass. Clutch: three to four; reddish-white, spotted reddish-brown. Breeding season: July to December, sometimes later.

26:2 SPLENDID FAIRYWREN *Malurus splendens*

IDENTIFICATION. The male is entirely brilliant blue and black. The female is an immature mousy grey-brown, with dull blue tail, pale reddish bill, and dull rufous patch around the eye.

DISTRIBUTION. Southern Australia generally, except the south-east. In three populations, differing slightly in appearance: *M. s. melanotus* occurs from about Winton, Queensland, and near Griffith, New South Wales, west to south-eastern South Australia; *M. s. callainus* occurs from the Simpson Desert west to the Gibson and Great Victoria Deserts; and *M. s. splendens* inhabits southern Western Australia, north to about Shark Bay.

NOTES. Seen in pairs or family parties, it inhabits low bushes on plains, in mallee, mulga and brigalow scrubs, in thickets on slopes of hills, and (in the south-west) the undergrowth of forests and woodlands. Similar in calls and habits to the Superb Fairywren, but much more retiring.

BREEDING. Nest: domed, with a side entrance near the top; made of dry grass, lined with feathers, fine grass and fur; placed in tangled grass or a low bush near the ground. Clutch: three to four; white or pale pinkish, spotted and marked, reddish or purplish brown. Breeding season: mainly August to December.

26:3 WHITE-WINGED FAIRYWREN *Malurus leucopterus*

IDENTIFICATION. The male is a rich blue, with white back and wings. The female is a very plain, pale grey-brown, with pinkish bill and powder blue tail. Males of the population on Dirk Hartog and Barrow Islands, Western Australia (subspecies *leucopterus*) are glossy black, with white wings.

DISTRIBUTION. Most of interior and western Australia.

NOTES. Usually seen in family parties seldom containing more than one fully plumaged adult male. It frequents saltbush and bluebush plains and open roly-poly country. The song is a rapid reeling trill; calls include a thin abrupt 'prr'p'. The population on Dirk Hartog and Barrow Islands, Western Australia, happened to be formally described first, so the species as a whole must take its name *leucopterus*.

BREEDING. Nest: loosely built, domed, with a side entrance; made of soft dry grass, lined with finer grass and a few feathers; placed near the ground in a low bush. Clutch: two to four; white, sparingly blotched and marked with reddish-brown. Breeding season: mainly August to November.

26:4 VARIEGATED FAIRYWREN *Malurus lamberti*

IDENTIFICATION. The male has a white belly, black throat, red shoulders, and brilliant blue crown and ear coverts, the crown a noticeably darker, richer blue than the ear coverts. The female is mousy grey-brown above, dingy white below, with a dull pinkish bill, chestnut patch around the eye, and distinct blue tinge in the dark tail.

DISTRIBUTION. Australia generally, except Tasmania, Victoria, north-eastern Queensland and the far south-west of Western Australia. There are four groups of populations, their classification vexed and controversial, and sometimes regarded as distinct species: *M. l. lamberti* (Variegated Fairywren) of the east coast, *M. l. assimilis* (Purple-backed Fairywren) of most of Australia, *M. l. dulcis* (Lavender-flanked Fairywren, not illustrated) of Arnhem Land, and *M. l. rogersi* (not illustrated) of the Kimberley.

NOTES. Common and sedentary, it is seen in pairs or family parties, frequenting undergrowth, heathlands, and undergrowth at the margins of rainforests. It is much shyer than the Superb Fairywren and its call is rather lighter.

BREEDING. Nest: dome-shaped, with an entrance near the top; constructed of dried grasses or plant-down; placed near the ground in a low bush, tuft of grass, or clump of ferns. Clutch: three to four; white or reddish-white, spotted with different shades of red. Breeding season: September to December, sometimes later.

26:5 LOVELY FAIRYWREN *Malurus amabilis*

IDENTIFICATION. The male is very similar to the male Variegated Fairywren, but with ear coverts the same shade of blue as the crown, and the tail white tipped and edged. The female is dusky blue above, white below, with white lores.

DISTRIBUTION. Coastal lowlands of Cape York Peninsula, south on the west coast to about the Edward River (possibly as far as the Norman River) and on the east coast to about Townsville, Queensland.

NOTES. Seen in pairs or family parties, it frequents the fringes of rainforests and adjacent heathland or shrubbery, lantana thickets, and landward fringes of mangroves; mainly coastal, but extending locally into highlands up to about 550 metres altitude. Generally uncommon and patchy in distribution. It spends relatively more time in trees (rather than in the underbrush) than other wrens.

BREEDING. Nest: dome-shaped; constructed of dried grasses and skeletons of leaves, hidden in undergrowth. Clutch: three; white or pinkish-white, sprinkled reddish-brown. Breeding season: September to December.

26:6 RED-WINGED FAIRYWREN *Malurus elegans*

IDENTIFICATION. A large, very long-tailed fairywren, the male very like Blue-breasted Fairywren, but with cheeks and crown silvery blue (not deep blue), and flanks pale buff (not white). The female and young have rather dark grey heads, brown back, and black bill.

DISTRIBUTION. Coastal districts of south-western Australia from Moora to the Stirling Range.

NOTES. Found in pairs or family parties, it inhabits dense scrub, thickets and heathlands bordering swamps and streams.

BREEDING. Nest: dome-shaped; constructed of grass and strips of bark; placed in a low bush near the ground. Clutch: three to four; pinkish-white, with spots of reddish-brown. Breeding season: September to December.

26:7 BLUE-BREASTED FAIRYWREN *Malurus pulcherrimus*

IDENTIFICATION. The male has a white belly, dark blue throat, uniform bright blue cheeks and crown, and red shoulders. The female and young are very difficult to distinguish from female Variegated Fairywren.

DISTRIBUTION. Southern Eyre Peninsula, South Australia, and south-western Australia (except the forested south-west corner) north to about Shark Bay and east possibly as far as Eucla.

NOTES. Locally common and sedentary, it is usually seen in family parties. Favourite haunts are dwarf marlock or mallee scrubs growing in patches on or about hills and dry creek-beds. The male bird especially is very secretive in its movements. In general the habits of the species are similar to those of the Variegated Wren.

BREEDING. Nest: domed, loosely built of grass, lined with finer materials and a few feathers; placed close to the ground in a low bush. Clutch: three; white, spotted reddish-brown. Breeding season: September to December.

26:8 RED-BACKED FAIRYWREN *Malurus melanocephalus*

IDENTIFICATION. The breeding male is unmistakable, being jet black with a brilliant red mantle. The immature males, females and juveniles closely resemble other fairywrens, but are somewhat darker, browner, shorter-tailed, with brown bill, plain face, and no hint of blue in the dark brown tail.

DISTRIBUTION. Northern and eastern Australia, west to about Broome, Western Australia and south to about Taree, New South Wales.

NOTES. Common, usually seen in family parties, it frequents dwarf scrub and blady grass, mainly in damp places. Because the reeling calls of most fairywrens are similar it is sometimes difficult, in the sub-tropics, to determine whether an unseen bird is a Red-backed Wren or a Variegated Wren; but if the undergrowth is heavy and damp, the caller is likely to be a Red-back.

BREEDING. Nest: dome-shaped; constructed of grass and lined with finer grass; placed in a tussock, sometimes above water. Clutch: three to four; white, spotted reddish-brown. Breeding season: August to February.

26:9 LILAC-CROWNED FAIRYWREN *Malurus coronatus*

IDENTIFICATION. The male is brown above, sandy white below, with blue tail, black mask, and strikingly brilliant violet crown. The female is similar but crown is grey and mask reddish-brown.

DISTRIBUTION. Tropical northern Australia, from the Fitzroy River, Western Australia, east to the Gregory River, north-western Queensland.

NOTES. Usually seen in family parties, it inhabits canegrass, pandanus palms, and paperbark thickets near rivers. Locally common, it is sedentary. As other wrens, adult males are shy and difficult to observe, females and immatures are usually much more confiding. The song is a shrill high-pitched reel, 'cheepa–cheepa–cheepa'; calls include an abrupt soft 'drrt'.

BREEDING. Nest: bulky, with a side entrance near the top; constructed of paperbark and canegrass; lined with fine grass roots; usually placed in a tussock. Clutch: three; pinkish-white, with spots of brownish-pink. Breeding season: mainly January to June.

PLATE 27

SOME BIRDS OF THE AIR AND OPEN SPACES

27:1 LITTLE WOODSWALLOW *Artamus minor*

IDENTIFICATION. This bird resembles Dusky Woodswallow but is smaller, much darker, and without any white in the wings. Sexes are similar.

DISTRIBUTION. Northern Australia, south to about Grafton and Bourke, New South Wales; Renmark, South Australia, and the Murchison River, Western Australia.

NOTES. Usually found in pairs or small flocks, it frequents open country studded with trees and the rugged ranges of the interior. Mainly sedentary in the west, but it is apparently partially migratory in the east. Its general habits are similar to those of the Dusky Woodswallow.

BREEDING. Nest: open, cup-shaped; constructed of small twigs and plant stems and lined with rootlets; placed in a tree cavity or crevice. Clutch: three; dull white, spotted and blotched brown and with underlying markings of slaty-grey. Breeding season: October to January.

27:2 DUSKY WOODSWALLOW *Artamus cyanopterus*

IDENTIFICATION. This is a plain, dusky brown woodswallow, with outer webs of the outermost wing feathers white, producing a distinct white line along the folded wing. Sexes are similar.

DISTRIBUTION. Eastern Australia from near Cairns south to Tasmania and west to Kangaroo Island and Eyre Peninsula, South Australia; also extreme south-western Australia.

NOTES. Found in pairs or flocks, it frequents open spaces in forest country, also partly cleared lands, orchards and parks. Like other woodswallows, it flies very gracefully. Its seasonal movements are nomadic. Birds of this species have the habit of roosting clustered together on the rough bark of a tree trunk. Food: insects and nectar.

BREEDING. Nest: open, cup-shaped; constructed of slender twigs and lined with grass; placed in a tree cavity or crevice. Clutch: three to four; creamy-white, with varying shades of brown, black, and grey. Breeding season: September to January.

27:3 GREY SWIFTLET *Collocalia spodiopygia*

IDENTIFICATION. This is a small, dark grey swift with pale greyish rump. Sexes are similar.

DISTRIBUTION. North-eastern Australia, from Cape York south to about Mackay, Queensland (sporadically further south). It also inhabits New Guinea and islands of the south-western Pacific.

NOTES. Common in flocks over open spaces of coastal ranges, rainforest, or about the precipitous sides of rocky ridges, it flies rapidly and captures small insects on the wing. The species nests in colonies (sometimes exceeding 200 pairs) in caves; the bird uses incessant high-pitched 'clicking' notes as an echo-location device to help it manoeuvre in pitch darkness. The bird's calls also include a high-pitched 'cheep–cheep'. Food: small flying insects.

BREEDING. Nest: a small cup of moss, bark, and feathers, cemented together with saliva, and fastened to the sloping roof of a cave or rocky recess. Clutch: one; white. Breeding season: October to March.

27:4 FORK-TAILED SWIFT *Apus pacificus*

IDENTIFICATION. This bird is mainly black, with a conspicuous white rump and a long-forked tail. Sexes are similar.

DISTRIBUTION. Breeds in Siberia, Mongolia, northern China, Japan and Taiwan, migrating south to Australia, where it occurs mainly in the centre and west; more erratic and in smaller numbers along the east coast.

NOTES. In flocks, which visit Australia during late spring and summer, this bird is usually seen hawking for insects high in the air, or just above the tree tops; at times, close to the ground. It is usual for large (sometimes huge) flocks to appear during unsettled weather conditions. Food: insects, caught on the wing.

BREEDING. Nest: a shallow saucer of vegetation cemented with saliva; placed in a cranny of a cliff. Clutch: one to three; pure white. Breeding season: June to July.

27:5 SPINE-TAILED SWIFT *Hirundapus caudacutus*

IDENTIFICATION. This bird has a greyish, cigar-shaped body with short blunt tail. The chin and undertail coverts are white. Sexes are similar.

DISTRIBUTION. Breeds in eastern Siberia, Mongolia and Japan, migrating to eastern Australia in the southern summer.

NOTES. Seen in flocks visiting Australia during late spring and summer, it is similar in habits to the Fork-tailed Swift, but faster and more direct in flight, with characteristic hurtling glides on motionless wings. It is on the wing throughout the day, but has been recorded clinging at night to the face of cliffs, against the bark of large trees, or in thick foliage. Food: small flying insects.

BREEDING. Nest: a shallow saucer of scraps of vegetation cemented with saliva; in crevices of cliffs. Clutch: two to three; dull white. Breeding season: May to August.

27:6 WELCOME SWALLOW *Hirundo neoxena*

IDENTIFICATION. This bird is glossy blue-black above, sandy white below, with a dull rufous face and throat, and long, deeply forked tail. Sexes are similar.

DISTRIBUTION. Southern and eastern Australia generally, including Tasmania; absent from much of the centre and north-west. It also inhabits New Zealand (self-introduced), Lord Howe Island and Norfolk Island.

NOTES. A common and well-known bird, it frequents parklands and settled areas. It is, for the most part, a migratory species — prior to departing for northern Australia in autumn, the birds congregate in large flocks — but in many districts numbers remain throughout the year. The species has a sweet, twittering song. Food: small flying insects.

BREEDING. Nest: cup-shaped; constructed of mud pellets, reinforced and lined with grass, horsehair, and feathers; built under eaves of buildings, verandas, bridges, and in caves and mining shafts. Clutch: four to five; white, spotted purplish-brown with underlying markings of lavender. Breeding season: may nest at any time, but especially August to December.

27:7 BARN SWALLOW *Hirundo rustica*

IDENTIFICATION. This species is very similar to Welcome Swallow except for a narrow blue-black band across the upper breast. Sexes are similar.

DISTRIBUTION. Widespread across the Northern Hemisphere, wintering south to South America, Africa, India, Indonesia, Australia, and Micronesia. In Australia records are comparatively few, but it apparently winters in fair numbers in coastal regions of the north-west; also the Top End and north-eastern Queensland. Scattered records further south.

NOTES. Previously known from only a single specimen from Cape York, but now has been recorded with increasing frequency since about 1960. It is very similar in habits to the Welcome Swallow with which it often associates.

BREEDING. Nest: a bulky cup of grass and mud pellets, lined with feathers and other soft materials, usually plastered to the wall of a house or barn. Clutch: four to six; white, speckled with shades of reddish brown or grey. Breeding season: generally April to June.

27:8 FAIRY MARTIN *Cecropis ariel*

IDENTIFICATION. This bird has a square tail, white rump, and bright rufous crown. Sexes are similar.

DISTRIBUTION. Almost throughout Australia; rare in Tasmania.

NOTES. Seen in flocks, it frequents open country, chiefly in the neighbourhood of streams and lakes. Migratory in southern Australia (often in large flocks, sometimes with other swallows), it is sedentary or locally nomadic elsewhere. Food: insects, caught on the wing.

BREEDING. Colonial. Nest: a retort or bottle-shaped structure; constructed of mud pellets and lined with grass and feathers. Clutch: four to five; dull white, freckled yellowish or faint reddish-brown. Breeding season: September to January.

27:9 WHITE-BACKED SWALLOW *Cheramoeca leucosterna*

IDENTIFICATION. This species resembles Welcome Swallow in size and shape, but is mainly black, with a white back, crown and throat. Sexes are similar.

DISTRIBUTION. Australia generally, except Tasmania and the tropical north.

NOTES. Found in small flocks or colonies, it inhabits chiefly open country in the vicinity of streams, mainly in the interior but locally in coastal regions. Apparently it is mainly sedentary or locally nomadic. In cold windy weather several birds may shelter in an old nesting burrow. Food: small insects, caught on the wing.

BREEDING. Nest: of grass and small leaves, in a burrow in the vertical bank of a creek. Clutch: five to seven; white. Breeding season: August to December.

27:10 RICHARD'S PIPIT *Anthus novaeseelandiae*

IDENTIFICATION. This is a nondescript, streaked, brownish, sparrow-sized bird of open country, with a slender bill and white outer tail feathers. It is conspicuous in flight and persistently wags its tail up and down. Sexes are similar.

DISTRIBUTION. Virtually found throughout Australia, including Tasmania. It is also widespread in the Old World from Africa across Asia to New Zealand.

NOTES. Singly or in pairs, it is widely distributed and very common in all kinds of open country, from suburban golf courses to arid plains, and from the highest ranges to the seashore. When flushed it rises with an undulating flight, sometimes uttering warbling notes, then suddenly drops to the ground. Occasionally it perches on a post or the branch of a tree, and sometimes sings while there. Usually, however, it relies on short flights or running to keep out of harm's way. Food: insects and seeds.

BREEDING. Nest: cup-shaped; constructed of grass; placed in a hollow in the ground near or under a tuft of grass. Clutch: three to four; greyish-white, spotted pale umber and dull slate-grey. Breeding season: August to January.

27:11 YELLOW WAGTAIL *Motacilla flava*

IDENTIFICATION. This is a slender, long-tailed bird of open country. In breeding, its plumage is olive green above, and bright yellow below. In winter, it is olive above, dull white below, with white throat and superciliary. Sexes are similar, but females are duller than males.

DISTRIBUTION. Breeds in Alaska and across Europe and northern Asia; winters south throughout Africa and across southern Asia to Indonesia, New Guinea and northern Australia.

NOTES. Status in Australia uncertain (recorded mainly in the Kimberley, around Darwin and in north-eastern Queensland), but probably an annual visitor in small numbers. A terrestrial bird, it frequents airfields, water meadows or the margins of swamps and lagoons; the tail is wagged up and down almost incessantly — hence the name. The chief call is a shrill, high-pitched 'tzweeep'.

BREEDING. Nest: cup-shaped; of grass and plant stems, thickly lined with hair; placed in a depression in the ground, usually sheltered by a tussock. Clutch: five to six; buff or ochre, mottled or finely streaked. Breeding season: May to July.

27:12 BUFF-BREASTED BUTTONQUAIL *Turnix olivei*

IDENTIFICATION. This species is very similar to Chestnut-backed Buttonquail, but its breast is a plain dingy buff. The male is similar to the female but duller. The female is larger than the male.

DISTRIBUTION. Central and western Cape York Peninsula.

NOTES. Seen in pairs or small coveys, it inhabits rank grass in open forest country. Little is known of its habits. It is shy and difficult to flush. Food: seeds; fine gravel is swallowed to aid digestion.

BREEDING. Nest: an ovate structure with an entrance at the side; constructed of fine grass; placed in a shallow depression in the ground. Clutch: usually four; whitish, speckled reddish-brown, bluish-grey, and black. Breeding season: usually late summer and early autumn.

27:13 CHESTNUT-BACKED BUTTONQUAIL *Turnix castanota*

IDENTIFICATION. The bird is reddish above, grey below, intricately marked and spangled grey, white, slate and chestnut. In flight, its rump and wing coverts look strongly reddish. Sexes are similar but the female is brighter and larger than the male.

DISTRIBUTION. Tropical northern Australia from the Kimberley to Arnhem Land.

NOTES. Seen in pairs or small coveys, it frequents sandstone country. When disturbed, the birds seldom rise together, but run along the ground. It is only when closely pressed that they take wing, and then they merely fly a short distance. Food: seeds and insects.

BREEDING. Nest: a depression beneath a tussock or in a clump of grass; usually in the vicinity of water. Clutch: usually four; greenish-white, sometimes speckled dark brown; others have faint spots of purplish-brown. Breeding season: January to March.

27:14 RED-CHESTED BUTTONQUAIL *Turnix pyrrhothorax*

IDENTIFICATION. This species is very like Little Buttonquail, but much darker and more richly coloured, with a conspicuous pale superciliary. In flight, its upperparts look distinctly olive grey. Sexes are similar, but the female is brighter than the male.

DISTRIBUTION. Eastern Australia generally, from Arnhem Land and Cape York Peninsula south to Victoria, mainly west of the Great Dividing Range.

NOTES. Seen in pairs or small coveys, it inhabits grasslands, high dry country, river flats or pasture and wheat stubble. Locally common, it is highly nomadic in habits. Secretive and difficult to flush, it then only flies for a short distance, often uttering a sharp dry chattering call. Food: seeds and insects.

BREEDING. Nest: a slight depression in the ground; scantily lined with grass; usually sheltered by a tussock. Clutch: usually four; buff-white, spotted slate-grey, chestnut, and dark brown. Breeding season: September to December.

27:15 LITTLE BUTTONQUAIL *Turnix velox*

IDENTIFICATION. This is a small buttonquail with white belly and flanks and rather plain, sandy red head and breast. In flight it looks sandy brown, its white flanks often obvious. Sexes are similar, but the female is brighter and larger than the male.

DISTRIBUTION. Australia generally, except the tropical north, Tasmania, and the extreme south-east.

NOTES. Usually seen in coveys, large or small, it inhabits open plains. It is nomadic, its appearance being regulated by rainfall. If the season is good, large flocks appear. The bird lies close, and when flushed it flies only short distances. The flocks usually scatter when disturbed, making it difficult to flush them again. Food: seeds and insects. The female does the courting and leaves to the male the care of the young.

BREEDING. Nest: a slight depression in the ground; lined with grass; usually under a tussock. Clutch: four; buff-white, thickly spotted slate-grey, chestnut, and purplish-brown. Breeding season: September to December, but individual pairs may be found breeding throughout most of the year.

27:16 RED-BACKED BUTTONQUAIL *Turnix maculosa*

IDENTIFICATION. This is a small buttonquail with plain dull rufous face and breast, yellowish bill, dark crown, and rich rufous nape. In flight, its buff wing coverts contrast strongly with its olive grey back, rump and flight feathers. Sexes are similar but the female is brighter than the male.

DISTRIBUTION. Northern and eastern Australia (occasionally as far south as northern Victoria). It is also found in New Guinea and Timor.

NOTES. Seen in pairs or small coveys, it chiefly inhabits marshy lands studded with low scrub, especially in coastal districts. It is shy, lies very close, and is difficult to flush. The call is a monotonous 'oom–oom–oom'. Food: seeds and insects.

BREEDING. Nest: a hollow in the ground; scantily lined with grass; in the shelter of a tussock. Clutch: usually four; greyish-white to stone-grey with numerous freckles of pale umber and grey. Breeding season: October to February.

27:17 STUBBLE QUAIL *Coturnix novaezelandiae*

IDENTIFICATION. This species is grey-brown above, strongly streaked below, with a pale superciliary. The male has a warm sandy brown face and throat. In flight it looks grey-brown, with distinct buff-white streaks on its back and rump.

DISTRIBUTION. Australia and Tasmania; generally widespread and common in southern Queensland, New South Wales, Victoria, south-eastern South Australia, and coastal Western Australia north to about Shark Bay; erratic and highly local elsewhere. It once also inhabited New Zealand (now extinct).

NOTES. Usually seen in coveys, large or small, it inhabits open plains, well-grassed lands and cultivated paddocks. It is nomadic, often appearing in flocks in good seasons. The chief call is a loud clear 'pippy–wheep!'. Food: seeds, green grasses, and insects.

BREEDING. Nest: a grass-lined depression in the ground; sheltered by a tussock or a low bush; sometimes situated in standing crops. Clutch: seven to eight; buff, freckled reddish-brown. Breeding season: usually September to January or February.

27:18 PLAINS-WANDERER *Pedionomus torquatus*

IDENTIFICATION. This bird has an alert, upright 'tip-toe' stance which is distinctive. The female has a white-spangled black collar and dull rufous throat patch.

DISTRIBUTION. Eastern Australia (inland) from southern South Australia and Victoria to (probably) central Queensland.

NOTES. Found alone or in pairs, it inhabits open plains and level grassed lands. It flies only under compulsion and when disturbed hides itself in the grass. When running about it has the habit of raising itself on its toes, to enable it to make a survey of its surroundings. This curious bird was once fairly common but has become rare. Food: seeds and insects.

BREEDING. Nest: a grass-lined depression in the ground; usually sheltered by a tussock or low bush. Clutch: usually four; stone-coloured or yellowish-white, thickly freckled with various shades of umber and slate-grey. Breeding season: September to January or February.

27:19 BROWN SONGLARK *Cinclorhamphus cruralis*

IDENTIFICATION. The male is dark sooty brown, almost black below, with a long untidy tail often held cocked. The female is much smaller and is easily confused with Rufous Songlark (No. 11:10, p. 82), but is a much colder brown, with a greyish rump and a dark patch on its belly.

DISTRIBUTION. Australia generally, except Tasmania and Cape York Peninsula.

NOTES. An inhabitant of open grasslands and cultivation paddocks, it is generally rare and local in the north, common in the south. It is a partially migratory species, usually arriving in the more southerly portions of Australia during September and departing for the plains of the interior about February. It spends much time on the ground, but frequently perches on fences and stumps, or in dead trees. It ascends fairly high in the air, singing in a curious clattering and creaking fashion as it rises, or while hovering; it then descends in a fluttering flight, uttering meanwhile a chuckling sound. The species appears to be polygamous. Food: seeds and insects.

BREEDING. Nest: cup-shaped; constructed of dried grasses and softer materials, built in a depression in the ground, usually near a tuft of grass or a low shrub. Clutch: three to four; salmon-pink, with pinkish-red markings. Breeding season: September to January.

27:20 SINGING BUSHLARK *Mirafra javanica*

IDENTIFICATION. The plumage of this bird is very variable — very similar to Skylark, but smaller and darker, with a shorter, stubbier bill and reddish or cinnamon shoulder patch. Sexes are similar.

DISTRIBUTION. Australia generally, except the centre and south-west, Tasmania, and Cape York Peninsula. It is also widespread across Asia.

NOTES. Found in pairs or small parties (sometimes large numbers in the non-breeding season), it inhabits open plains, grassy flats, and cultivation paddocks. It is generally inconspicuous and often overlooked. Like the Skylark (which has been introduced to Australia) this bird soars at a considerable height and sings continuously; its spirited melody, which often extends into mimicry of other birds' voices, is heard to advantage on moonlit nights of late spring and early summer. Size and pattern in this species remains fairly constant across Australia, but the ground colour of the plumage varies widely — tending to buff, brown, rufous or grey — from place to place, in general conforming with the prevailing colour of the region's soil. Food: seeds and insects.

BREEDING. Nest: small, rounded, domed, with a large side entrance; constructed of grass, lined with finer grasses; built in a slight depression scraped by the bird in the ground. Clutch: three to five; greyish-white, freckled dark grey or greyish-brown. Breeding season: October to February.

PLATE 28

BIRDS OF REED-BEDS AND GRASSLANDS

28:1 DOUBLE-BARRED FINCH *Poephila bichenovii*

IDENTIFICATION. This finch is mainly white below, with a 'clown' face and two narrow black bars on its breast. Those found in eastern Australia have white rumps, those in the tropical north (west of the Gulf of Carpentaria, subspecies *annulosa*) have black rumps.

DISTRIBUTION. Northern and eastern Australia, west to about Broome, Western Australia and south to about Moruya, New South Wales. Gradually expanding southward in the south-east.

NOTES. Common, it is mainly sedentary or locally nomadic. Seen in pairs or flocks, it frequents grasslands bordering watercourses preferring tall grass or low thickets. The call is a soft, kitten-like mewing. Food: seeds.

BREEDING. Nest: bottle-shaped, made of dry grass and lined with finer materials; placed in a grass tussock or a small bush, sometimes near a wasp nest. Clutch: four to eight; white. Breeding season: variable, but mainly February to June in the north and August to November in the south-east.

28:2 ZEBRA FINCH *Poephila guttata*

IDENTIFICATION. This species has a red bill, banded black-and-white tail, vertical black streak below eye and (in males) chestnut ear patch.

DISTRIBUTION. Australia generally, except Tasmania and high-rainfall areas of the far north, south-east and south-west. It is also found in Timor.

NOTES. Common, it is seen in pairs or small parties, occasionally large flocks, frequenting grasslands bordering watercourses and arid plains intersected with scrub. It is also common in partly cleared and cultivated lands. Nomadic, it spends much time on the ground feeding chiefly on the seeds of grasses. The call is a soft trumpet-like note.

BREEDING. Nest: domed, with a side entrance; constructed of grass and lined with feathers or other soft material; placed in undergrowth or tree cavity. Clutch: four to eight; faint bluish-white. Breeding season: very variable, but mainly August to December.

28:3 PAINTED FIRETAIL *Emblema pictum*

IDENTIFICATION. This bird is striking with a red face, black breast and white iris.

DISTRIBUTION. North-western Australia, southern Northern Territory, western Queensland, and northern South Australia.

NOTES. Found in pairs or small flocks, it frequents stony hillsides where spinifex flourishes, and grasslands bordering watercourses. It utters a pleasing twitter when flushed. Locally common, but it is patchy in distribution. Food: insects and seeds.

BREEDING. Nest: bottle-shaped, with a short entrance tunnel; made of twigs, bark fragments, spinifex stems and grass, on a platform of small stones and pieces of soil, placed at the base of a clump of spinifex. Clutch: three to five; white, lustreless. Breeding season: variable.

28:4 RED-BROWED FINCH *Aegintha temporalis*

IDENTIFICATION. This is a small greenish finch with a bright red rump and red eyebrow stripe.

DISTRIBUTION. Eastern Australia from Cape York Peninsula south to the Riverina and Victoria and west to Kangaroo Island and near Adelaide, South Australia; introduced near Perth, Western Australia.

NOTES. Found in pairs or flocks, it frequents grasslands, partly cleared and cultivated lands, open forest, and the fringes of scrub. It is generally common, and abundant in the neighbourhood of certain towns and cities. It spends much time on the ground, feeding on seeds and flying into adjacent shrubbery when disturbed. The call is a high-pitched 'seeee'.

BREEDING. Nest: bulky, bottle-shaped; constructed of dried and green grasses and lined with feathers and fine grass; placed in a small tree or bush. Clutch: five to eight; white. Breeding season: mainly September to January.

28:5 STAR FINCH *Neochmia ruficauda*

IDENTIFICATION. This finch has a red face and bill, dull green back, and a head and underparts profusely spotted white. Northern birds (subspecies *clarescens*) have yellowish bellies; north-eastern birds have dull white bellies and somewhat browner backs.

DISTRIBUTION. Tropical northern Australia from the Pilbara, Western Australia, to Cape York Peninsula, south through central Queensland; now rare, local and erratic in occurrence over much of its range.

NOTES. Seen in pairs or flocks, it frequents chiefly tall grass and dense vegetation bordering watercourses. Call is a soft, high-pitched 'tseet'. Food: seeds and flying insects.

BREEDING. Nest: bottle-shaped; constructed of dry grass and lined with fine grass and feathers; placed in a low tree or a bush. Clutch: three to five; white. Breeding season: September to January.

28:6 BLUE-FACED PARROTFINCH *Erythrura trichroa*

IDENTIFICATION. This bird has plumage which is mainly green, with a dark red tail and blue face. Sexes are similar.

DISTRIBUTION. North-eastern Queensland from Cape York to the Atherton Tableland. It also inhabits New Guinea, the Solomons, and various other islands.

NOTES. Rare and local in Australia, although it is fairly common in New Guinea and elsewhere. It frequents mangrove fringes and clearings in dense rainforest. Usually seen in small parties, it forages in low vegetation, seldom on the ground. Food: insects and seeds.

BREEDING. Nest: neat, rounded, with a small side entrance; constructed of fibre or grass and lined with soft materials, placed in a shrub or in a mangrove. Clutch: three to six; white. Breeding season: March and November are the only months on record in Australia.

28:7 PLUM-HEADED FINCH *Aidemosyne modesta*

IDENTIFICATION. This finch is mainly brown above, and white below, with underparts closely barred brown, and a dark purple crown. Sexes are similar but the female has a white superciliary.

DISTRIBUTION. Eastern Australia, mainly west of the Great Dividing Range, from about Rockhampton, Queensland, south to near Canberra, exceptionally north to about Cairns.

NOTES. Found in pairs or small flocks, it frequents savannah and grassland bordering watercourses. It is generally uncommon and patchily distributed. Food: seeds of grasses and other plants.

BREEDING. Nest: bottle-shaped; constructed of dried grasses and lined with feathers; built in tall grass, among thistles, or in a low bush. Clutch: four to seven; white. Breeding season: mainly September to January.

28:8 DIAMOND FIRETAIL *Emblema guttatum*

IDENTIFICATION. This bird is mainly brown above, white below, with a grey head. Its rump is bright red and it has a broad black band across its breast, extending along its flanks, boldly spotted white. Sexes are similar.

DISTRIBUTION. South-central Queensland to South Australia and Kangaroo Island, west to Eyre Peninsula.

NOTES. Found in pairs or small flocks, it frequents open spaces and grasslands with large trees. Feeding mainly on the ground, it usually flies to a high perch when disturbed. The call-note is a plaintive, long-drawn-out 'kweet'. Food: seeds and insects.

BREEDING. Nest: bottle-shaped, placed on its side; constructed of grass and lined with feathers; built in a bush or tree in thick foliage, sometimes in the outer loose material of the nest of an eagle or crow. Clutch: four to seven; white. Breeding season: mainly August to January.

28:9 MASKED FINCH *Poephila personata*

IDENTIFICATION. This finch has a yellow bill, brown head, white rump, and a black mask reaching only to the chin. Sexes are similar.

DISTRIBUTION. Tropical northern Australia from about Derby, Western Australia, to western Cape York Peninsula.

NOTES. Usually found in pairs or flocks, it frequents lightly timbered grasslands bordering watercourses, feeding mostly on the ground. When in flight it utters a feeble call-note, and at other times a drawn out, mournful note. Food: seeds and insects.

BREEDING. Nest: bulky, bottle-shaped; constructed of grass and lined with feathers; built in grass, near or upon the ground, sometimes in a small tree or bush. Small pieces of charcoal are often placed in the nest chamber. Clutch: five to six; white, which soon become discoloured through contact with charcoal. Breeding season: August to December, and often as late as April or June.

28:10 BLACK-THROATED FINCH *Poephila cincta*

IDENTIFICATION. This finch is brown above, sandy below, with a grey head and black throat, and a black bill. Sexes are similar. Populations of western Cape York Peninsula (subspecies *atropygialis*) have black rumps.

DISTRIBUTION. Eastern Australia from Cape York to about Inverell, New South Wales, though generally avoiding humid coastal lowlands.

NOTES. Seen in pairs or flocks, it frequents grasslands bordering watercourses and open country. It is similar in habits to the Masked Finch. Food: seeds and insects.

BREEDING. Nest: bottle-shaped; constructed of dry grasses and lined with feathers; built in tall grass, a low bush, or a small tree, and occasionally in a hollow limb of a dead tree. Clutch: five to nine; white. Breeding season: usually August to December.

28:11 LONG-TAILED FINCH *Poephila acuticauda*

IDENTIFICATION. This bird resembles Black-throated Finch except for its long pointed tail and yellow (Kimberley population, subspecies *hecki*) or red (Top End and Queensland populations) bill. Sexes are similar.

DISTRIBUTION. North-western Australia to north-western Queensland.

NOTES. It frequents open country and grass bordering watercourses, foraging mainly on bare ground. It is similar in habits to the Black-throated Finch. Food: seeds and insects. Calls include a brief attractive warbled song and a loud 'tee–wheet'.

BREEDING. Nest: bottle-shaped; constructed of dried grasses and lined with feathers; built in tall grass, a low bush, or a palm tree. Clutch: five to six; white. Breeding season: usually September to January.

28:12 YELLOW-RUMPED MANNIKIN *Lonchura flaviprymna*

IDENTIFICATION. This bird has a brown back, plain creamy underparts, pale grey head and a buff rump. Sexes are similar.

DISTRIBUTION. North-western Australia and the Northern Territory.

NOTES. Found in pairs or flocks, it frequents chiefly tall canegrass at the margins of swamps and rivers, mainly in the interior, but in times of drought it visits coastal districts. It is closely related to the Chestnut-breasted Mannikin with which it commonly flocks and sometimes interbreeds.

BREEDING. Nest: large, bottle-shaped; constructed of dried grasses and lined with finer grasses and a few feathers; built in tall grass or a low bush. Clutch: four to six; white. Breeding season: July to January.

28:13 PICTORELLA MANNIKIN *Lonchura pectoralis*

IDENTIFICATION. This bird is mainly grey above, with a black face, pale pinkish underparts, and a white breast, scaled black. Sexes are similar.

DISTRIBUTION. Northern Australia, from about Derby, Western Australia across the Northern Territory, sporadically east to about Croydon, Queensland.

NOTES. Seen in pairs or flocks, it frequents dense grass bordering watercourses and open areas. It has a feeble call-note, 'chip, chip, chip'. Food: seeds of grasses and other plants; also insects.

BREEDING. Nest: large, bottle-shaped; constructed of grass stems; built in a tussock of grass. Clutch: four to six; white. Breeding season: July to December, sometimes as late as March and April.

28:14 CHESTNUT-BREASTED MANNIKIN *Lonchura castaneothorax*

IDENTIFICATION. This bird has a yellowish rump and tail, with a brown back, black face, and rich rufous breast. Sexes are similar.

DISTRIBUTION. Northern and eastern Australia (mainly coastal) west to Derby, Western Australia, and south to about Nowra, New South Wales. It also inhabits New Guinea.

NOTES. It frequents reed-beds, canefields and grasslands, chiefly in coastal districts. The male and female are very attached to each other during the breeding season, but during late autumn and winter the species congregates in large flocks. The call, often uttered during flight, is a simple 'tare, tare'. Food: seeds of grasses and sometimes those of sorghum and other cultivated crops.

BREEDING. Nest: bulky, oval, with a side entrance; constructed of grass and plant tendrils cleverly interwoven, and lined with finer grasses; placed in a low bush, in a tuft of tall grass, or among weeds. Clutch: four to eight; white. Breeding season: usually July to December.

28:15 GOULDIAN FINCH *Chloebia gouldiae*

IDENTIFICATION. This finch is unmistakable, with a bright green back, yellow underparts and a purple breast, and a pale bill. Most individuals have black faces, others red or (very rarely) dull yellow. Sexes are similar.

DISTRIBUTION. Tropical northern Australia from Derby, Western Australia, across the Northern Territory, east (sporadically) to the Atherton Tableland, Queensland.

NOTES. Seen in pairs or flocks, it frequents open country, dry ridges where spinifex flourishes, or grasslands bordering watercourses. It feeds on or near the ground on the seeds of grasses and other plants, often far from water, which it visits at dusk. This beautiful bird has been extensively bred in aviaries since the 1920s. The black-faced morph outnumbers the red-faced morph by about 3:1.

BREEDING. Nest: bottle-shaped; constructed of dried grasses; placed in a variety of situations — in tall grass, a bush, a small tree, but more often in the hollow limb of a tree, with scanty lining added. Clutch: four to eight; white. Breeding season: mainly January to April.

28:16 CRIMSON FINCH *Neochmia phaeton*

IDENTIFICATION. This finch is rather slim and long-tailed, mainly bright red, with a light grey crown and nape, and brownish back; flanks spotted white. Birds inhabiting western Cape York Peninsula (subspecies *albiventer*) have white bellies; populations elsewhere have black bellies.

DISTRIBUTION. Tropical northern and eastern Australia, west to about Broome, Western Australia, and south to about Proserpine, Queensland. It is also found in New Guinea.

NOTES. It is generally common, but not gregarious, and seldom forms flocks. Usually seen in pairs or small parties, frequenting canefields, grass bordering watercourses and also pandanus trees. Calls include a loud 'chee–chee–chee'. Food: seeds (mainly of grasses), also termites and other insects.

BREEDING. Nest: bulky, bottle-shaped; constructed of dried grasses, bark, and leaves; lined with grass and feathers or fur; normally built in tall grass, a bush, or a pandanus tree. Clutch: five to eight; white. Breeding season: mainly August to December.

28:17 ZITTING CISTICOLA *Cisticola juncidis*

IDENTIFICATION. This species is almost impossible to distinguish from Golden-headed Cisticola except by its calls, habitat and distribution.

DISTRIBUTION. The Darwin area, Northern Territory, the head of the Gulf of Carpentaria, and the north-east coast of Australia from about Townsville to Rockhampton, Queensland. It is also widespread from Africa east to Japan and Indonesia.

NOTES. Very similar to the Golden-headed Cisticola, it cannot be reliably distinguished from that species on appearance alone, except in the case of males in breeding plumage. The songs, nests and eggs are, however very distinct; the song of the Zitting Cisticola has been transcribed as 'lik–lik–lik', or 'tink–tink–tink', with a musical but insect-like quality. It frequents the grassy margins of coastal salt flats, water meadows, and open fields. Food: small insects.

BREEDING. Nest: a deep cup-shaped structure of grass, bound with cobweb and lined with rootlets and fine grass; woven into a grass tussock. Clutch: four to five; pale blue, only faintly lustrous, sparsely spotted and freckled with pale brown. Breeding season: December to April.

28:18 GOLDEN-HEADED CISTICOLA *Cisticola exilis*

IDENTIFICATION. A common, small, nondescript bird of rank grasslands, it is streaked above, plain below. The adult male in breeding plumage is easily identifiable by its rich, warm golden-buff head. Females and immatures are almost impossible to distinguish from Zitting Cisticola on appearance alone (note habitat, distribution and calls).

DISTRIBUTION. Northern and eastern Australia, west to about Broome, Western Australia, south to Tasmania, and west to about Adelaide, South Australia; apparently extending its range westward in New South Wales. It is also widespread from India to the Bismarck Archipelago.

NOTES. It frequents rank herbage bordering swamps and standing crops, including canefields. The male has an animated song when breeding — a buzzing note followed by two or three sharp piping calls, usually uttered while flying on tremulous wings, but sometimes also while perched on a telephone wire or the top of a shrub; the flight ends in a rapid dive to the grass, over which the bird often 'hedge-hops'. It is secretive when not breeding. Food: small insects.

BREEDING. Nest: among the most complex of Australian nests; about the size of a tennis ball, placed in dense vegetation close to ground or water; built of fine grass, bound with cobweb and lined with plant down and feathers. Often green leaves of living plants are stitched into the walls or made to form a roof over the entrance. Clutch: three to five; bluish-green, spotted reddish or purplish-brown. Breeding season: September to March.

28:19 CLAMOROUS REED WARBLER *Acrocephalus stentoreus*

IDENTIFICATION. This bird has an olive brown back, unstreaked, a pale superciliary, and plain, pale brownish underparts. Sexes are similar.

DISTRIBUTION. Australia generally. It is also widespread across Africa and Asia to New Guinea.

NOTES. Seen in pairs, it frequents reed-beds. Very common, it is usually skulking and very difficult to observe, but has a loud, vigorous song. It is a migrant, arriving in southern Australia during August or September and departing in March or April. Occasionally some birds winter in the south. Half-fledged young are apt to leave a nest and clamber expertly among reeds.

BREEDING. Nest: deep, cup-shaped, constructed of soft paper-like sheaths of reeds and dead aquatic plants, firmly woven round the stems of the reeds between which it is placed; lined with fine grass. Clutch: three to four; varying from bluish-white or greyish-white to pale yellowish-brown, spotted reddish-brown and lavender. Breeding season: September to December.

28:20 LITTLE GRASSBIRD *Megalurus gramineus*

IDENTIFICATION. This bird is dull brown, streaked with black on crown, back and breast. Sexes are similar.

DISTRIBUTION. Widespread in New South Wales, Victoria, Tasmania, and far south-western Australia; also recorded at widely scattered localities (at bore-drains and similar situations) across the interior of Western Australia, the Northern Territory, and Queensland. It also inhabits New Guinea.

NOTES. Found alone or in pairs, it frequents reed-beds and rank grass. Common and widespread, it is secretive, skulking and keeps closely to dense cover. The call is very distinctive — a mournful whistle of two or three notes.

The bird is very inquisitive, and can often be coaxed into full view by a patient observer mimicking this call. The bird also utters a harsh chatter in alarm. Food: insects and seeds.

BREEDING. Nest: a deep cup, narrower at the rim; constructed of grasses and aquatic plants and lined with feathers; built in a tussock of rushes in or near water, in a swamp tea-tree, or in a mangrove. Clutch: three to five; reddish-white, almost obscured with freckles of purplish-red. Breeding season: August to January.

28:21 TAWNY GRASSBIRD *Megalurus timoriensis*

IDENTIFICATION. Rather like Little Grassbird but substantially larger, this species has a plain, dingy white breast and unstreaked, rich tawny crown. Sexes are similar.

DISTRIBUTION. Northern and eastern Australia (mainly coastal) west to the Kimberley and south to about Wollongong, New South Wales. It also inhabits Indonesia and New Guinea.

NOTES. Usually seen in pairs, it frequents reed-beds and rank grass. It is a shy bird, difficult to observe. Its call is a harsh and rapidly repeated 'chutch', but it often sings, during short and rapid flights over grass, a spirited lark-like song. Food: insects and seeds.

BREEDING. Nest: deep, cup-shaped; constructed of dried swamp grasses and lined with finer dried grasses and rootlets; built at the base of a tuft of grass or rushes, usually very well hidden. Clutch: three to four; reddish-white, freckled all over with purplish-red. Breeding season: mainly October to February.

28:22 BROWN QUAIL *Coturnix ypsilophorus*

IDENTIFICATION. This bird is a rich brown, intricately marked with slate, white, and grey. In flight it looks a plain, rich brown (Stubble Quail looks grey-brown, with prominent pale streaks). Sexes are similar.

DISTRIBUTION. Mainly coastal lowlands, of northern, eastern and south-western Australia, including Tasmania. It is also found in New Guinea.

NOTES. Usually seen in coveys or flocks, it frequents rank grass, heavy pasture, and swampy localities. Sedentary or nomadic, its movements from one locality to another are regulated by the supply of seeds and insects. It has a loud double-whistle, 'tu–wheep', uttered especially at dawn and at dusk, often at night. Food: seeds of grasses and other plants, also insects.

BREEDING. Nest: a depression in the ground; lined with grass; placed in the shelter of a tuft of grass or rushes. Clutch: six to twelve; dull white or bluish-white, usually finely freckled olive or light brown. Breeding season: mainly October to February.

28:23 KING QUAIL *Coturnix chinensis*

IDENTIFICATION. This species is very small and dark. The adult male has a mahogany belly, rich blue-grey breast and flanks, and a black and white face. The female is conspicuously barred below, its face buff and throat white.

DISTRIBUTION. Northern, eastern and southern Australia to as far west as Adelaide, South Australia. It is also found from India and China to New Guinea.

NOTES. Usually seen in coveys, it frequents heaths, dense weedy pastures and swampy areas. It is shy, secretive and difficult to flush. It is chiefly nomadic in southern Australia. It has a mournful call which is uttered at intervals during the night and at daybreak. Food: seeds of grasses and other plants, also insects.

BREEDING. Nest: a depression in the ground; lined with dried grasses; sheltered by a tuft of grass. Clutch: usually four; pale brown, more or less covered with spots and small markings of blackish-brown. Breeding season: mainly September to March.

PLATE 29

DIURNAL BIRDS OF PREY

29:1 NANKEEN KESTREL *Falco cenchroides*

IDENTIFICATION. A small, slender falcon, it is sandy rufous above. Sexes are similar, but male has a grey head and tail (dull rufous in female).

DISTRIBUTION. Australia, including Tasmania; accidental to New Zealand.

NOTES. Seen singly or in pairs, it frequents open and lightly timbered country. It is a common and familiar species, being numerous in cultivated areas. It is usually seen skimming or hovering over paddocks, crops and grasslands, every now and again dropping down to capture its prey. The call is a peculiar chatter. Food: grasshoppers and other insects, small reptiles, rodents and occasionally small birds.

BREEDING. Nest: in a hollow limb of a tree or a crevice in a rock; sometimes a deserted nest of a crow or magpie is used. Clutch: four to five; dull white or buff, blotched and freckled with reddish-brown. Breeding season: variable across Australia, mainly August to November in the south.

29:2 PEREGRINE FALCON *Falco peregrinus*

IDENTIFICATION. A large, dark, powerful falcon, its upperparts are iron grey, underparts dingy white or buff, narrowly barred black, with black crown and cheek. Sexes are similar, but juveniles are dark brown above, heavily streaked below.

DISTRIBUTION. The Australian mainland generally (except central Australia and western South Australia) and Tasmania. It also occurs in North America, Europe, Africa, and Asia.

NOTES. Seen singly or in pairs, it frequents alike inland and coastal districts, but shows a decided preference for heavily timbered and ruggedly mountainous country. It is bold and fearless and in flight is one of the strongest and swiftest of all Australian hawks. It preys upon various species of birds, such as ducks and parrots, which are usually killed in mid-air by a blow with the hind claw struck after a high-speed dive on the victim. Small mammals, reptiles and insects are also eaten. The call is a loud, harsh rattling 'chak–chak–chak–chak'.

BREEDING. Nest: usually on the ledge of a horizontal crevice on a precipitous rocky cliff; sometimes in a hollow of a tree or in an old nest of another bird. Nest sites are used for many years in succession. Clutch: two to three; buff, covered with reddish-brown markings. Breeding season: August to November.

29:3 LITTLE FALCON *Falco longipennis*

IDENTIFICATION. This falcon resembles Peregrine but is much smaller, more slender-winged, with rich reddish underparts, buff forehead, and pale reddish patch behind ear coverts, almost meeting across the nape.

DISTRIBUTION. Throughout Australia, including Tasmania.

NOTES. Seen singly or in pairs, it frequents open and lightly timbered country, also mountain ranges; often seen over towns and cities. The flight is characteristically dashing and impetuous. The call is a peevish high-pitched chatter. Food: chiefly small birds, caught on the wing; also large insects.

BREEDING. Nest: a large, loosely made platform of sticks and twigs without a lining; seldom, if ever, builds it own nest, preferring to use the abandoned nest of some other bird of prey or of a raven. Clutch: three; buff-white, almost hidden by reddish-brown markings. Breeding season: variable; usually July to October in the south, April to June in the north.

29:4 GREY FALCON *Falco hypoleucus*

IDENTIFICATION. This falcon resembles Peregrine in size, proportions and general appearance, but is more or less uniform pale grey above, white below, with darker wingtips. Sexes are similar.

DISTRIBUTION. The inland parts of Australia generally, but extending to coastal areas in parts of Western Australia.

NOTES. Seen singly or in pairs, it frequents open plains, semi-desert and lightly timbered country or mountain ranges. It is generally rare and confined to arid regions. Its flight is slower and more leisurely than that of other falcons. The call of the species is a loud 'cluck–cluck–cluck'. Food: small birds, reptiles and small mammals.

BREEDING. Nest: large; loosely built of sticks and twigs, lined with soft bark or wool; generally placed at the top of a tall tree. Often uses the abandoned nests of hawks. Clutch: two to four; buff or buff-white, covered with small spots and blotches of rusty-red. Breeding season: July to October.

29:5 BLACK FALCON *Falco subniger*

IDENTIFICATION. A large, powerfully built, more or less evenly coloured dark dusky brown falcon, with paler chin and (in very old birds) throat. Sexes are similar.

DISTRIBUTION. Inland areas of eastern and southern Australia chiefly, but also extending to some coastal localities; rare in Western Australia and Tasmania.

NOTES. Seen singly or in pairs, it frequents open and lightly timbered country, chiefly of inland districts. It is nomadic and generally uncommon. Its flight is normally leisurely, but is capable of spectacular bursts of speed while hunting, often soaring. It feeds mainly on young rabbits, quail and other small birds. The call is a hoarse 'gak–gak–gak–gak', similar to that of the Peregrine Falcon, but more subdued and not so freely used.

BREEDING. Nest: usually refurbishes the deserted nest of some other bird, such as a crow or raven. Clutch: two to five; buff, with spots of reddish brown and a few purplish-brown markings. Breeding season: variable, but mainly June to December.

29:6 BROWN FALCON *Falco berigora*

IDENTIFICATION. This falcon has very variable plumage ranging from dark to light brown or reddish-brown, and is often difficult to distinguish from Black Falcon. It is much less solidly built. Its upperparts are usually much paler than its underparts. It has a pale face with dark brown cheeks and malar streak, with tail and underwing prominently barred. Sexes are similar.

DISTRIBUTION. Australia generally, including Tasmania. It is also found in New Guinea.

NOTES. Seen singly or in pairs, it frequents open and lightly timbered country. It is usually seen flying over open spaces, or perched upon telegraph posts and wires or fences. It feeds upon snakes, grasshoppers, mice, and small birds; it catches birds by pouncing on them instead of taking them on the wing. The call is a loud cackling.

BREEDING. Nest: a platform of sticks and twigs; lined with bark fragments; usually the abandoned nest of some other bird of prey or raven is used. Clutch: two to four; buff, usually covered with reddish-brown blotches. Breeding season: mainly June to November.

29:7 BLACK-SHOULDERED KITE *Elanus notatus*

IDENTIFICATION. This bird has mainly white plumage; its upperwing pale grey, with a prominent black patch; its underwing pale, with dusky outer primaries and black patch at wrist. Sexes are similar; juveniles are like adults but with head and upper breast strongly washed golden reddish.

DISTRIBUTION. Australia generally; absent from Tasmania and most of the arid interior.

NOTES. Seen singly or in pairs, it frequents open and lightly timbered country in coastal areas. It is nomadic, moving from district to district according to food supplies. It is frequently seen in the neighbourhood of farms, either flying or hovering over paddocks and crops or perched on fences, stumps or dead trees. Its call is a chicken-like 'cheep–cheep–cheep'. Food: mice, lizards, grasshoppers, and other insects.

BREEDING. Nest: a platform made of sticks and twigs; lined with leaves; often the deserted nest of a crow or magpie is used. Clutch: three to four; whitish, blotched reddish-brown. Breeding season: mainly March to September.

29:8 LETTER-WINGED KITE *Elanus scriptus*

IDENTIFICATION. In flight overhead the black wing linings of this kite are diagnostic, but at rest it is very difficult to distinguish from Black-shouldered Kite. The black patch in front of the eye does not extend behind the eye. Sexes are similar.

DISTRIBUTION. Centred on the Simpson Desert, the Channel Country of western Queensland, and the Barkly Tableland, Northern Territory; subject to periodic irruptions, when individuals or flocks may appear almost anywhere in eastern Australia.

NOTES. Gregarious and mainly nocturnal, it is typically seen in loose flocks, frequenting open and lightly timbered country of the arid interior. It usually hunts at night, roosting in groups in trees during the day. It is mainly dependent for food on the Long-haired Rat *Rattus villosissimus*, which periodically reaches plague proportions, with a corresponding increase in the number of Letter-winged Kites. When the rat plague subsequently collapses, large numbers of kites are forced to roam widely in search of food, when individuals or groups may appear almost anywhere across mainland Australia, although the main movements tend to be south and eastwards. Calls include a high-pitched 'chip–chip' and a harsh, rasping 'kar–kar–kar'.

BREEDING. Nest: a platform constructed of fine sticks and lined with leaves and fur. Clutch: three to six; bluish-white, with brown and red markings. Breeding season: at various periods according to available food supplies.

29:9 COLLARED SPARROWHAWK *Accipiter cirrhocephalus*

IDENTIFICATION. The adults are dull grey above, narrowly barred rufous below, with a reddish collar around the neck. Immatures are dark brown above, heavily streaked and barred brown below. It is difficult to distinguish from Brown Goshawk, but smaller and less powerfully built, its tail tip square or slightly notched (rounded in Brown Goshawk). Within the genus *Accipiter*, the male bird is considerably smaller than the female, and a female sparrowhawk is approximately the size of a male Brown Goshawk.

DISTRIBUTION. Australia generally, including Tasmania. It also inhabits Indonesia and New Guinea.

NOTES. Seen singly or in pairs, it frequents most kinds of wooded country. It is usually seen skimming above the surface of the ground or in and about timbered areas; often soaring. During flight it is remarkably quick in its movements, and fearless when in pursuit of prey. Its food consists mainly of small birds. The call is a shrill chatter.

BREEDING. Nest: a platform constructed of thin twigs, either dead or green, and lined with leaves; placed on a thin forked limb of a tall tree; occasionally the deserted nest of a Whistling Kite or a raven is used. Clutch: two to four; dull white or bluish white, sometimes spotted or blotched reddish-brown or lavender. Breeding season: usually September to December.

29:10 GREY GOSHAWK *Accipiter novaehollandiae*

IDENTIFICATION. This bird has plumage either entirely white, or pale grey above and white below; with legs and feet bright yellow, and eye bright red. Sexes are similar.

DISTRIBUTION. Northern and eastern Australia, west to the Kimberley and south to Tasmania, west to Kangaroo Island and about Adelaide, South Australia.

NOTES. Seen singly or in pairs, it frequents chiefly rainforests, thickly timbered coastal districts and inland forest country. It attacks small birds (including domestic chickens) and also feeds on insects such as grasshoppers, cicadas and beetles. The call is a slow mellow 'yuik, yuik, yuik'; also a brisk chatter. The species is polymorphic, some individuals being white, others grey; the ratio of white birds to grey varies throughout the range, with white birds predominating in the Kimberley and Tasmania.

BREEDING. Nest: a large structure of sticks; lined with leaves; usually placed among the topmost branches of a tall tree. Clutch: two to three; faint bluish-white. Breeding season: August to December.

29:11 BROWN GOSHAWK *Accipiter fasciatus*

IDENTIFICATION. This species is very similar to Collared Sparrowhawk, but is larger, and the tail tip is rounded, not square or notched. Sexes are similar.

DISTRIBUTION. The Australian mainland generally, and Tasmania. It is also found from Timor to New Guinea and New Caledonia.

NOTES. Found singly or in pairs, it frequents heavily timbered districts, the margins of watercourses, and scrub. Dreaded by all the smaller birds, it procures its prey in sudden surprise attacks from cover. Food: mainly small birds. The female is considerably larger than the male. The call is a shrill chatter.

BREEDING. Nest: small, flat; constructed of sticks and lined with leaves; placed among the topmost branches of a tree. Clutch: two to four; bluish-white, sometimes spotted and blotched reddish-brown or lavender. Breeding season: September to January.

29:12 RED GOSHAWK *Erythrotriorchis radiatus*

IDENTIFICATION. This species has rich reddish brown plumage, streaked on the breast and intricately marked slate, brown and grey on the back with heavily barred wings and tail, and large, powerful, yellow legs and feet. Sexes are similar.

DISTRIBUTION. Northern and eastern Australia, from the Kimberley to north-eastern New South Wales.

NOTES. A rare and little-known species, usually seen singly or in pairs, it frequents rainforests, the margins of swamps and belts of timber bordering open country. The call is similar to that of the Brown Goshawk, but slower and deeper. Food: birds, reptiles, and small mammals.

BREEDING. Nest: large; constructed of sticks and lined with leaves; placed among the branches of a tall tree. Clutch: usually two; bluish-white, sometimes faintly smeared with pale brown or lavender. Breeding season: mainly April to September in the north-west, August to November in the east.

29:13 SWAMP HARRIER *Circus approximans*

IDENTIFICATION. This bird is mainly brown, with a white rump. The tail is plain or only obscurely barred. Sexes are similar.

DISTRIBUTION. The Australian mainland generally (except the interior) and Tasmania. It also inhabits New Caledonia, Lord Howe Island, Norfolk Island, New Zealand, and Fiji.

NOTES. Found singly or in pairs, it frequents swamps, reed-beds and cultivated lands. Harriers have long, broad wings and long tails, and their hunting behaviour is distinctive: they fly low over reed-beds, grassland, crops or other open country, slowly and methodically covering the ground in search of small animals, especially rodents and small reptiles, often gliding on upswept wings, or rocking slightly from side to side, occasionally hovering clumsily.

BREEDING. Nest: bulky; constructed of sticks, reeds, weeds, and long grass; placed on the ground among long rushes growing in a swamp or in a standing crop. Clutch: three to five; bluish-white, without gloss. Breeding season: September to January.

29:14 SPOTTED HARRIER *Circus assimilis*

IDENTIFICATION. This species is mainly mid-grey above, chestnut below, and profusely spotted white. Its tail is heavily barred and slightly wedge-shaped. Sexes are similar.

DISTRIBUTION. Australia generally, although less common in coastal areas; vagrant to Tasmania. It is also found in Indonesia.

NOTES. Usually seen singly or in pairs, it frequents open country. It is mostly observed flying slowly, periodically hovering, low over open plains, swamps and cultivated lands. Prey is procured both on the wing and on the ground. It consists of birds, reptiles, and small mammals.

BREEDING. Nest: loosely constructed of sticks, and lined with leaves; usually well-concealed in a bushy tree. Clutch: two to four; bluish-white, without gloss. Breeding season: variable, but mainly August to October.

PLATE 30

DIURNAL BIRDS OF PREY

30:1 CRESTED HAWK *Aviceda subcristata*

IDENTIFICATION. This is the only Australian raptor with a distinct crest, spiky and prominent. Its breast, head and back are plain grey; its underparts boldly barred. Sexes are similar.

DISTRIBUTION. Northern and eastern Australia, west to the Kimberley and south to about Sydney, New South Wales.

NOTES. Usually seen in pairs or small parties, it frequents margins of rainforests and belts of timber bordering rivers and plains. Its flight is usually slow and gliding; often soaring. It indulges in peculiar tumbling displays in flight, uttering the while a mellow double whistle, 'wee–choo, wee–choo, wee–choo', a call very different from that of any other Australian hawk. Food: chiefly insects snatched from the outer foliage of trees; also lizards and mice.

BREEDING. Nest: a flimsy, shallow structure of sticks, twigs and leaves; lined with leaves; usually placed on a horizontal limb and supported by several upright leafy twigs. Clutch: two to three; uniform bluish-white, unless nest-stained. Breeding season: October to December.

30:2 OSPREY *Pandion haliaetus*

IDENTIFICATION. This bird has a white head and underparts, with dark brown upperparts, dark band through the eye, and 'necklace' of dusky brown mottling across upper breast. In flight, it has distinctive kinked wings, with a prominent dark brown patch at the wrists. Sexes are similar.

DISTRIBUTION. Coastal Australia and Tasmania (but absent from most of south-eastern Australia). Cosmopolitan, except southern South America and the Pacific islands.

NOTES. Seen singly or in pairs, it frequents borders of rivers, lakes, inlets of the sea, and small islands lying off the coast. Its food consists almost entirely of fish, caught by plunging from above and grasping them with its talons.

BREEDING. Nest: large and bulky; composed of sticks and lined with seaweed, occasionally with palm leaves; usually placed on a rock overlooking the sea, but sometimes in a tree, and on the ground on islands. Clutch: two to four; buff, heavily blotched at the larger end with reddish-purple. Breeding season: May to September.

30:3 BLACK-BREASTED BUZZARD *Hamirostra melanosternon*

IDENTIFICATION. This bird is mainly black above, rufous below, with a golden nape. There is considerable colour variation in the plumage of this species; some birds have little or no black on the breast. Its flight silhouette is distinctive, with long broad wings and short, chopped-off tail, soaring on markedly upswept wings, a prominent white 'bulls-eye' towards the tip of each wing. Sexes are similar, but juveniles are mainly dull rufous. The female is larger and more conspicuously coloured than the male.

DISTRIBUTION. Australia generally, especially northern interior, and avoiding eastern and southern coastal regions; not recorded in Tasmania.

NOTES. Uncommon and mainly sedentary, it is seen singly or in pairs, frequenting open country and nesting in belts of timber growing on plains or along watercourses, mainly in the north and the arid interior. It is usually seen soaring high, after the manner of the Wedge-tailed Eagle. Food: reptiles (chiefly lizards) and mammals (mostly rabbits); it has the singular habit of robbing the nests of emus and bustards by breaking the eggs with a stone grasped in its talons and dropped onto the eggs.

BREEDING. Nest: large, flat; constructed of sticks and lined with leaves; placed in a horizontal fork of a tree; an old nest of another bird is sometimes used. Clutch: usually two; white to buff, blotched reddish-purple and lavender. Breeding season: July to November.

30:4 BLACK KITE *Milvus migrans*

IDENTIFICATION. This bird is nondescript dingy brown, with a forked tail. Sexes are similar.

DISTRIBUTION. Northern and central Australia, south to Point Cloates, Western Australia, northern South Australia and central-western New South Wales, but south to Tasmania at times of sporadic irruptions. It also occurs in Europe, north-western Africa, and Asia to Indonesia.

NOTES. Seen in pairs or flocks, it frequents inland districts chiefly. It is a common species about homesteads and camps (especially when grass is fired) and is a well-known scavenger. Its food consists of carrion, small mammals, reptiles, and grasshoppers, also garbage.

BREEDING. Nest: small, flat, compact; constructed of sticks and lined with wool or fur; placed in a high tree fork. Old nests are often relined and used year after year. Clutch: two to three; dull white, with spots, blotches and streaks of umber or reddish-brown. Breeding season: September to January (south), May to July (north).

30:5 SQUARE-TAILED KITE *Lophoictinia isura*

IDENTIFICATION. This species is not easy to distinguish from Whistling Kite or immature Brahminy Kite, but is distinctly rufous below, with paler patch on shoulder and much white on the face and crown. In flight it shows long slender wings and a rather square-tipped tail, with dark terminal bar; an obscure white 'bulls-eye' towards the tip of each wing. Sexes are similar.

DISTRIBUTION. Australia generally, except Tasmania.

NOTES. Solitary or in pairs, it frequents alike coastal districts and open woodlands (especially *Callitris* and *Eucalyptus*) of the interior, avoiding dense forest and treeless plains. Rare and elusive, and frequently misidentified, it is apparently mainly migratory in southern regions. It shows a marked preference for smaller watercourses, where it breeds in adjoining belts of timber. Food: insects, reptiles and nestling birds.

BREEDING. Nest: a substantial structure of sticks; lined with green leaves; usually placed on a high horizontal limb; the nest may be re-used in subsequent seasons. Clutch: two to three; dull white, boldly spotted red-brown and lavender. Breeding season: August to December.

30:6 BRAHMINY KITE *Haliastur indus*

IDENTIFICATION. The adult is mainly rich rufous, with a pure white head and breast. Sexes are similar, but juveniles are dull brown, and difficult to distinguish from Whistling Kite except for a short, blunt tail.

DISTRIBUTION. Northern and eastern Australia, west to about Shark Bay, Western Australia, and south to about Port Macquarie, New South Wales. It is also widespread from India to the Philippines and the Solomon Islands.

NOTES. Seen singly or in pairs, it frequents inlets, estuaries and islands off the coast, and particularly mangrove swamps. Mainly a scavenger, it forages along tide-lines for carrion, occasionally catching fish, crabs, sea snakes and cuttlefish. Its call is a curiously modulated 'pee–ah–h–h–h', the last syllable rather drawn-out and tremulous.

BREEDING. Nest: large; constructed of sticks and lined with fine bark, grass or leaves, and occasionally decorated on the sides with bleached seaweed; placed near the top of a tree. Clutch: usually two; bluish-white, sparingly marked chestnut or brown. Breeding season: April or May to September (north); August to October (east).

30:7 WHISTLING KITE *Haliastur sphenurus*

IDENTIFICATION. This bird is nondescript brown, with a long tail, rounded, pale, and unbarred. In flight, its underwing pattern is distinctive: inner primaries very pale, contrasting with brownish wing lining and slate brown secondaries and outer primaries. Sexes are similar. Its distinctive call is often uttered in flight.

DISTRIBUTION. Australia generally, very rare in Tasmania. It also occurs in New Guinea and New Caledonia.

NOTES. Common and widespread, usually in pairs, it frequents alike coastal and inland districts. Its flight is buoyant and easy and it often soars to a great height, uttering a shrill whistling cry that is audible at a distance of a kilometre or more. In coastal districts it is a confirmed scavenger, feeding upon dead fish and offal left by the tides. It also feeds on small mammals, birds, lizards, carrion, and insects; in many districts rabbits are its chief prey. In all cases the prey appears to be taken on the ground.

BREEDING. Nest: large, rather flat; constructed of sticks and lined with leaves; placed on a horizontal branch of a tall tree; occasionally an old nest of another bird is used. Clutch: two to three; white or bluish-white, sparsely spotted lavender and reddish-brown. Breeding season: practically throughout the year.

30:8 LITTLE EAGLE *Hieraaetus morphnoides*

IDENTIFICATION. The plumage of this species is very variable. Its crown feathers are blackish and rather long, often producing a short, shaggy crest. Its tail is short, square-cut, and obscurely barred. In flight it shows a distinctive underwing pattern: rufous leading edge contrasting with white wing panel, dark secondaries and dark-tipped, white primaries. Sexes are similar.

DISTRIBUTION. Inland areas of Australia generally, extending to the coast in the west and north-west, and occasionally in eastern Australia. It also inhabits New Guinea.

NOTES. Usually seen in pairs, it frequents chiefly inland districts, showing a preference for country intersected by creeks. Usually seen high in slow wheeling flight, soaring and gliding with level wings. It performs spectacular courtship display flights. In some districts it subsists almost entirely on rabbits; it also feeds on other small mammals and reptiles. The call is a shrill rapid double whistle.

BREEDING. Nest: large, compact; made of sticks and twigs, lined with green leaves; usually high in a leafy tree; occasionally uses the abandoned nest of some other species. Clutch: one to two; bluish-white, with reddish-brown spots. Breeding season: August to November.

30:9 WHITE-BELLIED SEA-EAGLE *Haliaeetus leucogaster*

IDENTIFICATION. The adult is very large, with head and underparts white, upperparts grey. Its distinctive flight silhouette shows long, very broad wings and a proportionately very small, short, diamond-shaped tail. Sexes are similar, but juveniles are brownish.

DISTRIBUTION. Throughout the coastal mainland of Australia and in Tasmania and about some of the larger inland rivers and lakes; also in south-east Asia and Oceania.

NOTES. It is usually found in pairs and observed flying slowly above foreshores, mud-flats, or sand-spits, or wheeling high in the sky in slow majestic circles. It scavenges along beaches searching for offal and carrion left by the tides. Food includes various mammals, tortoises, sea-snakes, fish, eels, and the larger crustaceans. It also occurs at major rivers and larger bodies of water inland. The species has a peculiar metallic cackling cry. The female is larger than the male.

BREEDING. Nest: huge (often two metres across); of sticks, lined with leaves; placed high in a tall tree, on ledges of cliffs, or (on off-shore islands) on the ground. Nests are used for years in succession. Clutch: usually two; faint bluish-white. Breeding season: usually May to October.

30:10 WEDGE-TAILED EAGLE *Aquila audax*

IDENTIFICATION. This is a large, very dark eagle with distinctive long, wedge-shaped tail. Sexes are similar.

DISTRIBUTION. Australia, including Tasmania.

NOTES. It frequents alike timbered country and plains and is usually observed singly or in pairs soaring high on motionless wings, but nevertheless travelling with rapidity. Capable of impressive bursts of speed in attacking a victim, it has a bad reputation as a lamb-killer in some districts, but rabbits and carrion are the most important items of its diet; also young dingos, marsupials, and birds such as galahs. The female is larger than the male.

BREEDING. Nest: very large; constructed of sticks and lined with soft bark and leaves, especially green leaves when young are in the nest; placed in a large tree; usually one that is isolated or so situated that the sitting bird has a clear view of the surrounding country. Clutch: one to three; white or light buff, often spotted or blotched lavender and dull red. Breeding season: usually June to July.

BIRDS OF LAKES, STREAMS AND SWAMPS

PLATE 31

BIRDS OF LAKES, STREAMS AND SWAMPS

31:1 LITTLE KINGFISHER *Ceyx pusillus*

IDENTIFICATION. This tiny bird is bright blue above, white below, with a white plume below the eye, and a long black bill. Sexes are similar.

DISTRIBUTION. Coastal Northern Territory and north-eastern Queensland, south to about Mackay. It also inhabits Indonesia, New Guinea and the Solomon Islands.

NOTES. Seen singly or in pairs, it frequents streams in dense rainforests, and particularly small creeks running through mangrove swamps. It is secretive and inconspicuous. Its note is a shrill, piping cry, uttered mostly while the bird is on the wing. Food: small fishes.

BREEDING. Nest: in a hole in a bank of a creek; sometimes an old stump. Clutch: usually five; white, rounded, glossy. Breeding season: November to February.

31:2 AZURE KINGFISHER *Ceyx azureus*

IDENTIFICATION. This small bird is bright blue above, rich rufous below with a white plume below the eye, and a long black bill. Sexes are similar.

DISTRIBUTION. Northern and eastern Australia, from about Derby, Western Australia to Tasmania and about Adelaide, South Australia. It is also found in Indonesia and New Guinea.

NOTES. Found singly or in pairs, it frequents fresh and saltwater streams and inlets. Its flight is swift and it usually keeps close to the surface of the water as it travels up or down a stream. While in flight it utters a shrill call. Food: small fishes, crustaceans, and insects.

BREEDING. Nest: a chamber at the end of a tunnel in the bank of a stream. Clutch: five to six; white, rounded and glossy. Breeding season: variable, mainly September to January in the south, probably October to April in the north.

31:3 **AUSTRALIAN CRAKE** *Porzana fluminea*

IDENTIFICATION. This small bird has a short bill. Its face and underparts are bluish slate, flecked white; its undertail coverts are white, its bill green and red. Sexes are similar.

DISTRIBUTION. Australia generally, but especially widespread in Tasmania and the south-east.

NOTES. Seen singly or in pairs, it frequents marshy localities overgrown with rank herbage, or the reed-lined banks of streams and swamps. It often feeds on open mud or floating vegetation near dense cover, and will often ignore a cautious observer, but when startled it disappears from sight very quickly. Young of all crakes appear to leave the nest almost immediately after hatching. Food: aquatic insects and the green shoots of aquatic plants.

BREEDING. Nest: open; constructed of coarse grass; placed at the base of a tussock surrounded by water. Clutch: four to six; stone-brown, spotted and blotched purplish-brown and grey. Breeding season: August to January.

31:4 **MARSH CRAKE** *Porzana pusilla*

IDENTIFICATION. Small, with a short bill, this bird's upperparts are warm brown, streaked black and rusty at nape. Its face and underparts are pale grey, and bill dull green.

DISTRIBUTION. Coastal and near-inland areas of the Australian mainland (rarely noted in the north), and Tasmania. It is also found in Europe, Africa, Asia and New Zealand.

NOTES. Usually seen singly or in pairs, it frequents swamps and reed or mangrove-lined streams and inlets. Elusive and shy, but very inquisitive, it will often ignore a careful observer. Although it swims and dives expertly, it prefers to keep to the shallows, seeking its food while wading along the fringes of reed-beds, or on floating mats of aquatic vegetation. The chief note is a sharp 'krek', or 'crake'; the bird also calls 'whee–whee–whee', followed by a harsh 'chrrr'. Food: aquatic insects, small freshwater molluscs, and green shoots of aquatic plants.

BREEDING. Nest: slightly concave; constructed of dried coarse grasses and aquatic plants, built in a clump of reeds or a low bush growing in water. Clutch: five to six; variable, from pale brown tinged with olive to dark olive brown; some closely resemble pebbles, others are slightly covered with streaks of a darker shade of the ground colour. Breeding season: October to January.

31:5 SPOTLESS CRAKE *Porzana tabuensis*

IDENTIFICATION. This small bird is very dark brown above, and plain slate grey below with a bright red eye, and black bill. Sexes are similar.

DISTRIBUTION. Eastern and south-eastern Australia to south-eastern South Australia, south-western Australia and Tasmania. It is also found in Indonesia and the Philippines to Tonga, New Zealand, and the Chatham Islands.

NOTES. Found singly or in pairs, it frequents swamps and the reed-lined margins of streams. Very secretive, it remains in dense cover, perhaps less inclined to feed in the open than other crakes. Its calls are very varied, including some that suggest a motorbike starting up. Food: aquatic insects and vegetable material.

BREEDING. Nest: open; constructed of coarse grass stalks; built low in a tussock of grass. Clutch: four to seven; pale creamy-brown, covered with faint markings of chestnut-brown. Breeding season: September to January.

31:6 RED-NECKED RAIL *Rallina tricolor*

IDENTIFICATION. This bird has a head and breast of reddish chestnut, its body plain dark brown, with few obvious markings. Sexes are similar.

DISTRIBUTION. Coastal areas of Cape York Peninsula, south to Cardwell. It is also found in the Aru Islands and New Guinea.

NOTES. Seen singly or in pairs, it frequents dense tropical rainforests bordering creeks or on the sides of stony ridges. It is noisy but shy, and difficult to observe. It is crepuscular and partly nocturnal. Its call is a loud 'gurk' and also 'clock, clock', repeated several times, as well as curious grunting notes. Food: insects, snails, and freshwater animals of various kinds.

BREEDING. Nest: a hole scooped in the ground, in which a few dead leaves are placed; usually situated at the foot of a tree. Clutch: three to five; white. Breeding season: January to April.

31:7 LEWIN'S RAIL *Rallus pectoralis*

IDENTIFICATION. This bird is closely barred black and white below, streaked olive and black above, with a grey breast and rusty crown and nape. The bill is long and pinkish. Sexes are similar.

DISTRIBUTION. Coastal eastern and south-eastern Australia to south-eastern South Australia, south-western Australia (rare), Kangaroo Island and Tasmania. It is also found in New Guinea.

NOTES. Seen singly or in pairs, it frequents swamps and reed-lined margins of streams. It is exceedingly shy and difficult to observe. If flushed it rarely flies far, but seeks refuge among tall grasses. When in flight its long legs hang down. Although not web-footed, it swims with facility and dives if closely pursued. When startled it utters a loud, abrupt alarm note, resembling 'tick, tick, tick'. Food: worms, freshwater snails, and insects.

BREEDING. Nest: shallow, saucer-shaped; constructed of coarse plant stalks and grass stems; well concealed among rushes, grass, or aquatic plants. Clutch: three to five; dull white or warm creamy-white, covered with freckles and streaks of purplish-brown, chestnut-brown, and violet-grey. Breeding season: August to December.

31:8 BANDED RAIL *Rallus philippensis*

IDENTIFICATION. This species is closely barred black and white below, with a dull orange patch across its upper breast; its throat and superciliary are bluish grey; its crown and cheeks are rich red; its bill is stout and pinkish. Sexes are similar.

DISTRIBUTION. Australia generally, including Tasmania, but absent from most of the arid interior. It is also widespread in south-east Asia and the south-west Pacific.

NOTES. Usually found singly or in pairs, it frequents scrub and rank herbage in swampy localities, and the margins of streams and cultivation paddocks. It also occurs on many sand cays and islands on the Great Barrier Reef. It often feeds in the open, but is timid, and will dash into dense cover at the least disturbance. When startled, it utters an alarm note, 'krek', which is often answered by other birds in the vicinity. Its calls are varied and include a loud abrupt squeak and 'deep thudding grunts'. Food: insects, seeds and small freshwater molluscs, and the green shoots of various plants.

BREEDING. Nest: saucer-shaped; constructed of grass and herbage, well-hidden in grass or undergrowth. Clutch: usually five to six; creamy-buff or buff-white, spotted and blotched with various shades of brown and purplish-grey. Breeding season: variable, but mainly September to March in the south.

31:9 AUSTRALIAN PRATINCOLE *Stiltia isabella*

IDENTIFICATION. This bird is very slender, graceful and long-legged, with long pointed wings. Its plumage is mainly warm sandy brown; its belly deep chestnut. Sexes are similar.

DISTRIBUTION. Australia generally, except much of southern Western Australia and the humid south-east. It is also found in Indonesia and New Guinea.

NOTES. It mainly frequents dry plains, either inland or near the coast, there feeding on insects of both the ground and the air. The bird has an odd see-sawing motion when standing, it runs rapidly, and flies gracefully with frequent zig-zagging. When breeding, it is much given to the 'broken-wing' trick. The name Road-runner arises from its habit of running on or near roads and jumping away from vehicles at the last moment. Seasonal movements of the species are partly migratory (north-south) and partly nomadic. Calls of this bird, in both sexes, are spirited and pleasant.

BREEDING. Nest: a bare space on the ground. Clutch: two to three; pale stone-colour, with markings of dark brown, underlined grey. Breeding season: August to January, mainly October and November.

31:10 INLAND DOTTEREL *Peltohyas australis*

IDENTIFICATION. This bird is sandy brown above, reddish below, with a dull white face and throat and bold black breast-band. Its bill is black. Sexes are similar.

DISTRIBUTION. Australia generally, mainly south of the Tropic of Capricorn, and excluding the humid south-west and south-east.

NOTES. Found in pairs or small flocks, it inhabits mainly the arid interior, where it frequents plains and margins of lakes and streams. It appears to be nomadic, although it is found in some localities throughout the year. The plumage pattern is strongly cryptic, and the bird is very difficult to see. If approached carefully, it is not timid, but when startled it flies a considerable distance before alighting. Its call resembles 'quick', uttered in a slightly metallic tone, and it also has a low note, like 'kr–root'. Food: insects and seeds.

BREEDING. Nest: a depression in the ground. Clutch: usually three; rich cream or buff, sparingly sprinkled with spots of chocolate-black, with a few dots of a lighter tint. When the bird leaves the nest it covers the eggs with surrounding soil. Breeding season: April to October.

31:11 LOTUSBIRD *Irediparra gallinacea*

IDENTIFICATION. This species is brown above, white below, with black cap and breast, and a prominent red comb on its forehead. Sexes are similar.

DISTRIBUTION. Northern and eastern Australia (mainly coastal) west to the Kimberley and south to about Sydney, New South Wales. It is also found in Indonesia and the Philippines to New Guinea.

NOTES. Seen in pairs or small flocks, it frequents swamps, lagoons, and streams, chiefly those covered with aquatic vegetation. It is usually observed walking over the broad leaves of waterlilies or similar plants. Habitually wary, when disturbed it utters a shrill chattering call and flies to another part of the swamp or stream. Its flight is direct, with quick wingbeats, and the long legs and long toes trail behind the body. Food: aquatic life and plants.

BREEDING. Nest: flat; constructed of sedge, grass, and aquatic plants, and built upon leaves or grass growing in water. Clutch: four; pale brown, pale yellowish-brown, or brownish-red, covered with black lines criss-crossing the surface; the surface is smooth, appearing as if varnished. Breeding season: September to January, sometimes later.

31:12 BUSH-HEN *Gallinula olivacea*

IDENTIFICATION. This bird is dark and plain, deep brown above, slate grey below, with deep buff undertail coverts. Sexes are similar.

DISTRIBUTION. Coastal eastern Australia from Cape York to about Ballina, New South Wales; possibly also coastal Northern Territory. It also inhabits Indonesia and the Philippines to the Solomon Islands.

NOTES. Found singly or in pairs, it frequents swampy areas, chiefly of coastal districts. Noisy (at least when breeding), but very secretive and difficult to observe. It is sedentary, and at least partly nocturnal. Calls are varied including a loud, harsh 'knee–you', often in series, and a persistent 'tok'. Food: mainly small invertebrates.

BREEDING. Nest: open; constructed of coarse grass and other herbage; built in a tussock of grass. Clutch: four to six; white or creamy-white, spotted pale purplish-red and purplish-grey. Breeding season: October to March.

31:13 JAPANESE SNIPE *Gallinago hardwickii*

IDENTIFICATION. This is a short-legged, stocky, skulking wader of boggy places, with a very long, straight bill. Seldom seen unless accidentally flushed, it then flies off with a distinctive zig-zagging flight and harsh, rasping call. Almost impossible to distinguish from Swinhoe's Snipe in the field. When examined in the hand, it is identified by 16-18 tail feathers, the outermost four barred dull brown and white. Sexes are similar.

DISTRIBUTION. Japan (breeding), migrating to eastern Australia and Tasmania; accidental to New Zealand.

NOTES. Seen singly or in small parties, it arrives in Australia during September and departs in March or April. It frequents overgrown river flats, swamps and marshes, and is a very wary bird. The species was formerly a favourite target of game shooters. Food: insects and aquatic life.

BREEDING. Nest: a depression in the ground. Clutch: three to four; pale stone colour, with purplish-red spots and underlying markings of lavender. Breeding season: May and June (Japan).

31:14 SWINHOE'S SNIPE *Gallinago megala*

IDENTIFICATION. This bird is virtually impossible to distinguish from the Japanese Snipe, unless examined in the hand. It has 20-24 tail feathers, the outermost three or four being substantially narrower than the others. Sexes are similar.

DISTRIBUTION. Central Siberia, migrating to New Guinea and occasionally to north-western Australia.

NOTES. Seen singly or in flocks, it arrives in Australia during September or October and departs in March or April. Its status in Australia is uncertain, and it has so far not been recorded outside the tropics (the Japanese Snipe is most common in the south-east). It frequents marshy country and swamps, and is similar in habits to the Japanese Snipe.

BREEDING. Nest: a depression in the ground; lined with grass. Clutch: four; creamy-white or pale ochre, spotted reddish-brown. Breeding season: June (Asia).

31:15 PAINTED SNIPE *Rostratula benghalensis*

IDENTIFICATION. This bird is dull greenish above, intricately marked with black and buff. The head and breast are a deep, rich chestnut, contrasting with a white belly and broad white eye-ring, extending backwards almost to the nape. Sexes are similar, but the female is very much duller than the male.

DISTRIBUTION. Australia generally (although mainly eastern, and no recent records from Western Australia). It is also widespread in Africa and Asia.

NOTES. Usually found in pairs, it frequents the margins of swamps and streams, chiefly those covered with low and stunted vegetation. Little is known of its movements, but it appears to be nomadic. It is generally secretive and difficult to observe. The species is polyandrous and the male broods the eggs. The trachea of the adult female is highly convoluted, a fact suggesting that she is the author of a deep hollow sound uttered by the species, usually at night. Food: aquatic animals and plants.

BREEDING. Nest: a shallow depression in the ground; lined with grass or leaves, usually in the shelter of a tussock or low bush. Clutch: four; creamy-white or yellowish-stone, covered with spots and blotches of black, a few spots of brown, and underlying markings of grey. Breeding season: variable; generally March to May in the north, October to December in the south.

31:16 AUSTRALASIAN GREBE *Tachybaptus novaehollandiae*

IDENTIFICATION. In breeding plumage, this bird is mainly deep, sooty grey-brown, blackish on head and neck, with dull chestnut band along the neck. A small yellowish white patch at gape is diagnostic. In winter it is mainly dull grey, with white cheeks and throat, and very difficult to distinguish from Hoary-headed Grebe, though somewhat browner, with a dark cap 'pulled down' to eye but not beyond it. Sexes are similar.

DISTRIBUTION. Australia generally, including Tasmania. Found also in Indonesia, New Guinea, Vanuatu, and New Caledonia.

NOTES. Usually seen in pairs or small parties, it frequents still waters of lakes, swampy lagoons, dams and estuaries; often on ornamental pools in city parks. It is mostly seen in water, rarely on land. When disturbed it suddenly disappears under the water, to reappear some distance away. Food: aquatic animals, especially small fishes.

BREEDING. Nest: a floating, raft-like structure of aquatic plants, moored reeds, twigs of a fallen branch of a tree, or other debris. Clutch: four to seven; white, soon becoming stained due to a thick coating of lime. Breeding season: October to March or April.

31:17 HOARY-HEADED GREBE *Poliocephalus poliocephalus*

IDENTIFICATION. In breeding this bird's plumage is striking, with a black head densely covered with narrow white streaks. At other seasons it is very difficult to distinguish it from Australasian Grebe, but it is slightly greyer, and with a dark cap 'pulled down' level with the lower rim of the eye. Sexes are similar.

DISTRIBUTION. Australia generally, including Tasmania.

NOTES. Seen in pairs or flocks, it frequents lakes and streams, saltwater inlets, and estuaries or rivers. It is similar in habits to the Australasian Grebe, but it shows a distinct preference for extensive bodies of water and is less prone to occur on stock dams or small ponds. It is also less vocal, much more gregarious, and much less reluctant to fly. It is nomadic. Food: aquatic animals, especially invertebrates.

BREEDING. Nest: similar to that of the Australasian Grebe. Clutch: four to six; white, soon becoming nest-stained. Breeding season: variable, influenced by rainfall; mainly November to January.

31:18 WOOD SANDPIPER *Tringa glareola*

IDENTIFICATION. This bird is most similar to Marsh Sandpiper, but its bill is stouter and less needle-like; its upperparts are usually more profusely spotted. In flight it reveals a prominent square white rump (in Marsh Sandpiper the white extends in a narrow V well up on to the back). Sexes are similar.

DISTRIBUTION. Northern Europe and northern Asia, migrating to South Africa, India, Malaysia, and Australia (has been recorded from all mainland States and Tasmania).

NOTES. An uncommon bird in Australia, it is usually encountered alone. It frequents freshwater swamps, particularly where there is aquatic vegetation. It occurs mainly in summer. It swims well, and also perches on trees. The chief call is a shrill 'chiff–iff–iff'. Food: shell fish and insects.

BREEDING. Nest: a depression in the ground. Clutch: four; bluish, with spots and blotches of dark purplish-red. Breeding season: May and June (Siberia).

31:19 MARSH SANDPIPER *Tringa stagnatilis*

IDENTIFICATION. This species resembles Wood Sandpiper but is somewhat smaller, more slender in build, with a long needle-like bill. Its upperparts are greyish, and rather plain. In flight it reveals a prominent white rump, extending in a sharp V well up on to the back. Sexes are similar.

DISTRIBUTION. Central Europe and northern Asia, migrating to South Africa, India, Malaysia and Australia (occurs sporadically in the various mainland States).

NOTES. It occurs singly or in flocks, but is generally uncommon in Australia, although locally in good numbers. Mainly during spring and summer, it frequents both salt marshes and freshwater swamps and lagoons. Active, it feeds mainly in shallow water, often belly-deep. The chief call is a mellow, whistled 'tui–eu'.

BREEDING. Nest: a depression in the ground among grass. Clutch: four; pale yellow, with spots of brown and underlying markings of grey. Breeding season: June (Siberia).

31:20 BLACK-WINGED STILT *Himantopus leucocephalus*

IDENTIFICATION. Head, neck and underparts of this bird are white, black at nape and across hind neck. Its bill is long and very slender. Its legs are very long and deep pink. Sexes are similar, but juveniles are scruffier.

DISTRIBUTION. Australia generally, including Tasmania; local and patchy over much of the arid interior. Closely related forms occur almost throughout the world.

NOTES. Generally common; it occurs in pairs or flocks, frequenting shallow lakes, swamps and tidal flats. Noisy and demonstrative, the incessant call is not unlike the yapping of a small dog. Food: aquatic animals and plants.

BREEDING. Usually loosely colonial. Nest: variable, from a simple depression in the ground to a compact, substantial structure of dried aquatic plants, built in a swamp. Clutch: four; greenish-stone, with spots and blotches of purplish-brown and underlying markings of lavender. Breeding season: August to December.

31:21 RED-NECKED AVOCET *Recurvirostra novaehollandiae*

IDENTIFICATION. This bird is boldly black and white, with a deep chestnut head and neck, and slender upturned bill. Sexes are similar.

DISTRIBUTION. Australia generally, except northern and eastern coastal regions.

NOTES. Found in pairs or flocks, it frequents lakes, streams and swamps. It feeds while wading in shallow water, occasionally swimming, swinging the bill from side to side. Nomadic, it breeds locally in the interior, tending to wander coastwards after breeding. Usually shy and quiet, it becomes noisy if its nest is approached. Besides its chief call, which is somewhat like the bark of a dog, it utters a trumpet-like whistle, usually during flight. Food: aquatic animals and plants.

BREEDING. Colonial. Nest: variable, from a simple grass-lined depression to a substantial saucer of local vegetation, usually on small islands in swamps. Clutch: four; yellowish-stone to creamy-brown, with freckles and blotches of black and underlying markings of inky-grey. Breeding season: August to December.

31:22 BANDED STILT *Cladorhynchus leucocephalus*

IDENTIFICATION. This species resembles the more common and widespread Black-winged Stilt in size and general appearance, but its head, neck and back are entirely white, the adults having deep chestnut breastband, shading to a black line down the centre of the belly. Sexes are similar.

DISTRIBUTION. Southern Australia, north on the west coast to about Point Cloates and east to Melbourne, Victoria; highly nomadic, and individuals or small parties may occur erratically almost anywhere in southern Australia.

NOTES. Usually seen in often large flocks, frequenting shallow lakes, swamps, and tidal flats. It is similar in habits to the Black-winged Stilt, but much more gregarious, and generally feeds in deeper water, often swimming. It has a marked preference for salt lakes, where it feeds on brine-shrimps and other small crustaceans. Breeds irregularly at remote salt lakes in the interior (only a few localities known), wandering unpredictably to coastal localities (especially commercial salt fields) after breeding.

BREEDING. Colonial. Nest: a slight depression in the ground. Clutch: two to four; dull white or creamy, with twisted lines of black or brown and underlying markings of grey. Breeding season: very erratic.

31:23 MASKED LAPWING *Vanellus miles*

IDENTIFICATION. This species is sandy above, white below, with prominent fleshy yellow facial wattles. Northern form (subspecies *miles*) has black cap; south-eastern form (subspecies *novaehollandiae*) has fuller black cap and nape, extending well down on to the shoulders. Sexes are similar.

DISTRIBUTION. Australia generally, except the centre and south-west. It also inhabits Indonesia and (self-introduced) New Zealand. In two well-marked populations: *V. m. miles* ('Masked Plover') in northern Australia, and *V. m. novaehollandiae* ('Spur-winged Plover') throughout the south-east.

NOTES. Seen in pairs or flocks, it frequents wetlands generally, including lush pastures, golf courses, playing fields and city parks. Common and familiar, it is wary, noisy and highly demonstrative. It is nomadic, although odd pairs will remain in a district throughout the year. The usual call is a loud, strident, incessant 'keerk, keerk, keerk', uttered when the bird is alarmed or in flight. Food: insects, small crustaceans, and herbage.

BREEDING. Nest: a depression in the ground, lined with short grass stems or cattle dung. Clutch: usually four; greenish-olive or yellowish-stone, spotted and blotched dark-brown, with underlying marks of dull grey. Breeding season: variable, generally June to January in the south-east.

31:24 BANDED LAPWING *Vanellus tricolor*

IDENTIFICATION. This species somewhat resembles Masked Lapwing, but has a broad black band across breast, a small red wattle in front of the eye; and in flight, shows a broad white wingbar. Sexes are similar.

DISTRIBUTION. Australia (rare in the northern portion), and Tasmania.

NOTES. Seen in pairs or flocks, it frequents plains, bare paddocks, airfields, and other areas of short grass. It is partly nomadic, its movements from one district to another being influenced by seasonal conditions. Like other species of lapwing, it strongly resents any interference with eggs or young, and employs various wiles to lure the intruder away, or, protesting loudly, makes bold swoops at the observer. Food: insects and seeds.

BREEDING. Nest: a depression in the ground; lined with short grass stems. Clutch: four; light brown, with spots and blotches of brown and blackish-brown and underlying markings of grey. Breeding season: June to November.

31:25 GULL-BILLED TERN *Gelochelidon nilotica*

IDENTIFICATION. This is a large, silvery grey tern with a very large, stout, black bill. Sexes are similar.

DISTRIBUTION. Mainland Australia generally. It is also found in North America, Europe, Africa and Asia.

NOTES. Usually appearing in flocks, it frequents wetlands generally. Nomadic and erratic in occurrence, it breeds in colonies at lakes and swamps in the interior, wandering northward and coastward in autumn and winter. It skims in hawk-like fashion over the swamps, lakes, or surrounding plains, or above saltwater marshes and estuaries. Unusual among terns, it often feeds over mud-flats, ploughed land and plains rather than water. Food: fish, insects, and small reptiles.

BREEDING. Colonial. Nest: a depression in the soil; surrounded by debris, which is added to as incubation proceeds. Clutch: two to four; buff-white or whitish-brown, with light umber markings, over which are splashes and spots of purplish-red and purplish-grey. Breeding season: October to March (eastern Australia); May (north-western Australia).

31:26 ROSEATE TERN *Sterna dougallii*

IDENTIFICATION. This species is very similar to Common and White-fronted Terns, but smaller, more delicate in build and proportions, and slightly paler grey above. At rest the tail extends well beyond the tips of the folded wings. In breeding plumage the underparts are delicately flushed pink. The bill is black with a red base. The legs and feet are red. Sexes are similar.

DISTRIBUTION. Almost cosmopolitan. In Australia it breeds on several islands on the Great Barrier Reef and off the Western Australian coast (especially the Abrolhos Group); non-breeding birds occur along the coast of northern Australia, south to about Perth on the west coast and Brisbane on the east coast.

NOTES. Generally uncommon, it is almost exclusively marine, frequenting chiefly sand cays, coral reefs, and off-shore islands. Gregarious, it breeds, roosts, and feeds in flocks. It is extremely graceful in flight. Food: chiefly fish.

BREEDING. Colonial. Nest: a slight depression in sand or on a ridge of dead coral; sometimes lined with fine pieces of coral or shells. Clutch: one to two; from light yellowish to a faint greyish-stone, with markings of inky-black and faint blue. Breeding season: generally September to January in the east and February to May in the west.

31:27 WHISKERED TERN *Chlidonias hybrida*

IDENTIFICATION. In breeding plumage this species has dark grey underparts, with a conspicuous white cheek. Its bill is bright red. At other seasons it is mainly grey above, white below, with forehead white, and crown heavily streaked white. Sexes are similar.

DISTRIBUTION. Mainland Australia generally. It is also widespread across Europe, Africa and Asia.

NOTES. Usually seen in flocks, it frequents chiefly lakes and swamps of inland districts. It has an easy and graceful flight as it passes over the lakes, every now and then darting into the water after food, which consists mostly of fish and aquatic insects. Generally migratory in the south, it breeds in loose colonies at freshwater swamps in the interior, wandering northward and coastward in autumn and winter.

BREEDING. Colonial. Nest: constructed of rushes or aquatic plants, forming a flat and (usually) floating structure; sometimes placed among rushes growing in deep water. Clutch: two to three; greenish-buff, blotched blackish-brown, with underlying markings of grey. Breeding season: October to December.

31:28 WHITE-WINGED TERN *Chlidonias leucoptera*

IDENTIFICATION. In breeding plumage this species is mainly black, with white wings, but in Australia it is usually seen in non-breeding plumage, when it is very difficult to distinguish from non-breeding Whiskered Tern (the two species sometimes congregate in mixed flocks): its white rump contrasts with a grey back (Whiskered Tern has grey rump); it usually has a black mark on its cheeks (Whiskered Tern has white cheeks). Sexes are similar.

DISTRIBUTION. Breeds across Europe and Asia, wintering in Africa, India, Indonesia, and Australia; especially the north and east, regularly south to about Newcastle, New South Wales, more erratically further south.

NOTES. It frequents mainly estuaries and coastal lagoons and swamps, usually seen feeding in hovering flocks over shallow water. Sometimes it associates with the Whiskered Tern. Both have a confusing array of different plumages and, except in breeding plumage, are difficult to tell apart.

BREEDING. Colonial. Nest: constructed of vegetable debris placed on water-surrounded clumps of fixed vegetation, occasionally on accumulations of pond material floating on the surface. Clutch: three; deep olive or pale chocolate to greenish-grey or buff, with blotches or dots of black or umber. Breeding season: May to July.

PLATE 32

BIRDS OF SWAMPS, LAKES AND RIVERS

32:1 BLACK-TAILED NATIVE-HEN *Gallinula ventralis*

IDENTIFICATION. Its plumage is blackish, with several large, tear-shaped spots along the flanks. Its legs are bright pink, bill green, and lower mandible red at the base.

DISTRIBUTION. Throughout Australia (mainly interior), except Tasmania; accidental to New Zealand.

NOTES. Seen in pairs or flocks, it frequents swamps, lakes, the reed-beds and backwaters of rivers, and grassy plains. It is nomadic, often appearing after local floods in huge flocks in districts where it has not been seen, perhaps, for decades. It is an active bird, flicking its tail as it runs nimbly in and out of the reeds, and flying only when hard-pressed. Food: grass and aquatic plants and animals.

BREEDING. Nest: saucer-shaped, deep; constructed of plant stems, dried grasses, or rushes; placed on the ground in a clump of reeds or under a low bush. Clutch: five to nine; from light green to pale sage green, sparsely blotched purplish-brown and violet-grey. Breeding season: highly variable and erratic, strongly influenced by local rainfall.

32:2 TASMANIAN NATIVE-HEN *Gallinula mortierii*

IDENTIFICATION. This species is large, stocky, and flightless. Its plumage is blackish, with a white splash along its flanks. Its bill is dull yellow. Sexes are similar.

DISTRIBUTION. Tasmania.

NOTES. Common and sedentary, it occurs in pairs or small parties, frequenting marshes and reedy margins of lakes and streams. It is shy, disappearing in rank herbage when disturbed. The call resembles the sound of steel being sharpened; another note is a resonant 'cluck'. Like certain of its relatives on other islands (some now extinct), this species is flightless. Food: aquatic plants and insects, mixed with gravel.

BREEDING. Nest: open, bulky; constructed of dry herbage and reed stalks; built on the ground beneath a clump of rushes or a low bush. Clutch: five to eight; from yellowish-stone to buffy-brown, spotted and blotched brown. Breeding season: September to December.

32:3 DUSKY MOORHEN *Gallinula tenebrosa*

IDENTIFICATION. This species is dusky black, with a red and yellow bill and narrow white patch on each side of the tail. Sexes are similar.

DISTRIBUTION. Eastern and south-eastern Australia from the Gulf of Carpentaria to Eyre Peninsula and Kangaroo Island, South Australia; including King Island but not Tasmania. It also inhabits Indonesia and New Guinea.

NOTES. Seen in pairs or flocks, it frequents swamps and the margins of lakes and streams. Common, even on ornamental ponds in city parks, it runs, swims or dives with equal rapidity. Occasionally when disturbed it flies in a laboured fashion. Food: aquatic plants and insects.

BREEDING. Nest: open; constructed of reed stems and dried grasses; placed on a broken-down tussock of grass or rushes. Clutch: five to seven, but several females often lay in the same nest; usually creamy-white, with spots and blotches of reddish-brown. Breeding season: August to December.

32:4 EURASIAN COOT *Fulica atra*

IDENTIFICATION. Plumage of this species is entirely dusky black. The bill and frontal shield are white. Sexes are similar.

DISTRIBUTION. The Australian mainland generally (where conditions are suitable) and Tasmania. It is also found in Europe, northern Africa, and Asia; straggler to New Zealand.

NOTES. A common and familiar sight in pairs or flocks, sometimes forming large rafts of birds on open water, it frequents wetlands generally. An expert swimmer and diver, it is a graceful bird in the water but has a rather clumsy gait on land. When swimming it constantly jerks its head backward and forward, apparently keeping time with the paddle-like strokes of its feet. It is noisy, with a variety of loud, strident and abrupt notes. Food: aquatic plants and animals.

BREEDING. Nest: open, bulky; constructed of aquatic plants and lined with sheaths and leaves of reeds; built in a bunch of reeds or on top of a low bush growing in water. Clutch: seven to ten; whitish-brown, covered with spots of purplish-brown and faint markings of violet-grey. Breeding season: August to February.

32:5 CHESTNUT RAIL *Eulabeornis castaneiventris*

IDENTIFICATION. A large (about Swamphen-sized) rail of tropical mangroves, this species is mainly rufous, with a grey head and rather long, stout greenish bill. Sexes are similar.

DISTRIBUTION. Coastal northern Australia, from the Kimberley to the Gulf of Carpentaria. It is also found in the Aru Islands.

NOTES. Seen singly or in pairs, it frequents dense mangroves, emerging at low tide to feed on mud flats. Wary, secretive and extremely difficult to observe, it rarely takes to the wing when alarmed, usually seeking safety by running. Its calls include loud screeches and low grunts. Food: insects, crustaceans, etc.

BREEDING. Nest: flat; constructed of sticks; placed on a low branch of a mangrove. Clutch: four; pinkish-white, spotted reddish-brown. Breeding season: mainly November to January.

32:6 PURPLE SWAMPHEN *Porphyrio porphyrio*

IDENTIFICATION. This species is large and dark, with a deep rich blue head and underparts and prominent white undertail coverts. It has a large, stout, bright red bill. Sexes are similar.

DISTRIBUTION. In Australia, it occurs in two populations: subspecies *melanotus* in northern and eastern Australia, from the Kimberley to Cape York, south to Tasmania and Kangaroo Island and Eyre Peninsula, South Australia; and subspecies *bellus* in south-western Australia. It is also widespread from Europe and Africa across Asia to islands of the south-west Pacific.

NOTES. Seen in pairs or flocks, it frequents reedy margins and flats of wetlands generally; often common at ornamental ponds in city parks. It sometimes congregates in large flocks and occasionally does damage to crops and gardens. The call is loud and resonant and is usually uttered during the night or when the bird is startled. It swims readily and is also able to perch in trees. When walking it flicks its tail continually. Food: grass, aquatic plants, and freshwater molluscs.

BREEDING. Nest: open; constructed of reeds, rushes, and other plant material; placed on a platform of broken-down reeds or in a tussock. Clutch: five to seven; pale brown to creamy-brown, with spots of purplish-brown and faint markings of slate-grey. Breeding season: variable.

32:7 GREAT CRESTED GREBE *Podiceps cristatus*

IDENTIFICATION. This bird has a long slender bill, reddish-black ear tufts, and a prominent, twin-pointed black crest. Sexes are similar.

DISTRIBUTION. South-western Australia; eastern and south-eastern Australia, and Tasmania. It is also found in New Zealand and throughout most of the eastern hemisphere.

NOTES. Occurring singly or in pairs, sometimes gathering in loose flocks on larger lakes in winter, it frequents swamps and lagoons. Deep pools and reaches are its favourite haunts. It dives freely, and can swim great distances underwater. It has spectacular displays during the breeding season. Food: aquatic plants and animals.

BREEDING. Nest: a flat, floating platform of green rushes, reeds and other water plants, moored to rushes or the branches of a floating tree. Clutch: five to seven; greenish-white, soon becoming nest-stained. Breeding season: November to January.

32:8 GLOSSY IBIS *Plegadis falcinellus*

IDENTIFICATION. This species has glossy brown plumage (looks black at a distance), and a slender downcurved bill. Sexes are similar.

DISTRIBUTION. Mainland Australia generally, especially the north-west and interior south-east; erratic and local elsewhere. It also inhabits Central America, Africa and Asia.

NOTES. Found in pairs or flocks, it frequents swamps, margins of lakes and streams, and adjoining grasslands. Highly nomadic and erratic, it is nowhere especially common. It sometimes visits farms to follow the plough and to feed on insects that are disturbed.

BREEDING. Colonial. Nest: a platform of sticks, lined with reeds and other aquatic plants; placed in an upright tree fork, or upon lignum bushes, usually in the centre of a large swamp. Clutch: three to four; deep greenish-blue, the surface being slightly rough and lustreless. Breeding season: September to December, sometimes later.

32:9 SACRED IBIS *Threskiornis aethiopica*

IDENTIFICATION. This species is mainly dingy white, with a naked black head and long downcurved bill. Sexes are similar.

DISTRIBUTION. Eastern Australia generally, from the Kimberley south to Eyre Peninsula, South Australia. It is also widespread in Africa and Asia.

NOTES. Common, and locally abundant, it is nomadic. Usually seen in flocks, it frequents swamps or the margins of streams and lakes which adjoin grasslands. Generally it prefers secluded situations where it can search for food and breed undisturbed, but in some districts it has become a scavenger, common in paddocks, cultivated areas, garbage dumps and even city parks.

BREEDING. Colonial. Nest: a platform made by bending down aquatic herbage; breeding colonies usually are situated in low vegetation in the centre of a swamp. Clutch: two to five; dull white and lustreless. Breeding season: variable, but mainly September to December.

32:10 STRAW-NECKED IBIS *Threskiornis spinicollis*

IDENTIFICATION. This species is black above, strongly glossed green and purple. It has a white neck and breast, and a naked black head with long, downcurved bill. Sexes are similar.

DISTRIBUTION. The Australian mainland generally; straggler to Tasmania.

NOTES. Found in pairs or flocks (sometimes very large), it frequents swamps, the margins of streams and lakes, and pastoral lands. Sometimes it occurs in mixed flocks with Sacred Ibis, but in general it prefers slightly drier, less marshy habitats. Often it feeds in paddocks or grassy plains, catching insects, especially locusts, grasshoppers and their larvae. Common and familiar, it is nomadic and ranges widely.

BREEDING. Colonial. Nest: similar to that of the Sacred Ibis. Clutch: three to five; dull white and lustreless. Breeding season: variable, but usually September to December.

32:11 CATTLE EGRET *Bubulcus ibis*

IDENTIFICATION. This small, stocky white egret often associates with cattle and other stock. It is unmistakable in breeding plumage, when its head, breast and back are a strongly washed, rich buff. At other seasons it is difficult to distinguish it from other small egrets, but it is noticeably shorter necked. White feathers extend well along the lower surface of the bill, producing a distinctive heavy-jowled look. Sexes are similar.

DISTRIBUTION. Coastal Australia generally; common and widespread in the north and east, less so in the west and south. Almost cosmopolitan.

NOTES. Usually seen in small groups, it associates with cattle and feeds on grasshoppers and other large insects disturbed by the cattle as they graze. From its former home in Africa, about the turn of the century, the Cattle Egret began a dramatic expansion of its range, which now sees it widespread in tropical and sub-tropical regions almost throughout the world. The species has become common over much of Australia within the past half-century; it was deliberately introduced in the Kimberley in 1933 in the hope of controlling the cattle tick, but there is reason to believe the bird may also have reached Australia unaided from Asia.

BREEDING. Colonial, usually with other waterbirds. Nest: a platform of sticks and twigs; placed in a tree. Clutch: three to six; greenish-white. Breeding season: variable, mainly November to February in the south-east.

32:12 LITTLE EGRET *Egretta garzetta*

IDENTIFICATION. This small, graceful, snowy-white egret has a long, slender black bill.

DISTRIBUTION. Australia generally, especially the north and east; mainly coastal but extending inland over much of Queensland and New South Wales. It is also widespread from Europe and Africa across Asia to New Guinea.

NOTES. Seen singly, in pairs, or in small flocks, it frequents swamps or margins of lakes and streams. It is nomadic and nowhere particularly numerous. Unlike most other herons and egrets, it often actively chases prey in shallow water. The ornamental plumes on the crown, throat and back are shed when incubation of the eggs begins. Food. aquatic animals.

BREEDING. Colonial, usually with other waterbirds. Nest: a platform of sticks; placed in the branches of a tree, usually over water. Clutch: three to five; pale bluish-green, the surface slightly glossy and minutely pitted. Breeding season: variable.

32:13 PLUMED EGRET *Egretta intermedia*

IDENTIFICATION. A medium-sized egret, it is easily confused with Great Egret, but its neck is proportionately shorter and thicker, seldom showing the abrupt kink typical of Great Egret. It often stands for long periods with its neck straight, extended at an angle away from the body. Sexes are similar.

DISTRIBUTION. Northern and eastern Australia, west to the Kimberley and south (irregularly) to Tasmania and about Adelaide, South Australia. It is also widespread in Africa and Asia.

NOTES. Seen in pairs or flocks, it frequents swamps and the margins of lakes and streams. It is similar in general habits to the Great Egret, although much more gregarious. Especially in northern Australia, numbers often occur in damp pastures with cattle. The ornamental plumes on the neck and back are shed when incubation of the eggs begins. Food: aquatic animals.

BREEDING. Colonial, usually with other waterbirds. Nest: an almost flat structure of thin sticks and twigs, in some instances with leaves attached; placed in the branches of a tree growing in or near water. Clutch: three to five; pale bluish-green. Breeding season: variable.

32:14 GREAT EGRET *Egretta alba*

IDENTIFICATION. This is a large, snowy white egret with a very long, slender neck, characteristically held with an acute kink about a third of the way down. Sexes are similar.

DISTRIBUTION. Continental Australia and Tasmania. It is also widespread in Eurasia, Africa and the oriental region.

NOTES. Occurring singly, in pairs, or in flocks, it frequents swamps or the margins of lakes and streams. When not breeding it is generally seen frequenting shallow waters of lakes and swamps, silently wading in quest of prey. An adult in non-breeding plumage does not possess the plumes on the back. Food: fish, frogs, and aquatic insects.

BREEDING. Colonial, usually with other waterbirds. Nest: a platform of sticks; placed in the branches of a tree growing in or near water; breeds in colonies, often in association with other wading birds. Clutch: three to five; pale bluish-green, the surface minutely pitted. Breeding season: variable.

32:15 ROYAL SPOONBILL *Platalea regia*

IDENTIFICATION. The plumage of this species is white. It has a long, spoon-shaped black bill. In breeding plumage it has a long shaggy crest. Sexes are similar.

DISTRIBUTION. Australia generally. It also inhabits Indonesia and New Guinea.

NOTES. Common, nomadic and widespread, although erratic and local over much of the arid interior of the continent, it occurs in pairs or small flocks, frequenting swamps, lagoons, and reed-covered margins of rivers. It stalks its prey in shallow, weed-covered swamps, showing a preference for extensive swampy areas, where it can keep far out from the margins. Food: small fish, aquatic insects, and molluscs.

BREEDING. Colonial, usually with other waterbirds. Nest: a platform of broken-down reeds and twigs; placed a few metres above water among the branches of leafy trees, or even at considerable heights in trees. Clutch: three to four; dull chalky-white, with spots and smears of yellowish-brown or reddish-brown. Breeding season: variable, but mainly October to April.

32:16 YELLOW-BILLED SPOONBILL *Platalea flavipes*

IDENTIFICATION. This species has white plumage, with a long, spoon-shaped, pale yellow bill. Plumage often looks dingy, creamy white, contrasting with the pure white plumage of Royal Spoonbill. Sexes are similar.

DISTRIBUTION. Throughout most of Australia but apparently absent from Cape York Peninsula, central Australia, and the inland parts of Western Australia.

NOTES. Generally common, but highly nomadic and erratic in occurrence, it is seen singly, in pairs, or in flocks, frequenting swamps, margins of lakes and streams, and flood-covered flats. It is usually seen stalking about the edge of a swamp in search of food, often in the company of other wading birds. Similar in general habits to the Royal Spoonbill, but rather less gregarious, it tends to favour smaller bodies of water. Except when breeding, it is extremely wary, and its habit of perching on the branch of a dead tree usually affords it a good view. Food: fish, aquatic insects, and molluscs.

BREEDING. Colonial, usually with other waterbirds. Nest: a large structure of sticks, loosely interlaced; placed in an upright forked branch of a tree, usually over water. Clutch: three to four; dull chalky-white and lustreless. Breeding season: September to January, or according to conditions.

32:17 DARTER *Anhinga melanogaster*

IDENTIFICATION. This bird is mainly black or dull grey, with silvery feathers in the wings. Its long full tail, slender snake-like neck, and long dagger-like bill are distinctive.

DISTRIBUTION. Mainland Australia generally. It is also widespread in Africa and Asia.

NOTES. Seen singly, in pairs or small groups, it frequents chiefly inland lakes, streams and swamps. Its favourite haunts are deep pools and secluded reaches. It is wary, and if disturbed while swimming immediately sinks its body beneath the water, leaving only the head and neck above the surface, or it dives, to reappear some distance away. When flying it usually makes a few flapping motions and then glides; often soaring to great heights. Food: fish and aquatic animals.

BREEDING. Nest: a substantial platform of twigs and sticks, covered with green branchlets which droop over the sides; placed in a low tree over water. Clutch: three to five; greenish and covered with a coating of whitish lime. Breeding season: very variable.

32:18 PIED HERON *Ardea picata*

IDENTIFICATION. A small gregarious heron of tropical swamps and lagoons, it is mainly black, with a white throat, neck and breast. Sexes are similar.

DISTRIBUTION. Tropical northern Australia, from about Wyndham, Western Australia, to the Gulf of Carpentaria, erratically to eastern Queensland, south to about Townsville. It is also found in Indonesia and New Guinea.

NOTES. Gregarious, usually found in groups, occasionally in flocks of a hundred birds or more, it frequents chiefly lagoons, mangroves and tropical wetlands generally. Habits are little studied. Possibly it is partially migratory.

BREEDING. Nest: slightly concave; constructed of twigs; placed in a mangrove tree several metres from the ground. Clutch: three to four; deep blue-green. Breeding season: usually March to May.

32:19 GREAT-BILLED HERON *Ardea sumatrana*

IDENTIFICATION. Australia's largest heron, this bird is dull grey-brown, with a very large, dagger-like bill. Sexes are similar.

DISTRIBUTION. Tropical northern Australia, west to Derby, Western Australia, and south to about Rockhampton, Queensland. It is also found from Burma to Indonesia and New Guinea.

NOTES. Generally uncommon, it is solitary and secretive, inhabiting chiefly mangrove swamps. A shy bird, it frequents the quiet reaches and tidal channels which intersect large areas of mangroves. When disturbed, it moves with a rather ungainly flight to a more secluded part of the swamp. The call-note is a hoarse croak. Food: no detailed information; apparently mainly crabs and other marine invertebrates.

BREEDING. Nest: a flat, bulky structure of coarse sticks; placed in a mangrove tree, usually one overhanging a narrow channel. Clutch: two; light bluish-green, the surface being slightly glossy and minutely pitted. Breeding season: variable, strongly influenced by local conditions.

32:20 WHITE-FACED HERON *Ardea novaehollandiae*

IDENTIFICATION. This species is plain bluish-grey, with white face and chin. Sexes are similar.

DISTRIBUTION. Continental Australia generally and Tasmania. It is also found in New Zealand and numerous islands adjacent to Australia.

NOTES. Common and familiar, it is almost ubiquitous in wetlands generally. Found singly, in pairs or small flocks, it frequents swamps, the margins of lakes and streams, wet paddocks, mud flats, and mangroves. It is usually seen wading in shallow water or perched on a dead limb near water. When disturbed it utters a loud croaking note and rises with a laboured flight. Food: yabbies, freshwater snails, frogs, and insects.

BREEDING. Colonial. Nest: a platform of sticks; placed in the branches of a tree, sometimes well away from water. Clutch: three to six; pale bluish-green, smooth and lustreless. Breeding season: variable.

32:21 PACIFIC HERON *Ardea pacifica*

IDENTIFICATION. Substantially larger than White-faced Heron, this species has head, neck and breast almost entirely white (often appearing creamy or dingy white), and back and wings deep grey. Sexes are similar. In flight, note conspicuous white 'headlights' on the leading edge of the wing.

DISTRIBUTION. Australia generally. It is also found in New Guinea.

NOTES. Seen in pairs or small flocks, it frequents swamps or the margins of lakes and streams. It is shy and wary, keeping to situations where it has a clear view of its surroundings. Similar in general habits to the White-faced Heron, but less common, and rather less gregarious, it is usually seen wading in shallow water, but also often in paddocks and open fields. Food: fish, small reptiles, freshwater molluscs, frogs and aquatic insects.

BREEDING. Colonial. Nest: a rather bulky platform of sticks; placed in the branches of a tree growing in or near water. Clutch: four to six; pale greenish-blue, smooth and lustreless. Breeding season: variable.

32:22 LITTLE BLACK CORMORANT *Phalacrocorax sulcirostris*

IDENTIFICATION. The plumage of this bird is almost entirely black, glossed green. Very like Great Cormorant, it is much smaller, slimmer, and with a slender, completely dark bill. Sexes are similar.

DISTRIBUTION. Australia generally. It is also found in Indonesia, New Guinea and New Zealand.

NOTES. Common and widespread, it is usually seen in flocks or small parties, frequenting lakes, streams, inlets and rocky islets. It is similar in habits to the Great Cormorant, although the Great Cormorant is common along the coast, whereas its smaller relative in general tends to avoid marine environments. Food: aquatic life, especially fish.

BREEDING. Colonial. Nest: a platform of sticks, often with leaves attached; placed on a horizontal branch of a tree. Clutch: three to six; pale green, coated with lime. Breeding season: variable.

32:23 LITTLE PIED CORMORANT *Phalacrocorax melanoleucos*

IDENTIFICATION. Same size as Little Black Cormorant, but its face and underparts are white (often rust-stained). It has a stubby yellowish bill. It can be confused with Pied Cormorant — despite the fact that it too has a black cap and nape, the Pied Cormorant usually looks substantially white-headed at a distance, whereas the Little Pied Cormorant looks dusky-headed. Pied Cormorant has conspicuous black thighs, like shaggy trousers. Sexes are similar.

DISTRIBUTION. Australia generally. It is also found from Malaysia, through Indonesia and New Guinea to the Solomon Islands, New Caledonia and New Zealand.

NOTES. Seen in pairs or flocks, it frequents lakes, streams, swamps, inlets, and rocky islets. Common, widespread and familiar, it occurs freely on stock dams and ponds in city parks or golf courses. It usually fishes alone, but joins other cormorants at favourite loafing spots. Food: aquatic life.

BREEDING. Colonial, usually with other waterbirds. Nest: a platform of sticks and small green twigs; placed on a branch of a tree, usually one growing in or near water. Clutch: four to seven, usually five; pale bluish-white, more or less obscured with a coating of lime. Breeding season: variable.

32:24 GREAT CORMORANT *Phalacrocorax carbo*

IDENTIFICATION. A large, robust cormorant, this species is mainly greenish-black, with dark, stout bill and yellow face. Breeding adults have a white face and chin. Sexes are similar.

DISTRIBUTION. Australia generally. It is also widespread in North America, Europe, Africa and Asia to New Zealand.

NOTES. Seen singly or in small flocks, it frequents lakes, streams, the coastline, and inlets. It is usually seen perched on poles or snags in streams, on rocks, or resting on sandbanks and mud flats. This bird sometimes dives from its perch after fish and yabbies, though the usual method of securing food is to pursue it under water.

BREEDING. Colonial. Nest: open, almost flat; constructed of sticks, aquatic herbage, and debris; placed on a horizontal branch of a tree, in a low bush, or on a ledge of rock. Clutch: three to five; pale bluish-white, thickly and often roughly coated with lime; the eggs soon become scratched and nest-stained. Breeding season: variable.

32:25 PIED CORMORANT *Phalacrocorax varius*

IDENTIFICATION. This bird is a large, crisply black-and-white cormorant, with blue, yellow and pink on the face and black thighs. Sexes are similar. Little Pied Cormorant is similar but much smaller, with stubby yellowish bill.

DISTRIBUTION. Mainland Australia generally; mainly coastal but, especially in the south-east, occurs also on larger inland bodies of water. It is also found in New Zealand.

NOTES. Found singly or in flocks, it frequents swamps, lakes, streams, inlets, or rocky islands. It is similar in habits to the other species of cormorants, with which it often congregates. Like other cormorants, it is often seen loafing in loose companies on reefs, sandbanks or dead trees, with wings outspread as though to dry. Food: aquatic life.

BREEDING. Colonial. Nest: substantial; built on a firm foundation of sticks; lined with green eucalypt leaves and the bird's quill-feathers; placed on a horizontal branch of a tree, on a low bush, or on the ground. Clutch: three to five; pale bluish-white, thickly and often roughly coated with lime. Breeding season: variable.

32:26 BLACK-FACED CORMORANT *Leucocarbo fuscescens*

IDENTIFICATION. This species resembles Pied Cormorant but has a plain, dark grey face. Sexes are similar.

DISTRIBUTION. Coastal Victoria and South Australia (west to Gulf St Vincent); also in the Recherche Archipelago and the adjacent mainland coast of Western Australia; coastal Tasmania and the Bass Strait Islands.

NOTES. Occurring singly or in flocks, it frequents rocky islands and inlets. It is similar in habits to other cormorants, except that its habitat is almost exclusively marine. Food: aquatic life, especially fish.

BREEDING. Colonial. Nest: flat; constructed of seaweed and flotsam and placed on a ledge of rock. Clutch: two to four; pale bluish-white, coated with lime; the eggs soon become scratched and nest-stained. Breeding season: variable, mainly September to January.

P L A T E 3 3

B I R D S O F S W A M P S , L A K E S A N D R I V E R S

33:1 HARDHEAD *Aythya australis*

IDENTIFICATION. The bird is mainly rich mahogany, with white under the tail, dark head and white eye. Sexes are similar, but the female is duller than the male, and has a dark eye. In flight it shows a broad white band extending almost the entire length of the wing.

DISTRIBUTION. Continental Australia (except the far interior) and Tasmania. It is also found in Indonesia, New Guinea, New Caledonia, Vanuatu, and New Zealand.

NOTES. Seen in pairs or flocks (sometimes very large), it frequents pools, swamps, and streams. It is shy and wary, as well as being perhaps the fastest flier among Australian ducks. Most of its food is procured by diving; it remains under water for some time, raking the mud in search of vegetable and animal food.

BREEDING. Nest: a slight depression in the ground, lined with grass mixed with feathers; often in lignum or canegrass, well concealed, and constructed of grass with very little down; sometimes in a hollow spout of a tree. Clutch: usually nine to twelve; light creamy-white. Breeding season: variable; mainly October to November in the south-west, January and February in the south-east, and April and May in the north.

33:2 FRECKLED DUCK *Stictonetta naevosa*

IDENTIFICATION. This duck looks entirely dark grey at a distance, but intricately barred and freckled buff. It has a distinctive head shape, shaggy and pointed at the nape, with a deeply scooped bill, plain grey in females, pink-based in males.

DISTRIBUTION. Mainly south-western Australia and the basin of the Murray, Murrumbidgee and the lower Darling Rivers; vagrants occur erratically across Australia.

NOTES. Found in pairs or small flocks, it frequents chiefly lakes and swamps of inland districts. It is mainly sedentary, but vagrants occur widely throughout Australia. It is a rare species in coastal areas. Generally quiet and unobtrusive, it often prefers to be in the centre of wetlands, far from the margins. Food: aquatic plants and animals.

BREEDING. Nest: flat; constructed of grass and herbage and lined with down; usually well-hidden near water, and sometimes with a platform leading to it. Clutch: five to twelve; creamy-brown, smooth and lustrous. Breeding season: September to December.

33:3 GREY TEAL *Anas gibberifrons*

IDENTIFICATION. This is a small grey-brown duck, with a pale, almost white, face, chin and throat. Sexes are similar. In flight, a narrow white bar along the underwing can be seen. Its upperwing patch (speculum) is metallic green, edged white fore and aft.

DISTRIBUTION. Continental Australia generally and Tasmania. It is also found in various islands, including New Zealand.

NOTES. Usually seen in flocks, it frequents streams, swamps and lagoons, either inland or near the coast.Though highly nomadic, it usually congregates in large numbers and is fairly tame unless disturbed by shooting. The call is a peculiar 'cack–cack–cack', repeated quickly. Food: aquatic animals and vegetation.

BREEDING. Nest: of grass, lined with down; placed in a hollow limb or in lignum or grass. Clutch: usually ten to twelve; creamy-white (unless nest-stained), smooth and slightly glossy. Breeding season: practically throughout the year, influenced by rainfall.

33:4 CHESTNUT TEAL *Anas castanea*

IDENTIFICATION. The male is mainly deep chestnut, with black and white under the tail and a glossy bottle-green head. The female is very difficult to distinguish from Grey Teal, but somewhat darker, plainer brown, with little contrast between dark cap and lighter chin.

DISTRIBUTION. South-eastern Queensland to Victoria, southern South Australia, south and mid-western Australia, and Tasmania.

NOTES. Usually seen in small flocks, often in the company of Grey Teal, it frequents saltwater lakes, inlets and swamps, generally coastal but occasionally on inland streams and lagoons. Food: aquatic vegetation and animal life.

BREEDING. Nest: in a hollow limb or hole in a tree, but occasionally on the ground in herbage near water; lined with down. Clutch: nine to thirteen; cream-coloured (unless nest-stained), glossy. Breeding season: June to December.

33:5 GARGANEY *Anas querquedula*

IDENTIFICATION. This species is like Grey Teal but with a prominent powder-blue patch on the forewing. The male has a deep brown head with bold white superciliary extending almost to the nape. The female has an obscure pale eyebrow stripe and a dark line through the eye.

DISTRIBUTION. Northern Europe, Asia, tropical Africa to New Guinea; apparently accidental to Australia.

NOTES. A vagrant to Australia, but its status is uncertain, possibly being a regular migrant to the far north. Food: aquatic vegetation and animal life.

BREEDING. Nest: a depression in the ground among grass or herbage; lined with grass and down. Clutch: eight to fourteen; buffish-white or cream-coloured (unless nest-stained), smooth and glossy. Breeding season: June to September (Siberia).

33:6 BLUE-BILLED DUCK *Oxyura australis*

IDENTIFICATION. This is a small, dumpy, diving duck with black head, dull chestnut body, and bright blue or blue-grey bill. It could conceivably be mistaken for Hardhead, but has no white under the tail. Sexes are similar.

DISTRIBUTION. South-western Australia and south-eastern Australia to southern Queensland; also Tasmania.

NOTES. Seen in pairs or small flocks, it frequents lakes, lagoons or swamps. It is secretive and wary, usually keeping to deep reaches and pools or to small islands of reeds away from the margins of lakes and swamps. Most of its food is procured by diving, at which the bird is highly expert; it remains under water for considerable periods. Usually silent, the male in display has a low-pitched rattling call, the female a soft quack. Food: aquatic vegetation and animal life.

BREEDING. Nest: bulky; constructed of flags or reeds, and lined with down; the nest is made by bending down and interlacing the flags. Clutch: four to six; greenish-white (unless nest-stained), slightly glossy and rough. Breeding season: October to December or January.

33:7 MANED DUCK *Chenonetta jubata*

IDENTIFICATION. This duck is mainly pale grey, with a brown head and stubby dark grey bill. The male has a short shaggy crest at the nape. The female is extensively mottled white below, and with a narrow pale line above and below the eye.

DISTRIBUTION. Australia generally, including Tasmania.

NOTES. Common and familiar, seen in pairs or flocks, it shows a preference for the upper reaches of streams and timbered margins of swamps. It is also often around stock-dams. It procures most of its food on land, feeding on grass and herbage growing on the margins of streams and swamps. It often frequents flats some distance from water. The call is an extended 'quarck'.

BREEDING. Nest: in a hole in a tree; lined with down and feathers; often high up, and sometimes far from water. Clutch: six to twelve; creamy-white, smooth and lustrous. Breeding season: at any time of year, dependent on rainfall.

33:8 WHITE PYGMY-GOOSE *Nettapus coromandelianus*

IDENTIFICATION. This species is very small and toy-like, its back bottle-green; crown dark; head, neck and underparts otherwise pure white. The male has a narrow green band across the breast. The female is somewhat duller than the male, with a narrow dark line through the eye. In flight, a white wingbar extends the length of the upperwing.

DISTRIBUTION. North-eastern Queensland, south to about Rockhampton (formerly to about Grafton, New South Wales). It is also found in India and southern China to New Guinea.

NOTES. It frequents lakes, streams and swamps, where it congregates in small flocks, usually out in the centre, well away from the margins. It is usually seen floating among waterlilies, or loafing on partly submerged logs. Food: aquatic vegetation and animals.

BREEDING. Nest: in a hole in a tree; lined with grass. Clutch: eight to twelve; ivory-white, with very smooth texture. Breeding season: usually October to January.

33:9 GREEN PYGMY-GOOSE *Nettapus pulchellus*

IDENTIFICATION. This species is tiny and toy-like. Its head, neck and upperparts are mainly bottle-green; its underparts white, finely vermiculated slate-grey. The male has a white cheek patch; the female has a white face, chin and throat. In flight it reveals a white patch along the trailing edge of the inner wing.

DISTRIBUTION. Tropical northern and eastern Australia, west to about Broome, Western Australia and south to about Rockhampton, Queensland. It is also found in Indonesia and New Guinea.

NOTES. Seen in pairs or small groups, it frequents mainly deep, permanent lagoons of the tropics, but also smaller ponds and wetlands during the wet season. It is among the most aquatic of ducks, and seldom leaves the water. Like the White Pygmy-goose, it is usually seen floating among waterlily pads well away from the margins of lagoons. Not especially shy, but alert and difficult to approach, when disturbed it rises quickly and utters a peculiar whistling note while on the wing. Food: aquatic animals and plants.

BREEDING. Nest: flat, occasionally with a slight cavity; constructed of long grass and lined with feathers and down; placed among herbage growing in water or in a hole in a tree. Clutch: four to eleven; creamy-white (unless nest-stained), smooth and lustrous. Breeding season: January to March, or after rain.

33:10 WANDERING WHISTLING-DUCK *Dendrocygna arcuata*

IDENTIFICATION. This is a rather large duck with an alert, long-necked stance, mainly reddish below, with dark crown and short, buffy flank plumes. Its bill and legs are near black. Sexes are similar.

DISTRIBUTION. Northern and eastern Australia, west to the Kimberley and south to about Rockhampton, Queensland. It is also found in the Philippines, Indonesia, Borneo and Papua New Guinea.

NOTES. Highly gregarious, usually seen in dense flocks, it frequents streams, lakes, or lagoons of the inland districts. Feeding is by upending, dabbling or diving in shallow water. The name refers to the incessant shrill whistling notes uttered by flocks. Food: chiefly grass and other herbage.

BREEDING. Nest: an unlined depression in grass, often at a considerable distance from water. Clutch: eight to twelve; creamy white, slightly glossy, and pointed at both ends. Breeding season: almost any time according to seasonal conditions.

33:11 PLUMED WHISTLING-DUCK *Dendrocygna eytoni*

IDENTIFICATION. This species is like Wandering Whistling-duck but paler. Its back is greyish, head buffy; with long creamy plumes along flank. The bill and legs are pinkish. Sexes are similar.

DISTRIBUTION. North-western, northern and eastern Australia, occasionally extending into southern areas and also to central Australia; accidental to Tasmania and New Zealand.

NOTES. Largely nocturnal, it camps during the day in dense flocks, often very large, near secluded streams, lakes, swamps, or waterholes of the northern inland districts. It prefers shallow water near the margins of streams or swamps, except during the breeding season, when it resorts to well-grassed lands some distance from water. It also perches in trees. Like the Wandering Whistling-duck, it has a loud twittering, whistling call. Food: chiefly grass and other herbage.

BREEDING. Nest: a slight hollow in the ground; lined with dried grasses; placed among grass or herbage growing upon plains, and often far from water. Clutch: eight to twelve; pale cream colour, with a glossy surface; sometimes minutely spotted light brown. Breeding season: September to December, occasionally later.

33:12 PINK-EARED DUCK *Malacorhynchus membranaceus*

IDENTIFICATION. This species is dark brown above, boldy barred ('zebra-like') below. Its face is white, with a dark patch around the eye. The bill is broad, greyish, with leathery flaps at tip. Sexes are similar.

DISTRIBUTION. Australia generally, but mainly interior south-eastern Australia in the basin of the Murray, Murrumbidgee and Darling rivers. Vagrants occur erratically across Australia.

NOTES. Found in pairs or small groups, sometimes large flocks, it frequents chiefly shallow lakes and swamps, especially residual floodwaters. Highly nomadic, its movements are influenced by local flooding. It is mostly confined to the inland districts and only rarely visits the coast. Most of its food is procured by 'shovelling' with its bill in the mud in shallow water. It often keeps its head below the surface for lengthy periods. Food: aquatic plants and animals.

BREEDING. Nest: a rounded mass of down plucked from the breasts of the parent birds and placed among grass or herbage growing in water, or on a deserted platform-shaped nest of another species; sometimes in a tree cavity. Clutch: six to eight; creamy-white. Breeding season: variable, in response to floods.

33:13 PACIFIC BLACK DUCK *Anas superciliosa*

IDENTIFICATION. This duck is mainly dark brown, its head paler, with a distinctive face pattern: a dark crown, line through the eye, and malar streak. Sexes are similar. Underwing coverts are white; upperwing has large metallic green patch, but no white.

DISTRIBUTION. Continental Australia generally and Tasmania. It is also found in islands to the north and east, including New Zealand.

NOTES. Seen in pairs or flocks, it frequents streams, lakes or swamps, both inland and coastal, reaching maximum densities in extensive southern wetlands, but it is extraordinarily versatile, occurring at least casually in any kind of water, even narrow rainforest streams or roadside puddles. It is the best-known and, with the possible exception of the Grey Teal, probably the commonest of Australia's ducks. Food: grass, herbage, and aquatic plants and animals.

BREEDING. Nest: open, but sometimes partly domed; constructed of grass and lined with feathers; placed on the ground among rushes or grass growing near water, in herbage growing in a field far from water, on a deserted platform-shaped nest of another species, or in a hollow stump or limb of a tree. Clutch: eight to fourteen; creamy-white, occasionally tinged with green. Breeding season: in normal times, July to December.

33:14 BLUE-WINGED SHOVELER *Anas rhynchotis*

IDENTIFICATION. Its bill is uniquely long, straight and flattened, producing an unmistakable silhouette. The male has a blue head with narrow white crescent, chestnut underparts, and white flank patch. The female is dull brown. Both sexes have a large powder-blue patch on forewing, obvious in flight.

DISTRIBUTION. Continental Australia (except the far north), Tasmania and New Zealand.

NOTES. Found in pairs or flocks, it frequents swamps, lagoons, and freshwater lakes, both near the coast and inland. It is very wary, mostly keeping to open spaces far out from the water's edge, often with other waterfowl. In flight, it makes a distinctive whistling or humming noise with its wings. Food: aquatic plants and animals.

BREEDING. Nest: a grass-lined depression in the ground; placed under the shelter of a tussock of grass or clump of low herbage, sometimes out on an open plain, but usually not far from the water. Clutch: four to eleven; creamy-white. Breeding season: variable, in response to floods.

33:15 MUSK DUCK *Biziura lobata*

IDENTIFICATION. This is a bulky, low-slung, dark, bizarre-looking duck, the male having a large, dark, leathery pouch under the bill.

DISTRIBUTION. South-eastern Australia, from Fraser Island, Queensland, to Eyre Peninsula and Kangaroo Island, South Australia. It is also found in south-western Australia from about Esperance to Moora.

NOTES. Common, mainly sedentary, it is seen singly or in pairs, occasionally in small flocks, frequenting wetlands generally. Completely aquatic, it is very seldom seen on land. Males have an extraordinary courtship display in which jets of water are thrown out on each side with a rapid back-kick of the feet, accompanied by a deep, resonant 'plonk' and a piercing whistle, the broad tail fanned and cocked well forward over the back. Food: aquatic plants and animals.

BREEDING. Nest: a bulky structure; placed among reeds and made by bending down and interlacing the stems, forming a cup-shaped mass which is lined with grass and down. Clutch: usually two to three; pale green, rough and slightly glossy. Breeding season: August to December.

33:16 LITTLE BITTERN *Ixobrychus minutus*

IDENTIFICATION. This is a tiny, very secretive heron of dense reed-beds. It has a warm buff face, neck and wing patches. The back is black in the male, dark brown in the female.

DISTRIBUTION. South-western Australia (north to the Murchison River) and eastern and south-eastern Australia. It is also found in New Zealand, Europe, Africa, and Asia.

NOTES. Found singly or in pairs, it frequents the margins of streams and swamps. It is very secretive but may sometimes be seen flying over reed-beds. For the most part it remains hidden among the reeds. Apparently it is migratory, but its movements are not well understood. Food: small fish and aquatic animals.

BREEDING. Nest: open; constructed of dead pieces of aquatic plants and grasses, and usually in reeds over water. Clutch: four to five; white. Breeding season: October to December.

33:17 NANKEEN NIGHT-HERON *Nycticorax caledonicus*

IDENTIFICATION. This is a squat, stocky heron with a deep, stout bill. The adults are buff below, rufous above, with a black cap and wispy white plumes at the nape. Juveniles are dull brown, and heavily streaked. It is often confused with Brown Bittern, but has a spotted back.

DISTRIBUTION. Australia generally. It also inhabits Indonesia and the Philippines and islands of the south-western Pacific.

NOTES. Common and widespread, it frequents wetlands generally. It is mainly nocturnal, but may be seen during the day roosting in trees growing in or near water (especially weeping willows) or in reed-beds, often in groups. Towards dusk it emerges from cover and flies to feeding grounds. It utters a harsh croaking note during the night or when disturbed at its roosting place. Food: yabbies, freshwater molluscs, frogs, and aquatic insects.

BREEDING. Colonial. Nest: a scanty platform of sticks; placed on a horizontal branch of a tree. Clutch: two to four; pale bluish-green. Breeding season: usually September to January.

33:18 MANGROVE HERON *Butorides striatus*

IDENTIFICATION. This is a small, stocky, plain dusky heron, greyish below, greenish above, with a black cap. A reddish morph occurs in north-western Australia.

DISTRIBUTION. Coastal Australia, south to about Shark Bay, Western Australia, in the west and Jervis Bay, New South Wales, in the east. Almost cosmopolitan.

NOTES. Seen singly or in pairs, it frequents muddy foreshores and flats of inlets and rivers, particularly localities thickly covered with mangroves. Typically seen on tidal mudflats near mangroves, it stalks prey with crouched posture and apparently infinite caution, though it not infrequently scuttles about after crabs or mudskippers with a distinctive hobbling gait. It perches, hunch-backed, in branches of trees growing in or near water, or on mooring posts. When disturbed it utters a loud squawking note. Food: fish and crustaceans.

BREEDING. Nest: a loosely constructed platform of sticks; placed in a tree, usually a mangrove, growing in or near water. Clutch: two to four; pale bluish-green, dull. Breeding season: September to December.

33:19 BLACK BITTERN *Dupetor flavicollis*

IDENTIFICATION. This is a very dark, almost black, heron, with streaked breast and prominent buff streak down the side of the neck. Sexes are similar.

DISTRIBUTION. Western, northern and eastern Australia (chiefly coastal areas) to the Shoalhaven River, New South Wales, in the east. It is also found in India, China, and Malaysia to New Guinea.

NOTES. Seen singly or in pairs, it frequents timbered margins of streams, mangrove flats, and tree and reed-lined lakes and swamps, mainly in coastal lowlands. Extremely secretive, during the day it perches in a tree or rests among reeds, and when startled usually assumes the stick-like attitude common to bitterns. Food: fish, frogs, aquatic insects.

BREEDING. Nest: a platform of sticks; placed in a tree, usually on a branch overhanging water. Clutch: three to five; white, with a greenish tinge inside the shell. Breeding season: September to January.

33:20 BROWN BITTERN *Botaurus poiciloptilus*

IDENTIFICATION. The plumage of this species is mainly dull brown, intricately mottled, streaked and banded with golden buff. The breast is streaked, with a large dark streak down the side of the neck. Sexes are similar.

DISTRIBUTION. South-western Australia and from south-eastern South Australia (west to the Adelaide plains) to north-eastern New South Wales. It is also found in New Caledonia and New Zealand.

NOTES. Found singly or in pairs, it frequents margins of streams, lakes and swamps. It is partly nocturnal in habits, and seldom emerges from the cover of dense reed-beds. When disturbed it freezes, stiffly extending neck and bill vertically, even swaying gently if wind is moving the reeds: in this posture it is almost impossible to see. The call consists of three or four deep 'booms', with a distinct interval between each, suggesting the bellowing of a bull; suggested as the origin of the fabulous bunyip, said to dwell in swamps and such places. Food: fish, frogs, yabbies, and other aquatic life.

BREEDING. Nest: a platform of bent-over and interlaced reeds and rushes; usually placed barely above water-level in the densest part of a swamp. Clutch: four to six; olive green, smooth and lustrous. Breeding season: October to January or February.

33:21 PHEASANT COUCAL *Centropus phasianinus*

IDENTIFICATION. This is a large, long-tailed, dark, clumsy, untidy-looking bird of dense grassland. Breeding birds are mainly black, with reddish brown upperparts and narrowly banded tail. The plumage at seasons is mainly reddish brown, intricately streaked and barred.

DISTRIBUTION. Northern and eastern Australia, west to about Shark Bay, Western Australia, and south to about Ulladulla, New South Wales. It is also found in New Guinea.

NOTES. Common, mainly sedentary, it frequents swamps and rank, dense grasslands, mainly in coastal lowlands. Generally secretive, it may often be seen sitting watchfully in the tops of bushes, or scuttling clumsily across roads. The loud whooping call suggests water gurgling out of an upturned bottle. This species is the only Australian cuckoo that does not deposit its eggs in nests of other birds. Food: frogs, small reptiles and aquatic insects, also eggs and young of other birds.

BREEDING. Nest: a large, globular structure; built in a tussock of tall grass, formed by drawing the tops of grasses together, and lining the inside with leaves; sometimes in a low bush. Clutch: three to five; dull white, smooth and slightly lustrous. Breeding season: September to March.

33:22 BURDEKIN SHELDUCK *Tadorna radjah*

IDENTIFICATION. This species has white head, neck and underparts, its back mainly brown, a narrow brown band across the breast, and with a pink bill and legs. Sexes are similar.

DISTRIBUTION. Coastal northern Australia, west to the Kimberley and south to about Bowen, Queensland; also inhabits Indonesia and New Guinea.

NOTES. Seen in pairs or flocks, it frequents lakes and swamps. It prefers shallow water and often resorts to adjacent grasslands and mangrove swamps. Food: aquatic plants, crabs, molluscs and other marine life.

BREEDING. Nest: in a hole in a tree. Clutch: six to twelve; rich creamy-white. Breeding season: February to July.

33:23 AUSTRALIAN SHELDUCK *Tadorna tadornoides*

IDENTIFICATION. This large goose-like duck is boldly patterned in black, white and chestnut. Sexes are similar, but the female has a white ring around the eye. In flight, it shows large white patches in the upperwing. It has a narrow white collar.

DISTRIBUTION. Eastern Australia (rare in Queensland), Victoria, South Australia, Western Australia (as far north as the Tropic of Capricorn), and Tasmania.

NOTES. Found in pairs or flocks, it frequents lakes, swamps, or open plains. It is shy and wary and keeps far out on the shallow lakes or swamps. When disturbed it rises quickly, uttering a harsh cry resembling 'chank, chank'. Large flocks gather after breeding on certain favoured lakes (for example, Lake George, New South Wales and the Coorong, South Australia) to moult, when they are for a time, like most other wildfowl, flightless. Food: chiefly grass and other herbage.

BREEDING. Nest: of grass, lined with down; usually in a hole in a tree, sometimes in or near water, often far from it; occasionally on the ground or in a rabbit burrow. Clutch: eight to fourteen; creamy-white, with a glossy surface. Breeding season: July to December.

BIRDS OF THE OCEAN AND SHORE

PLATE 34

BIRDS OF SHORES AND RIVER MARGINS

34:1 GREY PLOVER *Pluvialis squatarola*

IDENTIFICATION. This is like Pacific Golden Plover but slightly larger and stockier, with a stout black bill. Its plumage is mainly grey, intricately spangled white. In its breeding plumage (infrequently seen in Australia) it has face, throat, breast and belly black. It is easily distinguished from Pacific Golden Plover in flight, when it reveals its white rump and bold white wingbar. Black axillaries (in the 'armpit') are also diagnostic.

DISTRIBUTION. Breeds in the high Arctic; widespread in winter across North, Central and South America, Eurasia, Africa, southern Asia and Australasia.

NOTES. Generally uncommon in Australia, it is usually alone or in small groups, seldom associating with other waders. It arrives in Australia during August and departs in March or April. It frequents the seashore and contiguous salt marshes and grassy flats, seldom occurring inland. It is very timid and wary. Its call-note is a piping whistle, not unlike that of the Pacific Golden Plover, a species which it resembles in habits. Food: aquatic animal life.

BREEDING. Nest: a depression in the ground; lined with dry leaves and lichen. Clutch: four; yellowish-grey, covered with brown spots. Breeding season: June and July (Arctic regions).

34:2 PACIFIC GOLDEN PLOVER *Pluvialis dominica*

IDENTIFICATION. This plover is mainly brownish-grey, freckled and spangled golden-buff, while in breeding plumage (not commonly seen in Australia) has black face, throat and breast. In flight it reveals a narrow, rather obscure pale wingbar. Its rump is the same colour as the back. Sexes are similar.

DISTRIBUTION. Breeds in Alaska and northern Siberia; winters in South America and across the Pacific to New Zealand and Australia.

NOTES. Usually seen in flocks, it arrives in southern Australia during August or September and departs in April. It frequents beaches, sand flats of inlets and rivers, salt marshes, and the grassy margins of shallow lagoons, occasionally airfields or golf courses, mostly in coastal regions but locally inland. During low tide it feeds along the sand flats, leaving for marshes and grassy flats as the tide rises. It is common and widespread in Australia. Food: insects, small crustaceans and worms.

BREEDING. Nest: a hollow in the ground in tundra; lined with broken stalks of moss. Clutch: four; buff, with purplish-brown markings. Breeding season: June-July (north-eastern Siberia and Alaska).

34:3 ORIENTAL PLOVER *Charadrius veredus*

IDENTIFICATION. Long-legged and slender in build, this species is not much smaller than a Pacific Golden Plover, but plain sandy brown above (not spangled), with obscure buffy superciliary and yellowish legs. In flight it shows a plain upperwing, lacking a pale wingbar. Unmistakable in its breeding plumage: it has a broad chestnut band across the breast and is bordered below with a narrower black band.

DISTRIBUTION. Breeds in Mongolia; winters mainly in Malaysia, Indonesia and north-western Australia.

NOTES. Singly or in flocks, it arrives in Australia during September and departs in March. Most common in the north-west, where large flocks may occur, it is reported from all mainland States. It frequents tidal flats, salt marshes, clay pans, and airfields, not necessarily on the coast. Its flight is swift and often erratic. When at rest it stands erect and motionless with a characteristic alert stance. It is extremely wary, and when disturbed utters a sharp whistling note. Food: insects, worms, and small crustaceans.

BREEDING. Nest: not recorded. Clutch: not recorded.

34:4 RINGED PLOVER *Charadrius hiaticula*

IDENTIFICATION. This species is much like Doubled-banded or Mongolian Plover in size, shape and general appearance, but it has yellowish (not black) legs. A white band completely encircles the neck, bordered below by a broad dark band (jet black in breeding adults, duller and greyer, but usually at least obscurely visible, in non-breeding adults or juveniles). A dark cheek patch contrasts markedly with a white forehead and line behind and above the eye. The bill is yellowish, tipped black. In flight it reveals a narrow white wingbar. Sexes are similar.

DISTRIBUTION. Breeds across northern Europe and Asia; winters from Africa to western India, less commonly further east. Rare vagrant to Australia.

NOTES. It occurs alone or in pairs. On its wintering grounds it frequents mainly coastal environments; tidal mud flats, sandbanks, estuaries, and occasionally shingle beaches. There are very few Australian records.

BREEDING. Nest: a hollow in sand or shingle; lined with small pebbles or shell fragments. Clutch: usually four; stone-buff blotched with dark brown and grey. Breeding season: May to July.

34:5 LITTLE RINGED PLOVER *Charadrius dubius*

IDENTIFICATION. This species is very like Ringed Plover, but slightly smaller, with a black bill and narrow yellow eye-ring. In flight it reveals plain upperwing, with no pale wingbar. Sexes are similar.

DISTRIBUTION. Breeds in Europe and across most of Asia to the Philippines and New Guinea. Vagrant to Australia.

NOTES. Usually seen alone or in pairs, it frequents mainly the sandy or pebbly banks of rivers, mud flats and occasionally arable land. In general, it favours freshwater, not coast. There are few Australian records, mainly from the Northern Territory.

BREEDING. Nest: a scrape in loose sand. Clutch: usually four; greenish-buff, densely spotted with umber-brown or black. Breeding season: variable, but mainly March to July.

34:6 RED-CAPPED PLOVER *Charadrius ruficapillus*

IDENTIFICATION. Very common, this species is pale sandy brown above, white below, with a white forehead. Breeding adults have rufous crowns. Sexes are similar.

DISTRIBUTION. Australia generally, including Tasmania; mainly coastal, but locally in the interior, especially in the south-east.

NOTES. Seen in pairs or flocks, it frequents shores of inlets or margins of lakes, rivers and beaches, preferring sand substrates rather than mud. It runs with quick little strides and sudden pauses, and if disturbed flies a few paces away, alights, and repeats these movements. Food: insects and small crustaceans.

BREEDING. Nest: a depression in the sand; usually lined with broken pieces of shell or tiny pebbles; the site is usually, but not always, near water. Clutch: usually two; sandy grey or pale green, with dots of dark brown and a few underlying spots of lavender. Breeding season: variable, mainly August to March in coastal regions, June to September in the interior.

34:7 DOUBLE-BANDED PLOVER *Charadrius bicinctus*

IDENTIFICATION. This species is unmistakable in its breeding plumage, with narrow black, white, and rufous bands across the breast. At other seasons it closely resembles Mongolian Plover, but a buffy wash at the nape and hind-neck is diagnostic. Sexes are similar.

DISTRIBUTION. Breeds in New Zealand; a trans-Tasman migrant, wintering in south-eastern Australia.

NOTES. Usually seen in small flocks, it arrives from New Zealand during February or March and departs in September or October. It is rarely seen during the summer months. It is most common on the east coast between Tasmania and about Noosa, Queensland, but occasionally it is seen further north and west. It is a vagrant inland. It frequents chiefly seashores and adjoining salt marshes. The call-note is a piping whistle, 'twit, twit'.

BREEDING. Nest: a depression in gravel or shingle of a river flat. Clutch: three; greenish-brown, with dark brown markings. Breeding season: August to December (New Zealand).

34:8 BLACK-FRONTED PLOVER *Charadrius melanops*

IDENTIFICATION. This plover is mainly white below, with a black forehead, a band through the eye extending to the nape and downwards across the breast. It has a chestnut patch on the wing. Sexes are similar.

DISTRIBUTION. Australia generally, including Tasmania. It is also found in New Zealand.

NOTES. Usually seen in pairs or family parties, it frequents chiefly shingly and muddy banks of rivers, lakes or waterholes, also the shores of inlets, and even storm channels in towns. It runs with great rapidity. When flushed it rises quickly, and frequently utters plaintive notes like 'chick, chick'. Food: aquatic life.

BREEDING. Nest: a slight depression in the ground; lined with tiny pebbles; favourite sites are shingly flats, rarely far from water. Clutch: usually three; stone-coloured or greyish-yellow, with markings of brown and lavender. Breeding season: September to December, sometimes later.

34:9 HOODED PLOVER *Charadrius rubricollis*

IDENTIFICATION. This species is pale sandy brown above, white below, with a black head and a broad white band across the nape. Sexes are similar.

DISTRIBUTION. Coastal southern Australia, including Tasmania, north to about Geraldton on the west coast and about Jervis Bay on the east coast.

NOTES. Found in pairs or family parties, it frequents chiefly sand beaches, dunes, occasionally margins of coastal lagoons, and (in the south-west) inland salt lakes. It is usually seen running along sandy beaches just clear of the waves, or among debris left by the tides. Generally it is rather silent, but calls include abrupt piping notes and a barking 'ker, kew'. Food: marine insects.

BREEDING. Nest: a depression in sand or among pebbles, shells, or seaweed. Clutch: two to three; pale stone-colour, covered with purplish-black and lavender markings. Breeding season: September to December or January.

34:10 MONGOLIAN PLOVER *Charadrius mongolus*

IDENTIFICATION. The breeding plumage of this species has black mask, white forehead, and broad red band across the breast, narrowly bordered above with black. At other seasons it is difficult to distinguish from Large Sand or Double-banded Plover.

DISTRIBUTION. Breeds in central Asia, winters in Africa, India, and southern Asia, east and south to Australia.

NOTES. Usually found in flocks, it arrives in Australia during September and departs in March, a few birds remaining throughout the year. Common in coastal regions of the north and east, it is less so in the west and south; and only sporadically found inland. It frequents mainly tidal sand and mud flats. The call is clear and musical. It is most often seen in winter plumage, but individuals may be seen in full breeding plumage just before leaving for the north in autumn.

BREEDING. Nest: a slight hollow in the ground; lined with leaves and stems of plants. Clutch: three; cream-buff, spotted brown. Breeding season: June (Siberia).

34:11 LARGE SAND PLOVER *Charadrius leschenaultii*

IDENTIFICATION. This plover's breeding plumage has a bright reddish band across the breast, not bordered with black either above or below. At other seasons it is extremely difficult to distinguish it from a non-breeding Mongolian Plover, but it is usually longer-legged, with markedly longer, stouter bill.

DISTRIBUTION. Breeds in central Asia, migrating to Africa, southern Asia and Australia; mainly in the north-west, progressively less common southwards.

NOTES. Seen singly or in flocks, often with other plovers, it frequents tidal salt creeks and seashores. It is fairly common during summer in north-western Australia, where it frequents mud banks and sandy or shingly beaches. It is much less common in the west and south. An adult in breeding plumage is cinnamon-rufous on the crown, the hind neck, and on a narrow collar around the upper breast.

BREEDING. Nest: a depression in the sand and fine shingle on the borders of a lake (Siberia). Clutch: four; ochre, with a greenish tint. Breeding season: June to July.

34:12 RED-KNEED DOTTEREL *Erythrogonys cinctus*

IDENTIFICATION. This bird has a black cap, white throat, and broad black breast band shading to chestnut flanks. Sexes are similar.

DISTRIBUTION. Mainland Australia generally.

NOTES. Found in wetlands of the interior, extending locally to coastal regions. Seen in pairs or small flocks, it frequents margins of swamps, lagoons, dams and river flats. It is seldom observed far from water. It runs with rather jerky movements, stopping suddenly to stand erect, or, with quick thrusts, striking at the ground in pursuit of insects.

BREEDING. Nest: a slight depression in the ground. Clutch: usually four; cream to creamy-brown, with a network of fine lines and freckles of black. Breeding season: October to December.

34:13 WANDERING TATTLER *Tringa incana*

IDENTIFICATION. This bird is very difficult to distinguish from the more common and widespread Grey-tailed Tattler, except by a call: a shrill, excited series of six to ten notes: 'ti–ti–ti–ti . . .'. Sexes are similar.

DISTRIBUTION. It breeds in Alaska, wintering widespread across the islands of the Pacific Ocean to New Zealand and the east coast of Australia.

NOTES. A comparatively rare bird in Australia, it is usually solitary or in company with Grey-tailed Tattlers, occurring chiefly on rocky coastal areas along the east coast (south to about Wollongong, New South Wales).

BREEDING. Nest: a shallow depression; usually on a gravel-bar in a mountain stream; lined with rootlets and grass. Clutch: four; greenish, spotted and blotched brown. Breeding season: June and July (Alaska).

34:14 GREY-TAILED TATTLER *Tringa brevipes*

IDENTIFICATION. This species is a rather plump seaside wader, with rather short, yellowish legs and a long straight bill. It is mid-grey above, slightly paler grey below. This and the Wandering Tattler are the only two waders that show an entirely plain, unmarked upper surface in flight. The two tattlers are very difficult to tell apart. Calls provide the most reliable distinguishing feature, a whistled 'pyuee' in this species, a rapid 'ti–ti–ti–ti–ti' in the Wandering Tattler.

DISTRIBUTION. Breeds in north-eastern Siberia; winters south through the Philippines, Indonesia and New Guinea to Australia; mainly the north and east coasts between about Shark Bay, Western Australia, and Sydney, New South Wales; less common further south.

NOTES. One of the commonest of the migratory waders in Australia, it is usually seen in flocks, arriving in Australia during September or October and departing in April or May, although many commonly over-winter. It frequents mainly coastal mangrove swamps, rocky seashores and mud flats. The call is a liquid whistle of one or two notes, 'tlooeep', occasionally a more strident series of notes.

BREEDING. Nest: a hollow among stones, or in the abandoned nest of a song bird. Clutch: four; pale buff, blotched with dark brown. Breeding season: probably June to July (Siberia).

34:15 GREENSHANK *Tringa nebularia*

IDENTIFICATION. This is a rather large sandpiper, with long, rather stout, faintly upcurved bill. Its plumage is mainly grey above, and white below. In flight it reveals a white rump, extending well up the back in an acute V. Sexes are similar.

DISTRIBUTION. Breeds across northern Europe and Asia; winters from the Mediterranean across southern Asia to New Guinea and Australia.

NOTES. It is wary, active and excitable, with a loud ringing call, 'teu–teu–teu'. Usually seen alone or in small groups, occasionally in large flocks, it arrives in Australia during September and departs in March or April. Widespread, mainly in coastal regions, it is also locally common at suitable wetlands in the interior. It frequents mud flats, sand spits, salt marshes, and shallow lagoons. It is usually seen wading in shallow water, much less often on muddy margins. Food: aquatic life.

BREEDING. Nest: a depression in grass. Clutch: four; stone-colour, with dark red blotches and underlying markings of lavender. Breeding season: May and June (northern Europe and Asia).

34:16 COMMON SANDPIPER *Tringa hypoleucos*

IDENTIFICATION. This species is mainly brown above, and white below. A smudgy brown patch on the side of the breast produces a distinct white 'tab' extending towards the back, just in front of the shoulder. It has a white eye-ring. Sexes are similar.

DISTRIBUTION. Breeds across Europe and northern Asia; winters from the Mediterranean across southern Asia to Japan, New Guinea and Australia.

NOTES. A spring and summer migrant (generally July to May, but a few over-winter) to Australia, it is common in the north, becoming progressively less common southwards. Usually solitary, it tends to shun the company of other waders. It frequents rocky or muddy inlets, mangrove swamps, or the margins of stock-dams, streams or drainage channels, both coastal and inland. Characterised by constant nervous teetering and rapid flight, straight and low, on stiff down-curved vibrating wings. The call-note is a tremulous whistle. Food: small aquatic animals.

BREEDING. Nest: a depression in grass or on the ground; lined with dead grass, moss, or leaves. Clutch: four; creamy-buff, with spots of grey and brown. Breeding season: June and July (Europe and northern Asia).

34:17 TEREK SANDPIPER *Tringa terek*

IDENTIFICATION. This species is a small greyish shorebird, readily identified by yellow-orange legs and long, slightly upturned bill. In flight it shows a white panel along the trailing edge of the wings. Sexes are similar.

DISTRIBUTION. Breeds across northern Russia; winters in Africa, India and across south-east Asia to New Guinea, Australia and New Zealand.

NOTES. Generally uncommon and local, it is mainly found on northern and eastern coasts (south to about Newcastle, New South Wales). Seen singly or in small flocks, although larger numbers congregate at especially favoured localities, it frequents tidal mud flats and estuaries. It arrives in Australia during September and departs in March or April. Food: aquatic animal life.

BREEDING. Nest: a depression in the ground among grass. Clutch: four; pale stone-colour, covered with blotches of dark purplish-red and underlying ones of lavender. Breeding season: June and July.

34:18 RED KNOT *Calidris canutus*

IDENTIFICATION. This species is difficult to distinguish from Great Knot (except in breeding plumage, when face, neck and underparts are brick red), but is distinctly smaller, with plain grey crown (unstreaked), proportionately shorter bill, and dusky greyish rump. Sexes are similar.

DISTRIBUTION. Breeds in the high Arctic; winters widely in South America, Africa and southern Asia, east and south to Australia and New Zealand.

NOTES. It is a visitor to the shores of Australia generally, where it frequents coastal sand flats and the margins of inlets and rivers. It is rare and erratic inland. It usually arrives from the north during August and departs about April, although a few remain during the southern winter. It is usually seen in small parties, often in company with other waders, occasionally in dense flocks. Food: aquatic life.

BREEDING. Nest: a small scrape in the ground. Clutch: usually four; greyish-green to olive-buff, spotted brown and grey. Breeding season: June and July (Siberia).

34:19 GREAT KNOT *Calidris tenuirostris*

IDENTIFICATION. This bird is rather large, of long tubby build, with a moderately long, faintly drooped bill. Non-breeding plumage is mainly dull grey, dingy white below, its crown grey, narrowly dark-streaked and rump white. In breeding plumage, the breast is boldy scalloped dark grey. Sexes are similar.

DISTRIBUTION. Breeds in north-eastern Siberia. Winters south through south-eastern Asia to Australia, especially the north-west; in fewer numbers elsewhere along the Australian coastline.

NOTES. Generally seen in small groups, often in company with godwits, large flocks occurring in the north-west. It frequents mainly estuaries and tidal mud flats, occasionally seen inland. Present mainly from September to March, a few over-wintering.

BREEDING. Nest: a slight depression in reindeer moss. Clutch: four; greyish-yellow, speckled reddish-brown. Breeding season: June and July (Siberia).

34:20 CURLEW SANDPIPER *Calidris ferruginea*

IDENTIFICATION. In non-breeding plumage this species is mainly dull grey above, dingy white below, with a moderately long, slender, delicately downcurved bill. It is the only common small migratory wader with a white rump. In breeding plumage, its head, neck and underparts are deep red. Sexes are similar.

DISTRIBUTION. Northern Siberia, migrating to Africa, Australia and Tasmania; accidental to New Zealand.

NOTES. Usually found in flocks, often with other small waders, it frequents seashores, estuaries and adjacent marshes. Common and widespread around the coasts of Australia, it is only occasional in the interior. It is most commonly seen from September to April, but recorded during every month of the year. It procures its food on sandy and muddy shores and flats, usually making its appearance on feeding grounds as the tide begins to fall. At high tide it goes to higher ground or adjacent marshes, where it rests until the ebb commences again.

BREEDING. Nest: a depression in the ground. Clutch: four; greenish-grey, with rufous-brown markings and underlying spots of purplish-grey. Breeding season: June and July (northern Siberia).

34:21 RED-NECKED STINT *Calidris ruficollis*

IDENTIFICATION. In non-breeding plumage this species is mainly white below, pale grey above, without any obvious markings. In flight it reveals a narrow white wingbar. In breeding plumage, it is suffused dull red on the head and breast, with a white face. Sexes are similar.

DISTRIBUTION. North-eastern Siberia, migrating to India, continental Australia, Tasmania, and New Zealand.

NOTES. Usually appearing in flocks, it arrives in southern Australia about August and departs in April, although a fair number of the birds usually remain throughout the year. It frequents open marshy swamp lands, estuaries and beaches, where it feeds on small marine crustaceans and aquatic insects and worms. One of the most numerous and ubiquitous migrant waders around the coasts of Australia, it is more erratic and local in occurrence at suitable wetlands inland.

BREEDING. Nest: a hollow in the ground; lined with dwarf willow leaves. Clutch: four; light buff, heavily spotted reddish-brown. Breeding season: June and July (Siberia).

34:22 LONG-TOED STINT *Calidris subminuta*

IDENTIFICATION. This bird is very small and difficult to distinguish from Red-necked Stint, but it has dull yellowish legs, and favours muddy freshwater swamps. Sexes are similar.

DISTRIBUTION. Breeds in north-eastern Siberia; winters from China and the Philippines to India, Indonesia and Australia.

NOTES. Usually found in small flocks, it is more likely to be seen singly in Australia; recorded more frequently in Western Australia than in the east. It often associates with other waders. It frequents boggy meadows, margins of swamps and lagoons, sewage farms, and seaweed along tidelines. It often feeds in an inconspicuous and mouse-like manner.

BREEDING. Nest: a depression in the ground; lined with grass. Clutch: four; olive-buff, blotched with shades of brown. Breeding season: June and July (Siberia).

34:23 SANDERLING *Calidris alba*

IDENTIFICATION. This bird is a very small wader, with comparatively stout black bill and short black legs. In non-breeding plumage it is white below, very pale grey above, with dusky shoulder. In breeding plumage the head and breast are strongly suffused reddish. Sexes are similar.

DISTRIBUTION. Arctic regions, migrating to South America, Africa, and Australia; rare in Tasmania and New Zealand.

NOTES. This is mainly a bird of coastal beaches and tidal sand flats in estuaries. It is widely distributed, though not common, along the coasts of Australia, occurring mainly from September to April. Foraging behaviour is very distinctive. Almost alone among the small waders, it favours sandy ocean beaches, often with heavy surf. It chases out-going waves, jabbing rapidly at prey in the ebbing shallows, and retreats up the beach before the next, running on twinkling feet like a little clockwork toy. Food: aquatic animal life.

BREEDING. Nest: a hollow in the ground; lined with small leaves and fibre. Clutch: four; greenish, with markings of reddish-grey, brown and blackish-brown. Breeding season: June and July (Arctic regions).

34:24 BROAD-BILLED SANDPIPER *Limicola falcinellus*

IDENTIFICATION. This species is about midway between Red-necked Stint and Curlew Sandpiper in size, with a long bill, faintly drooped at the tip. It is rather dark greyish above, and faintly streaked across the breast. In breeding plumage it has a double white eyebrow stripe. Sexes are similar.

DISTRIBUTION. Breeds across northern Europe and Asia; winters from the Mediterranean across southern Asia to Australasia.

NOTES. It is generally uncommon to rare in Australia, and highly local. It is seen alone or in small groups, often with other waders. It frequents tidal mud flats, favouring muddy rather than sandy environments.

BREEDING. Nest: a hollow scooped in the ground; lined with dry grass; usually situated on a low sedge-clothed hummock of mountain marsh. Clutch: usually four; stone-buff to brown, spotted dark-brown. Breeding season: June and July.

34:25 RUDDY TURNSTONE *Arenaria interpres*

IDENTIFICATION. This species is a stocky shorebird with short yellow-orange legs and dusky breast. It is variably black and chestnut above, according to age or season; with a white rump and wingbar. Sexes are similar.

DISTRIBUTION. Breeds in the high Arctic; wintering distribution virtually worldwide.

NOTES. Common and widespread in Australia, it is mainly coastal but occasionally occurs inland. Usually seen in small flocks, but often solitary, or associated with other waders, it arrives during September and departs in March or April, many individuals over-wintering. It frequents beaches, coral cays, rocky coasts, and estuaries, feeding upon small marine animals. It has the characteristic habit of turning over small stones and shells with its bill.

BREEDING. Nest: a slight depression in the ground; sometimes lined with grass. Clutch: four; pale green, marked olive-brown and lavender. Breeding season: June and July (Arctic regions).

34:26 ORIENTAL PRATINCOLE *Glareola pratincola*

IDENTIFICATION. This species is mainly dull neutral brown, with buff chin and throat, narrowly rimmed black. It has a long forked tail and very long slender wings. Sexes are similar.

DISTRIBUTION. Southern Europe and eastern Asia, migrating to Australia (chiefly the north-west and north, but occasionally south as far as Victoria, South Australia, and Western Australia).

NOTES. Usually seen in flocks, it arrives in northern Australia during December or January and departs in March or April. It frequents marshes, plains, and river flats, and is often in the company of the Australian Pratincole. Much of its food is caught on the wing, in a manner similar to that of swallows.

BREEDING. Nest: a depression in the ground. Clutch: two; pale stone-colour, with markings of purplish-black and underlying ones of smoky-grey. Breeding season: April and May (Northern Hemisphere).

PLATE 35

BIRDS OF THE OCEAN AND SEASHORE

35:1 ASIAN DOWITCHER *Limnodromus semipalmatus*

IDENTIFICATION. This bird is rather like a small, dumpy godwit, with a slightly darker crown, and a long, straight, slender black bill, noticeably bulbous at the tip. Sexes are similar.

DISTRIBUTION. Breeds in north-eastern Asia; winters from eastern India to Indonesia and (rarely) to northern and eastern Australia.

NOTES. Usually seen singly or in small groups. It is recorded only a few times in Australia, but it is very similar to the Bar-tailed Godwit (with which it often associates) in appearance, and may often be overlooked. It frequents tidal mud flats, estuaries and sand or shingle-banks. It wades in shallow water, moving its bill up and down in a manner suggesting a sewing machine.

BREEDING. Nest: sometimes a platform of grass stalks and dead leaves over shallow water, or a scrape in the ground. Clutch: two to three; light olive, blotched reddish-brown. Breeding season: May to July (Siberia).

35:2 BLACK-TAILED GODWIT *Limosa limosa*

IDENTIFICATION. This bird is a rather large wader, with long, slender, slightly upturned bill; at rest it is very difficult to distinguish from Bar-tailed Godwit, but in flight it reveals a diagnostic black tail, white rump and bold white wingbar. Sexes are similar.

DISTRIBUTION. Breeds in northern Europe and Asia; winters across Africa and southern Asia to Australia.

NOTES. Usually seen in small flocks, it arrives in Australia during September and departs in May. Widespread in coastal regions, it is most common along the northern and eastern coasts (south to about Newcastle, New South Wales). It frequents especially estuaries with extensive mud flats and sand spits of inlets. It is often seen in the company of other waders, especially Bar-tailed Godwits. In habits it resembles that species, but is generally less common.

BREEDING. Nest: a depression in grass. Clutch: four; olive green to pale yellowish, spotted olive brown. Breeding season: June and July (northern Europe and northern Asia).

35:3 BAR-TAILED GODWIT *Limosa lapponica*

IDENTIFICATION. This rather large, brownish wader is paler below, with a long, slender, slightly upturned, pinkish bill. It resembles Black-tailed Godwit, but in flight reveals plain brownish upperwings (with no white wingbar), whitish rump faintly mottled brown, and barred brownish tail. In breeding plumage, the head, neck and underparts are brick red. Sexes are similar.

DISTRIBUTION. Breeds in northern Europe and Asia, wintering across Africa and southern Asia to Australasia and the south-west Pacific.

NOTES. Usually seen in flocks, it arrives in Australia during September and departs in April; many individuals remain throughout the year. It is widespread and common in Australia (although less so in the south-west), mainly occurring in coastal regions, but often recorded inland. It favours sand and mud flats in estuaries, where flocks of thousands may congregate. Often seen in the company of other waders. Food: small crustaceans and worms.

BREEDING. Nest: a depression in grass. Clutch: four; greenish, spotted umber-brown. Breeding season: June and July.

35:4 EASTERN CURLEW *Numenius madagascariensis*

IDENTIFICATION. This bird is very large, dull brownish, with plain brownish rump and extremely long, down-curved bill.

DISTRIBUTION. Breeds in eastern Siberia; winters from Taiwan and the Philippines south to Australia and New Zealand.

NOTES. It is common along the northern and eastern coasts of Australia, though seldom in large numbers. It is less common on the west and south coasts. Seen alone or in flocks, it arrives during September and departs in April or May; a few birds may, however, remain throughout the year. It frequents beaches and sand flats near the coast, only occasionally straying to inland lakes. Wary, it usually keeps far out on the flats. Its call resembles 'ker-loo', or 'kor-lew', often uttered at night or when the bird is alarmed. Food: marine crustaceans and worms.

BREEDING. Nest: a hollow scooped in the ground; lined with grass or leaves. Clutch: four; olive green, with greenish-brown markings. Breeding season: June and July (Siberia).

35:5 WHIMBREL *Numenius phaeopus*

IDENTIFICATION. This species is like Eastern Curlew but much smaller, with a proportionately shorter bill with markedly shallower curve. In flight it reveals a whitish rump. Sexes are similar.

DISTRIBUTION. Breeds in Scandinavia, northern Russia, Alaska and northern Canada; winters in Central and South America, Africa and across southern Asia to Australasia.

NOTES. It usually arrives during September and departs in March or April. Mostly coastal, it is common along the northern and eastern coasts, less so in the south and west. Seen alone or in small groups, often with other waders, it is generally extremely wary. It frequents beaches, coral cays, mud and sand flats of estuaries, and salt marshes. Its call-note is a high, clear whistle, repeated seven or eight times. Food: aquatic life.

BREEDING. Nest: a depression in the ground, scantily lined with grass. Clutch: three; olive, blotched brown and slate-grey. Breeding season: June and July.

35:6 LITTLE CURLEW *Numenius minutus*

IDENTIFICATION. This curlew is like a small whimbrel, but with a shorter bill only faintly down-curved.

DISTRIBUTION. Breeds in north-eastern Siberia; winters mainly in Indonesia, New Guinea and northern Australia.

NOTES. Common in north-western Australia, it becomes decidedly rare south of about the Tropic of Capricorn. It arrives during September and departs in March or April. Usually found in small groups, although very large flocks occur in the north-west, it frequents floodplains, paddocks, airfields and playing fields, and other open areas of short grass. This bird is a close relative of the rare Eskimo Curlew of North America.

BREEDING. Nest: a depression in the ground. Clutch: three; olive-buff, with brown and slate-grey markings. Breeding season: June and July.

35:7 REDSHANK *Tringa totanus*

IDENTIFICATION. This species is rather like a Greenshank but is brownish rather than grey, with a shorter, straight bill, reddish at the base. It has long red legs. In flight it reveals a white rump and diagnostic white panel along the trailing edge of the inner wing.

DISTRIBUTION. Breeds across Europe and northern Asia; winter south to Africa, India and Indonesia; vagrant to Australia.

NOTES. A wary, excitable species, it occurs singly or in small flocks. Common and familiar throughout much of its normal range, it frequents mud flats, tidal estuaries and salt marshes. There are few Australian records to date, but it may be a more frequent visitor than these records suggest, especially in the far north-west.

BREEDING. Nest: at the base of a clump of grass; the stems often intertwined for concealment from above. Clutch: usually four; stone, buff or greenish, spotted and blotched dark brown. Breeding season: generally April to July.

35:8 SHARP-TAILED SANDPIPER *Calidris acuminata*

IDENTIFICATION. This bird is a small brownish wader with a distinctly reddish crown and obscurely streaked breast, straight black bill and dull greenish legs. Sexes are similar.

DISTRIBUTION. Breeds in north-eastern Siberia, wintering south to Australia and New Zealand.

NOTES. Usually seen in flocks, it arrives in southern Australia during August and departs in April or May. It often associates with other small waders. Perhaps the commonest and most widespead of migratory waders in Australia, both along the coasts and at suitable wetlands in the interior. The call-note is a piping whistle. Food: aquatic life.

BREEDING. Nest: a shallow hollow in the ground, lined with a few willow leaves. Clutch: four; olive green or brown, dotted and splotched with dark-brown. Breeding season: June to July (Siberia).

35:9 PECTORAL SANDPIPER *Calidris melanotus*

IDENTIFICATION. This species is very similar to Sharp-tailed Sandpiper, but its bill is slightly longer; its plumage is generally slightly browner in tone, less rufous; the crown is dull brown, not chestnut; the legs are yellowish; the heavily streaked breast is sharply demarcated from the white underparts. Sexes are similar.

DISTRIBUTION. Breeds in northern Siberia, Alaska and Canada; winters mainly in South America, also islands of the southern Pacific, New Zealand, and Australia.

NOTES. Usually seen singly, occasionally in small groups, it sometimes joins flocks of Sharp-tailed Sandpipers. It frequents flooded pastures, margins of lagoons and swamps, sewage farms, less commonly on tidal mud flats or estuaries. Although mainly coastal in distribution, it tends to prefer fresh to saltwater habitats. It is rare but regular in occurrence in Australia.

BREEDING. Nest: a depression in the ground, lined with grass; hidden in a grass tussock. Clutch: usually four; varying from dull white to olive-buff, splotched with shades of dark brown. Breeding season: June and July (North America).

35:10 BUFF-BREASTED SANDPIPER *Tryngites subruficollis*

IDENTIFICATION. The upperparts are brown, scaled buff; the head, neck and underparts buff, variably spotted black at the sides of the breast. It has a pale face; a short slim black bill, and yellowish legs. Sexes are similar.

DISTRIBUTION. Breeds in far northern Canada and Alaska; winters in Argentina, Paraguay and Uruguay. Vagrant to Australia.

NOTES. It frequents short-grass habitats often well away from water; also margins of freshwater lagoons or swamps, occasionally tidal mud flats. Gregarious, usually found in flocks, it is most likely to be seen singly in Australia, but usually associates with other waders. Rare vagrant in Australia, most records are from the south-east.

BREEDING. Nest: a depression in the ground, lined with grass and leaves. Clutch: four; pale buff, splotched with shades of brown. Breeding season: June and July (North America).

35:11 CASPIAN TERN *Hydroprogne caspia*

IDENTIFICATION. This species is a very large, powerfully built tern with shaggy black cap, immediately identifiable by its large, bright red bill. Sexes are similar.

DISTRIBUTION. Continental Australia (chiefly coastal) and Tasmania. It also inhabits North America, Europe, Asia, Africa, and New Zealand.

NOTES. Usually found in pairs, occasionally in small flocks, it frequents chiefly coasts and adjacent islands, and also some of the larger inland rivers and lakes. It feeds almost entirely on small fishes, which it obtains by diving from the air. It breeds either in colonies or as isolated pairs. Widespread but generally uncommon.

BREEDING. Colonial. Nest: a scrape in the ground; often ringed with bones and twigs as incubation proceeds. Clutch: two to three; greenish-grey, spotted umber and blackish-brown, with underlying markings of dull grey. Breeding season: October to February (southern Australia and Tasmania); March to November (north-western Australia).

35:12 CRESTED TERN *Sterna bergii*

IDENTIFICATION. This species is a large (about the size of a Silver Gull) but elegant, slender tern with shaggy black cap. It is difficult to distinguish from Lesser Crested Tern, but is slightly larger; the upperparts perceptibly darker grey; the bill pale yellow (Lesser Crested Tern has rich, orange-yellow bill). Sexes are similar.

DISTRIBUTION. Widespread from Africa across India and south-east Asia to Fiji and Australia.

NOTES. This is the commonest and most widespread Australian tern. Mainly coastal, it occurs singly or in small flocks, but is not especially gregarious, except when breeding. It breeds in large colonies on islands off the coasts throughout its range. Food: mainly fish, obtained by diving.

BREEDING. Colonial. Nest: a depression in sand or earth. Clutch: one or two; light to dark stone, spotted and blotched umber and brownish-black, and having underlying markings of pale lavender. Breeding season: October to January (Australia).

35:13 LESSER CRESTED TERN *Sterna bengalensis*

IDENTIFICATION. This bird is very similar to Crested Tern but slightly smaller and paler, with rich orange-yellow bill. Sexes are similar.

DISTRIBUTION. Widespread from the Mediterranean and eastern Africa to New Guinea and northern Australia, south to about Shark Bay on the west coast and about Fraser Island in the east.

NOTES. It is similar to the Crested Tern in general appearance and habits, but generally scarcer and (in Australia) less widely distributed, being essentially tropical in distribution. It breeds in colonies, often with other terns, on coastal islands throughout its range. Apparently it is mainly sedentary.

BREEDING. Colonial. Nest: a depression in the ground; usually on bare ground surrounded with herbage. Clutch: one; varying from white to reddish-white, with spots of purplish and reddish-brown and underlying markings of grey. Breeding season: May to November.

35:14 BLACK-NAPED TERN *Sterna sumatrana*

IDENTIFICATION. This is a small, delicate tern with very pale grey upperparts and white head, with a narrow black band extending through the eye and across lower nape. Sexes are similar.

DISTRIBUTION. Widespread in the tropical Indian and Pacific Oceans; northeastern Australia, mainly at islands in Torres Strait and along the Great Barrier Reef, south to the Capricorn and Bunker Groups.

NOTES. A characteristic tern of the shallow lagoons and coral cays of the Great Barrier Reef and Torres Strait, it is occasionally recorded along nearby mainland coasts. Usually seen fishing in association with noddies and other terns, or loafing in small flocks on sand cays, it breeds in colonies on coral islands throughout its range, often in association with other terns.

BREEDING. Colonial. Nest: a depression in coral fragments or in sand; placed just above high-water mark. Clutch: usually two; white or creamy-white, with spots and blotches of purplish-black, purplish-grey, or dark umber, and underlying markings of lavender. Breeding season: September to December (north-eastern Australia).

35:15 SOOTY TERN *Sterna fuscata*

IDENTIFICATION. This species is a black-backed tern with a white forehead, confusable only with Bridled Tern (which is slightly smaller, sooty brown above, and white forehead extending in a narrow line over the eye). Its underparts are pure white. Juvenile birds are entirely sooty black except for white underwing and vent, upperparts scaled buff. Sexes are similar.

DISTRIBUTION. Widespread in tropical and subtropical seas around the world; in Australia it breeds at Lord Howe and Norfolk Islands, at several islands in the Coral Sea, at islands of the northern Great Barrier Reef and Torres Strait, and off the coast of northern and western Australia to the Houtman Abrolhos Group, Western Australia.

NOTES. Usually seen in flocks, often in company with other species of terns, it frequents chiefly the seas in the vicinity of islands on which it breeds. It breeds in immense colonies on islands throughout its range. Noisy and demonstrative, calls include a sharp, grating 'wide–a–wake'. Occasionally recorded off the mainland coast south to about Sydney, New South Wales.

BREEDING. Colonial. Nest: a depression on bare ground, in grass, or under the shelter of a tussock. Clutch: usually one; colour highly variable, generally off-white, blotched and spotted shades of red, brown or purple. Breeding season: complex, varying somewhat from colony to colony (on Ascension Island in the South Atlantic, breeding takes place on a nine-month cycle rather than the annual cycle common to most birds); in Australia, generally two annual peaks, in spring and autumn.

35:16 BRIDLED TERN *Sterna anaethetus*

IDENTIFICATION. This species is similar to Sooty Tern but slightly smaller. Its underparts are greyish white; upperparts sooty brown. It has a black cap and white forehead, which extends in a narrow band over the eye.

DISTRIBUTION. Widespread in tropical seas around the world; in Australia it occurs along the northern coast, south in the west to Cape Leeuwin, Western

Australia, and in the east to the Bunker Group, Queensland; apparently extending its range in Western Australia.

NOTES. Usually seen in flocks, it frequents seas in the vicinity of islands on which it breeds. Similar in general habits to the Sooty Tern, but in general it is shyer, less common, and less widespread. Its note is very distinctive, suggesting the yapping of a puppy.

BREEDING. Colonial. Nest: a depression in sand; concealed under a tussock of grass; sometimes in a crevice between rocks, or under bushes. Clutch: one; very variable, but often dull white with spots of reddish-purple and underlying markings of purplish-grey. Breeding season: September to January (Australia).

35:17 WHITE-FRONTED TERN *Sterna striata*

IDENTIFICATION. The upperparts are pale grey; the underparts are white. With a black crown, and white forehead; it is very difficult to distinguish from Common Tern, but is slightly larger. In flight overhead it reveals featureless translucent white underwings. Sexes are similar.

DISTRIBUTION. Breeds in New Zealand; many winter along coasts of south-eastern Australia.

NOTES. Mainly coastal, it is often seen in flocks. It feeds offshore, often well out to sea, and often in the company of Crested Terns. Birds which cross the Tasman to winter in Australian waters are mainly immature, most adults remaining in New Zealand.

BREEDING. Colonial. Nest: a depression in sand or gravel; mainly on beaches, just above high-water mark. Clutch: two; varying from yellowish-stone to greenish-grey or coffee-brown, covered with spots and underlying markings of grey. Breeding season: November and December.

35:18 LITTLE TERN *Sterna albifrons*

IDENTIFICATION. This is a very small tern, with mid-grey upperparts, white underparts, and black cap. The bill is yellow, with a black tip. The forehead is white, but a black band extends from the bill through the eye to the nape. In non-breeding plumage the crown is largely white, and bill black. Sexes are similar.

DISTRIBUTION. Widespread across Europe, Africa, Asia and Australasia; in Australia it occurs along the northern and eastern coasts, west to about Broome, Western Australia and south to Tasmania.

NOTES. Usually found in flocks, it frequents chiefly inlets and beaches. Usually it breeds in loose colonies — sand spits near the entrance of inlets are its favourite nesting sites. It also breeds on beaches of coastal islands. The resident breeding population is apparently augmented by wintering migrants from the Northern Hemisphere. The call is a high-pitched yapping note.

BREEDING. Colonial. Nest: a depression in sand; usually just above high-water mark. Clutch: two to three; creamy-white to stone-grey or coffee-brown, with spots and blotches of blackish-brown, umber and grey. Breeding season: October to January.

35:19 FAIRY TERN *Sterna nereis*

IDENTIFICATION. This bird is very similar to Little Tern, but its upperparts are slightly paler grey; its lores white, not black; its bill a rich yellow (lacking black tip in breeding plumage), not pale yellow. Sexes are similar.

DISTRIBUTION. Australia, New Zealand and New Caledonia; in Australia, mainly the western and southern coasts, from about Derby, Western Australia, to about Port Albert, Victoria, and Tasmania.

NOTES. It is similar in habits to the Little Tern. It breeds in colonies in a similar situation to those selected by the Little Tern, but with a marked preference for offshore islands and reefs.

BREEDING. Colonial. Nest: a depression in sand. Clutch: usually two, similar to those of the Little Tern. Breeding season: November to February.

35:20 COMMON TERN *Sterna hirundo*

IDENTIFICATION. This tern is very difficult to distinguish from White-fronted or Arctic Tern, but its upperparts are mid-grey, not pale grey. At rest, tail tips do not quite reach wing tips. In flight overhead it reveals dusky outermost primaries, tipped grey, but white innermost primaries, producing a distinct panel or 'window' in the wing.

DISTRIBUTION. Breeds across Europe, Asia and North America; winters widely in the Southern Hemisphere, including Australia.

NOTES. Distribution is mainly coastal, frequenting estuaries, reefs, bays, salt fields, and salt marshes. Usually seen in flocks. Common (but local) in the east, less so in the west and south; mostly September to May. Calls include a high-pitched 'ki–ki–ki–ki' and a harsh drawn-out 'keeeeyah'.

BREEDING. Colonial. Nest: a scrape in sand or shingle; sometimes lined with grass or feathers. Clutch: usually three; stone, greyish or dull brown, blotched and marked with shades of dark brown. Breeding season: April to July.

35:21 ARCTIC TERN *Sterna paradisaea*

IDENTIFICATION. This tern is very similar to Common Tern, but its legs are shorter and bill stubbier. In flight overhead it shows dark-tipped outer primaries, producing a narrow dusky trailing edge along most of the outer wing.

DISTRIBUTION. Breeds across northern Europe, Asia and Africa; winters mainly in seas around Antarctica.

NOTES. Rare vagrant to Australia, mainly in the south-west and south-east; records span the period September to May. Very difficult to distinguish from the Common Tern, with which it occasionally associates, it frequents beaches, estuaries, reefs and salt marshes.

BREEDING. Loosely colonial. Nest: a scrape in sand or shingle. Clutch: usually two; variable in colour, pale-blue to stone or dull brown, splotched with dark brown. Breeding season: June and July.

35:22 RUFF *Philomachus pugnax*

IDENTIFICATION. This bird is rather like a large Sharp-tailed Sandpiper, but is smaller headed and longer necked. Its upperparts look scaled rather than streaked; its head is more evenly coloured, with no obvious superciliary or dark crown; its underparts are unstreaked, dingy buff or mottled greyish. In flight it reveals a rather plain upperwing; a white rump, with dark brown band up the centre. The male is much larger than the female.

DISTRIBUTION. Breeds across northern Europe and Asia; winters from the British Isles to southern Africa and across southern Asia to Indonesia and Australia.

NOTES. It frequents the grassy margins of swamps and lagoons, sewage farms, tidal mud flats and salt marshes. It often associates with other waders, particularly Sharp-tailed Sandpipers. The name Ruff applies to the male, the female is called a Reeve. The breeding plumage (unlikely to be seen in Australia) is especially striking in this species: a dense ruff of elongated feathers around the neck, with long ear tufts; these adornments are highly variable in colour and pattern, ranging from black-and-white to rufous, or even pure white.

BREEDING. Nest: a depression in the ground, lined with grass, often hidden in grass. Clutch: usually four; ground colour variable shades of ochre, grey or pale green, blotched with dark brown. Breeding season: May to July.

35:23 WILSON'S PHALAROPE *Phalaropus tricolor*

IDENTIFICATION. This species is similar to Red-necked Phalarope in non-breeding plumage, but somewhat larger, and lankier, with longer bill and a pale grey (not black) cheek patch. In flight it reveals plain grey upperparts, with a white rump and pale grey tail; no white wingbar.

DISTRIBUTION. Breeds in central North America; winters in southern South America. Rare vagrant to Australia.

NOTES. It is similar in habits to other phalaropes, although it is more inclined to feed on land. It frequents the margins of shallow lakes and swamps, salt marshes and other wetlands. Only a few records in Australia, mainly in the south-east.

BREEDING. Nest: a depression in the ground, lined with grass, usually well-hidden in grass tussocks. Clutch: four; olive-buff blotched with dark brown. Breeding season: May to July (Arctic regions).

35:24 RED-NECKED PHALAROPE *Phalaropus lobatus*

IDENTIFICATION. This is a small, delicate wader that spends most of its time swimming. In breeding plumage it is mainly deep grey, with a white chin and bright rufous patch on the side of the neck. In non-breeding plumage it is mainly plain pale grey above, white below, with a black patch through the eye. It has a slender needle-like bill.

DISTRIBUTION. Breeds across northern Europe, Asia and North America; winters at sea, mainly in the eastern Pacific and off the west coast of Africa. Vagrant to Australia.

NOTES. Gregarious outside the breeding season, it is usually seen in flocks. A rare vagrant in Australia, it is likely to be seen singly, but often associates with other waders. Phalaropes have a characteristic method of feeding — swimming in shallow water, spinning rapidly around like a top, and jabbing at the surface. Insects constitute a major component of the diet. Usually very tame.

BREEDING. Nest: a depression in the ground, lined with grass. Clutch: four; olive-buff blotched with dark brown. Breeding season: June and July (Arctic regions).

35:25 COMMON NODDY *Anous stolidus*

IDENTIFICATION. This bird is dull brown, paler at nape and merging gradually on to a dull white crown. The tail is long, full, wedge-shaped but with a shallow central notch. Sexes are similar.

DISTRIBUTION. Widespread in tropical seas around the world; in Australia it breeds at Bedout and Lacepede islands and the Houtman Abrolhos Group, Western Australia, and at islands in Torres Strait, the Coral Sea and the Great Barrier Reef south to Michaelmas Cay, near Cairns, Queensland; also Lord Howe Island.

NOTES. Usually seen in flocks, it frequents seas in the vicinity of its breeding places. It procures its food, consisting of small fishes and other marine life, mostly from the surface of the open seas beyond the reefs. Breeds in colonies, often very large.

BREEDING. Colonial. Nest: a flat structure of seaweed and dried grass, loosely packed together, with a slight depression in the centre, usually lined with small sea-shells; placed on the ground, on grass, or upon a low shrubby bush. Clutch: one; very variable, but often dull white or buff-white, spotted and blotched purplish-brown. Breeding season: July to January (Australia).

35:26 LESSER NODDY *Anous tenuirostris*

IDENTIFICATION. This bird is very similar to White-capped Noddy.

DISTRIBUTION. The coast of mid-western and north-western Australia. It occurs generally in the Indian Ocean.

NOTES. Sedentary, it usually appears in large flocks, frequenting the seas in the vicinity of the Houtman Abrolhos Islands, the only known breeding place of this species in Australia, although it also breeds in the Seychelles. It is similar in habits to the Common Noddy.

BREEDING. Colonial. Nest: a loosely made structure of seaweed; placed on a mangrove branch. Clutch: one; very variable, but often reddish-white with spots and blotches of reddish-brown. Breeding season: September to December.

35:27 GREY NODDY *Procelsterna albivittata*

IDENTIFICATION. This species is plain blue-grey, with a shallow forked tail and an eye rimmed with black feathers. Sexes are similar.

DISTRIBUTION. Breeds at various islands in the South Pacific, including the Kermadecs, Norfolk and Lord Howe Islands; vagrant to eastern Australia.

NOTES. It is generally seen in loose flocks around the breeding colonies, but often encountered singly at sea. Its flight is fluttering and graceful. It seldom calls. It is mainly sedentary, although there is some dispersal of young birds. Recorded as beach-washed derelicts in New South Wales and southern Queensland, there are also several sight records, especially at Stradbroke Island, Queensland. These records span the months December to May, and are especially numerous in January.

BREEDING. Nest: on a cliff ledge or rock crevice. Clutch: one; greyish-white, sometimes with a few reddish markings. Breeding season: mainly September to December.

35:28 WHITE-CAPPED NODDY *Anous minutus*

IDENTIFICATION. This species is similar to Common Noddy, but its crown is whiter, offering crisper contrast with a blackish head and nape. The bill is more slender, shorter, narrower and slightly forked. Sexes are similar.

DISTRIBUTION. Widespread in the tropical Atlantic and Pacific Oceans; occurs in north-eastern Australia from Torres Strait and the Coral Sea to the southern end of the Great Barrier Reef.

NOTES. Mainly sedentary, it usually occurs in large flocks, frequenting the seas in the vicinity of its breeding islands. During the night it rests in trees, leaving at daybreak for the open seas beyond the reefs. It breeds in large colonies on islands and reefs. On some islands birds are often rendered helpless by the sticky seeds of pisonia trees.

BREEDING. Colonial. Nest: an almost flat structure; of the leaves of the tree on which it is built, laid on one another, with a very slight addition of seaweed, and cemented together with the bird's excrement. Clutch: one; white or buff-white, with spots and blotches of purplish-grey. Breeding season: September to December (Australia).

35:29 WHITE TERN *Gygis alba*

IDENTIFICATION. The plumage of this tern is entirely white, with a black bill. Sexes are similar.

DISTRIBUTION. Breeds at many islands in the tropical Atlantic, Indian and Pacific Oceans, including the Kermadecs, Norfolk and Lord Howe Islands. Vagrant to the coast of eastern Australia.

NOTES. Usually seen in small flocks, its flight is light and airy; its plumage is pure white and wings and tail transluscent against a blue sky. Calls include a quiet chatter and a soft, vibrant 'tung', like plucking a guitar string. Several records from coastal New South Wales. It usually breeds in colonies; on Norfolk Island it breeds in pine groves. Food: mainly small fish, plucked from the surface.

BREEDING. Nest: none made, the egg being laid in a shallow crevice or fork in a horizontal limb of a tree. Clutch: one; greyish or pale buff, splotched and scrolled with various shades of brown. Breeding season: October to March.

PLATE 36

BIRDS OF THE OCEAN AND SEASHORE

36:1 SOUTHERN FULMAR *Fulmarus glacialoides*

IDENTIFICATION. The tail and upperparts are grey. The head and underparts are white. It has a white flash towards the tip of each wing; black secondaries; and pink bill and legs. Sexes are similar.

DISTRIBUTION. Breeds in Antarctica and at various sub-antarctic islands; vagrant to seas off southern Australia.

NOTES. It occurs in Australian seas mainly during the winter. Gregarious, it is usually seen in small flocks. It follows ships. Food: mainly shrimps and other crustaceans.

BREEDING. Colonial. Nest: on a cliff ledge. Clutch: one; white. Breeding season: November to December.

36:2 CAPE PETREL *Daption capense*

IDENTIFICATION. The head, breast and upperparts are mainly dark grey; back and rump white, heavily scaled black. It has two irregular white patches in each upperwing; underparts are white. Sexes are similar.

DISTRIBUTION. Breeds in Antarctica and at various sub-antarctic islands, including Macquarie and Heard islands. Disperses widely over southern oceans; common off the southern and eastern coasts of Australia, north to about Geraldton in the west and Fraser Island in the east.

NOTES. Gregarious at sea, it is usually seen in flocks, and often follows ships. It is very aggressive, and feeding flocks usually involve much squabbling. Food: fish, crustaceans and squid; also offal, carrion and galley refuse.

BREEDING. Colonial. Nest: a slight structure of a few small stones and a little earth; placed on a ledge of a cliff. Clutch: one; white. Breeding season: November to January.

36:3 GREAT-WINGED PETREL *Pterodroma macroptera*

IDENTIFICATION. This petrel is almost entirely dark brown (Australian subspecies *macroptera*) or with faintly pale face (New Zealand subspecies *gouldii*); it tends to fly with wings thrown well forward. Sexes are similar.

DISTRIBUTION. Breeds at islands in the sub-antarctic, the South Atlantic, around New Zealand, and along the southern coast of Western Australia; relatively sedentary.

NOTES. Usually seen alone or in small groups, it is generally uninterested in ships or fishing vessels. Its flight is dramatic, impetuous, towering high above the sea, then diving back close to the surface, progressing in a series of high-speed arcs. Strictly pelagic, it is seldom in off-shore waters over the continental shelf, except when visiting breeding islands.

BREEDING. Colonial. Nest: either on the surface (in niches between rocks or between the roots of trees) or in a chamber at the end of a burrow perhaps a metre long; lined with a few leaves. Clutch: one; white. Breeding season: May.

36:4 WHITE-HEADED PETREL *Pterodroma lessonii*

IDENTIFICATION. The head and underparts are white, upperparts mainly dark grey, with an almost uniform dark underwing, and a black patch around the eye. Sexes are similar.

DISTRIBUTION. Breeds at various sub-antarctic islands, including Macquarie Island. It is relatively sedentary, and disperses to seas around New Zealand and off the southern coasts of Australia.

NOTES. Uncommon in Australian seas, it is most frequent off Tasmania. Recorded all months, but perhaps most numerous from June to September. Its flight is swift, usually in great wheeling arcs, similar to Great-winged Petrel. It usually ignores shipping.

BREEDING. Colonial. Nest: in a large chamber at the end of a burrow. Clutch: one; white. Breeding season: November to February.

36:5 KERMADEC PETREL *Pterodroma neglecta*

IDENTIFICATION. Plumage of this species is very variable, but shafts of outermost primaries are white, producing a conspicuous white flash towards the tip of each wing.

DISTRIBUTION. Breeds at various islands in the South Pacific, including the Kermadecs and Lord Howe Island; rare vagrant to seas off eastern Australia.

NOTES. This species is very variable in plumage pattern, and individuals may be dark, light or intermediate. A small colony breeds at Balls Pyramid near Lord Howe Island, but birds apparently disperse mainly eastwards into the Tasman Sea with a rare vagrant westwards.

BREEDING. Colonial. Nest: a depression on the ground, sparsely lined with twigs and leaves. Clutch: one; white. Breeding season: apparently January to July at Lord Howe Island, but elsewhere nesting shows no seasonal pattern.

36:6 PROVIDENCE PETREL *Pterodroma solandri*

IDENTIFICATION. Plumage of this species is mainly very dark grey, the head slightly browner. The base of primaries is white; primary coverts (underwing) are also white, dark-tipped, the combination producing a white flash in underwing, dissected by a narrow dark bar.

DISTRIBUTION. Breeds at Lord Howe Island; regular visitor to seas off eastern Australia.

NOTES. Breeds in winter in colonies on the forested upper slopes of Mount Gower and Mount Lidgbird at Lord Howe Island. Formerly bred also at Norfolk Island, but was exterminated there in the late 1700s. Its oceanic range outside the breeding season is largely unknown, although it has been recorded in Japanese waters in July. Strictly pelagic, it is seldom recorded in inshore waters over the continental shelf.

BREEDING. Colonial. Nest: a pile of leaves and palm frond fragments in a chamber at the end of a tunnel. Clutch: one; white. Breeding season: February to November.

36:7 KERGUELEN PETREL *Pterodroma brevirostris*

IDENTIFICATION. This species is mainly dark grey. In flight it looks big-headed, with a small stubby bill. It has a pale leading edge of inner wing.

DISTRIBUTION. Breeds at islands in the South Atlantic and the southern Indian Ocean; oceanic range little known, but apparently disperses widely in sub-antarctic waters; rare visitor to seas off southern Australia.

NOTES. Usually solitary and highly pelagic, it approaches ships but seldom follows them persistently. In calm weather it flies close to the surface with a weaving, bat-like flight. In strong winds it towers high above the surface. It is difficult to distinguish at sea from several other dark-plumaged petrels. Fairly common off south-western Australia, north to about Fremantle, Western Australia; less common in the south-east.

BREEDING. Colonial. Nest: a chamber at the end of a tunnel, lined with leaves. Clutch: one; white. Breeding season: mainly October and November.

36:8 HERALD PETREL *Pterodroma arminjoniana*

IDENTIFICATION. Plumage of this species is very variable, but in flight it shows a narrow central white band along almost the entire length of the underwing.

DISTRIBUTION. Breeds at various islands in the tropical Atlantic, Indian and Pacific oceans; pelagic range largely unknown, possibly sedentary. Two subspecies, occasionally regarded as distinct species: *P.a. arminjoniana* (Trinidade Petrel) of the South Atlantic and Indian oceans, and *P.a. heraldica* (Herald Petrel) of the Pacific.

NOTES. There are only a scattering of records in Australian seas (all off the east coast), but it breeds on at least one island along the Great Barrier Reef, and may be more common than available data suggest. It occurs in several colour morphs (dark, light and intermediate), with much individual variation. Field identification is difficult and complicated; dark morphs are especially difficult to distinguish from the Providence Petrel or dark morphs of the Kermadec Petrel. Flight and general behaviour are much like other petrels. Occasionally it follows ships.

BREEDING. Colonial. Nest: a chamber at the end of a burrow. Clutch: one, white. Breeding season: inadequately known; eggs recorded September, November, March and April.

36:9   SOFT-PLUMAGED PETREL *Pterodroma mollis*

IDENTIFICATION. This bird is grey above, white below, with a narrow grey band across the upper breast. The underwing is almost uniformly dark, the head grey, with a black mark through the eye.

DISTRIBUTION. Breeds at islands in the Atlantic and Indian Oceans (possibly also the South Pacific); disperses widely in the South Atlantic and Indian Oceans, east to seas off southern Australia.

NOTES. Relatively common off southern Western Australia, it is frequently washed up dead or dying on beaches. It is progressively less common further east. Usually seen in small flocks, it ignores shipping.

BREEDING. Colonial. Nest: a chamber, lined with grass, at the end of a burrow. Clutch: one; white. Breeding season: November to December.

36:10 MOTTLED PETREL *Pterodroma inexpectata*

IDENTIFICATION. This petrel is dark grey above, with a blackish M-shaped band across upperwings; underparts white, belly mottled dusky grey; underwing white, primaries black-tipped, and black bar extending from carpal joint along inner wing to armpit.

DISTRIBUTION. Breeds on islands around New Zealand; apparently disperses widely over the eastern Pacific, from the Antarctic to the Bering Sea; recorded off south-eastern Australia.

NOTES. Generally solitary, it has very swift flight in great arcs, towering high above the sea then swooping low to the surface. It seldom follows ships. Once widespread as a breeding bird in New Zealand, now much reduced, and extant colonies now mainly in Foveaux Strait and on islands off Stewart Island. Several records occur from New South Wales, Victoria and Tasmania, mainly beach-washed derelicts. It is possibly a more regular visitor than records indicate.

BREEDING. Colonial. Nest: a chamber at the end of a tunnel, lined with grass or leaves. Clutch: one; white. Breeding season: December to February.

36:11 GOULD'S PETREL *Pterodroma leucoptera*

IDENTIFICATION. The upperparts are grey, head is black; chin, throat and underparts are white; underwing white, with narrow central black band extending almost to the axillaries.

DISTRIBUTION. Breeds at various islands in the south-west Pacific, and at Cabbage Tree Island, off Port Stephens, New South Wales; winter dispersal little known, but apparently relatively sedentary.

NOTES. Seldom reported at sea, like many other petrels and shearwaters, it waits for darkness before visiting its breeding islands. Birds can be heard circling in the darkness overhead, calling 'ki–ki–ki–ki', rapid and high-pitched, before crash-landing through the trees to the ground. Unlike many shearwaters, which struggle and bite viciously when handled, this species is docile and quiet in the hand. The total breeding population on Cabbage Tree Island (the only known Australian breeding site) has been estimated at 250-300 pairs.

BREEDING. Colonial. Nest: in a crevice among rocks; sometimes lined with a few scraps of palm fronds or other leaves. Clutch: one; chalky-white. Breeding season: November to January.

36:12 BLACK-WINGED PETREL *Pterodroma nigripennis*

IDENTIFICATION. The upperparts are grey; the head is grey with a black patch through eye; underparts are white, underwing with bold central black band extending from carpal joint to axillaries.

DISTRIBUTION. Breeds at various islands in the south-western Pacific, including Norfolk and Lord Howe Islands; rare but regular off eastern Australia.

NOTES. This species is apparently expanding its range southwards and westwards. Since the 1970s it has begun breeding at Norfolk and Lord Howe islands. It is a regular visitor to Mutton Bird Island, near Coffs Harbour, New South Wales, and the possibility has been raised that these visits are 'prospecting' for further new nesting sites. Records in Australian waters mainly span the months December to April. Unlike many other petrels, it is often seen over its breeding grounds by day.

BREEDING. Colonial. Nest: in a chamber at the end of a burrow. Clutch: one; white. Breeding season: December to January.

36:13 SALVIN'S PRION *Pachyptila salvini*

IDENTIFICATION. Virtually unidentifiable at sea.

DISTRIBUTION. Breeds only on Marion Island and the Crozets in the southern Indian Ocean; apparently fairly common in seas off southern Australia, but recorded mainly as dead or dying birds washed up on beaches.

NOTES. Like other prions, it is almost impossible to identify the species at sea. It breeds in colonies and disperses northwards after the breeding season.

BREEDING. Colonial. Nest: a chamber at the end of a burrow. Clutch: one; white. Breeding season: October to January.

36:14 BROAD-BILLED PRION *Pachyptila vittata*

IDENTIFICATION. Very similar to other prions, it is almost impossible to identify at sea. If examined in the hand, it has an extraordinary, huge black bill.

DISTRIBUTION. Breeds at various islands in southern oceans, including several around New Zealand; disperses widely over southern oceans.

NOTES. Usually seen in flocks, it is generally uncommon in Australian seas; occurring mainly in the winter. During stormy weather numbers of these birds are sometimes washed up on beaches along the coast. Its food consists chiefly of plankton, procured from the surface of the sea.

BREEDING. Colonial. Nest: in a hollow at the end of a rat-like burrow; made in slanting soil, in a natural cavity in rocks, or under matted stems and roots of weeds. Clutch: one; white. Breeding season: September to January.

36:15 ANTARCTIC PRION *Pachyptila desolata*

IDENTIFICATION. Almost impossible to distinguish from other prions at sea.

DISTRIBUTION. Breeds in Antarctica and at various sub-antarctic islands, including Macquarie and Heard islands; disperses widely over southern oceans, including seas off the southern and eastern coasts of Australia.

NOTES. One of the most abundant of the seabirds of sub-antarctic regions, it is often recorded as derelicts washed up on Australian beaches. It is similar in habits to other prions.

BREEDING. Colonial. Nest: in a cavity at the end of a burrow. Clutch: one; white. Breeding season: November to February.

36:16 FAIRY PRION *Pachyptila turtur*

IDENTIFICATION. This species is blue-grey above, white below. Almost impossible to distinguish from other prions at sea, under exceptionally favourable circumstances it can sometimes be identified by its broad black tail band (other prions have narrow tail bands), bold black M-band across the upperwings, and faint white superciliary.

DISTRIBUTION. Breeds at Marion Island in the Indian Ocean, at various islands around New Zealand, along the coast of Victoria, in Bass Strait and around Tasmania; limited dispersal over nearby seas.

NOTES. Usually found in flocks, its flight is swift, weaving and low. When feeding, it flutters and bounces over the waves or swims just under the surface. Like other small petrels, it waits until dark before visiting its breeding islands to feed the young or to change shifts with its mate to incubate the eggs. All of the prion species are extremely difficult or impossible to distinguish at sea.

BREEDING. Colonial. Nest: in a natural cavity in rocks or under densely matted stems or roots. Clutch: one; white. Breeding season: October to December.

36:17 BLUE PETREL *Halobaena caerulea*

IDENTIFICATION. This petrel is mainly blue-grey above, white below, with a dark grey head and a diagnostic white tip to its grey tail. Sexes are similar.

DISTRIBUTION. Breeds at various sub-antarctic islands; disperses widely over seas around Antarctica.

NOTES. An irregular visitor to the seas off southern Australia, it is mainly in the south-west, becoming progressively less common further east. Usually seen in flocks, it is similar in flight to the prions, but distinguished chiefly by its white-tipped tail. Occasionally it follows ships.

BREEDING. Colonial. Nest: in a large cavity at the end of a burrow; lined with fine root-fibres, twigs or leaves; burrows are usually beneath plants growing on hillsides. Clutch: one; white. Breeding season: September to November.

36:18 GREY PETREL *Procellaria cinerea*

IDENTIFICATION. This species is brownish-grey above, dingy white below, with an almost uniformly dark underwing; the bill is diagnostic, dull green, yellowish at the tip.

DISTRIBUTION. Breeds at various sub-antarctic islands, including (possibly) Macquarie Island; disperses over southern oceans.

NOTES. It is usually seen in small flocks, which freely follow ships, scavenging galley refuse. Also, like many small petrels, it commonly associates with whales. Very rare in Australian seas. Food: mainly fish and squid, obtained by diving.

BREEDING. Colonial. Nest: in a large chamber at the end of a burrow. Clutch: one; white. Breeding season: generally April to July.

36:19 WESTLAND PETREL *Procellaria westlandica*

IDENTIFICATION. This is a large, burly black petrel with a stout, pale, black-tipped bill.

DISTRIBUTION. Breeds only on South Island, New Zealand; apparently not recorded outside the Tasman Sea; rare vagrant to eastern Australia.

NOTES. Very closely related to both the Black Petrel and the White-chinned Petrel, it is not safely distinguishable at sea except under unusual circumstances. This species differs from both in being a winter breeder.

BREEDING. Colonial. Nest: a chamber at the end of a burrow. Clutch: one; white. Breeding season: May and June.

36:20 WHITE-CHINNED PETREL *Procellaria aequinoctialis*

IDENTIFICATION. This is a large, burly, black petrel with a pale yellowish bill and a white chin, diagnostic when present, but many individuals are dark-chinned. Otherwise it is almost impossible to distinguish it from Black or Westland Petrels.

DISTRIBUTION. Breeds at various sub-antarctic islands; disperses widely over southern oceans; uncommon in seas off southern Australia.

NOTES. White-chinned Petrels fly with slow, deliberate and graceful wingbeats, generally close to the sea. Food: mainly fish, squid and other cephalopods.

BREEDING. Colonial. Nest: a saucer-shaped structure of grass, in a chamber at the end of a burrow. Clutch: one; white. Breeding season: generally November to January.

36:21 WILSON'S STORMPETREL *Oceanites oceanicus*

IDENTIFICATION. This species is a small, dark stormpetrel with rounded wings, square-tipped tail, white rump, and greyish wing coverts. The toes are joined with yellow webs, diagnostic but almost impossible to see.

DISTRIBUTION. Breeds in Antarctica and various sub-antarctic islands; widespread as a winter migrant over the oceans of the world; common in Australian seas, though uncommon along the southern coast.

NOTES. Found singly or in flocks, chiefly along the eastern and western coasts, and wintering in the seas off northern Australia, it is common in waters over the continental shelf. Its flight when feeding is very erratic and fluttering with wings held high, somewhat like the flight of a butterfly. It pats the water with its feet, dancing and skipping over the surface. Food: surface plankton, the fat from dead whales or seals, and refuse from ships' galleys.

BREEDING. Colonial. Nest: in a chamber at the end of a tunnel; lined with feathers. Clutch: one; dull white, sometimes with reddish dots. Breeding season: December to February.

36:22 GREY-BACKED STORMPETREL *Oceanites nereis*

IDENTIFICATION. This species is mainly plain grey above, head and breast blackish; rest of underparts white, including underwing.

DISTRIBUTION. Antarctic and sub-antarctic seas; recorded in winter in Bass Strait and Tasmanian seas.

NOTES. Occurring singly or in flocks, the flight when feeding is a buoyant, erratic fluttering over the surface of the water. Apparently it is relatively sedentary.

BREEDING. Colonial. Nest: in a chamber at the end of a tunnel. Clutch: one; white, with reddish-brown and lavender dots. Breeding season: November to January.

36:23 WHITE-FACED STORMPETREL *Pelagodroma marina*

IDENTIFICATION. The upperparts are brownish-grey; the head is mainly white, with grey crown and nape, and a dusky patch around the eye.

DISTRIBUTION. Breeds at many off-shore islands along the southern Australian coast from Houtman Abrolhos Group, Western Australia, to Broughton Island, New South Wales. Also several islands in the New Zealand region, and in the North Atlantic. The Australian population apparently winters widely in the Indian Ocean, but movements are little known.

NOTES. It occurs singly or in flocks, is mainly pelagic, and seldom seen in inshore waters. Its flight when feeding is low and fluttering, skipping with both feet together over the water; otherwise strong and wheeling. It is similar in habits to other stormpetrels. It breeds in colonies, which it visits after dark.

BREEDING. Colonial. Nest: in a chamber, lined with dry grass, at the end of a rat-like burrow. Clutch: one; white, occasionally with reddish-brown spots on the larger end. Breeding season: October to February (Southern Hemisphere); March to April (Northern Hemisphere).

36:24 BLACK-BELLIED STORMPETREL *Fregetta tropica*

IDENTIFICATION. The head, breast and upperparts are black. It has a narrow white rump, with white underparts, with a narrow black streak down the centre.

DISTRIBUTION. Breeds at various sub-antarctic islands, including several in the New Zealand region; winters in tropical seas.

NOTES. Rather solitary, but occasionally it is seen in groups at sea. Its flight is agile, rapid and erratic. Vagrant to the seas off southern Australia and Tasmania.

BREEDING. Colonial. Nest: in a crevice among rocks. Clutch: one; white, with small pink spots. Breeding season: December to February.

36:25 WHITE-BELLIED STORMPETREL *Fregetta grallaria*

IDENTIFICATION. Very similar to Black-bellied Stormpetrel, this species lacks a black streak down the centre of the belly. Some individuals breeding at Lord Howe Island are of the rare dark morph, which is almost entirely dark dusky grey.

DISTRIBUTION. Breeds at various islands in the South Atlantic and southern Pacific Oceans, including Lord Howe Island; oceanic range poorly understood. Rare vagrant to seas off south-eastern Australia.

NOTES. This is similar in general habits to other stormpetrels, but little known in detail. Not uncommon in the Coral Sea, and there are several reports from coastal waters of New South Wales. It is difficult to distinguish it at sea from its close relative the Black-bellied Stormpetrel. A dark phase of this species occurs at Lord Howe Island.

BREEDING. Colonial. Nest: a chamber at the end of a tunnel, or in deep crevices between rocks. Clutch: one; white. Breeding season: January to March.

36:26 COMMON DIVING-PETREL *Pelecanoides urinatrix*

IDENTIFICATION. This species is dark grey above, and dingy white below.

DISTRIBUTION. Breeds at various sub-antarctic islands, including Macquarie and Heard islands, and at various islands in Bass Strait and off Tasmania; mainly sedentary.

NOTES. Seen singly or in small scattered flocks, it rests on the surface of the water or dives for small fishes and other marine organisms. It has a characteristic buzzy flight, very low on the surface of the water. It plunges into water from flight. It is difficult to detect at sea.

BREEDING. Colonial. Nest: in a cavity at the end of a crooked burrow. Clutch: one; white. Breeding season: July to November.

PLATE 37

BIRDS OF THE OCEAN AND SEASHORE

37:1 WANDERING ALBATROSS *Diomedea exulans*

IDENTIFICATION. Juveniles of this species are unmistakable, mainly dark brown, with a white face and underwings. Adults and immatures are identifiable by sheer size from all but Royal Albatross, but distinguishable from that species only with difficulty: diagnostic features include plain pinkish bill (Royal Albatross has narrow black line along the cutting edge of the upper mandible), and black outer tail feathers.

DISTRIBUTION. Breeds on various sub-antarctic islands, including Macquarie Island; common in southern Australian seas, north to about Fremantle, Western Australia, and Sydney, New South Wales; progressively less common further north.

NOTES. Common in Australian seas, mainly in winter and spring, but recorded in all months. It follows ships, and occasionally is seen in harbours and bays during stormy weather. It has graceful and effortless flight on slightly drooped, almost motionless wings. Usually solitary, but it congregates, often with other species of albatross, at floating refuse and other concentrations of food. Food: cuttlefish and other marine animals, as well as galley refuse from ships.

BREEDING. Loosely colonial. Nest: large, cone-shaped; composed of earth and grass cemented with excreta; placed on the ground. Clutch: one; white, but mostly nest-stained, the surface being rough and lustreless. Breeding season: December to February.

37:2 ROYAL ALBATROSS *Diomedea epomophora*

IDENTIFICATION. The adults are mainly white, with plain black upperwings. Immatures very difficult to distinguish from adults of the more common Wandering Albatross, and the only feature reliable in all cases is the dark cutting edges of both mandibles in this species. Sexes are similar; but immatures resemble adults.

DISTRIBUTION. Breeds at various islands around New Zealand; mainly sedentary, but occasionally recorded in seas off southern Australia.

NOTES. Restricted in range and generally uncommon. It is apparently sedentary, although recoveries of banded birds in Western Australia and elsewhere demonstrate that the species may wander widely on occasion. It follows ships. Like the Wandering Albatross, individuals of this species breed only every second year.

BREEDING. Loosely colonial. Nest: a truncated cone of mud and grass. Clutch: one; white with pinkish-brown spots. Breeding season: November to December.

37:3 BLACK-BROWED ALBATROSS *Diomedea melanophrys*

IDENTIFICATION. Adults of this species may be distinguished by their bright orange-yellow bills and mostly dark underwings. Immatures have dull olive, black-tipped bills.

DISTRIBUTION. Breeds on various sub-antarctic islands, including Macquarie Island; very common in Australian seas, north to about Fremantle, Western Australia and Sydney, New South-Wales, progressively less common further north.

NOTES. This albatross is often seen following ships and near fishing vessels, often in small groups. Recorded all months, but most common between May and October. It is similar in habits to other albatrosses.

BREEDING. Colonial. Nest: large, cone-shaped; composed of mud mixed with vegetable material. Clutch: one; dull white, with a zone of reddish-brown specks and blotches at the larger end. Breeding season: October to December.

37:4 GREY-HEADED ALBATROSS *Diomedea chrysostoma*

IDENTIFICATION. The adults may be distinguished from other albatrosses by a combination of grey head, broad black leading edge to the underwing, and black bill with a narrow orange-yellow line along both upper and lower ridges.

DISTRIBUTION. Breeds on various sub-antarctic islands, including Macquarie Island; fairly common in Australian seas, mainly the west (north to about Shark Bay) and south coasts and off Tasmania; much less common off the east coast.

NOTES. Generally solitary, it may approach ships but seldom follows them persistently. Most common between May and November. Similar in habits and general appearance to the Black-browed Albatross.

BREEDING. Colonial. Nest: a raised mound of earth mixed with grass and having a shallow cup for the egg. Clutch: one; white, with a band of brown spots at the larger end. Breeding season: October to September.

37:5 YELLOW-NOSED ALBATROSS *Diomedea chlororhynchos*

IDENTIFICATION. This species is the smallest of the albatrosses. The adults are identifiable by their white heads, mainly white underwing, and black bill with yellow line along the upper ridge.

DISTRIBUTION. Breeds on various sub-antarctic islands; common in Australian seas, north to about Shark Bay, Western Australia, and Sydney, New South Wales, progressively less common further north.

NOTES. Seen alone or in flocks, it is recorded in all months in Australian waters, but is most common between May and October. Much less inclined to follow ships than other albatrosses.

BREEDING. Loosely colonial. Nest: a cylindrical column of earth; about 30 to 60 centimetres in height. Clutch: one; white with tiny reddish spots. Breeding season: September to December.

37:6 SHY ALBATROSS *Diomedea cauta*

IDENTIFICATION. This is a large albatross with dull brownish-grey upperwings and mainly white underwings, very narrowly bordered black. The best single fieldmark is the small black mark (more conspicuous than might be expected from its size) in the 'armpit', at the base of the leading edge of the underwing.

DISTRIBUTION. Breeds on islands off Tasmania and New Zealand; common in Australian seas, north to about Fremantle, Western Australia, and Sydney, New South Wales, progressively less common further north. There are three distinct subspecies: *D. c. cauta* breeds at Albatross Island, the Mewstone, and Pedra Blanca, Tasmania and at Auckland Island, New Zealand; *D. c. salvini* breeds at Bounty and Snares islands; and *D. c. eremita* breeds at Pyramid Rock in the Chatham Islands. The pelagic distribution of the three forms is imperfectly known.

NOTES. Perhaps less often seen inshore than other albatrosses, it is generally solitary, following ships but not persistently. It loiters about fishing vessels.

BREEDING. Colonial. Nest: flat, bowl-shaped; built of soil and excrement mixed with roots and grasses; placed on the ground. Clutch: one; creamy-white, capped with reddish-brown surface markings. Breeding season: August to December.

37:7 BULLER'S ALBATROSS *Diomedea bulleri*

IDENTIFICATION. This species is very similar to Grey-headed Albatross but with a more distinctly white cap; white underwing more narrowly bordered black, and broader yellow band along the upper ridge of the bill.

DISTRIBUTION. Breeds at Solander, Snares and Chatham islands, New Zealand; apparently disperses eastwards into the southern Pacific. Rare vagrant to seas off south-eastern Australia, north to about Byron Bay, New South Wales; scattered records further north.

NOTES. Rare visitor to Australian seas, records span the period March to October. Seen singly or in small groups, it often follows ships and approaches fishing vessels. It breeds in loose colonies. Food: fish and squid.

BREEDING. Colonial. Nest: a conical mound of earth and grass with a central depression. Clutch: one; creamy-white, sometimes speckled reddish. Breeding season: January to February at the Snares, one or two months earlier at the Chatham Islands.

37:8 NORTHERN GIANT-PETREL *Macronectes halli*

IDENTIFICATION. This bird is very similar in appearance to the Southern Giant-petrel. The colour of the tip of the bill (dull reddish in this species, pale greenish in the Southern Giant-petrel) is the most conspicuous feature separating them. Also, this species is not known to have a white morph, so that any all-white bird must be a Southern Giant-petrel.

DISTRIBUTION. Breeds at various sub-antarctic islands; disperses widely over southern oceans. Regular visitor to seas off southern Australia.

NOTES. So similar are the two forms that it was only when their breeding biology was systematically studied that it became apparent that there are in fact two species. This species breeds about a month earlier than its relative, and is less inclined to breed in colonies — although the two species do sometimes breed together.

BREEDING. Loosely colonial. Nest: a rough heap of grass and other plant debris surrounding a central depression. Clutch: one; white. Breeding season: July to February.

37:9 SOUTHERN GIANT-PETREL *Macronectes giganteus*

IDENTIFICATION. This bird is very like Northern Giant-petrel, but its pale bill has a faintly greenish tip. The uncommon white morph usually has dark feathers scattered randomly over the body.

DISTRIBUTION. Breeds in Antarctica and at various sub-antarctic islands, including Macquarie and Heard islands; disperses widely over southern oceans. Common in Australian seas, north to about Fremantle in the west and Sydney in the east; progressively less common further north.

NOTES. There is a white phase of the species which is confined mainly to the neighbourhood of the Antarctic Circle. Numbers of these birds banded as nestlings on Heard, Macquarie, and the Falkland islands have been recovered in South America, South Africa, southern Australia, and other places, including Tahiti. Food: fish, squid and other marine life; offal and galley refuse, and (at the breeding grounds) eggs, chicks, dead seabirds and other carrion.

BREEDING. Colonial. Nest: a hollowed, cone-shaped structure; composed of earth and excreta. Clutch: one; white. Breeding season: October to November.

37:10 SOOTY ALBATROSS *Phoebetria fusca*

IDENTIFICATION. Plumage of this species is dark sooty brown, except for narrow, broken white eye-ring.

DISTRIBUTION. Breeds on various sub-antarctic islands; seldom recorded but perhaps fairly regular in seas off the southern coast of Australia, especially in the south-west and off Tasmania.

NOTES. Usually silent and solitary at sea, it often follows ships. This species and its close relative the Light-mantled Albatross are easily told from other albatrosses by their dark plumage, long wedge-shaped tails, and extraordinarily graceful flight.

BREEDING. Loosely colonial. Nest: a conical mound of earth, mixed with vegetation; usually built on cliffs. Clutch: one; greyish-white, covered with grey-brown specks. Breeding season: September to November.

37:11 LIGHT-MANTLED ALBATROSS *Phoebetria palpebrata*

IDENTIFICATION. This species is very like Sooty Albatross, but nape, back, rump and underparts are frosty grey.

DISTRIBUTION. Breeds on various sub-antarctic islands, including Macquarie and Heard islands; seldom recorded in Australian seas.

NOTES. It resembles the Sooty Albatross in habits, but its range is more southern than that species. Unlike the Sooty Albatross, it usually nests as single pairs, or as loose groups of pairs, rather than in colonies.

BREEDING. Nest: either a slight flattish platform or a mound of mud and grass; up to 30 centimetres in height, the bowl sometimes being lined with grass. Clutch: one; whitish, with small reddish-brown spots. Breeding season: October to January.

37:12 GREATER FRIGATEBIRD *Fregata minor*

IDENTIFICATION. The male has plumage entirely black; the female has a dusky grey throat and white breast.

DISTRIBUTION. Widespread in the tropical Atlantic, Indian and Pacific Oceans; breeds at several islands in the Coral Sea; regular visitor to the northern and eastern coasts of Australia, west to about Point Cloates, Western Australia, and south to about Rockhampton, Queensland.

NOTES. Usually seen soaring over the sea or circling an island, it is often so high as to appear a mere speck against the sky. Its flight is remarkably swift and graceful, and it remains on the wing throughout practically the whole day. It procures its food from the surface of the water or by compelling terns, gannets and other seabirds to disgorge their prey, which it adroitly catches. Food: young turtles, fish, cuttlefish, etc.

BREEDING. Colonial. Nest: bulky; composed of sticks, grass, and other herbage; placed on the ground or on top of a small bush. Clutch: one; white. Breeding season: March to July.

37:13 LESSER FRIGATEBIRD *Fregata ariel*

IDENTIFICATION. The male is entirely black except for a narrow white patch at the base of the underwing; the female is very similar to the female Great Frigatebird, but has a black throat and white collar.

DISTRIBUTION. Widespread in the tropical Atlantic, Indian and Pacific Oceans; breeds at various islands in the Coral Sea, along the Great Barrier Reef, and along the coast of northern Australia west to Bedout Island, Western Australia.

NOTES. It is similar in habits to the Greater Frigatebird, but generally more common and widespread.

BREEDING. Colonial. Nest: bulky; composed of small sticks, grass, and other herbage; placed on the ground or on top of a low bush. Clutch: one to two; white, with a slight coating of lime. Breeding season: April to July.

37:14 RED-TAILED TROPICBIRD *Phaethon rubricaudus*

IDENTIFICATION. This species is most easily distinguished from the smaller White-tailed Tropicbird by the pure white wings (White-tailed Tropicbirds have much black on the wing). Sexes are similar.

DISTRIBUTION. Widespread in the tropical Pacific and Indian Oceans; in the Australian region breeding stations include Norfolk, Lord Howe and Raine Islands in the east and at the Houtman Abrolhos Group (now possibly abandoned) and Rottnest Island in the west; vagrant to coastal waters north of Perth, Western Australia, and Sydney, New South Wales.

NOTES. Usually solitary at sea, it often ranges far from the breeding island. It breeds either as single pairs or in loose colonies; breeding pairs indulge in display flights, in which the displaying bird beats its wings rapidly and in a wide arc, causing the bird to rise and causing a 'back-pedalling' effect. Food: mainly fish and squid, obtained by diving from a height of about 10 metres above the sea.

BREEDING. Nest: a depression in the ground; sheltered by a bush or rock; sometimes on a ledge or in a crevice of a rocky cliff. Clutch: one; dull white or pinkish-red, almost obscured by minute marks of pinkish-red to blackish-brown. Breeding season: September to March (Lord Howe Island); practically throughout the year elsewhere.

37:15 WHITE-TAILED TROPICBIRD *Phaethon lepturus*

IDENTIFICATION. This bird is similar to Red-tailed Tropicbird but is smaller and more slender; with bold black patches in upper wing. Sexes are similar.

DISTRIBUTION. Tropical Atlantic, Indian and western Pacific Oceans; does not breed in Australian seas (the nearest breeding stations being Christmas and Cocos Keeling Islands in the Indian Ocean and Walpole Island south-east of New Caledonia), but recorded regularly in the Coral Sea, and vagrant to the eastern coast of Australia, south to about Batemans Bay, New South Wales.

NOTES. A vagrant to the coast of eastern Australia, occurrences often in the form of 'wrecks', when dead and dying birds may be found almost simultaneously at widely scattered localities, many often inland. Similar in general habits to the Red-tailed Tropicbird.

BREEDING. Nest: a depression in sand or on the floor of a crevice in a rocky cliff. Clutch: one; buff, with purplish-brown markings. Breeding season: December to September.

37:16 AUSTRALASIAN GANNET *Morus serrator*

IDENTIFICATION. The adult is mainly white, with head strongly washed rich yellow; primaries and secondaries black; tail white, central feathers black. Sexes are similar; but immatures are white below, brown above, and speckled white.

DISTRIBUTION. Coasts of southern Australia (south of Point Cloates, Western Australia, and Mackay, Queensland), Tasmania, and New Zealand.

NOTES. A fairly common species in coastal waters, it occurs singly, in small groups or flocks. It dives for fish from a considerable height, its skull being equipped with a maze of bony tissue that absorbs the impact of the head against the water. The species breeds in colonies on islands in Bass Strait, off Tasmania, on Lawrence Rock (off Portland, Victoria) and in New Zealand. Many birds banded as nestlings in New Zealand have been recorded in eastern and southern Australia, and one such recovery has been reported from Western Australia.

BREEDING. Strongly colonial. Nest: usually a well-built structure; composed of kelp, twigs, grass, and other plants; placed on a flat cone-shaped mound of earth and guano. Clutch: one; bluish-white. Breeding season: October to December.

37:17 BROWN BOOBY *Sula leucogaster*

IDENTIFICATION. The head, breast and upperparts are uniform dark brown, the belly white, the underwing largely white. Sexes are similar.

DISTRIBUTION. Tropical oceans around the world; in Australian seas, breeds at off-shore islands along the north-western coast of Western Australia, in Torres Strait, and along the Great Barrier Reef south to the Bunker Group; common south to the Dampier Archipelago in the west and Moreton Bay, Queensland; stragglers further south.

NOTES. Seen in small parties or large flocks, flying with direct, steady flight close to the surface of the water. Its food consists of fish, which it obtains by diving from the air. Commonly seen loafing on ships' rigging, channel markers and buoys and on sand cays. It breeds in colonies. (Booby is an old name referring to its tameness.)

BREEDING. Colonial. Nest: a depression in soil or sand, around which is placed any suitable material near at hand. Clutch: usually two; greenish white, with a coating of lime. Breeding season: throughout the year, with peaks in spring and autumn.

37:18 RED-FOOTED BOOBY *Sula sula*

IDENTIFICATION. Plumage of this species is very variable, occurring in several morphs. Most individuals are identifiable by a white rump and tail; red feet are diagnostic. Sexes are similar.

DISTRIBUTION. Tropical Atlantic, Pacific and Indian Oceans; breeds at islands in the Coral Sea, at Raine Island, Queensland, and at Ashmore Reefs, Western Australia.

NOTES. Similar in general habits to other boobies, but it apparently feeds mainly by night, and spends most of its time far out at sea.

BREEDING. Colonial. Nest: a substantial platform of interwoven sticks, with a shallow depression in the centre; placed in a shrubby bush, well off the ground. Clutch: one; pale greenish or bluish-white, with a coating of lime. Breeding season: May to September.

37:19 MASKED BOOBY *Sula dactylatra*

IDENTIFICATION. Largest of the boobies, this species is mainly white with black primaries, secondaries, and tail feathers; black face; and yellow bill.

DISTRIBUTION. Tropical oceans around the world; in Australian seas, breeds at off-shore islands along the north-western coast of Western Australia, in Torres Strait, the Coral Sea, and along the Great Barrier Reef; also at Norfolk and Lord Howe islands; uncommon in coastal waters off the mainland.

NOTES. It is similar in habits to other boobies, but forages far at sea in deep water.

BREEDING. Loosely colonial. Nest: a depression in sand or earth, around which twigs, grass, or weeds are strewn. Clutch: usually two; pale bluish-white, more or less covered with lime. Breeding season: variable, but mainly July to December.

PLATE 38

BIRDS OF THE OCEAN AND SEASHORE

38:1 FIORDLAND PENGUIN *Eudyptes pachyrhynchus*

IDENTIFICATION. This species is extremely difficult to distinguish from other *Eudyptes* penguins. Its cheeks are dull black, obscurely streaked white. The yellow superciliary is of more or less constant width from bill almost to nape, then broadens abruptly to form a drooping, bushy tassle. Sexes are similar.

DISTRIBUTION. New Zealand.

NOTES. This species breeds on the coast of South Island and on Stewart Island, New Zealand. The rather loose colonies are generally near the sea on forested headlands or on off-shore islands. It is rather sedentary, but stragglers occasionally reach south-eastern Australia and Tasmania.

BREEDING. Colonial. Nest: a depression in a cave or deep between the roots of a tree, sometimes lined with grass or a few sticks. Clutch: two; greenish-white, with a coating of lime. Breeding season: June to August.

38:2 ROCKHOPPER PENGUIN *Eudyptes chrysocome*

IDENTIFICATION. This species is extremely similar to other *Eudyptes* penguins: glossy jet black cheeks; yellow superciliary very narrow, fragments just before the nape to form a loose, disordered, frizzy tassel. Sexes are similar.

DISTRIBUTION. Circumpolar in sub-antarctic seas, breeding at a number of islands including the Falklands, Tristan da Cunha, Marion, Heard, Macquarie and islands south of New Zealand. Pelagic range little known; vagrant to Australia (Tasmania and the south coast) and New Zealand.

NOTES. It breeds in dense colonies which are often very large, and usually on boulder-strewn slopes near the sea. The name is apt — on land it usually hops with both feet together, 'like a man running in a sack race'. Food: mainly crustaceans; also squid.

BREEDING. Colonial. Nest: a depression, among rocks, on a ledge, or in a cave (sometimes in burrows), lined with a few pebbles and sometimes grass. Clutch: two to three at colonies in the South Atlantic); white or greenish-white. Breeding season: October to March.

38:3 LITTLE PENGUIN *Eudyptula minor*

IDENTIFICATION. This is a very small penguin, with blue-grey above, and white below. Sexes are similar.

DISTRIBUTION. Coasts of southern Australia from about Fremantle, Western Australia, to about Port Stephens, New South Wales, casually further north. It also inhabits New Zealand.

NOTES. It frequents Australian seas throughout the year, inhabiting well-established rookeries extending along the coast and on many islands. It is very quick and agile underwater. When disturbed at its nest, or when sporting in the water, it utters a sharp barking note, suggesting a small dog. It comes ashore to visit its colonies at night, and evening parades of this dapper little bird on Phillip Island, Victoria, have become a popular tourist attraction.

BREEDING. Colonial. Nest: a little dry grass or seaweed placed in a cavity between rocks or in a burrow scraped out underneath tussock grass or other vegetation. Clutch: two to three; dull white. Breeding season: August to March.

38:4 BULLER'S SHEARWATER *Puffinus bulleri*

IDENTIFICATION. This species is relatively easily identified by its white underparts, dark cap and striking grey and black upperwing pattern. Sexes are similar.

DISTRIBUTION. Breeds at the Poor Knights Islands, New Zealand; disperses into the North Pacific, and recorded with increasing frequency along the coast of eastern Australia, north to about Stradbroke Island, Queensland.

NOTES. First recorded in Australian seas in 1954, but it has since been recorded with increasing frequency; most records span the months October to June. It is gregarious, though seldom seen in large flocks. In Australian waters it often associates with Wedge-tailed or Short-tailed Shearwaters. Its flight is usually close to the surface, with wingbeats easy, measured, and graceful.

BREEDING. Colonial. Nest: in a chamber at the end of a burrow, occasionally in crevices between rocks. Clutch: one; white. Breeding season: November to January.

38:5 WEDGE-TAILED SHEARWATER *Puffinus pacificus*

IDENTIFICATION. Plumage of this bird is entirely dusky brown. It is very similar in appearance to other shearwaters, but it has a distinctive flight, drifting and buoyant, with wings curved well forward. Sexes are similar.

DISTRIBUTION. Widespread in the tropical Indian and Pacific oceans. In Australia, it breeds on numerous off-shore islands south to Montague Island (off Narooma, New South Wales) on the east coast and to Carnac Island (off Fremantle, Western Australia) in the west.

NOTES. Southern populations are migratory, dispersing northwards into the western Pacific. Both sexes take part in incubation, one remaining in the burrow all day while its mate ranges the ocean for food, which consists of fish and various floating or surface-living organisms, and also scraps from ships. Although a rookery is a silent place during the day, throughout the night it is noisy with the wail of birds, so that the species is sometimes termed Ghostbird. In many areas, including the Shark Bay region of Western Australia, two colour morphs occur, one being all dark, the other extensively white below.

BREEDING. Colonial. Nest: in a hollow at the end of a burrow or in a natural cavity; lined with grass or feathers. Clutch: one; white. Breeding season: October to March (Australia).

38:6 FLESH-FOOTED SHEARWATER *Puffinus carneipes*

IDENTIFICATION. Plumage of this species is entirely dusky brown. It closely resembles other shearwaters, but the large pale bill is a helpful fieldmark. Sexes are similar.

DISTRIBUTION. Coasts of south-western and southern Australia, New South Wales, Lord Howe Island, and New Zealand, migrating to the eastern Indian Ocean and through the Pacific Ocean to Japan and California.

NOTES. Common during the summer off the coasts of south-eastern and south-western Australia, it is usually seen in flocks. It breeds in large numbers on Lord Howe Island, on islands lying off the south-west of Western Australia and about New Zealand.

BREEDING. Colonial. Nest: a hollow at the end of a burrow in soil; lined with grass or feathers. Clutch: one; white. Breeding season: November to March.

38:7 SOOTY SHEARWATER *Puffinus griseus*

IDENTIFICATION. This species is difficult to distinguish from the more common (in Australian waters) Short-tailed Shearwater — the white underwing coverts of the present species is an obvious but very deceptive fieldmark, as Short-tailed Shearwaters can appear very light under the wing. Sexes are similar.

DISTRIBUTION. Breeds at islands near New Zealand and in South America, migrating to the North Pacific and North Atlantic oceans. Fairly common in seas off south-eastern Australia, breeding locally in small numbers on off-shore islands in New South Wales and Tasmania.

NOTES. Usually seen in flocks, the flight is brisk, stiff-winged, and direct, with frequent glides. This species, the common muttonbird of New Zealand, wanders to Australia mainly in spring and early summer. Not infrequently specimens are washed up on the beaches of New South Wales. The main breeding colonies are in New Zealand and southern South America, but small numbers breed at various islands along the south-eastern coast of Australia and in Tasmania. Migration extends to the North Pacific Ocean.

BREEDING. Colonial. Nest: in a hollow at the end of a burrow. Clutch: one; white. Breeding season: November to April.

38:8 SHORT-TAILED SHEARWATER *Puffinus tenuirostris*

IDENTIFICATION. Plumage of this bird is entirely sooty brown. It is very difficult to distinguish from Sooty Shearwater at sea, but it is very slightly smaller and slimmer, with dark underwings and a slender bill. Sexes are similar.

DISTRIBUTION. Bass Strait, the coasts of Tasmania, southern and south-eastern Australia (north to south-eastern Queensland), and New Zealand, and the north Pacific Ocean.

NOTES. This species, the muttonbird of commerce, migrates to the northern Pacific Ocean in autumn after breeding on islands off southern New South Wales, Victoria, Tasmania, and eastern South Australia. One bird, banded as a nestling on Ceduna Island, South Australia, was recorded in the Bering Sea (nearly 13,000 kilometres along the presumed migration route) about six weeks later. From September to November the returning migrants move down the eastern Australian coast in immense numbers to their breeding islands. Upwards of 500,000 young birds are collected each autumn and sold for food.

BREEDING. Colonial. Nest: in a hollow at the end of a burrow in soft soil. Clutch: one; white. Breeding season: November to March.

38:9 HUTTON'S SHEARWATER *Puffinus huttoni*

IDENTIFICATION. This species is very similar in appearance to the Fluttering Shearwater, but is somewhat larger, darker and longer tailed. Its underwing is mainly dusky grey. Sexes are similar.

DISTRIBUTION. Breeds in the Seaward Kaikoura Mountains, South Island, New Zealand; apparently mainly sedentary, but some disperse across the southern Tasman Sea to south- eastern Australia.

NOTES. Though it is usually seen in flocks, it appears that only occasional individuals reach the south-eastern coast of Australia (and, as rare vagrants, westward along the southern coast to Western Australia). Mixed flocks have been reported. The only known breeding colonies are high in the Seaward Kaikoura Range of New Zealand, where the first colonies were discovered in 1965.

BREEDING. Colonial. Nest: in a chamber at the end of a tunnel. Clutch: one; white. Breeding season: August to April.

38:10 LITTLE SHEARWATER *Puffinus assimilis*

IDENTIFICATION. This small shearwater is black above and white below, its underwing mainly white. Critical fieldmarks include the white undertail coverts, and the fact that the white face completely encircles the eye. Sexes are similar.

DISTRIBUTION. Breeds at islands in the South Atlantic and in Australasian seas, including Lord Howe Island, Norfolk Island, and islands off the coast of Western Australia; non-breeding birds range widely over southern oceans.

NOTES. It frequents the seas of south-western Australia, more rarely ranging to south-eastern Australia. Its flight is fast and low, on rapid fluttering wings. It often congregates in large flocks when feeding. Relatively sedentary, it remains in the vicinity of the breeding islands for much of the year. Food: small fish and cephalopods (squids).

BREEDING. Colonial. Nest: in a natural crevice or in a shallow burrow. Clutch: one; white. Breeding season: June and July.

38:11 FLUTTERING SHEARWATER *Puffinus gavia*

IDENTIFICATION. This species is dark grey above, including the head (except chin and throat). The underparts are white. It is very similar to Hutton's Shearwater but the underwing is mostly white. Sexes are similar.

DISTRIBUTION. Breeds at islands around New Zealand; disperses to seas off the southern and eastern coasts of Australia, west to about Fremantle, Western Australia, and north to about Fraser Island, Queensland.

NOTES. Common in coastal waters of south-eastern Australia, it is present throughout the year, but most numerous from July to November. Usually seen in flocks, sometimes quite large, its flight is low, direct, on briskly flapped wings, alternating with brief glides. It dives freely and expertly. It seldom approaches ships or fishing vessels.

BREEDING. Colonial. Nest: in a chamber at the end of a burrow; lined with a few leaves. Clutch: one; white. Breeding season: October to March (on islands adjacent to New Zealand).

38:12 STREAKED SHEARWATER *Calonectris leucomelas*

IDENTIFICATION. A rather large shearwater, it is greyish brown above and white below. The head is grey-brown, and profusely streaked white. The white face and forehead are diagnostic. Sexes are similar.

DISTRIBUTION. Breeds at various islands around Japan; disperses southwards at least to seas off New Guinea, recorded with increasing frequency off the east coast of Australia.

NOTES. This is the common shearwater of Japanese waters, where it is abundant in inshore waters, and breeds in large colonies on many islands. At many islands, young are gathered for their meat and oil in much the same manner as Short-tailed Shearwaters are harvested in the islands of Bass Strait.

BREEDING. Colonial. Nest: in a chamber at the end of a burrow. Clutch: one; white. Breeding season: June to August.

38:13 PIED OYSTERCATCHER *Haematopus ostralegus*

IDENTIFICATION. This is a large, boldly black-and-white shorebird with pinkish legs and long, pointed red bill. Sexes are similar.

DISTRIBUTION. Coastal Australia generally, including Tasmania. Closely related forms occur on all continents.

NOTES. Seen singly or in pairs, occasionally in parties (which in winter may contain up to fifty birds), it frequents seashores, preferring undisturbed beaches and sand spits, tidal mud flats and estuaries; occasionally reefs and rocky shores. The chief call is a ringing, high-pitched 'kl'eep, kl'eep' or 'peepapeepapeep'. Food: small molluscs, crustaceans, and other marine animals.

BREEDING. Nest: a depression in sand, usually on the beach above high-water mark. Clutch: two to three; very variable, but usually brownish-white, with blackish-brown spots and underlying markings of inky-grey. Breeding season: October to January (southern Australia); July to September (north-western Australia).

38:14 SOOTY OYSTERCATCHER *Haematopus fuliginosus*

IDENTIFICATION. This bird is like Pied Oystercatcher but its plumage is entirely black. Sexes are similar.

DISTRIBUTION. Coastal Australia generally, including Tasmania. Closely related (and possibly conspecific) forms occur elsewhere in the world.

NOTES. Generally uncommon, it occurs alone or in pairs, occasionally in small flocks during the winter. It frequents chiefly rocky shores, islands, and reefs. It is similar in habits to the Pied Oystercatcher, but it is even more wary than that species.

BREEDING. Nest: a shallow depression in sand; lined with pieces of herbage, dried grass, seaweed, fragments of coral, or broken shells; usually on an off-shore island or reef often on a grass-covered ledge, at some height above the water. Clutch: two to three; pale brown, with spots and streaks of blackish-brown and a few underlying markings of light brown and inky-grey. Breeding season: October to January.

38:15 REEF HERON *Egretta sacra*

IDENTIFICATION. This is a medium-sized egret, either entirely dark grey or white, and seldom found away from the coast. White morph resembles other white egrets, but has proportionately much shorter legs and longer, heavier bill. Its posture is characteristically hunched, arthritic. Sexes are similar.

DISTRIBUTION. Coastal continental Australia generally (rare in the south) and Tasmania. It also inhabits New Zealand and is found in India, Japan and Malaysia to Oceania.

NOTES. The dark morph appears to be the only form frequenting the coasts and islands of southern Australia and Tasmania; white-plumaged birds are found in tropical regions. The species is usually seen singly or in pairs, frequenting rocky coasts, islands and reefs. When not stalking among rocks at low tide, it squats in a dejected-looking attitude on a rock. Food: small fishes, molluscs, crustaceans, and other marine life.

BREEDING. Nest: a platform of sticks; placed either on a rock or in the branches of a low bushy tree. Clutch: two to four; pale bluish-white. Breeding season: very extended, but usually September and October to January.

38:16 BEACH STONE-CURLEW *Esacus magnirostris*

IDENTIFICATION. This is a very large, sandy brown shorebird with a long stout bill and glaring yellow eye. It has a conspicuous dark brown bar on shoulder, edged white. Sexes are similar.

DISTRIBUTION. Northern and eastern Australia, west to Point Cloates, Western Australia, and south to about Coffs Harbour, New South Wales. It is also found in the Andaman Islands, Indonesia and the Philippines to New Caledonia.

NOTES. Seen singly or in pairs, it frequents undisturbed beaches of the mainland and islands off the coast. Its call is similar to that of the Bush Stone-curlew, but higher-pitched and harsher in tone. When disturbed it may emit in flight short, sharp notes — 'sit–sit–sit' — that suggest hissing. Generally uncommon and sedentary. Food: small crustaceans and shell-fish.

BREEDING. Nest: a depression in the sand, usually just above high-tide mark.

Clutch: one to two; creamy-white, with streaks and blotches of olive brown. Breeding season: October to February.

38:17 ARCTIC JAEGER *Stercorarius parasiticus*

IDENTIFICATION. This species is very similar to Pomarine Jaeger, but slightly smaller and less powerfully built. Its plumage is very variable, and identification is often difficult. Moderately long, sharply pointed, central tail feathers are diagnostic when present, but are often broken or in moult.

DISTRIBUTION. Breeds in the Arctic, wintering widely in the Southern Hemisphere; well-dispersed around the coasts of Australia, but especially common along the east coast.

NOTES. It usually arrives during October or November, departing about April or May. Found singly or in small groups, it often frequents inshore waters, including bays, harbours and inlets. It is swift and agile in flight, harassing gulls and terns and robbing them of their prey. There is a light phase, differing in having the sides of the head and neck straw-yellow, chin and breast dull white, and the remainder of the underparts ash-brown; intermediates also occur. 'Jaeger' is a German word meaning hunter.

BREEDING. Nest: a shallow depression in the ground, lined with grass or moss. Clutch: two; dark stone to greenish-buff, with dark brown to light grey markings. Breeding season: May to July.

38:18 POMARINE JAEGER *Stercorarius pomarinus*

IDENTIFICATION. This species is the largest jaeger, broad-winged and powerfully built. Its plumage is very variable, but in breeding plumage has black cap, yellowish cheeks, and white underparts, with greyish band across the breast. Long central tail feathers are broad, blunt-ended, and twisted; these are diagnostic, but are often missing, broken or in the process of replacement.

DISTRIBUTION. Breeds across northern Europe, Asia and North America; winters widely in the Southern Hemisphere, including Australia.

NOTES. Common off the east coast of Australia from September to April; less common in Bass Strait and along the southern coast to Western Australia. The species tends to prefer off-shore waters, in contrast to the closely similar Arctic Jaeger which tends to be more common in coastal waters. It often approaches fishing vessels, and harasses gulls and terns, robbing them of food.

BREEDING. Nest: a depression in the ground, lined with grass. Clutch: two to four; brown or greenish, blotched dark brown. Breeding season: May to July.

38:19 LONG-TAILED JAEGER *Stercorarius longicauda*

IDENTIFICATION. This is a small slender jaeger, variably dingy grey below, plain, cool grey-brown above, with darker primaries; outermost few primaries have white shafts.

DISTRIBUTION. Breeds in the high Arctic; winters at sea in the South Atlantic and the south-west Pacific. Vagrant to Australia.

NOTES. Similar in general habits and appearance to other jaegers, but it is more pelagic. This species is much smaller, slighter and more graceful in flight than the other two jaegers.

BREEDING. Nest: a depression in the ground, sometimes lined with grass. Clutch: usually two; greenish-brown, sparsely marked with dark brown. Breeding season: June and July.

38:20 SOUTHERN SKUA *Catharacta antarcticus*

IDENTIFICATION. This bird is a large, burly, very powerful gull-like seabird, uniformly dark brown, with a bold white flash towards the tip of each wing.

DISTRIBUTION. North and south Atlantic, southern oceans and sub-antarctic islands (including Macquarie and Heard islands), to southern Australia; extending from about Geraldton, Western Australia, to south-eastern Queensland.

NOTES. A visitor to Australian shores during winter, it is generally seen among flocks of gulls and terns, which it relentlessly pursues, bullying them until they yield any food they may have secured. It follows ships, congregates about fishing vessels, and is usually seen off-shore but in some areas may frequent wharves and beaches. It feeds on small mammals, insects, eggs, young birds, fish, carrion, and animal refuse.

BREEDING. Nest: a shallow depression in the ground, lined with grass. Clutch: two; glossy dark stone, heavily marked brown. Breeding season: November to January.

38:21 KELP GULL *Larus dominicanus*

IDENTIFICATION. This bird is a large, black-backed seagull with plain white tail. Sexes are similar; but immatures are dull brown, variably streaked and mottled dark grey.

DISTRIBUTION. Southern coasts of Australia from about Wollongong, New South Wales to Jurien Bay, Western Australia; scattered records further north. Also South America, southern Africa, New Zealand, and various subantarctic islands.

NOTES. A recent colonist, presumably from New Zealand, it was first found breeding in Australia (at Moon Island, New South Wales) in 1958. Now it is most common in Tasmania and Bass Strait, and appears to be gaining ground, largely at the expense of the endemic Pacific Gull. Not especially gregarious, it is usually seen in small groups. The most characteristic call is a long choking, yelping 'yo–yo–yo–yo–yo–yo'.

BREEDING. Colonial. Nest: a substantial structure of grass and plant stems, on the ground. Clutch: usually three; stone to greenish-buff, blotched with shades of brown. Breeding season: November to January.

38:22 PACIFIC GULL *Larus pacificus*

IDENTIFICATION. This species is a large black-backed seagull, best identified by its enormously deep bill, yellow with red spot in adults, pinkish, black-tipped in immatures; legs yellow; white tail with narrow black subterminal band. Immature birds are dull brown; both this species and the Kelp Gull reach maturity through a confusing series of immature plumages, some very similar to each other; identification of such young birds requires caution.

DISTRIBUTION. Breeds on islands off the southern coast of Australia; occurs north to about Shark Bay in the west and about Sydney in the east.

NOTES. Not especially gregarious, it is usually seen singly, in pairs or sometimes loose groups. It patrols tide lines. Most of its food is procured from the surface of the water, and consists of fish and marine animals, also galley refuse from ships; it also robs the nests of other birds. Adults are sedentary, but young birds tend to wander further afield.

BREEDING. Colonial. Nest: a depression in the ground; lined with grass or other herbage; usually situated in the shelter of a tussock of grass or a low bush. Clutch: one to three; grey to olive brown, blotched with reddish-brown and lavender. Breeding season: September to January.

38:23 SILVER GULL *Larus novaehollandiae*

IDENTIFICATION. This is a 'seagull' with bright red bill and legs; white eye and narrow red eye-ring. Sexes are similar; immatures resemble adults but have dusky black bill and legs.

DISTRIBUTION. Continental Australia generally (chiefly coastal) and Tasmania. It also inhabits New Caledonia and New Zealand.

NOTES. Widespread and familiar, it is abundant throughout the year on harbours, inlets and coastal rivers, and at times in large flocks on inland lakes and rivers. Its natural food consists principally of small fishes and other marine-life, but it is also a versatile scavenger. It is also a notorious nest-robber, taking the eggs of other seabirds. It breeds in colonies, sometimes on headlands and occasionally on lakes, but mostly on small islands throughout its range.

BREEDING. Colonial. Nest: varying from a slight depression in the ground to a substantial saucer of grass, lined with grass or dried seaweed. Clutch: two to three; extremely variable, generally pale green or brown, spotted and blotched with umber or dark brown. Breeding season: variable; in parts of Western Australia the species is double-brooded (a characteristic unique among gulls), in other areas some breeding may take place throughout the year, with a peak in spring.

38:24 FRANKLIN'S GULL *Larus pipixcan*

IDENTIFICATION. This species is smaller than Silver Gull, with darker grey upperparts. In breeding plumage it has a black head; in non-breeding plumage it is restricted to a dark grey smudge around the eye and over the crown; one white crescent over the eye and another below it. Sexes are similar.

DISTRIBUTION. Breeds in central North America; winters mainly in South America. Vagrant to Australia.

NOTES. A common gull of the prairies of western Canada and the United States, it often follows the plough. Sociable, it breeds in dense colonies at lagoons and swamps. Vagrants have shown up at widespread localities around the world, including Europe, islands of the central Pacific, and Marion Island in the southern Indian Ocean. Few Australian records, mainly in the south-west and south-east; these records have been of single birds, associating with Silver Gulls.

BREEDING. Colonial. Nest: a floating mass of vegetation in shallow water. Clutch: usually three; buff or greenish-brown, spotted and blotched with various shades of brown. Breeding season: May to July.

APPENDIX

PLATE 39

BIRDS INTRODUCED TO AUSTRALIA

In a process beginning shortly after European settlement, many species of birds were deliberately introduced into Australia from various parts of the world. A number of clubs and societies rapidly came into being, whose entire purpose was to foster, encourage and facilitate such introductions. These clubs were especially active during the late 1800s and the first decade or two of the twentieth century. It is now illegal to import exotic birds into Australia for release.

Most introductions were unsuccessful, but a few birds quickly established themselves in a feral state, and subsequently prospered. The following species represent the most successful and widespread of these introduced birds. There are, however, a number of other species that are not mentioned because, although a few individuals may survive in a purely local context, they cannot be said to have established a viable, permanent breeding population in Australia, while certain others seem so well known as not to need detailed treatment. These birds include the domestic Pigeon or Rock Dove; the domestic Fowl, which occasionally lives in a feral state; the Common Peafowl, which has sometimes been allowed to run wild in certain areas; the Mute Swan; the old-world duck known as the Mallard, which frequents lakes in various parks; the Ring-necked Pheasant, which was released for sporting purposes in a number of places and still exists in some of them; and the Ostrich, numbers of which (descended from birds formerly farmed for their feathers) exist in a wild state in the Port Augusta and Coorong districts of South Australia.

Other introductions include the African Grenadier Weaver (*Euplectes orix*), which appears to have become lightly established, from aviary escapees, along portions of the Murray River region of South Australia; the African White-shouldered Wydah (*Coliuspasser albonotatus*), which formed small colonies in swampy areas near Sydney but appears now to have died out; the Asiatic Black-headed Mannikin (*Lonchura atricapilla*), which is lightly established

333

near Sydney; and the Californian Quail (*Lophortyx californica*), which has become established in parts of Victoria and on King Island in Bass Strait.

On the whole, Australia is in a comparatively fortunate position with respect to introduced birds. Although such species as the Starling and Indian Mynah are among our most common and conspicuous birds, they are so only in disturbed environments highly modified, in one sense or another, by the activities of human beings. These, of course, are precisely the areas in which we spend most of our time, and this familiarity tends to disguise the fact that few introduced birds have succeeded in establishing vigorous and widespread populations in habitats that have not been modified by human beings. In short, broadly speaking, introduced species are rare 'in the bush', no matter how common and ubiquitous they may seem to us in the cities, suburbs and farmlands in which we spend most of our time.

39:1 HOUSE SPARROW *Passer domesticus*

IDENTIFICATION: This bird is small, active, and 'cheeky'. The male has a grey crown, chestnut nape, white cheek and a black bib. Females are rather plain mousy grey.

DISTRIBUTION. Eurasia; introduced widely throughout the world. In Australia widespread in the eastern half of the continent, penetrating occasionally into Western Australia and the Northern Territory.

NOTES. First introduced to Australia in 1863. For some time thereafter shooting the bird was considered a serious offence. It rapidly established a vigorous population, and by the turn of the century had become abundant and widely distributed in urban and country areas throughout most of eastern Australia. It is seldom encountered far from human habitation. It lives in small groups and feeds largely on the ground on seeds and insects, but occasionally also fruit. Calls include a harsh 'chee–ip' and a chattering song.

BREEDING: Nest: an untidy structure of straw and other soft material, usually with a side entrance; lined with feathers; placed in a cavity or crevice of almost any kind, or in the fork of a tree or shrub. Clutch: usually five to six; variable in colour but often greyish-white finely spotted ashy-grey and brown. Breeding season: at any time, but mainly spring and summer.

39:2 TREE SPARROW *Passer montanus*

IDENTIFICATION: This bird closely resembles the familiar House Sparrow, but has a chestnut (not grey) crown, and a black mark on a white cheek. Sexes are similar (unlike the House Sparrow).

DISTRIBUTION. Europe and Asia; in Australia sparsely distributed (although common locally) in the south-east, approximately from Melbourne, Victoria, north to Hay, New South Wales, and east to Sydney.

NOTES. Although closely related to the House Sparrow, the Tree Sparrow is much less bold and enterprising, and is not especially common nor widely distributed. It frequents parks and gardens in various towns and cities, especially in Victoria and the Riverina.

BREEDING: Nest: similar to that of the House Sparrow, but smaller; usually placed in a cavity in a tree, sometimes in crevices in buildings. Clutch: four to six; smaller than those of the House Sparrow, browner in general tint, and more glossy. Breeding season: September to January.

39:3 RED-WHISKERED BULBUL *Pycnonotus jocosus*

IDENTIFICATION: This slender, alert, jaunty bird has a pointed crest, white throat, mainly black head, and bright red undertail coverts. Sexes are similar, but immatures are plainer and duller.

DISTRIBUTION. South-east Asia; introduced in Australia, where well-established in and around Adelaide, South Australia, Melbourne, Victoria, and Sydney and Coffs Harbour, New South Wales; locally elsewhere.

NOTES. First released near Sydney in the 1880s, the Red-whiskered Bulbul did not become established until early in the present century, and then probably through escapees or later releases. Even now it is not especially common or widespread away from major urban centres. It inhabits shrubbery in gardens and parks, feeding mainly on insects and fruit. Common calls include chirping notes and a melodious whistled song.

BREEDING. Nest: cup-shaped, made of strips of bark and rootlets, generally with a few large dead leaves or a piece of rag or paper forming a base; lined with fine rootlets; usually placed in a dense bush several metres from the ground. Clutch: two to four; white, glossy, profusely spotted or heavily blotched reddish-brown. Breeding season: September to February.

39:4 GREENFINCH *Carduelis chloris*

IDENTIFICATION. This sturdy, sparrow-sized finch is mainly dull green with yellow patches on the wings and tail. Sexes are similar, but immatures are dull brown, faintly streaked on the breast.

DISTRIBUTION. Western Eurasia and North Africa; in Australia mainly in Victoria, extending sparingly to Tasmania, southern South Australia, and south-eastern New South Wales.

NOTES. Generally uncommon, quiet and unobtrusive in habits, it inhabits trees and shrubbery, mainly in gardens and parks. Calls include a simple, nasal 'dwee–ee' and a light trill. Food: mainly seeds and insects.

BREEDING: Nest: cup-shaped, made of twigs and moss lined with rootlets and feathers; placed in a shrub or tree a few metres from the ground. Clutch: four to six; dull white to greenish-blue, sparingly marked red-brown and pale violet. Breeding season: September to January.

39:5 GOLDFINCH *Carduelis carduelis*

IDENTIFICATION. This sparrow-sized finch has body plumage mainly warm brown, with a white rump, red face, and large yellow patches on the wing. Sexes are similar, but immatures are duller.

DISTRIBUTION. Europe and Asia; in Australia from south-eastern Queensland through New South Wales and Victoria to Tasmania, southern South Australia, and the south-west of Western Australia (established near Perth and Albany).

NOTES. Abundant in many rural areas, especially in Tasmania and the south-east, it inhabits mainly parks, gardens, orchards, weed-choked roadsides and rough pastures. It usually encountered in pairs or small flocks. Calls include a light twitter and a liquid chattering song. Food: seeds (especially thistles and sunflowers).

BREEDING: Nest: deep cup-shaped, constructed of fibrous material and thickly lined with fluffy plant material; usually placed in a fruit tree or a shrub several metres from the ground. Clutch: usually five; bluish-white, spotted brown and chestnut, mainly around the larger end. Breeding season: October to January, often later.

39:6 NUTMEG MANNIKIN *Lonchura punctulata*

IDENTIFICATION. A small, plain finch, its head and upperparts are brown, its underparts light, heavily scaled brown. It persistently flicks its tail. Sexes are similar, but immature birds are without markings on their underparts.

DISTRIBUTION. South-east Asia; in Australia from about Moruya, New South Wales, north to Cooktown, Queensland.

NOTES. The early history of introduction is not well documented, but apparently it was first noted near Brisbane, Queensland, in 1937, apparently originating from aviary escapees. It is now common over much of coastal eastern Australia. It frequents reed-beds, rough grassland, scrubby areas, orchards and arable land. Usually found in flocks, often associating with the native Chestnut-breasted Mannikin (28:14, p. 219). The call is short, clear 'chip–chip', or 'chippy–chippy'. Food: mainly seeds.

BREEDING: Nest: compact and globular, with a side entrance; made of leaves and coarse grasses and lined with fine grass; usually placed in a small shrub or bushy tree several metres from the ground. Clutch: four to eight, sometimes more; white, rather elongated oval. Breeding season: mainly October to April.

39:7 COMMON STARLING *Sturnus vulgaris*

IDENTIFICATION: This bird is robust and short-tailed. Its plumage is black, glossed green and purple, with a yellow bill. After moulting the body feathers are tipped dull white, producing a strongly speckled appearance. Sexes are similar, but juveniles are mouse-grey, with slate bills.

DISTRIBUTION. Eurasia. Introduced to Australia (and widely elsewhere in the world); common virtually throughout the south-eastern States, from near Rockhampton, Queensland to the Eyre Peninsula, South Australia; local and erratic elsewhere.

NOTES. The Common Starling spread rapidly after its introduction to Victoria in 1861 and later years, and is now common and familiar in urban and rural areas almost everywhere in eastern Australia, though much less common in the tropics. Strongly gregarious, it roosts communally and feeds in small groups to large flocks, mainly on open ground. It has a long, rambling song, wheezy, chattering and whistled. Food: mainly insects (especially larvae) and fruit.

BREEDING: Nest: an untidy assortment of straw and feathers; placed in a cavity in a tree or in a building. Clutch: five to seven; pale blue, sometimes almost white. Breeding season: variable, but mainly September to January.

39:8 LAUGHING TURTLEDOVE *Streptopelia senegalensis*

IDENTIFICATION. The upperparts of this species are mainly pale warm tan; the head and breast dull pink, and the rump grey; a diagnostic patch of black-spotted buff is on the breast. Sexes are similar, but immatures duller and plainer.

DISTRIBUTION. From North Africa across southern Asia to India; in Australia confined mainly to the vicinity of Perth, Western Australia, though it extends to some country centres and to Rottnest and Garden islands.

NOTES. The Laughing Turtledove became established in parts of south-western Australia through birds that escaped or were released from the Perth Zoological Gardens in or about 1898, and is now common in the metropolitan area and nearby rural areas. Usually seen in pairs or small parties, it frequents parks and gardens. Calls include a musical, bubbling series of cooing notes. Food: mainly seeds.

BREEDING: Nest: a crude, open structure of small sticks; placed in a tree or shrub. Clutch: two; white. Breeding season: variable, but mainly spring–summer.

39:9 SPOTTED TURTLEDOVE *Streptopelia chinensis*

IDENTIFICATION. This species is mainly brown above, with a dull pink head and underparts; a diagnostic patch of black, spotted white, is on the sides of the neck. Sexes are similar, but immatures are duller and plainer.

DISTRIBUTION. Southern Asia and Indonesia, introduced to Australia; now well-established, especially in urban areas, along most of the east coast from Cairns, Queensland to Melbourne, Victoria, in Tasmania, south-eastern South Australia, in the Perth area, Western Australia and at various other centres.

NOTES. It is now very common in many urban and rural areas, apparently as a result of multiple introductions dating from 1870 onward. Usually seen in pairs or small groups, it feeds mainly on the ground. The call is a simple cooing. Males of both this species and the Laughing Turtledove have a conspicuous display flight, flapping hurridly to a height of about ten metres, then sailing down on stiffly downcurved wings. Food: mainly seeds and green shoots.

BREEDING: Nest: a slight structure of sticks; placed in a tree or shrub. Clutch: two; white. Breeding season: variable, but usually October to January.

39:10 SKYLARK *Alauda arvensis*

IDENTIFICATION. This is a rather stocky, small, nondescript bird of open grassland; not easy to distinguish from Singing Bushlark, but larger, paler, and more conspicuously streaked on the breast; with white outer tail feathers. Sexes are similar.

DISTRIBUTION. Eurasia; introduced to Australia; now well-established and common in south-eastern Australia north to about Newcastle, New South Wales and west to Adelaide, South Australia.

NOTES. Introduced to Victoria from Britain in the early 1850s, this famous bird is fairly abundant in open grassy places. Usually seen alone or in pairs; the male has a distinctive song, uttered in circling flight high in the sky. Food: seeds and insects.

BREEDING: Nest: a cup-shaped depression in grass. Clutch: four to five; grey, spotted dark brown. Breeding season: September to January.

39:11 COMMON MYNA *Acridotheres tristis*

IDENTIFICATION: Plumage of this bird is mainly cocoa-brown, with a black head and conspicuous white flashes in the wings. The bill, legs and patch behind the eye are yellow.

DISTRIBUTION. Southern Asia from Afghanistan to southern China; now well-established and common (especially in coastal areas and in major cities) over much of eastern Australia.

NOTES. Apparently first introduced in Victoria in 1862, this species rapidly became established around Melbourne and in 1883 many were collected there and liberated in northern Queensland in an attempt to control insect pests attacking sugar cane. Vigorous, enterprising, and often very abundant, it is still expanding its range in many areas. It roosts communally but otherwise seldom forms large flocks, and feeds almost entirely on open ground. Noisy and conspicuous, it feeds mainly on insects and fruit.

BREEDING: Nest: an untidy cluster of dried grass, placed in a cavity in a tree or building, or in thick vegetation such as that of palm trees. Clutch: four to five; glossy blue. Breeding season: variable, but mainly in spring and summer.

39:12 SONG THRUSH *Turdus philomelos*

IDENTIFICATION. This bird is plain grey-brown above; its underparts creamy white, and copiously marked with bold rounded spots. Sexes are similar.

DISTRIBUTION. Europe; in Australia chiefly in the vicinity of Melbourne but extending to some country districts.

NOTES. Another early introduction to Victoria, this thrush from Britain (the Mavis and the Throstle of poets) has remained largely restricted to the parks and gardens of Melbourne. Unlike its relative the Blackbird, it rarely if ever troubles fruit growers. Like the Blackbird, it tends to skulk in shrubbery, emerging to forage over lawns and flowerbeds. Calls include a high-pitched 'seee' and a superb, spirited and musical song. Food: mainly insects and other small invertebrates (especially snails).

BREEDING: Nest: bowl-shaped, made of grass and bark fragments reinforced with mud; placed in a bush a metre or so from the ground; sometimes in a building. Clutch: three to five; deep blue, spotted black at the larger end. Breeding season: September to January.

39:13 BLACKBIRD *Turdus merula*

IDENTIFICATION: The male is entirely black, with yellow bill and legs. The female is dingy brown. Immatures are dark, nondescript, obscurely mottled.

DISTRIBUTION. Eurasia; in Australia now well-established in Tasmania and over much of the south-east from Adelaide, South Australia, to Armidale and Sydney, New South Wales.

NOTES. Originating from specimens introduced in the 1860s, the Blackbird has long been common in Melbourne and has extended to most other parts of the State; it is also abundant in Tasmania — originating there from a batch released from the Hobart Zoo — and is common in parts of South Australia (mainly in and near Adelaide). It is still relatively uncommon around Sydney, but is widespread (and apparently expanding its range) over much of the interior of New South Wales, west to Broken Hill and north to Armidale. It skulks in dense undergrowth, forages over open lawns, flowerbeds and vegetable patches; and frequently cocks its tail. Calls include a rich, melodious and complex song (rendered mainly from August to December), and an abrupt scolding 'chak!'. Instances of a partial albinism in this species, usually involving white feathers in the wings, are not uncommon. Food: insects and fruit (sometimes a nuisance to growers of soft fruits, especially in Tasmania).

BREEDING: Nest: a substantial bowl of grass and bark matted and reinforced with mud or manure; placed in a shrub or thicket (usually exotic) a metre or so from the ground. Clutch: three to five; bluish-green, with numerous small spots of brown. Breeding season: September to January.

SUPPLEMENTARY LIST

The list of birds of Australia now contains approximately one hundred species not illustrated or discussed in the body of the present book as originally issued in 1931. These include several native species relatively recently discovered, and also a number of vagrants whose presence was recorded years ago, but only as very rare stragglers. However, the bulk of these additions are vagrants detected in Australia only within the past decade or two, resulting mainly from ever more intensive and systematic field work. Most on the following list are known from only a few records, and must be classified as 'accidentals' — that is, the individuals concerned were lost, and there is no particular reason to expect the species ever to occur again — although doubtless many will. However, it seems reasonable to suppose that several species on the list may well turn out to be regular visitors, whose presence has hitherto been obscured either by difficulties of identification, or by the fact that the species concerned occur regularly only in more remote parts of the country (such as the far north-west, for example).

The following is not a complete list of birds reported in Australian territory. A number of additional species might be included, except that — although perhaps valid — the reports are difficult to assess objectively and consistently. This list includes those species: (a) which are included (without brackets, which indicates doubt) in the official checklist of the Royal Australasian Ornithologists Union (except in four instances where reasonable doubt has since been indicated), (b) for which the occurrence is based on a specimen, (c) for which photographic evidence has been published, (d) for which the occurrence has been assessed and accepted by the RAOU Records Appraisal Committee. Any report which does not meet these criteria is not included.

1. King Penguin *Aptenodytes patagonicus*
Breeds at various sub-antarctic islands, including Heard and Macquarie islands. Vagrant to Australia, recorded Victoria and Tasmania.

2. Gentoo Penguin *Pygoscelis papua*
Breeds in Antarctica and at various sub-Antarctic islands, including Macquarie Island. Accidental, one record from Tasmania.

3. Chinstrap Penguin *Pygoscelis antarctica*

Breeds in Antarctica and at various sub-antarctic islands, including Heard Island. Vagrant Macquarie Island; several records from Tasmania.

4. Adelie Penguin *Pygoscelis adeliae*

Breeds in Antarctica. Two or three Australian records which may involve birds carried by whaling ships, then released.

5. Snares Penguin *Eudyptes robustus*

Breeds at several islands in the New Zealand region, including Macquarie Island. Recorded Tasmania and South Australia.

6. Erect-crested Penguin *Eudyptes sclateri*

Breeds at several islands near New Zealand. Regular vagrant to Macquarie Island; also recorded Western Australia and Victoria.

7. Royal Penguin *Eudyptes schlegeli*

Breeds only at Macquarie Island. Several records from Tasmania and one from South Australia.

8. Magellan Penguin *Spheniscus magellanicus*

Breeds in southern South America and the Falkland Islands. One Australian record: Phillip Island, Victoria, 1976.

9. Antarctic Petrel *Thalassoica antarctica*

Breeds in Antarctica. Rare vagrant to Australia, most records from Victoria.

10. Tahiti Petrel *Pterodroma rostrata*

Breeds at New Caledonia and associated islands, and in the Society and Marquesas groups. Two or three records from eastern Australia, possibly more regular than records suggest.

11. Cook's Petrel *Pterodroma cookii*

Breeds at offshore islands around New Zealand. Several Australian records, mainly from New South Wales.

12. Fulmar Prion *Pachyptila crassirostris*

Breeds at various sub-antarctic islands, including Heard Island. Rare vagrant to Australia.

13. Black Petrel *Procellaria parkinsoni*

Breeds at New Zealand and at various off-shore islands. One Australian record (Sydney, New South Wales, May 1875).

14. Manx Shearwater *Puffinus puffinus*
Breeds in Europe, the Caribbean and the Arabian Gulf; winters in the South Atlantic. One Australian record: a bird banded in Wales, September 1960 was found dead at Venus Bay, South Australia, in November 1961.

15. Audubon's Shearwater *Puffinus lherminieri*
Breeds at various islands in the Caribbean and tropical Indian and Pacific oceans, including Vanuatu. One very old Australian record (Halifax Bay, northern Queensland, June 1770).

16. Leach's Stormpetrel *Oceanodroma leucorrhoa*
Breeds in the northern Pacific and Atlantic oceans; disperses southwards. Several Australian and New Zealand records, including Victoria and Western Australia.

17. Georgian Diving-petrel *Pelecanoides georgicus*
Breeds at Auckland Island and at various islands in the southern Indian Ocean, including Heard Island. One Australian record: Bellambi Beach, New South Wales, December 1958.

18. Cape Gannet *Morus capensis*
Breeds in southern Africa. In 1980 one was discovered mated to an Australian Gannet at a small breeding colony in Port Phillip Bay, Victoria.

19. Christmas Frigatebird *Fregata andrewsi*
Breeds at Christmas Island, Indian Ocean. Several records from around Darwin, Northern Territory; possibly more regular than records suggest.

20. Yellow Bittern *Ixobrychus sinensis*
Breeds from China and Japan to India, Indonesia and New Guinea. At least one Australian record (Kalgoorlie, Western Australia, January 1967).

21. Northern Shoveler *Anas clypeata*
Breeds across North America, Europe and northern Asia; winters south to Mexico, central Africa, India and Indonesia. Recorded New South Wales (twice) and South Australia (once).

22. Red-legged Rail *Rallina fasciata*
Breeds in south-east Asia, winters south to Borneo and Indonesia. Vagrant to the Kimberley, Western Australia.

23. Corncrake *Crex crex*
Breeds Europe to central Asia, winters in Africa. Accidental to Australia.

24. Pheasant-tailed Jacana *Hydrophasianus chirurgus*
One Australian record (Paraburdoo, Western Australia, December 1974).

25. Caspian Plover *Charadrius asiaticus*
Breeds in central Asia, wintering in Africa. One old Australian record, a specimen from Pine Creek, Northern Territory, September 1896.

26. Eurasian Curlew *Numenius arquata*
Breeds across northern Eurasia, winters south to Indonesia, India and Africa. One Australian sight-record (near Darwin, Northern Territory, 1948).

27. Upland Sandpiper *Bartramia longicauda*
Breeds in North America, wintering in South America. One Australian record, a specimen from Sydney, New South Wales, in 1848.

28. Pintail Snipe *Gallinago stenura*
Breeds in northern Eurasia, winters south to the Philippines, Indonesia and India. Two specimen records from north-western Australia.

29. Baird's Sandpiper *Calidris bairdii*
Breeds in North America, wintering in South America. Several Australian records, from Western Australia, Tasmania and Victoria.

30. Dunlin *Calidris alpina*
Breeds in the high Arctic, wintering mainly in the Northern Hemisphere. Several Australian records, mainly from the east coast, including Cairns, Queensland, Port Phillip Bay, Victoria, and Hobart, Tasmania. These have recently been questioned due to the possibility of confusion with the next species.

31. Cox's Sandpiper *Calidris paramelanotus*
An enigmatic species recently described. Known only from two specimens taken in South Australia and several sight-records.

32. White-rumped Sandpiper *Calidris fuscicollis*
Breeds in North America, wintering in South America. Several Australian records, from Western Australia, Victoria and New South Wales.

33. Little Stint *Calidris minuta*
Breeds in northern Europe and Asia, wintering south to Africa and India. Several Australian records.

34. Stilt Sandpiper *Micropalama himantopus*

Breeds in North America, wintering in South America. One Australian record: Darwin, Northern Territory, August 1980.

35. Grey Phalarope *Phalaropus fulicarius*

Breeds in the high Arctic, wintering at sea, mainly in the eastern Atlantic and eastern Pacific oceans. One Australian record (near Swan Hill, Victoria, February 1976).

36. South Polar Skua *Catharacta maccormickii*

Breeds in Antarctica, winters mainly in the north Pacific. At least two Australian records.

37. Japanese Gull *Larus crassirostris*

Breeds in Japan, Korea and north-eastern China. Two Australian records (Melbourne, Victoria, 1978 and Darwin, Northern Territory, 1982).

38. Sabine's Gull *Xema sabini*

Breeds in the high Arctic, winters at sea off the west coasts of South America and Africa. One Australian record (Darwin, Northern Territory, 1982).

39. Black Tern *Chlidonias niger*

Breeds across North America, Europe and northern Asia; winters in South America, Africa and southern Asia. Accidental to Australia, at least three records.

40. Black-collared Pigeon *Ducula muellerii*

New Guinea; one sight record from Boigu, Queensland, 1980.

41. Brown Hawk-owl *Ninox scutullata*

Breeds from Japan and China to India and Indonesia; northern populations winter south to Indonesia. One Australian record: a specimen found at Ashmore Reef, north-western Australia in January 1973.

42. Glossy Swiftlet *Collocalia esculenta*

Occurs from south-eastern Asia to the Solomon Islands and New Caledonia. Several records from north-eastern Queensland.

43. Uniform Swiftlet *Collocalia vanikorensis*

Occurs from Indonesia to the Solomon Islands and New Caledonia. One record from Cape York Peninsula (specimen, Peak Point, September 1913).

44. House Swift *Apus affinis*
Occurs from Africa across southern Asia to Indonesia. One specimen found near Darwin, Northern Territory, in March 1979; several possible sight-records.

45. Blue-winged Pitta *Pitta moluccensis*
Occurs from the Himalayas and Japan south to Sri Lanka and Indonesia. Two old specimen records from north-western Australia.

46. Yellow-headed Wagtail *Motacilla citreola*
Breeds across the Soviet Union and China; winters mainly in India, Bangladesh and Burma. At least one Australian sight-record (Botany Bay, New South Wales, June-July 1962).

47. Grey Wagtail *Motacilla cinerea*
Breeds across Europe and northern Asia; winters south to Africa, India, south-east Asia, Indonesia and New Guinea. Several Australian sight-records.

48. White Wagtail *Motacilla alba*
Breeds across Europe and northern Asia; winters south to north Africa, India, and southern China. At least one Australian record.

49. Arctic Warbler *Phylloscopus borealis*
Breeds across northern Asia, wintering south to India. One specimen found near Darwin, Northern Territory.

50. Great Reed Warbler *Acrocephalus arundinaceus*
Breeds across southern Europe and Asia, wintering in Africa, India, south-east Asia to New Guinea. One Australian specimen (Melville Island, Northern Territory, 1912); recent studies suggest the species may occur more frequently.

PLATES

PLATE 1

AUSTRALIA'S LARGEST BIRDS

(Excluding seabirds)

7

PLATE 2

BIRDS OF RAINFORESTS AND SCRUBS

PLATE 3

BIRDS OF RAINFORESTS AND SCRUBS

PLATE 4

BIRDS OF RAINFORESTS AND SCRUBS

PLATE 5

NOCTURNAL BIRDS

PLATE 6

MOUND-BUILDING BIRDS

PLATE 7

GROUND-FREQUENTING BIRDS

7:1   **NULLARBOR QUAILTHRUSH** *Cinclosoma alisteri*
     A. male
     B. female

7:2   **CINNAMON QUAILTHRUSH** *Cinclosoma cinnamomeum*
     A. subspecies *cinnamomeum*, male
     B. subspecies *cinnamomeum*, female
     C. subspecies *castaneothorax*, male

7:3   **CHESTNUT QUAILTHRUSH** *Cinclosoma castanotum*

7:4   **SPOTTED QUAILTHRUSH** *Cinclosoma punctatum*

7:5   **BLACK-BREASTED BUTTONQUAIL** *Turnix melanogaster*

7:6   **PAINTED BUTTONQUAIL** *Turnix varia*

7:7   **RAINBOW PITTA** *Pitta iris*

7:8   **NOISY PITTA** *Pitta versicolor*

7:9   **BLUE-BREASTED PITTA** *Pitta erythrogaster*

7:10 **CHOWCHILLA** *Orthonyx spaldingii*
     A. male
     B. female

7:11 **LOGRUNNER** *Orthonyx temminckii*
     A. male
     B. female

7:12 **FERNWREN** *Oreoscopus gutturalis*

7:13 **ROCK WARBLER** *Origma solitaria*

7:14 **PILOTBIRD** *Pycnoptilus floccosus*

7:15 **SOUTHERN SCRUB-ROBIN** *Drymodes brunneopygia*

7:16 **NORTHERN SCRUB-ROBIN** *Drymodes superciliaris*

7:17 **NOISY SCRUB-BIRD** *Atrichornis clamosus*

7:18 **RUFOUS SCRUB-BIRD** *Atrichornis rufescens*

7:19 **BASSIAN THRUSH** *Zoothera lunulata**

7:20 **RUSSET-TAILED THRUSH** *Zoothera heinei**

7:21 **WHITE-THROATED NIGHTJAR** *Eurostopodus mystacalis*

7:22 **SPOTTED NIGHTJAR** *Eurostopodus argus*

7:23 **LARGE-TAILED NIGHTJAR** *Caprimulgus macrurus*

*almost impossible to distinguish by sight

PLATE 8

BIRDS OF THE OPEN FOREST

PLATE 9

BIRDS OF THE OPEN FOREST

BIRDS OF THE OPEN FOREST

SCALE
50
mm

PLATE 11

BIRDS OF THE OPEN FOREST

PLATE 12

SOME HONEYEATERS OF THE OPEN FOREST

PLATE 13

GROUND-FEEDING PIGEONS AND DOVES

BIRDS OF BLOSSOMS AND OUTER FOLIAGE

10

PLATE 15

BIRDS OF BLOSSOMS AND OUTER FOLIAGE

SCALE

25   50   75

mm

PLATE 16

BIRDS OF BLOSSOMS AND OUTER FOLIAGE

BIRDS OF TREE TRUNKS AND BRANCHES

1B

1A

1E

1C

1D

1F

1G

1H

2

3A

4A

4B

3C

5B

3B

7B

5A

7A

6

N·H·Cayley—

SCALE

25   50   75

mm

PLATE 18

SOME BIRDS OF SCRUBLANDS

PLATE 19

BIRDS OF FOREST BORDERS AND GRASSLANDS

SCALE

25   50   75

mm

PARROTS AND COCKATOOS OF FOREST LANDS

SCALE

100   200

mm

PLATE 21

PARROTS OF OPEN FOREST AND SCRUBLANDS

PLATE 22

PARROTS OF TREETOPS AND OPEN SPACES

SCALE
50
mm

PLATE 23

SOME BIRDS OF MANGROVES

SOME BIRDS OF HEATH AND UNDERGROWTH

5

PLATE 25

BIRDS OF THE HEATHLANDS

17

SCALE

25 50 75

mm

Plate 26

Fairywrens of Heath and Shrubs

SCALE

25   50   75

mm

PLATE 27

SOME BIRDS OF THE AIR AND OPEN SPACES

PLATE 28

BIRDS OF REED-BEDS AND GRASSLANDS

17

1A

1B

15A

15B

2B

2A

4

15C

3

8

18A

5

6

18B

9

7

12

20

13

10B

10A

14

19

11

16D

16B

16C

21

16A

22A

23B

23A

22B

N. R. Cayley

SCALE
50
mm

DIURNAL BIRDS OF PREY

SCALE

100   200

mm

N. W. Cayley

DIURNAL BIRDS OF PREY

PLATE 31

BIRDS OF LAKES, STREAMS AND SWAMPS

SCALE

100   200

mm

PLATE 32

BIRDS OF SWAMPS, LAKES AND RIVERS

PLATE 33

BIRDS OF SWAMPS, LAKES AND RIVERS

PLATE 34

BIRDS OF SHORES AND RIVER MARGINS

SCALE
50
mm

PLATE 35

BIRDS OF THE OCEAN AND SEASHORE

SCALE
150
mm

BIRDS OF THE OCEAN AND SEASHORE

PLATE 37

BIRDS OF THE OCEAN AND SEASHORE

SCALE

250

mm

BIRDS OF THE OCEAN AND SEASHORE

SCALE

250

mm

PLATE 39

BIRDS INTRODUCED TO AUSTRALIA

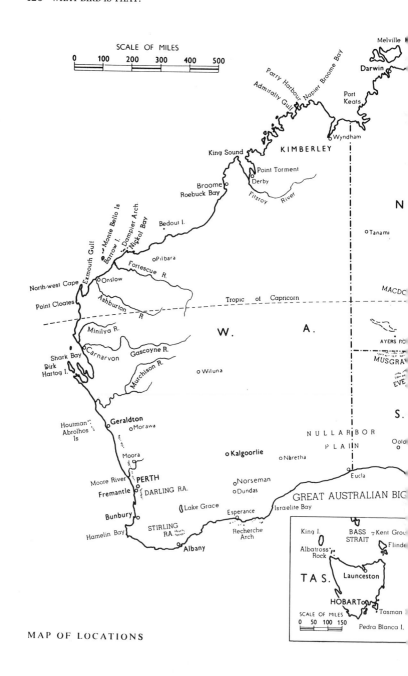

MAP OF LOCATIONS

TORRES STRAIT
C. York
Raine I.

Pascoe R.
Claudie R.
Watson R.

GULF OF
CARPENTARIA

Rocky R

GREAT BARRIER REEF

Cooktown

Normanton
ATHERTON
Herberton
TABLELAND

Cairns
Innisfail
Rockingham Bay
Cardwell
Herbert. R.
Townsville

Leichhardt. R.

Norman R.

Flinders R.

Cloncurry

Inkerman
Holbourne I.
Port Denison
Bowen

Burdekin R.

Sutton R.
Mackay

GREAT DIVIDING

Q   L   D

Percy Is.

Broad Sound

Fitzroy R.
Barren I.
Rockhampton

Gladstone

Masthead I.
Lady Musgrave I.
Lady Elliot I.

ngs

Birdsville

dnadatta
Lake Eyre

Charleville

Dawson R.
Chinchilla

Hervey
Bay
Fraser I.
Maryborough

BLACKALL RA.
BUNYA RA.
DARLING
DOWNS
Stanthorpe

Moreton Bay
BRISBANE
McPHERSON RA
Tweed R.

Richmond R.

Clarence R.

RA.

Lake
Frome

Augusta
FLINDERS
RA.

N.   S.   W.

Darling River

Macquarie R.

Castlereagh R.

Wellington

Rylstone

Bellinger R.
Nambucca R.
Macleay R.
Hastings R.

Manning R.
Williams R.
Port Stephens
Hunter R.

Spencer

G. St Vincent

Clare
MT LOFTY
RA.

Lachlan River

BLUE
MTS

Hawkesbury R.

YORK PEN

RE
N

MALLEE

Murrumbidgee R.

ADELAIDE

Kangaroo I.

GRAMPIANS
RA.

Murray R.

V.

C.

SYDNEY
ILLAWARRA
Shoalhaven R.
Conjola
Milton

OTWAY
RA.
Portland

MELBOURNE
DANDENONG RA.

Port Phillip

BASS
STRAIT
Kent Group

MAYO

INDEX